CONTEMPORARY PORTRAYALS OF
AUSCHWITZ

CONTEMPORARY PORTRAYALS OF
AUSCHWITZ

Philosophical Challenges

edited by
**Alan Rosenberg, James R. Watson
and Detlef Linke**

**Humanity
Books**

an imprint of Prometheus Books
59 John Glenn Drive, Amherst, New York 14228-2197

Published 2000 by Humanity Books, an imprint of Prometheus Books

Introduction:
"With a Variable Key," from *Poems of Paul Celan*. Translation copyright ©
1972, 1980, 1988, 1995 by Michael Hamburger. Reprinted by permission of the
translator, Persea Books, Inc. (USA) and Anvil Poetry Press Ltd. (UK)

"Poetry after Auschwitz: Paul Celan's Aesthetics of Hermetism":
"Todesfuge" and "Mit wechselndem Schlüssel," *Gesammelte Werken*, vol 1.
Translated by John Felstiner. Reprinted by permission of the translator.

"Homecoming," "An Eye, Open," from *Poems of Paul Celan*. Translation
copyright © 1972, 1980, 1988, 1995 by Michael Hamburger. Reprinted by
permission of the translator, Persea Books, Inc. (USA) and Anvil Poetry Press
Ltd. (UK)

Photographs by J. R. Watson.

04 03 02 01 00   5 4 3 2 1

Library of Congress Cataloging-in-Publication Data

Contemporary portrayals of Auschwitz : philosophical challenges / edited by
    Alan Rosenberg, James R. Watson, Detlef Linke.
        p.   cm.
    Includes bibliographical references.
    ISBN 1–57392–733–3
    1. Holocaust, Jewish (1939–1945)—Influence. 2. Holocaust, Jewish
(1939–1945)—Personal narratives—History and criticism. 3. Holocaust,
Jewish (1939–1945)—Moral and ethical aspects. 4. Genocide—Moral and ethical aspects. 5. Auschwitz (Concentration camp) 6. Holocaust, Jewish
(1939–1945), in literature. I. Rosenberg, Alan, 1939– II. Watson, James R.
III. Linke, Detlef, 1945–

D804.3 C67 2000
940.53'18—dc21   99–053621
                                                             CIP

Printed in the United States of America on acid-free paper

Contents

Part 3. Art and Poetry

Part 4. History and Memory

Part 5. The Crisis of Representation

Acknowledgments

The Society for the Philosophical Study of Genocide and the Holocaust would like to express its gratitude to Professor Dr. Rita Süssmuth, President of the German Parliament, for her patronage of the first SPSGH international conference. We would also like to offer our thanks to Mrs. Bärbel Reindl, Mayor of the City of Bonn, for making our stay in Bonn such a wonderful experience and to Professor Dr. Max G. Huber, Rektor of the Rheinische Friedrich-Wilhelms-Universität in Bonn, for providing us with the university's superb facilities for the conference. A special thanks to Ignatz Bubis, President of the Board of Directors of the Central Council of the Jews in Germany, and Professor Dr. Wolfgang Kluxen, Former President of the Allgemeine Gesellschaft für Philosophie in Deutschland, for their addresses to the conference.

Alan Rosenberg and James R. Watson would like to give special mention to Eugene O'Connor, our editor at Humanity Books, for seeing the book through from the beginning to the end. He made the process as painless as it could be. We would also like to give special mention to Morris Rabinowitz, whose meticulous proofreading of the galleys made the book as error-free as a book of this nature can be.

Without the meticulous and persistent efforts of Professor Dr. Detlef B. Linke our conference would not have been possible. A very special thanks to Dr. Linke.

Introduction

Interpretations are always situated between themselves and the cultural-historical conditions whose values they exploit. This is especially true for interpretations that understand themselves as interpretations of other interpretations. Add to this multilayered hermeneutic situation a series of troubling events, past and present, and the resultant constellation of readers and texts becomes even more complex and ambiguous. With the genocidal events of the 1990s, this is certainly the case with the series of texts presented in this volume. On the one hand, with respect to the "business-as-usual" operations of globalization since the fall of communism in 1989, it is clear that human rights at the end of this bloody century have exactly the same status as they did during the Holocaust. In this sense it is easy to compare what is happening in Rwanda, Bosnia, and Kosovo with the Holocaust. The former are thus understood as simply further genocidal episodes of the Nazi genocidal perfection called "the Holocaust," "Auschwitz," "Shoah," or "The Final Solution."

On the other hand, there are important differences between what has happened and what is happening, differences that cannot be ignored as they are by the operations of globalization. Globalization is indeed a meta-narrative at work. Genocide, on the other hand, has no meta-narrative. Meta-narratives conflate differences to the point of denying individual victims-survivors their own voice. Bosnia-Herzegovina, Kosovo, Bangladesh, and Rwanda (1994) are all cases of gender-specific genocide. The Nazi genocide against the Jews and the Khmer Rouge genocide in Kampuchea (1975–1979) were examples of gender-neutral genocide.[1] In the latter cases rapes were committed, but rape was not, as it is in gender-specific genocides, an instrumental policy of the perpetrators.

The primary target of the gender-specific genocide led by Slobodan Milošević was the Muslim family and the central role that women play in this family. In the case of Bosnia-Herzegovina and Kosovo a primary target was Muslim women: "Rapes spread fear and induce the flight of refugees; rapes humiliate, demoralize, and destroy not only the victim but also her family and community; and rapes stifle any wish to return."[2]

Milošević's grand narrative of "Greater Serbia," like all great myths, evolved as a fictional construction, "smoothing over" the differences disturbing the assemblage of domains it sought to unify. In this case, however, the grand narrative contains its rules of practice in the very heart of its foundational myth—the Battle of Kosovo.[3] The big picture— Greater Serbia—was in the making, a great war movie[4] launched in 1991 with tacit yet strong backing from the international "community." The grand narrative, as they all must do, unfolded, revealing its founding practical imperatives when General Ratko Mladić moved against the "peace keepers" and then launched his systematic massacre and rape of thousands at his death camps north of Srebrenica. Bosnia was now Greater Serbia's for the taking. The many differences now being "smoothed over" according to the dictates of the Serbian meta-narrative. "Ethnically cleansed," Bosnia was under new production values as a land in the making of mass graves and raped women, children, and men—a palimpsest for a Second Coming. In the summer of 1995 the international community did more than just tolerate a repeat of death camps in Bosnia (and that means in Europe); it also made clear its fondness for grand narratives. Of course it had not responded to the shelling of Dubrovnik or Sarajevo. Of course it would not interfere in the internal matters of a sovereign state. Of course what was happening in the "other" Europe, the ex-Yugoslavia, was of concern but not its responsibility. Everything was happening "of course" from the perspective of the grandstands filled with those playing out their roles according to the dictates of another (post WWII) grand narrative. On stage one meta-narrative, watched by those acting out another. Mladić knew he had humiliated the international community many times.[5] What he did not know, however, is why this humiliation serves the narcissism of the public viewing the results of his ethnic cleansing operations.

The Balkans of the 1990s are the "other" of the civilized world, the screen for the projection of self-hatreds, not so distant memories, and the nagging persistence of hate crimes, racism, and our cynical disregard for the homeless. In Slavoj Žižek's words: "Far from being the Other of Europe, ex-Yugoslavia was, rather, Europe itself in its Otherness, the screen on to which Europe projected its own repressed reverse."[6] Watching the Milošević-NATO war movie of Bosnia enables the "civilized West" a displacement of its own past, present, and future. The terror and atrocity "there" could never happen "here." And, as Žižek points out, it is precisely this displacement in the frames of televised effects of atrocities, these fantasy images of the civilized world, that thwart our ability to act.

In 1996, therefore, a conference on "Contemporary Portrayals of Auschwitz" might well have been seen in terms of the fantasy images of a West refusing to come to terms with its repressions in its fascination with the reverse coming through the televised screens of Bosnia. The question is whether this will change in 1999 or 2000, when this volume of selected essays from that conference comes before the public. What has changed in the interim? The great war movie has expanded its scope. Kosovo, it now seems, will be the quintessential scene, preceded of course by the special effects bombing of Belgrade.

As of this writing, victory has been declared in Kosovo. Victory? At least a million Kosovar Albanians in the tent cities of Albania, Macedonia, and Montenegro, together with the untold thousands in the forests and the still unknown numbers of the massacred and raped, are probably thinking in other terms. If ending the "tragedy" was, in President Bill Clinton's words, "a moral imperative," we must remember that the bombing campaign of seventy-nine days failed to stop Serb armies from killing, raping, and "removing" at least a million people from their land and homes. On the side of the Western alliance, however, neither a single loss or serious injury. It was indeed a *virtually* perfect war[7]: all victims remained on the side of the Other—the good Other, the sacrificed.[8] Here we arrive at the real meaning of universalization—universality is always constructed on the basis of sacrifices that never include those in charge of the ceremonies. Milošević wanted ethnic cleansing—removals—and NATO responded with a great war movie with a sacrificial cast of over a million. This is the precise sense of Clinton's "moral imperative." And, of course, all tragedies must end in the sacrifice of the others.

In 1944 the Allies refused requests to bomb the rail lines to Auschwitz. The reasons for declining this request are still debated today, but in all likelihood the primary reasons had to do with the probable ineffectiveness of such a bombing.[9] There is no evidence that the Allies refused because they did not want to risk military deaths in a military effort to save Jews. In fact, as Novick makes clear, European Jews were not seen, at least in the United States, as "other." There simply is no comparison between the Allies 1944 decision not to bomb the rail lines to Auschwitz and NATO's recent decision to bomb rather than deploy ground troops in Kosovo. The Western perception of ethnic Albanians is opposite to their perception of Jews.

Kosovar victims are not we. We, the master of ceremonies, are not they. We do not risk our lives for those who must die as others. Substitution in the case of those who really are other must always be discriminate. Universality is always staged for the benefit of the sacrificial spectacle, not for saving the flesh on stage. There have been exceptions to the logic of this sacrificial bloodbath so dearly loved by the Christianized world, but the exceptions seem always to prove the rule. Consider, for example, conservative columnist George Will's reaction to the killing and humiliation of American troops by Somali warlords during Operation Restore Hope. Will could only hope that this experience would "inoculate America's body politic against the temptations of humanitarian interventionism."[10] Novick is certainly on the mark regarding the basis of our actions "against" Serbian troops since 1992: "Hovering over everything were 'the lessons of Vietnam,' which trumped 'the lessons of the Holocaust.' "[11] The one possible exception to this is perhaps the effects of the images of refugees fleeing their homeland. These images in particular seemed to have evoked imagery of the Holocaust for many people.

The reader of *Contemporary Portrayals of Auschwitz* must knowingly confront what also confronts the writer on the manifold themes of the Nazi genocide against the Jews. Perhaps poet and Holocaust survivor Paul Celan said it best in 1952:

> With a variable key
> you unlock the house in which
> drifts the snow of that left unspoken.
> Always what key you choose
> depends on the blood that spurts
> from your eye or your mouth or your ear.
>
> You vary the key, you vary the word
> that is free to drift with the flakes.
> What snowball will form round the word
> depends on the wind that rebuffs you.[12]

The immense struggle undertaken by Celan to write after Auschwitz is something unknown to most philosophers today. In the United States, for example, there are over eleven thousand professional philosophers,[13] about 10 percent of whom gather annually for the annual meetings of the American Philosophical Association. In late December of 1988 a handful of this 10 percent met informally to plan a society that would position the Holocaust and genocide as its central philosophical issues. Sander Lee, Berel Lang, and Alan Rosenberg were among these few. With their leadership the Society for the Philosophic Study of Genocide and the Holocaust (SPSGH) was thus formed.

In addition to providing a place for the presentation of papers on the Holocaust and other genocides, the formation of the SPSGH also brought a new book series called "Holocaust and Genocide Studies" (HGS), edited by Alan Rosenberg and Alan Milchman. HGS is part of the "Value Inquiry Book Series" published by Rodopi Editions in Amsterdam and

Atlanta. Today, a little over ten years later, the SPSGH has more than fifty members representing the United States, Canada, England, Europe, and Australia, and the HGS has three volumes under its listing. The society has grown and become increasingly transdisciplinary, and that is as it should be. In October 1997, the SPSGH held its first international conference in Bonn, Germany, under the patronage of Dr. Rita Süssmuth, President of the German Parliament. The essays published in this volume are the result of that conference.

For the most part the profession of philosophy is sadly and shamefully still less than face-to-face with genocide and the Holocaust as central philosophical concerns. Considering only the professional philosophers who are now members of the SPSGH, the society's membership represents, at best, only about 2 percent of all professional philosophers in the United States. This is not to say, however, that only those who are members of the SPSGH are concerned with these issues.

At the same time, however, it must be admitted that very little has changed since 1974, when Elie Wiesel came to the conclusion that the world remains world, that the testimony of witnesses has made little or no difference.[14] And, indeed, why should philosophical business-as-usual be interrupted or challenged by something that happened over fifty years ago, "over there," so to speak, and largely the result of aberrant thinking and politics? Just as there was and remains a perspective of Israel as a terminus of Jewish history, a point from which the Holocaust is viewed as something that happened "over there,"[15] there is a New World Order perspective within which the Holocaust is something past in the sense of "over and done with," something superseded by the universalization of the "free market." Remembrance, yes, but critical reflections that implicate and complicate "business-as-usual" attitude—no.[16] In ways not yet fully understood, this "business-as-usual" is possible only because the disaster destroyed so much. The eradication of the others continues, of course, even as one of the world's poorest countries is bombarded by the world's wealthiest nation. Business-as-usual. We have no stomach for protracted conflicts that would require a significant number of casualties of our own. Thus genocide will continue and intensify.

Auschwitz problematized the Enlightenment concept of humanity. And not only this concept. The perfection of state-sponsored and administered mass death in industrially optimized death camps issued in new forms of language, moral indifference, and forgetting. The memory of the disaster was and continues to be erased in the smooth, uninterrupted communications of new language forms refined for optimized performativity precisely on the basis of language brought to ruination by the planning and secret implementation of industrialized murder. This ruination of language, reaching its penultimate stage with the Nazi invention of a language of genocide governed by speech rules that concealed the literal meaning of its key/code terms,[17] has now been advanced to the quintessential level of total transparency. The rationalization of production requisite for the task of mass extermination also required a rationalization of language whose words would then no longer referentially trace anything other than what the masters of this "regimented" language desired. If the product of rationalized labor sports only its "producer's" brand and no longer the mark/signature of the labor that made it, the communicative flow of linguistic products is equally regulated by the demands of the market and the imperative of forgetting whatever and whoever has been "bypassed" in the process.

The disaster called "Auschwitz" has been largely neutralized by the normalization of a ruined language under the spell of communicative transparency. In the United States especially, the fetish of clarity is not far removed from a ruination that the profession of philosophy has preferred to adopt rather than examine. Even with the so-called move to post-analytic philosophy (the dominant "brand" in the United States), the emphasis remains "technical" rather than historical, contextual, or Socratic in the sense of public matters crucial for the maintenance and futherance of political life. In a recent text subtitled "Conversations with Quine, Davidson, Putnam, Nozick, Danto, Rorty, Cavell, MacIntyre, and Kuhn,"[18] for example, there is mention and some discussion of National Socialism (and the case of Heidegger) but no mention or discussion of the Holocaust. In an influential text published in 1989, Richard Rorty provides his reflections on cruelty and solidarity without even mentioning the Holocaust.[19] Perhaps this omission is related to one of the central claims of his book, that

> our responsibilities to others constitute *only* the public side of our lives, a side which competes with our private affections and our private attempts at self-creation, and which has no *automatic* priority over such private motives. Whether it has priority in any given case is a matter for deliberation, a process which will usually not be aided by appeal to "classical first principles."[20]

That National Socialism was from beginning to end an attempt to permanently destroy public life seems to have no contextual bearing on Rorty's (ironic?) distinction of public and private life. Vito Acconci is closer to life with his observation: "Private space becomes public when the public wants it; public space become private when the public that has it won't give it up."[21] In 1946 John Dewey wrote:

> There are issues in the conduct of human affairs in their production of good and evil which, at a given time and place are so central, so strategic in position, that their urgency deserves, with respect to practice, the names ultimate and comprehensive. These issues demand the

most systematic reflective attention that can be given. It is relatively unimportant whether this attention be called philosophy or by some other name. It is of immense human importance that it be given, and that it be given by means of the best tested resources that inquiry has at command.[22]

Dewey is certainly right when he tells us that it is relatively unimportant whether systematic reflective attention on ultimate and comprehensive issues be called philosophy, but it is crucial for philosophy if it is to retain anything of its Platonic-Socratic legacy, it must not only give its reflective best to issues such as Auschwitz, it must make these reflections a decisive aspect of public discourse.

Communicative transparency is the modus operandi of business-as-usual. It is a communicative and hermeneutic fetishism demanding the appropriation, assimilation, and/or eradication of everything standing in the way of optimized performativity.[23] The force of this fetish of transparency is comparable to that of a society of "normalized" rapists confronting a few yet insistent "Noes." The normative generality always occupies the higher ground—the base of appropriation. Indeed, the Serbian rapists in Kosovo understood and "operated" within this normative generality. What used to be the unsurmountable barrier to imagination and comprehension that is Auschwitz has been surmounted by the administrators of optimized performativity. And for this decisive task, the dominant profession of philosophy played and is, of course, continuing to play an instrumental role.

Functionalized rationality today attempts to leave its metaphysical-ontological grounds "in the past." Consider the words of Francis Fukuyama:

> A Universal History is simply an intellectual tool; it cannot take the place of God in bringing personal redemption to every one of history's victims.
>
> Nor does the existence of discontinuities in historical development like the Holocaust—horrifying as they may be—nullify the obvious fact that modernity is a coherent and extremely powerful whole.[24]

This judgment—"modernity is a coherent and extremely powerful whole"—differs from Kant's judgment concerning history and progress in that Fukuyma's reflects something quite other than people's enthusiasm.[25] This instrumentalization of universal history is central to the program of the New World Order,[26] its normalization and neutralization of the Holocaust; it now knows better than to present itself in the metaphysical dress of traditional philosophy.

There is much at stake in the continuing unfolding of the legacy of Auschwitz. A good part of this legacy is the continuation of the Nazi program of "night and fog"—silence. As André Neher has written, the Nazi "night and fog" policy of secrecy and concealment with regard to the death camps was followed by the complete isolation of these camps from the rest of the world—"the silence of Auschwitz." This in turn was followed by

> the silence of those few who finally understood, but who took refuge in an attitude of prudence, perplexity, and incredulity. . . . Lastly, there is the silence of God, which continues when the other rings of silence have been broken, and by that very fact is all the more serious and alarming.[27]

The silence of philosophy, however, is complicitous with the silence of Auschwitz, the silence of "night and fog," the silence which maintains the abyss between Auschwitz, its victims, survivors, and "memorial candles," and the world. In this way, philosophy today has become anathema to the Socratic impulse concerned with what makes possible the form of living together we call the human world. After the "victory in Kosovo," the soft folds of "night and fog" will once again encompass the travesty we still call public life.

Philosophy, literature, art, religion, indeed all culture, cannot remain what they were before and during Auschwitz. Adolf Eichmann and others demonstrated that culture and barbarism can coexist. This does not mean that, to mention only a few canonical figures, Kant, Hegel, Goethe, and Rilke were protofascist. It does mean, however, that before Nazism no one anticipated the unthinkable—the mass murder of human beings who had contributed so much to the very culture that turned against *and* away from them. The "greatness" of Nazism lies not only in the fact that it thought the unthinkable. With the creation of the death camps—the Nazi *novum*—it also accomplished the unthinkable within the complicitous culture-world. To read Kant today, for example, as if nothing has happened is to leave Kant in Eichmann's hands. Today, with Kant *through* Auschwitz, we must ask "Wie ist ein Kategorischer Imperativ möglich? (How is a categorical imperative possible?)"

In George Steiner's words:

> The unspeakable being said, over and over, for twelve years. The unthinkable being written down, indexed, filed for reference. The men who poured quicklime down the openings of the sewers in Warsaw to kill the living and stifle the stink of the dead wrote home about it. They spoke of having to "liquidate vermin." In letters asking for family snapshots or sending season's greetings. Silent night, holy night, *Gemütlichkeit*. A language being used to run hell, getting the habits of hell into its syntax. Being used to destroy what there is in man of man and to restore to governance what there is of beast. Gradually, words lost their

original meaning and acquired nightmarish definitions. *Jude, Pole, Russe* came to mean two-legged lice, putrid vermin which good Aryans must squash, as a party manual said, "like roaches on a dirty wall." "Final solution," *endgültige Lösung*, came to signify the death of six million human beings in gas ovens.[28]

Getting the habits of hell into the syntax of language was accomplished, which is perhaps why today there is little if anything that shocks us. The disaster continues, the writing done by the disaster continues to ruin books, language, and culture. But before we can return to the refuse that culture has become[29] after the "utter-burn where all history took fire, where the movement of Meaning was swallowed up,"[30] we must first turn to the witnesses who bore testimony to the ruination *for us*. Thus, this volume begins by addressing the issues raised by witnesses of the Holocaust and their testimonies.

Alan Rosenberg and James R. Watson

Notes

1. See Helen Fein, "Genocide and Gender: The Uses of Women and Group Destiny," *Journal of Genocide Research* 1, no. 1 (March 1999): 43–63.
2. Alexandria Stiglmayer, "The Rapes in Bosnia-Herzegovina," in *Mass Rape: The War against Women in Bosnia-Herzegovina*, ed. Alexandria Stiglmayer, trans. Marion Faber (Lincoln and London: University of Nebraska Press, 1994), p. 85.
3. Concerning the absurdity of this founding myth, see Susan Sontag, "Why Are We in Kosovo?" *The New York Times Magazine*, May 2, 1999.
4. See Lewis H. Lapham, "War Movie," *Harper's Magazine*, July 1999, pp. 12–15.
5. For a more conventional explanation of Mladić's motives, see Jan Willem Honig and Norbert Both, *Srebrenica: Record of a War Crime* (New York: Penguin Books, 1997), pp. 179–83.
6. Slavoj Žižek, *The Metastases of Enjoyment* (London: Verso, 1994), p. 212.
7. See Mark Danner, "The Meaning of Victory," *The New York Review of Books*, July 15, 1999, pp. 53–54.
8. See Slavoj Žižek, "Die Nato—die linke Hand Gottes?," *Die Zeit*, 26 (24 June 1999).
9. A balanced account is provided by Peter Novick, *The Holocaust in American Life* (Boston and New York: Houghton Mifflin Company, 1999), pp. 54–58.
10. George Will, "America's Inoculation by Somalia," *Newsweek* 122 (6 September 1993): 62. As quoted by Novick, *The Holocaust in American Life*, p. 250.

11. Novick, *The Holocaust in American Life*, p. 251.

12. Paul Celan, "Mit wechselndem Schlüssel," *Gesammelte Werke*, Vol. 1 (Frankfurt am Main: Suhrkamp, 1983), p. 112. The translation is Michael Hamburger's, reproduced in *Art from the Ashes*, ed. Lawrence L. Langer (New York and Oxford: Oxford University Press, 1995), p. 604.

13. The source for the approximate numbers given here is the *Directory of American Philosophers 1996–1997*, ed. Archie J. Bahm (Bowling Green: Philosophy Documentation Center, 1996), p. 465.

14. Elie Wiesel, "Art and Culture after the Holocaust," in *Auschwitz: Beginning of a New Era?* ed. Eva Fleischner (New York: KTAV, 1977), p. 405.

15. See *Breaking Crystal: Writing and Memory after Auschwitz*, ed. Efraim Sicher (Urbana and Chicago: University of Illinois Press, 1998), pp. 39–52.

16. For a description of the "business-as-usual" loop and its neutralization of the disaster, see James R. Watson, *Between Auschwitz and Tradition: Postmodern Reflections on the Task of Thinking* (Amsterdam and Atlanta: Editions Rodopi, 1994), "Introduction."

17. See Berel Lang, "Language and Genocide," in *Echoes of the Holocaust*, eds. Alan Rosenberg and Gerald E. Meyers (Philadelphia: Temple University Press, 1988).

18. Giovanna Borradori, *The American Philosopher*, trans. Rosanna Crocitto (Chicago and London: The University of Chicago Press, 1994). Stanley Cavell's observation is apropos here: "Philosophy is in some ways the last place in the American landscape that you would look in order to learn to write. Yet, in a sense, to write your own words, to write your own inner voice, is philosophy. But the disciplione most opposed to writing, and to life, is analytic philosophy" (p. 126).

19. Richard Rorty, *Contingency, Irony, and Solidarity* (New York: Cambridge University Press, 1989), Part III.

20. Ibid., p. 194.

21. Vito Acconci, "Public Space in a Private Time," *Critical Inquiry* 16, no. 4 (Summer 1990): 904.

22. John Dewey, *Problems of Men* (New York: Philosophical Library, 1946), pp. 11–12. This passage is also quoted by Alan Rosenberg and Paul Marcus, "The Holocaust as a Test of Philosophy," in *Echoes of the Holocaust*, p. 201.

23. See Jean-François Lyotard, *The Postmodern Condition: A Report on Knowledge*, trans. Geoff Bennington and Brian Massumi (Minneapolis: University of Minnesota Press, 1984), pp. 14–17.

24. Francis Fukuyama, *The End of History and The Last Man* (New York: The Free Press, 1992), p. 130.

25. See Immanuel Kant, "Der Streit der Fakultäten," *Werkausgabe*, XI, ed. Wilhelm Weischedel (Frankfurt am Main: Suhrkamp, 1978), especially sections 6 and 7, pp. 357–62. For a brilliant commentary on these and other passages in Kant's writings on history, see Jean-François Lyotard, *The Differend: Phrases in Dispute*, trans. Georges Van Den Abbeele (Minneapolis: University of Minnesota Press, 1988), pp. 151–81.

26. Fukuyama does not employ this term, preferring instead "the recent worldwide liberal revolution" (i.e., economic development)—see his last chapter of *The End of History*, "Immense Wars of the Spirit."

27. André Neher, "The Silence of Auschwitz," in *Holocaust: Religious &*

Philosophical Implications, eds. John K. Roth and Michael Berenbaum (New York: Paragon House, 1989), p. 10.

28. George Steiner, "The Hollow Miracle," in *George Steiner: A Reader* (New York: Oxford University Press, 1984), pp. 211–12.

29. Theodore W. Adorno, *Negative Dialectics*, trans. E. B. Ashton (New York: The Seabury Press, 1973) p. 367: "All post-Auschwitz culture, including its urgent critique, is garbage [*Müll*]."

30. Maurice Blanchot, *The Writing of the Disaster*, trans. Ann Smock (Lincoln and London: University of Nebraska Press, 1986), p. 47.

Part 1

Witnesses
and
Testimonies

Introduction

Debra Bergoffen responds to witnesses and testimonies with the recommendation that the unrepresentable be referred to as The Final Solution rather than as "Holocaust" or "Shoah." She makes this recommendation because she insists upon maintaining the absolute meaninglessness of The Final Solution—"The Useless." She thus suggests an eleventh commandment be added to the Mosaic ten: "Thou shalt not make use of The Final Solution/The Shoah/The Holocaust. Thou shalt not provide a place for it within the domains of intelligibility; neither within the rational/utilitarian form of intelligibility which dominates our times, nor within the more ancient and enduring sacrificial form which has come down to us through the centuries, nor any other form that has found, now finds or will find a place in the human community." The Final Solution "cannot find a home in the domain of meaning." Bergoffen responds with an attempt to prevent any appropriation of The Final Solution, any "explaining away" of the ruination we have inherited. It is her response and pledge to the witnesses and the ghosts of the *Musselmänner*.

Bergoffen's response is taken one step further by Hans Seigfried. After the senseless death of those "wasted" by The Final Solution and in the midst of ongoing genocidal pratices today, we cannot, argues Seigfried, simply remain in a state of numb agitation: "The anger over the wasting of victims soon becomes unbearable if it is not channeled into carefully considered actions that promise to forestall the recurrence of the destruction and to secure the protection of fundamental human rights." The latter, however, can no longer be understood or formulated on the basis of the concept of humanity since the viability of this concept was destroyed at Auschwitz. Seigfried's response to the victims and their testimonies is pragmatic rather than metaphysical. After Auschwitz there can be neither metaphysical truths about human nature nor a universalistic morality. What is needed is, rather, a turning toward an instrumental philosophy which furnishes "points of view and working ideas which may clarify and illuminate the actual and concrete course of life." Seigfried argues that such was the inspiration of the Western and non-Western representatives and founders of the United Nations Organization.

Ruth Liberman's "Of Testimony, Piles, and the Poetics of *Final Letters*," reveals "a complex and intricate relationship between witness and testimony," which in the case of a particular type of testimony—"last letters"—actively turns the reader of the testimony into a witness. The historical gap separating those who experienced what broke the very framework of traditional interpretation (indeed, broke language itself) is "joined" by the spacing/frame of then and now, author and reader. This implication of reader and testimony is further intensified by reproductions of the original testimonies (as in the case of *Final Letters*) because "the image of the letter as an object works more immediately on our emotional response than does the mediation of the text." Without this reader's response to the reproduction displays of piles of shoes, clothing, and the like could not serve as representations of what has been witnessed since the semantic bridge constituted by the symbolism of the *imagery* of the testimonies would be lacking. Testimony and its reproduction thus make representations of testimony possible, and then only insofar as the viewer/listener/reader is engaged as an *active participant* in the reproduced testimony.

Taking a somewhat different approach, Burkhard Liebsch's "Giving Testimony" begins with the contra-Hegelian observation that truth does not testify for itself. Truth becomes true "only through the witnesses' testimony," especially in the case when testimony speaks of what is without precedent in human experience. Because what was witnessed by victims of the Nazis so radically breaks with the flow of our everyday experience and interpretative framework, Liebsch argues that the traditional juridical model of testimony cannot be employed in attempts to understand Holocaust testimonies. The witnesses themselves did not understand what they reported. Nor do we. An unavoidable *Nachträglichkeit* or delay of the truth is inextricably connected to the witnesses' telling of the truth. What "remains to be said" is our task and responsibility, and neither will ever be at an end. Our debt is infinite. "We non-survivors and 'ordinary mortals,' to whom the testimonies are addressed, will thus, whether we like it or not, be the only ones who can preserve truth from falling into the paralysis of an indifferent unsayability or into the forgetfulness of *the written word*."

A.R./J.R.W.

Improper Sites

Debra B. Bergoffen

The problem of representing the unrepresentable is an ancient one. Within the Western philosophical tradition it dates back at least to Plato, who spoke of the possibility of seeing the Good and of the impossibility of adequately describing it. Within the biblical tradition, it is announced in the edict against graven images. In our times it concerns the Holocaust, the Shoah, the Final Solution. Between then and now the problem is only superficially the same. Then it was a matter of adequately expressing the fullness of Being; now it is a matter of portraying the Abyss. Then it was a matter of adequately referencing the source of the meaningful whole; now it is a matter of articulating the threat to the order of things. Then the desire to represent the unrepresentable could be traced to the conviction/belief that the unrepresentable was sublime/divine and/or the anchor of/for utopian visions and ethical hopes. Now the desire to represent the unrepresentable is tied to the biblical injunction to remember, to the survivors' imperative to witness, to demands for justice, to fear of/for the return/repetition of the traumatic event; to the desires of forgetfulness and consolation. Representations of the Holocaust, often ambiguous, sometimes suspicious, have been called upon to legitimate the liberating powers of the Allied war machine; to justify the birth of the state of Israel; to mourn the victimization of the Polish and German peoples; to celebrate the rebirth of German democracy and the reunification of the German state.

I want to interrogate our desire to represent The Final Solution, and I choose to call the unrepresentable of our times The Final Solution, rather than the Holocaust or the Shoah for several reasons. Each of these names, Holocaust, Shoah, The Final Solution, calls up the disaster of the

Third Reich; but each figures the disaster differently. The term Holocaust, meaning catastrophic destruction by fire, brings us face to face with the crematoria, the smoke, the ashes, the smell of burning flesh. The term Holocaust, however, is neither secular nor contemporary. It bears historical and theological weights that offer us a way to turn away from the catastrophe rather than face it; for holocaust calls up the image of a ritual sacrifice and with this vision of a religious burnt offering, it promises some comfort. In suggesting that institutionalized mass murder can be accounted for by the discourses of ritual and sacrifice, it situates the slaughter within the realm of religious intelligibility, allows us to see the victims as possibly redeemed and offers us the possibility of retrospective acceptance.[1] Even more troubling, it may privilege the Nazi perspective. For it if is true that the Holocaust was not experienced as a sacred or meaningful sacrifice by its victims, and if it is true that there was no sacrificial bond between those consumed by the flames and those lighting the pyre; it is also true that the Germans saw themselves as executing a necessary sacrifice and portrayed the camps in redemptive terms. They called it a purification.[2]

The term *Shoah*, meaning wasteland or destruction, carries different theological weight. Here the notion of sacrifice is rejected for the idea of a destruction that constitutes a breach in historical continuity (e.g., the destruction of the Temples). The breach, however, is not definitive. There is the promise that it can/will be healed. Further, there is the sense that it is somehow deserved. Again we are protected from the depth of the abyss. Again we may be guilty of privileging a particular perspective; this time, the perspective of some of the victims. In Berel Lang's words:

> [Shoah] references are confined to the viewpoint of the victims and they fail to suggest the specific role of genocide as it figured in the deeds of the Third Reich.[3]

The phrase *The Final Solution* cannot be traced to antiquity. It is a phrase of our times. Its history begins with a Nazi decision. No sacred roots anchor the cynicism of this euphemism for extermination. It resists all redemptive moves. In the phrase The Final Solution we hear the Nazis claiming the disaster for themselves, and we feel the Jews experiencing the disaster upon them. The phrase The Final Solution speaks of the terrible tie that binds perpetrator and victim as it exposes the chasm between them.

I do not know if the absence of historical echoes in the phrase *The Final Solution* is why it has not yet been appropriated for the politics of mourning or the discourses of redemption. I do not know if the phrase *The Final Solution* is too stark and too specific to circulate in the discourses of rhetorical overkill where political atrocities are indiscriminately referred to as Holocausts and where enemies are demonized as Nazis.[4] Perhaps it is simply a matter of time before the phrase The Final Solution is also appropriated for other ends. As yet, however, it remains unassimilated and as the not (yet) assimilated phrase it pushes the question of representability to the limit. Reminding us that we confront an absent meaning, it reminds us of the inadequacy of our heroic and redemptive vocabularies. It teaches us that new means of representation are required; and alerts us to the need for what Blanchot calls a "disaster notation."[5]

I do not come to these issues anonymously. I come as an American Jew born in 1941. Had I been born in Germany I would not be here. My coming speaks to/for/of the knots that bind Germany, the Jews, and America to each other. In coming, I come to ask whether or not we can remember/represent The Final Solution with/to/for each other without effacing the otherness we were and are to each other; without triggering the movement from otherness to contempt; and without falling prey to nostalgia. Guided by these questions and two stories, one by Elie Wiesel and one by Primo Levi, I try to think my way toward the possiblities of creating a disaster notation. Wiesel's story, "It Was Sufficient," links the Final Solution with other crises of Jewish history. It speaks of the possibilities of witnessing. Primo Levi's story questions these possibilities. Both Wiesel and Levi speak of the inadequacy of their speech, but where Wiesel believes that he will be heard, somehow understood, and ultimately acknowledged, Levi fears isolation. He fears his stories will be dismissed as impossible.

The Stories

Elie Wiesel has dedicated his life to bearing witness to the disaster. He knows that the age of witnesses is limited and that after they are gone the disaster itself may disappear. He is not naive when it comes to the question of memory. Reaching back to the Hasidic tradition he tells the following story. It is called "It was Sufficient." Originally it went like this:

> When the great Rabbi Israel Baal Shem-Tov saw misfortune threatening the Jews it was his custom to go into a certain part of the forest to meditate. There he would light a fire, say a special prayer and the miracle would be accomplished and the misfortune averted. Later when his disciple, the celebrated Magid of Mezrich had occasion for the same reason to intercede with heaven, he would go to the same place in the forest and say: "Master of the Universe, listen! I do not know how to light the fire but I am still able to say the prayer." And again the miracle would be accomplished. Still later, Rabbi Moshe-Leib of Sasov, in order to save

his people once more would go into the forest and say, "I do not know how to light the fire, I do not know the prayer but I know the place and this must be sufficient." And again the miracle occurred.

According to Wiesel, after Auschwitz, it is necessary to add a fourth part to the story which goes as follows:

Then it fell to Rabbi Israel of Rizhyn to overcome misfortune. Sitting in his armchair, his head in his hands, he spoke to God: "I am unable to light the fire, and I do not know the prayer; I cannot even find the place in the forest. All I can do is tell the story, and this must be sufficient." And it was sufficient.

For Wiesel, the horror of Auschwitz threatens but does not break the continuity of history. After Auschwitz the story continues, but the means of telling it, having been progressively impoverished by centuries of trauma, are now nearly depleted. The tale is almost obliterated by its silences and gaps. Julia Kristeva might well be commenting on the way the course of this story reflects the ways in which traumatic events disrupt our perceptual and representation systems when she writes:

From now on the difficulty in naming . . . opens . . . onto illogicality and silence . . . the actuality of the Second World War brutalized consciousness through an outburst of death and madness that no barrier seemed able to contain. . . . It was experienced as an inescapable emergency . . . invisible, nonrepresentable . . .[6]

and

As if overtaxed or destroyed by too powerful a breaker, our symbolic means find themselves hollowed out, nearly wiped out, paralyzed. On the edge of silence the word nothing emerges, a discrete defense in the face of so much disorder. . . . Never has a cataclysm been more apocalyptically outrageous; never has a representation been assumed by so few symbolic means.[7]

Wiesel confronts the problem of diminishing symbolic means with the question of sufficiency. He does not abandon the hope of the narrative. He believes that the story can be told. But it will be a story punctuated by loss. The question of memory is no longer a question of adequacy but of sufficiency and timing. It is a matter of recalling the proper story, or what is left of it, at the crucial moment. We are, Wiesel tells us, required to remember. We are, Wiesel tells us, incapable of adequately remembering; but our memory, with all its wounded gaps, must somehow be sufficient. Guided by the story "It Was Sufficient" we are left with the following questions: What constitutes a sufficient memory of The Final

Solution, that unintelligible reality which we can barely name and dare not forget? What constitutes a proper memorial to that monstrous time?

Primo Levi's story of remembering questions what Elie Wiesel's assumes. Wiesel raises the question of sufficiency, Levi raises the question of audience. Wiesel, a believer, is sure that (at least) God will hear him and respond. Levi, a non-believer, speaks only to us. He does not question his ability to witness; for him it is a matter of being believed. Can the impossible inhumanity/antihumanity of The Final Solution be taken up by/in human memory or will it be refused and thereby forgotten before it can be remembered?

Levi's story begins with a dream:

> This is my sister here, with some unidentifiable friend and many other people. They are all listening to me and it is this very story that I am telling: the whistle of three notes, the hard bed, my neighbor whom I would like to move but whom I am afraid to wake as he is stronger than me. I also speak diffusely of our hunger and of the lice control, and of the Kapo who hit me on the nose and then sent me to wash myself as I was bleeding. It is an intense pleasure, physical, inexpressible, to be at home, among friendly people, and to have so many things to recount: but I cannot help noticing that my listeners do not follow me. In fact they are completely indifferent: they speak confusedly of other things among themselves, as if I was not there. My sister looks at me, gets up and goes away without a word. . . . My dream stands in front of me, still warm, and although awake I still feel of its anguish: and then I remember that it is not a haphazard dream, but that I have dreamed it not once but many times since I arrived here. . . . I remember that I have recounted it to Alberto and that he confided to me, to my amazement, that it is also his dream and the dream of many others, perhaps everyone. . . . Why is the pain of every day translated so constantly into our dreams, in the ever-repeated scene of the unlistened-to story?[8]

As Levi tells his story, we find that the dream is also real; for he tells us that after the liberation he found himself in the midst of a group of curious Poles and that with a lawyer who spoke German and French acting as his interpreter he told them his story. Speaking of Auschwitz he says:

> I felt my sense of freedom, my sense of being a man among men, of being alive, like a warm tide ebb from me. . . . My listeners began to steal away; . . . I had dreamed, we had always dreamed of something like this in the nights at Auschwitz: of speaking and not being listened to, of finding liberty and remaining alone.[9]

Neither confined to the realm of dreams nor limited to individual incidents, the question of finding an audience played out on the stage of history. The conditions of the camps, described many times on Allied radio were not generally believed.[10] On April 14, 1944, U.S. reconnaissance planes took photos of Auschwitz that showed the gas chambers, crematoria, prisoners in line—but experts saw only a prison camp.[11] The Nazis, Levi tells us, counted on the public's disbelief. Victims and oppressors "had a keen awareness of the enormity and therefore the noncredibility of what took place in the Lagers [camps]."[12] Such things were unthinkable.

This awareness of The Final Solution as unthinkable, unbelievable, uncommunicable, and antihuman may be the only truth victim and murderer shared. They lived this truth differently. Nazis swore themselves to secrecy. Though there was nothing secret about the existence of the concentration camps, The Final Solution was an official state secret.[13] All SS accomplices were required to take specific vows of silence.[14] Himmler referred to The Final Solution as "an unwritten never to be written page of glory."[15] All witnesses and records were to be destroyed. Once the extermination was completed, the disappearance of the Jews would be called mysterious. Destroyed but not forgotten, Jewish history and traditions would be displayed in a Jewish museum in Prague.[16] Saul E. Friedlander believes that in insisting on secrecy and in intending to mystify their destruction of the Jews, the Nazis reveal the breach of The Final Solution. It must be kept secret because nothing can render it intelligible. It cannot be represented as serving any higher aim. It cannot be contained within the domains of politics or morality.[17]

As Germans were forbidden to use the phrase The Final Solution in public writings, Jews were forbidden to write. Knowing their annihilation was sealed if they obeyed the law of silence, Jews wrote in secret. They preserved and buried every scrap of evidence so that if the Nazis succeeded in destroying the Jews of Europe, they would not succeed in destroying Jewish memory.[18] Facing the secret of their extinction Jews staged Lager rebellions which were not intended to secure their freedom directly (a virtual impossibility given the camp system and the hostility and fear of the surrounding populations), but to save them indirectly by revealing the secret of the camps.[19]

In their witnessing Wiesel and Levi refuse to allow the rule of silence to prevail. Though their refusals draw on different traditions (Wiesel's story belongs to the rabbinic tradition of response to disaster.[20] Levi's to the secular tradition of Jewish remembrance[21]), their stories tie the questions of silence, speech and remembrance to the question of Jewish survival. Will there be a rabbi to remember what cannot be remembered? Will those who were not there listen to those who were?

I come from the stories of Wiesel and Levi haunted by the question of sufficiency, hounded by the problem of representation, and leery of the desire for community. I fear that guided by the best of intentions (the desire for the "we") we will mend the breach by covering it. I worry that in our desire to heal the wound of The Final Solution we will betray those destroyed by it. I ask whether lured by the desire for the "we," we will forget that The Final Solution destroyed the humanist idea/ideal of a common humanity.[22] Will we, for the sake of the "we," accept the consolations available in the terms Holocaust and Shoah? Will we, for the sake of the continuity of the "we" find a proper place for The Final Solution? Will we, for the sake of the "we," follow the temptation to find some common lesson in the disaster, lessons of tolerance, anti-Semitism or democracy? Will we, for the sake of the "we," find some good use for The Final Solution (the findings of the "medical experiments")? Will our nostalgia for the "we" lure us to forget the crack?

The witnesses are clear on this point. Life in the camps was brutal and senseless. The violence was either random or disproportionate to whatever purposes were invoked to justify it.[23] Under normal conditions life and meaningfulness are intertwined. Within the camps survival depended on not attempting to understand the horror; for according to the standards of logic and morality, the camps were impossible." In a world dedicated to utilitarian logic, the strategies of The Final Solution violated the criteria of purposeful action. The dying were transported to death camps.[25] Within the camps work was redundant, harsh and meaningless. No productive ends were served.[26]

We may counter Levi's claim that "the violence of the tattoo was *gratuitous*."[27] No, we may say, its purpose was to mark the victims for the count. We may quarrel with Levi's claim that the violated modesty that conditioned the existence of all Lagers was a useless cruelty. No, we may say, it served to degrade and dehumanize the victims and in this way justify their extermination. Our protests do not add up. They cannot transform The Final Solution into a pragmatic strategy that is immoral. They cannot erase the mark of uselessness that characterizes the brutality. Nothing is more telling in this regard than the actions of the German government itself, for toward the end of the war the purposeless savagery of The Final Solution overcame the practical imperatives of combat. Trains which could have been used in the war effort were used to carry Jews to their death. Jews whose forced labor could have been used to support the war machine were sent to the gas chambers; or if they had not yet been" selected," they were allowed to take shelter when the allies bombed the camps and forced, after the air raids were over, to return to their senseless work.[28]

The clarity of the witnesses and the evidence of the historical record establishes the parameters of the challenge. Can we comply with the mandate to remember, while remembering that The Final Solution:

> teaches us nothing commensurable with the very enormity of the event;
> . . . it does not help us to understand the present-day world or the

future of the human condition except that we know since "then" that such an event took place within modem industrial society . . . *A priori*, the "Final Solution" poses many questions concerning modernity, but either the linkages are kept at such a level of generality that they are irrelevant or the contradictions become insuperable.[29]

How can we think what is unthought as soon as we appropriate it for thinking? How can we think the unthinkable which, because it happened in our time, must now be thought?[30] One way, I think, is to represent The Final Solution as that which cannot be accommodated by the teleologies of reason—to represent its meaninglessness by representing it as The Useless.

In insisting on the absolute meaninglessness of The Final Solution, in insisting that it cannot be put to any good use, that it teaches us nothing, I am following the distinction Primo Levi makes between the drowned and the saved, though not the example of Levi himself. For, however powerfully he spoke as a witness to the senselessness of The Final Solution, upon reflection Levi could not see his experience as meaningless. It teaches us, he said, that:

> Whenever you begin by denying the fundamental liberties of mankind and equality among people you move toward the concentration camp system.[31]

Levi's "lesson" stops short of redeeming the victims, but it puts us on the path of a politics of consolation—a path I find too dangerous to tread; for it threatens to cover over the fact that the difference between the drowned and the saved was arbitrary; that the drowned were not martyrs in any meaningful sense of the term; that the saved were not chosen for either their merit or some historical purpose,

How then shall we remember? How shall we mark the breach? What can we do with these sites of useless, wanton terror? Our first impulse has been to preserve them; to mark them with monuments and transform them into museums; in short to put them to good use. Our first impulse may have betrayed us. For though the construction of monuments and museums seems to be an appropriate way to fulfill our obligation to remember, a survey of the histories of these monuments and museums exposes the ways in which institutionalized remembrance is always caught up in/with the teleologies of use and often captured by the desire to forget.

The history of the museum and of Holocaust museums is particularly instructive here. There is this fact:

> The number of monuments and memorial spaces in Europe, Israel and America dedicated specifically to the mass murder and resistance of

Jews during World War II now reaches into the thousands with dozens more being proposed and erected every year. Over one hundred museums and other memorial institutions devoted to this period have also been built, with many more planned.[32]

There is Carol Duncan's question, "What fundamental purposes do art museums serve in our culture and how do they use art objects to achieve those purposes?"[33] With this fact and this question we confront the problem of Holocaust museums: What fundamental purposes do Holocaust museums serve in our culture and how do they use The Final Solution to achieve these purposes?

Duncan interrogates the history of the art museum to answer her question. That history speaks to our question. Noting that the Louvre was created in 1793 when the French Revolutionary government nationalized the king's art collection and opened it to the public, Duncan tells us that this first modem art museum became a powerful symbol of the fall of the *ancien régime* and the creation of a new order. [34] The Louvre marked a break and represented a promise. Does the Holocaust museum perform an analogous function? Does it echo the revolution's desire to mark the end of an era of brutality and the beginning of an era of justice? Does it repeat this utopian desire by converting the horror of The Final Solution to the promise of "Never Again"? In repeating the utopian desire is it forgetting the difference between a break effected by the value of a common humanity and the chasm created by the terror of the anti-human?

By the middle of the nineteen the century almost every Western nation had a national museum or art gallery. These state sponsored galleries were public pronouncements of political virtue. They were offered as proof of a government that provided its people with the goods for the good life. Today, non-Western nations establish art museums as a way to signal the West that they are respectable governments and reliable allies. In Duncan's words:

> By providing a veneer of Western liberalism that entails few political risks and relatively small expense, art museums in the Third World can reassure the West that one is a safe bet for economic or military aid.[35]

As the non-Western nations use their art collections to assure the West of their respectability, Western nations continue to use the art museum to assure themselves and each other of their legitimacy. The museum fever of the West continues:

> As much as ever having a bigger and better art museum is a sign of political virtue and national identity—of being recognizably a member of the civilized community of modem liberal nations.[36]

After Auschwitz the art museum may not be up to its assigned task. The Western nations may need other institutions to signal their humanist credentials and political virtues. Holocaust museums perhaps? New collections of artifacts offered as collective proof of national innocence, virtue, contrition, or retribution? New testimonies to the triumph of good over evil?

These questions and this history mar our innocence. We are reminded that apparent and operative functions are not always the same. We realize that the event called the Final Solution can be betrayed by those claiming to protect it from oblivion. This insight is reflected in the concern of those Berliners who worry that monuments are replacing the sites themselves and that before long the marks of The Final Solution (e.g., the camps, the offices of the German high command, Nazi bunkers) will be sold to developers.[37] This worry might give us some direction. For the worry is not simply that the sites will be defamed by commercial interests (most of us are clear about this: no shopping malls at Auschwitz) but also that proper monuments betray the sites (if malls at Auschwitz are *verboten*, a museum, complete with a gift shop and cafeteria, appears to be acceptable). What if, led by the Berliners' worry, we insisted that Nazi sites neither be turned over to developers, nor be appropriated for proper monuments, memorials or museums? What if we abstained from using the sites for anything? What if we let them be what they are—eyesores; affronts to our sense of propriety; insults to our good sense? In confronting the waste of not being able to use the sites for either commercial, political or religious profit, might we begin to pay the only sort of reparation that can be paid to/for The Final Solution? Perhaps. Certainly the histories of Auschwitz and Birkenau are instructive here; for if they lead us to prefer the abandoned site to the preserved one, they show us that representing by letting be can also contribute to the covering over that covers up. That silence is not the answer. That the untouched site is inevitably touched by time; that some sort of intervention is necessary.

The question returns, what sort of intervention reveals the ways in which The Final Solution shatters all attempts to think it? What sort of intervention confronts the nightmare of the event with a scream of its own?[38] What sort of intervention respects the inscription from Job found on the plaque at Auschwitz:

> O Earth Cover not up my blood
> And let my cry never cease.

Surely not the intervention at Auschwitz, where state-run tourist itineraries give it half a day and where in that half day tourists find huts that have been cleaned and painted, grounds laid out with trees and flower beds and a museum in which pitiful relics, "tons of human hair, hundreds of thousands of eyeglasses, combs, shaving brushes, dolls, baby shoes" are laid out, neatly arranged.[39] Here, order contains the terror. No hint here of the diabolical caprice that marked Auschwitz and the other camps. No evidence here of The Final Solution. Auschwitz, the marker tells us:

> is a monument to the martyrdom and struggle of the Polish and other nations. The ashes of about four million victims of Hitler's genocides are buried in the area of the former extermination camp.[40]

No mention here of The Final Solution. And as if to underscore the effacement of the principle function of Auschwitz-Birkenau, the execution of The Final Solution, the sign at the entrance, written in a dozen languages, has no room for either Hebrew or Yiddish. The barbaric antiutilitarian logic of the camp gives way to a civilized utilitarianism.

> Thrift. Thrift. Speakers of Hebrew usually know some other language and there aren't enough speakers of Yiddish left to trouble a sign painter.[41]

Unlike the restored Auschwitz, Birkenau has been left unchanged. Primo Levi finds it as it was in 1945:

> There was mud and there is still mud or suffocating summer dust. The blocks of huts (those that weren't burned when the Front reached and passed this area) have remained as they were, low, dirty with droughty wooden sides and beaten earthen floors. There are no bunks but bare planks all the way to the ceiling.[42]

Birkenau confronts us with the fault line of The Final Solution. But, few visitors see it. No time for it in the prescribed half day excursion. Can a rarely visited place serve as a place of remembrance? Is it enough to know that it is there? And if those who come now find that grass is beginning to cover everything,[43] what will those who come fifty years from now find? Woods? Unrecognizable traces of tortured human lives? Is this what Wiesel means when he speaks of not being able to find the place? Between Auschwitz and Birkenau we confront unsatisfactory choices. With or without human intervention we are threatened with forgetfulness. Again, we are returned to the question: If forgetting is forbidden, how can we remember without forgetting?

Perhaps if we bring the worry of the Berliners to Emil Fackenheim's 614th commandment and then continue with a rule of our own we might discover a way. Fackenheim says that after the Holocaust we must add a new commandment to the rabbinic tradition's 613 commandments. This new commandment reads, "The authentic Jew of today is forbidden to hand Hitler yet another posthumous victory." By way of alerting us to what he might mean by "yet another," Fackenheim tells us that he has given up his earlier attempts to understand the radical evil of the Holocaust. Are we to infer that attempts to understand the Holocaust constitute a posthumous Nazi victory? Is the attempt to understand a way of avoiding the disaster? Does it allow us to escape the abyss through explanation?[44] Does inserting The Final Solution within the realm of intelligibility camouflage it in the trappings of legitimacy?

Provoked by these problems of understanding, intelligibility, and legitimacy, I suggest we adopt an eleventh commandment—a post-Holocaust supplement to the prohibition regarding graven images—which reads: Thou shalt not make use of The Final Solution/The Shoah/The Holocaust. Thou shalt not provide a place for it within the domains of intelligibility; neither within the rational/utilitarian form of intelligibility which dominates our times, nor within the more ancient and enduring sacrificial form which has come down to us through the centuries, nor any other form that has found, now finds or will in the future find a place in the human community.

In suggesting this supplement to the injunction against graven images, I do not intend to equate the domains of intelligibility with idolatry but rather to mark the excess that constitutes The Final Solution. There are many dimensions of reality that may appropriately be taken up in/by the province of intelligibility. The Final Solution, however, is *unheimlich*, it cannot find a home in the domain of meaning.

This supplementary commandment is haunted by the ghosts of the *Muselmänner*. For if I insist on the meaningless of The Final Solution, I do so, in part, on their account. There was nothing meaningful about the deaths of these men and women, "emaciated . . . with head dropped and shoulders curved, on whose face and in whose eyes not a trace of a thought is to be seen."[45] We are called by the *Muselmänner* to confront the silent, meaningless death of those who suffered the unspeakable horror of excremental degradation. Are piles of shoes sufficient? Would we dare to turn the sites that transformed solid articulated human bodies into dirty, flowing, abject, fluid masses into piles of shit?

Perhaps there are less offensive ways of bearing witness to the breach of the boxcars, the selections, the *Muselmänner*, the gas. Perhaps we can remember without forgetting if we attend to Lacan's account of the relationship between the signified and the signifier, to Levi's observations regarding language, and to Foucault's "Discourse on Language."

Reflecting on the relationship between the signifier and the signified, Lacan notes that it is the nature of the signified:

to take flight, to define itself as something that flees[46]

such that

the relationship between signifier and signified always appears fluid, always ready to come undone[47]

Further, he insists that:

the signifier doesn't just provide an envelope, a receptacle for meaning. It polarizes it, structures it and brings it into existence.[49]

Describing the relationship between the word (signifier) and the thing (signified) as inadequate and unstable, Lacan warns us against being duped by the apparent presence of the reality that is represented. There is never a full correspondence between the word or the image and that which it brings into view. If we forget that the relationship between the thing and its representations is fragile we risk losing it altogether; for we will equate the real with its representation and miss the gap between the name and its thing that keeps us tied to the world and sustains all living language.

Levi, without reference to Lacan's theory of signifier and signified, takes note of the gap between language and its objects and of the way in which language responds to this gap when pressed. He writes:

If the Lagers had lasted longer a new harsh language would have been born; and only this language could express what is means to toil the whole day in the wind with temperatures below freezing wearing only a shirt, underpants, cloth jacket and trousers and in one's body nothing but weakness and hunger and knowledge of the end drawing nearer.[49]

This observation belongs with Levi's story of not being heard. For though he speaks and we listen, the gap between our language and the breach of The Final Solution confounds his desire to be heard and our obligation to listen. If we attend to our failure, however, and understand it both as the inevitable failure of languages and images to appropriate reality, and as the unique failure of our languages and images in the face of this impossible reality, we may, perhaps, find ways to respect Fackenheim's 614th commandment and my eleventh one. We might mark the failure of all representations to present this disastrous event by calling the Final Solution monstrous and by remembering that the term monster refers to a being that cannot be properly named.[50] Abandoning the attempt to represent this monster properly, we might approach our obligation to remember by recalling the sixth-century Greek poets' description of true speech as discourse that inspires respect and terror.[51]

The modem museum and monument are associated with the Enlightenment distinction between the secular and the religious. As the cathedral, church and cloister were charged with representing the truth of the religious site, the monument and museum were commissioned to represent the truth of the secular site.[52] After Auschwitz a third site must be designated—a site of disaster, a monstrous site, an improper site. So far we have tried to mark the improper site with museums and monuments, markers of/for secular sites; or with cloisters, markers of/for religious sites. To date we have treated the controversies surrounding Final Solution memorials as signs of competing perspectives and agendas. Perhaps something else is happening. Perhaps it is the sites themselves that contest the propriety of these representations. Perhaps it is time to recognize the impropriety of assigning proper sacred or secular monuments the task of representing the monstrous.

The word "perhaps" betrays the urgency of the situation. "Proper" sites of remembrance proliferate as the survivors disappear. Their voices will soon be gone. Only ours will remain. If, sheared of our innocence, we fear that we are not prepared to remember without forgetting, we are called up short by Hillel's question, "If not now, when?" We are obliged to respond. For us it is not a matter of finding the place but of understanding how to confront the monster it houses. It is a matter of learning to tune our ears to the silence that cries out to be heard. It is a matter of clearing a space for an improper site.

Notes

1. Dominick La Capra, *Representing the Holocaust: History, Theory, Trauma* (Ithaca: Cornell University Press, 1994), p. 94.

2. For an alternative reading of the implications of the term *Holocaust*, see Berel Lang, *Act and Idea in the Nazi Genocide* (Chicago: The University of Chicago Press,1990), pp. xxi.

3. Ibid.

4. See, for example, Vladimor Nabokov's condemnation of the abuse of such words as *genocide, Auschwitz*, and *Holocaust* and his remarks on *Poshlost* as quoted in Lucy S. Davidowicz's *The Holocaust and the Historians* (Cambridge, Mass.: Harvard University Press, 1981), pp. 16–17. "*Poshlost* speaks in such concepts as America is no better than Russia or We all share in German guilt. . . . Listing in one breath Auschwitz, Hiroshima and Vietnam is seditious *poshlost.*"

5. Geoffrey H. Hartman, ed., *Holocaust Remembrance: The Shapes of Memory* (Cambridge: Basil Blackwell, 1994), "Introduction," pp. 5–6. For an objection to referring to the genocide as The Final Solution see Lang, *Act and Idea in the Nazi Genocide*, pp. 85–90, who argues that The Final Solution refers to German strategies regarding the Jews prior to their decision to exterminate the Jews of Europe, and that calling the genocide The Final Solution conceals and denies the extermination.

6. Julia Kristeva, *Black Sun: Depression and Melancholia*, trans., Leon S. Roudiez (New York: Columbia University Press, 1989), p. 222.

7. Ibid., p. 223.

8. Primo Levi, *If This Is a Man: Survival in Auschwitz* (New York: Summit Books, 1979), p. 43.

9. Levi, *The Reawakening*, p. 165.

10. For an account of the Allied reactions to information about the death camps see Martin Gilbert, *Auschwitz and the Allies* (New York: Henry Holt and Company, 1981).

11. Otto Friedrich, *The Kingdom of Auschwitz* (New York: Harper, 1982), pp. 71–74.

12. Primo Levi, *The Drowned and the Saved*, trans. Raymond Rosenthal (New York: Vintage International Books, 1988), p. 12.

13. Friedrich, *The Kingdom of Auschwitz*, p. 72.

14. Lang, *Act and Idea in the Nazi Genocide* , p. 25.

15. Alvin Rosenfeld, "Jean Améry as Witness," in *Holocaust Remembrance*, p. 60.

16. Lang, *Act and Idea in the Nazi Genocide*, p. 25.

17. Saul E. Friedlander, *Probing the Limits of Representation: Nazism and The Final Solution* (Cambridge, Mass.: Harvard University Press, 1992), pp. 104–107.

18. David G. Roskies, "The Library of Jewish Catastrophe," in Hartman, ed., *Holocaust Remembrance*, p. 41.

19. Levi, *The Drowned and the Saved*, p. 159.

20. Roskies, "Library," writes that in response to the disasters of the twentieth century beginning with the Kishinev pogrom of 1903, the rabbis asked the people to preserve all scraps of evidence and treat them as sacred documents/fragments, sheymes that bore the shem of God—p. 33.

21. Roskies, "Library," tells us that the literature of the Holocaust arises out of a "secular and revolutionary consciousness that taught Jews to make history by knowing their history . . . they derive their authority from the dead whose deeds they chronicle," p. 41.

22. Emil L. Fackenheim, *To Mend The World: Foundations of Post-Holocaust Jewish Thought* (Bloomington: Indiana University Press, 1994), p. 301.

23. Levi, *The Drowned and the Saved*, p. 106.

24. Ibid., pp. 142–43.

25. Ibid., p. 120.

26. Ibid., p. 121

27. Ibid., p. 119.

28. Levi, *If This Is a Man*, p. 90.

29. Saul Friedlander, *Memory, History and the Extermination of the Jews of Europe* (Bloomington: Indiana University Press, 1993), p. 112.

30. Fackenheim, *To Mend the World*, p. 299.

31. Levi, *The Drowned and the Saved*, "Afterward," p. 293.

32. James E. Young, *Holocaust Memorials and Meaning: The Texture of Memory* (New Haven: Yale University Press, 1993), p. ix.

33. Carol Duncan, "Art Museums and the Ritual of Citizenship," *Exhibiting Cultures* (Washington, D.C.: Smithsonian Institution Press, 1991), pp. 89–90.

34. Ibid., p. 93.

35. Ibid., p. 89.

36. Ibid.

37. Jane Kramer, "The Politics of Memory," *The New Yorker* (August 14, 1995), p. 56.

38. Fackenheim, *To Mend the World*, p. 263.

39. *Reawakening*, "Afterward," p. 292.

40. Chana Bloch, "Visiting the Burnt House," *Tikkun* 4, no. 3 (May 1989): 46.

41. Ibid.

42. *Reawakening*, "Afterward," p. 292.

43. Bloch, "Visiting the Burnt House," p. 123.

44. Fackenheim, *To Mend the World*, p. 193.

45. Levi, *If This Is a Man*, p. 67.

46. Jacques Lacan, *The Seminar of Jacques Lacan: Book III The Psychoses, 1955–1956,* ed. Jacques-Alain Miller, trans. Russell Grigg (New York: W. W. Norton, 1993), p. 260.

47. Ibid.

48. Ibid.

49. Levi, *If This Is a Man*, p. 93.

50. Foucault, "Discourse," p. 224.

51. Ibid., p. 218.

52. Duncan, "Art Museums and the Ritual of Citizenship," p. 90.

The Voices of the Victims

Hans Seigfried

Many who have survived the carnage of our time feel, or felt, the urge to tell their story and the story of those who perished. Others among the victims of crimes against humanity would not talk at all about their ordeal and would rather spit on anyone speaking about compassion and humanity. Women among the refugees from Srebrenica, for instance, were reported to have spat on Tadeusz Mazowiecki, a founding member of Solidarity and the first non-Communist premier of Poland, when he was presented to them in 1992 as the UN representative for human rights in the former Yugoslavia. Although this was not literally true, as Mazowiecki subsequently explained in an interview, some old women did point out to him what amounts to the same thing, namely, "that they simply didn't believe in anyone, had no confidence in anyone, and didn't want to talk to anyone anymore."[1]

In the end, so it seems, he himself came to feel as they did. On July 27, 1995, Mazowiecki resigned from his position as *Special Rapporteur* on the situation of human rights in the former Yugoslavia because he felt that he could not speak about the protection of human rights with credibility when confronted with "the lack of consistency and courage displayed by the international community and its leaders." For nearly three years he investigated crimes against humanity in the former Yugoslavia, eventually publishing eighteen reports. Crimes were committed "with swiftness and brutality," but the response of the international community was "slow and ineffectual." Mazowiecki said in his letter of resignation to the Secretary-General of the United Nations that he was not convinced "that the turning point hoped for will happen" and that he could not "continue to participate in the pretense of the protection of human rights."[2]

Mazowiecki's documentation and the coverage of the crimes in the media had perhaps a much greater effect on the present NATO intervention in Bosnia than he dared to believe. But I do not want to speculate about such possible connections, and no one can be sure yet that the terribly late measures taken will effectively stop the killings, massacres, and ethnic cleansing in the future.[3] Instead, I want to dwell on the despair of the women from Srebrenica, let them stand in for the victims of many similar atrocities that have followed seemingly without end, such as the ethnic cleansing of Albanians in Kosovo, and extrapolate from it some possibilities for keeping alive the memory of victims and for securing the effective recognition of their voices in the ongoing conversation of humanity and in the transaction of human affairs.

Of Stories Told, Archived, and Forgotten

It seems to me that the women of Srebrenica had no reason for doubting that their story was scrupulously reported and well known throughout the world. Yet the slaughter and the human rights violations continued all around them, and no one wanted to intervene. The presence of the UN representative for human rights violations and of the relatively passive UN peacekeepers made no difference to them. As people elsewhere, these violated women on the run must have asked: Why was there an immediate reaction in Kuwait but not in Bosnia? They were forced to realize that their begging for human compassion was simply ignored, and they consequently lost all faith in humanity.

Obviously, in their agony the women had expected that someone would hear their pleading voices and protect them. But their protection was not in the interest of those who could effectively act for them. It could not escape these women, then, that they were judged expendable and their loss an acceptable waste. In light of this, they must have felt that reporting the brutal violations of their human rights for UN records and worldwide television was the ultimate degradation and insult. Under these conditions, the women of Srebrenica definitely did not want their voices recorded and their story told. There was no point in telling their story merely for the records and archives. They wanted it to be used for the mobilization of human compassion and intervention, and short of that, "they didn't want to talk to anyone anymore," i.e., they wanted it to remain untold or be forgotten.

Of Memories and Memorials

But, of course, archiving the stories of the victims of crimes against humanity does not necessarily mean that their voices will be silenced and forgotten. With his letter of resignation Mazowiecki clearly showed that for him the purpose of the meticulous reporting of human rights violations in the former Yugoslavia for the records of the United Nations was the protection of the human rights of the living generation. He obviously believed that with his reporting they would get a voice in the ongoing conversation of humanity and a say in the transaction of human affairs. When he realized that under the given circumstances his reporting did not serve that purpose, he declined to continue with it and, in solidarity with the women of Srebrenica, rightly denounced it as a travesty of compassion and humanity. In the present context, I want to see in Mazowiecki's resignation only an illustration of the sense for the strong connection between keeping records of crimes against humanity and protecting the human rights of the living generation. It says that with the continued violation of human rights around us, mere documentation of crimes committed is simply inhuman. And some of us might agree that it belongs to those truths that we hold to be self-evident.

Naturally, what the victims voice in their stories varies tremendously and serves many other purposes in addition to the intervention in the continued violation of human rights around us today. Some stories are told simply to let us know what happened and what some people suffered from other people in the past. Others are told with a sense of urgency. They appeal to us for punishment, retribution, reparation, and justice. Still others implore us to get involved by pondering how people could commit such crimes in the past and by doing something to spare ourselves and future generations similar sorrows.

And the strategies for collecting the stories of the victims, together with tokens of their suffering, in libraries and museums, and for commemorating the crimes committed against them are even more complex and confusing, as Jane Kramer shows in "The Politics of Memory," a report on the controversies surrounding the building of Berlin's Holocaust memorial.[4] There is a troubling new trend in Germany's struggle to "manage" its past, she reports. Some Germans want to see Germany itself as a victim of the Nazi terror: "They want to have suffered from themselves the way everybody else suffered from them."[5] And in this context, many Germans are worried about the implications of the memorial. For it seems that the voices of the victims get muffled by the noise over the comparison of the depth of their suffering, the calculation of the relevant size of the crimes committed against different people, and the pomp of the "official" commemorations connected with such memorials.

Of course, the archives of the United States Holocaust Memorial Museum in Washington, D.C., do not include materials on such alleged victims, but only on the real victims of the Nazi terror. The museum is different from other memorials in that its documentation of genocide is not limited to Jews. It also documents what happened to Gypsies, Poles, the politically persecuted, homosexuals, and others. "What we want to do," says Sybil Milton, senior historian at the museum, "is *fully docu-ment* the racist urge for a homogeneous German society during the Nazi period. The willingness and readiness to murder other population groups as well as Jews."[6] According to Wesley Fisher, deputy director of the research institute in the museum's Wexner Learning Center, the goal is *a comprehensive archive.* But his following remarks show how easily such archiving becomes an end in itself. "The museum," he says, "has become something like a human rights symbol here in Washington. What I find quite interesting is that in addition to the heads of state, we are also getting visits from the heads of minorities, not only from the United States but also from other countries."[7] It is disappointing to read that an official of the museum is pleased to notice that his institution has become "something like" a human rights symbol. I would have liked to assume that a museum with a complete archive of Nazi crimes against humanity would want to be more than just "something like" a human rights symbol and, instead, see its *raison d'être* and prime purpose in the inspiration of actions for the worldwide protection of human rights. For without such protection, recording human rights violations would be mere busywork and pointless remembrance (*"unnützes Erinnern"*).[8]

Of Human Rights and Respect for Individuals

And yet, with our memories of the great wars' carnage fading, now nothing is needed more than institutions that keep alive all those memories that could inspire such actions. For today, as Mazowiecki observed about the situation in Bosnia in his August 1995 interview for *Le Figaro*: "There is a complete refusal to act, almost an aversion to it. No one wants to get involved."[9] Speaking against American involvement, Joe Klein last December claimed in his *Newsweek* column that "there *are* no good argu-ments for sending American troops to Bosnia. There are, however, several compelling not-so-good arguments. The most compelling, the polls say, is that American 'values'—not interests, mind you—are on the line. The 'value' in question apparently is the public's discomfort at watching the murder and mutilation of European civilians on television. Of course, this value was on the line three years ago—and it's on the line in lots of untele-vised non-European places where big tribes brutalize smaller ones. It's not the real reason Clinton is sending the troops."[10] Many of us would strongly disagree and contend that the defense of American values (respect for the individual, human rights, and democracy) *is* a good reason, and a far better one than the protection of narrowly conceived American interests (namely, trade and security) for sending American troops to stop crimes against humanity in places such as Somalia, Haiti, or Bosnia.

Fifty years ago, both survivors and witnesses were shocked when they learned about the scope of the total disregard for fundamental human rights and of the crimes against humanity committed during World War II. The emotional impact of the stories of the victims threatened to paralyze a whole generation. The disturbing thing was not so much that there were so many casualties, but that there were so many victims. Soldiers die for a cause and can be admired for their courage and noble deeds; their dying can have a redeeming quality. Victims are simply wasted and there is nothing ennobling in their destruction. The dead at Arlington National Cemetery could be remembered as heroes, but the dead victims at Auschwitz, Bergen-Belsen, Hiroshima, Gakovo, and the many other waste sites could only be bemoaned without consolation and in sheer unbearable anger.

The emotions aroused by the stories of the victims, then, had to be—and still have to be—mobilized into actions for the effective protection of the human rights of individuals. And it was this need that brought representatives from around the world to San Francisco in 1945, and then again to Paris in 1948.

In the preamble of the "Charter of the United Nations," written by Archibald MacLeish, it clearly states that the central aim of this "international organization" is "to save succeeding generations from the scourge of war" by reaffirming "faith in fundamental human rights, in the dignity and worth of the human person, in the equal rights of men and women and of nations large and small."[11] The representatives must have realized that such a reaffirmation makes sense only if they are able to secure with the very design and the operations of this international organization the effective and continued recognition of the voices of the victims in the ongoing conversation among the peoples of all nations and, more importantly, in the actual transaction of human affairs on the local and global scale. We can have faith in fundamental human rights again if we can be assured that there is an international tribunal that continues to hear the voices of the victims who plead for the protection of the dignity and worth of every human individual, in Bosnia and elsewhere.

In 1985 Irving Howe published an article on "How to Write About the Holocaust."[12] In this article he reflects on Primo Levi's way of "telling the story" of Auschwitz. He praises Levi for resisting the temptation to employ the Holocaust "as evidence for ready-made ideological and pietistic doctrines" or to "theorize" it into something ultimately comprehensible and therefore justifiable. What he admires most in Levi's writings is the tacit belief that "we cannot 'understand' the Holocaust, we can only live with it, in a state of numb agitation."[13] I do not believe that anyone can live for long in a state of numb agitation. The anger over the wasting of victims soon becomes unbearable if it is not channeled into carefully considered actions that promise to forestall the recurrence of the destruction and to secure the protection of fundamental human rights. It seems to me that it is much more appropriate to "tell the story" and voice the pleading of the victims in a way that transforms the numb agitation into a new sensibility and emotional power that searches and exposes—and thereby exorcizes—everywhere those (institutional) traits in our culture which, when the proper circumstances arise, very likely, if not necessarily, lead to the building of waste sites such as Auschwitz. Primo Levi's telling of the story of Auschwitz makes good sense only side by side with Eleanor Roosevelt's telling of the story—and what she did with it.

It seems to me that the closing of Auschwitz and the adoption and ratification of the "Charter of the United Nations" with its reaffirmation of faith in fundamental human rights fifty years ago is not a mere coincidence. And I wonder whether the founding of the United Nations at the closing of Auschwitz in 1945 and the Universal Declaration of Human Rights in 1948 could be regarded as our most effective effort to speak and act in the name of the victims of the most disturbing violation of human rights known to us.

It is not well known that the final adoption of the "Universal Declaration of Human Rights" in 1948 was largely a result of the vision, stamina, and personal diplomacy of Eleanor Roosevelt, then the United States representative to the United Nations. As one of her biographers writes, she "was among the first witnesses to speak with Holocaust survivors, to tour concentration camps, to consider the needs of the future as mandated by that historical moment."[14] And it was this mandate above all else that she represented at the United Nations and that she helped to *articulate* and *translate* into *definite* standards for human conduct in the "Universal Declaration of Human Rights." These standards, then, to the extent to which they actually direct our actions, effectively represent in our lives the voices of the victims of Auschwitz as well as the victims of the many other human waste sites.

With the victims and Eleanor Roosevelt I wonder: "When will our consciences grow so tender that we will act to prevent human misery rather than avenge it?" And I am tempted to answer, with the opening statement of the "Universal Declaration of Human Rights," when we have made this declaration of the victims of the Holocaust "a common standard of achievement for all peoples and all nations." In order to achieve this standard, "every individual and every organ of society, keeping this Declaration constantly in mind, shall strive by teaching and education to promote respect for these rights and freedoms and by progressive measures, national and international, to secure their universal and effective recognition and observance, both among the peoples of Member States themselves and among the peoples of territories under their jurisdiction."[15]

The United Nations as a corporate body, then, perhaps best represents the victims of the carnage of our time to the extent to which it continues to voice the concern for human rights and takes local and global measures to protect them.

Of Respect for Individuals and the Democratic Faith

The preamble of the "Universal Declaration of Human Rights" says that "the advent of a world in which human beings shall enjoy freedom of speech and belief and freedom from fear and want has been proclaimed as the highest aspiration of the common people."[16] Of course, this aspiration remains a mere pipe dream if it is not enacted in statutes and protected by the rule of law and, above all, if it is not operative in the attitudes which we display to one another in daily life.

Our reaffirmation of faith in fundamental human rights, in the dignity and worth of every person, is without basis and significance "save as it means faith in the potentialities of human nature as that nature is exhibited in every human being, irrespective of race, color, sex, birth and family, of material or cultural wealth," as John Dewey observed in his 1939 paper, "Creative Democracy—The Task Before Us." "To denounce Naziism," he explains, "for intolerance, cruelty and stimulation of hatred amounts to fostering insincerity, if in our personal relations to other persons, if in our daily walk and conversation, we are moved by racial, color or other class prejudice; indeed, by anything save a generous belief in their possibilities as human beings, a belief which brings with it the need for *providing conditions* which will enable these capacities to reach fulfillment."[17]

What I keep hearing, then, in the stories of the victims, just as did Irving Howe in the writings of Primo Levi,[18] are the voices of people pleading with us to develop and secure the conditions that enable all of us to live a full human life, the kind of life they were brutally prevented from living.

Of Human Rights, Self-Evident Truths, and Bloody Principles

The stories of the victims tell us that it is by no means self-evident what these conditions of a full human life are. Past efforts to definitively determine them with compelling arguments, fixed concepts, and universal principles not only failed us, but such principles inspired the very crimes they were designed to prevent. Some unguarded remarks in Jacques Maritain's exposition of the natural law indicate the reason for this disturbing result. The concept of the natural law, he explains, spells out the principles that determine human nature which is the same in all and according to which we must act. We obviously possess ends which correspond to our natural constitution and "which are the same for all—as all pianos, whatever their particular type and in whatever spot they may be, have as their end the production of certain attuned sounds. If they don't produce these sounds they must be tuned, or discarded as worthless."[19] Thus, the claim to knowledge of principles to which all human conduct must conform and of the necessary ends which all human beings must pursue is easily transformed into an appeal to a final solution by force and extermination.

There is perhaps no single idea that has done more harm in our bloody history than the belief that all individuals must be alike and pursue the same ends and that these ends define the idea of the good life. After the carnage of World War II, the United Nations Organization was established in response to the pleading voices of the victims, as it were, in order to produce and protect in concerted efforts conditions that in the future would allow all individuals to develop their possibilities as human beings. We can see at a glance that the conditions listed in the "Charter of the United Nations" and the "Universal Declaration of Human Rights" are neither self-evident truths nor universal moral principles, and to represent them as such in clear view of the continued and widespread violations of human rights, and of our reluctance to interfere, would unavoidably generate skepticism about them. And yet, we want them to be recognized by all. To help reaffirm faith in these rights and to make them a common standard of achievement for all, the preamble therefore asks "that every individual and every organ of society, keeping this Declaration constantly in mind, shall strive by teaching and education to promote respect for these rights and freedoms and by progressive measures . . . to secure their universal and effective recognition and observance. . . ."[20]

The philosophical challenge in this plea, i.e., the plea in the voices of the victims, is to develop an understanding of these conditions that does not discredit them as self-evident truths or mysterious metaphysical abstractions, but represents them in such a way that they can be recognized as matters of undeniable ordinary experience, open to public scrutiny and sensible legal measures on the local and global scale. We can easily do so by showing that the conditions listed in the thirty articles of the "Universal Declaration of Human Rights" are nothing but the positively restated conditions whose violations led to the suffering of the victims. We learn from the stories of the victims, for instance, that denying them rights and freedoms on the basis of "race, colour, sex, language, religion, political or other opinion, national or social origin, property, birth or other status" as a matter of fact prevented them from developing their possibilities as human beings. Article 2 simply restates as a common standard the empirical condition whose denial brought, as a matter of fact, "untold sorrow to mankind." Of course, we cannot be absolutely sure that producing the empirical conditions listed and securing them by progressive legal and institutional measures, both national and international, will really enable all of us to live a full human life, but it is the best we can do in compassion with the victims and in response to the horrors in their voices. For, as William James has said, we can "only know that if [we] make a bad mistake the cries of the wounded will soon inform [us] of the fact."[21] Abstract metaphysical and moral reason is not as forthcoming, and never was.

What the representatives spelled out in the "Charter of the United Nations" and in the "Universal Declaration of Human Rights" as the aims of politics and the standards of civic living are then nothing but the empirical and experimental conditions for avoiding the worst of "the bad" experienced in the two great wars, and not the contrived abstract conditions of "the good" that so many people claim to have inherited with their ethnic and/or moral codes. Politics, as Jean-François Lyotard puts it much later and in a different context, "cannot have the good at stake, but [it] ought to have the lesser evil. Or, if you prefer, the lesser evil ought to be the political good."[22] As Italo Calvino has put it, the best we can expect is to avoid the worst.[23] Postmodernists like Lyotard are not the first to fear that the complete and final realization of the good life, prescribed by ethnic and/or universal moral codes, will issue in a totalitarian suppression of all those who are ethnically different or do not conform to the locally accepted universal codes, as it has in the past. Human affairs are auspiciously managed not by the desired consequences that lie ahead, but by those that have followed in the past and that we have experienced. Today, while the memories of our horrible experiences of World War II slowly fade away and the voices of the victims are in danger of getting drowned out by noisy anniversary commemorations and silenced in archives, we hear again about violent efforts to establish nation-states on the basis of common local roots as well as philosophical endorsements of a universal moral code. Jürgen Habermas, for instance, believes that "only a universalistic morality, which demonstrates general norms, can be defended with good reasons."[24] And Vittorio Hösle declares that "the expansion of Western culture should be primarily devoted to the propagation of a universalistic morality."[25] Some of us might be tempted again to agree with them in despair when reading the recent reports on the cannibalism and the "fearsome cruelties" people engaged in during the cultural revolution in China for the sake of perfect socialism.[26]

But at the end of World War II in San Francisco, nothing could have been further from the minds of the Western and non-Western representatives and founders of the United Nations Organization than the promotion of a universalistic morality, which demonstrates general norms, based on metaphysical truths about human nature, that so many philosophers continue to propose as the only viable antidote against the experienced horrors and as the final solution of the problem of our dark age. As the opening statements of the "Charter of the United Nations" shows, their negotiations were inspired by the determination to avoid under similar empirical circumstances the repetition of the horrors experienced in the two world wars. Arguably, our human condition has immensely improved since then, yet ethnic cleansing and crimes against humanity are still with us today. Consequently, we have to reformulate and reinstitute the problem the UN representatives addressed then and reenvision and develop solutions in light of our present circumstances. Philosophers will be able to contribute to such efforts only if they don't close their ears to the haunting voices of the victims and if they aim, as John Dewey puts it, "at a philosophy which shall be instrumental rather than final, and instrumental not to establishing and warranting any particular set of truths, but instrumental in furnishing points of view and working ideas which may clarify and illuminate the actual and concrete course of life."[27]

Notes

1. Bernard Osser and Patrick de Saint-Exupéry, "The UN's Failure: An Interview with Tadeusz Mazowiecki" (conducted in August for *Le Figaro*), in *The New York Review of Books* 42 (September 21, 1995): 39.

2. See Tadeusz Mazowiecki's letter of resignation to the Secretary-General of The United Nations, in *The New York Review of Books* 42 (September 21, 1995): 39.

3. Even President Clinton admitted at the Paris signing ceremony that the Bosnian peace agreement might not settle things, after all: "We cannot guarantee the future of Bosnia." See "Peace at Last. But at What Cost?" in *Newsweek* (December 25, 1995): 9.

4. Jane Kramer, "The Politics of Memory," in *The New Yorker* 71 (August 14, 1995): 48–65.

5. Ibid., p. 49.

6. Quoted by Christian Göldenboog, "Confronting The Memory," in *Deutschland: Magazine on Politics, Culture, Business and Science* 5 (November 1995): 31. Emphasis added.

7. Ibid., pp. 29f.

8. See Johann Wolfgang Goethe, "Die Vereinigten Staaten" (The United States), in *Werke* (Hamburger Ausgabe), edited by Erich Trunz (Munich: Deutscher Taschenbuch Verlag, 1982), volume 1, p. 333: "Amerika, du hast es besser, / Als unser Kontinent, das alte, / . . . Dich stört nicht im Innern / Zu

lebendiger Zeit / *Unnützes Erinnern* / Und vergeblicher Streit* / America, you have it better, / Than our continent, the old one, / . . . / . . . . / You are not disturbed at heart / In your life time / By pointless remembrance / And futile quarrels . . ." Emphasis added.

9. Osser and Saint-Exupéry, "The UN's Failure," p. 38.

10. Joe Klein, "Looking at the Big 'But,'" *Newsweek* 126 (December 18, 1995): 35.

11. See "Charter of the United Nations," in *Charter of the United Nations and Statute of the International Court of Justice*, published by the United Nations Department of Public Information (New York: United Nations, 1994); also in *Webster's New Twentieth Century Dictionary of the English Language. Unabridged*, 2d edition (New York: Simon and Schuster, 1979), Supplements, 145.

12. Irving Howe, "How to Write about the Holocaust," in *The New York Review of Books*, 32 (March 28, 1985): 14–17. See also his "Writing and the Holocaust," in *Writing and the Holocaust*, edited by Berel Lang (New York: Holmes & Meier, 1988), pp. 175–99.

13. Ibid., pp. 15f.

14. Blanche Wiesen Cook, *Eleanor Roosevelt*, vol. 1: 1884–1933 (New York: Penguin Books, 1992), p.17.

15. *Universal Declaration of Human Rights* (New York: United Nations Department of Public Information, 1993), 6.

16. Ibid., p. 5.

17. John Dewey, "Creative Democracy—The Task Before Us" (1939), in *The Later Works*, vol. 14: 1925–1941, edited by Jo Ann Boydston (Carbondale: Southern Illinois University Press, 1988), p. 226. Emphasis added.

18. See Howe, "How to Write about the Holocaust," p. 17: "I kept hearing the voice of a man struggling to retrieve the sense of what it means in the twentieth century to be, or become, a *Mensch*."

19. Jacques Maritain, *The Rights of Man and Natural Law*, translated by Doris C. Anson (New York: Gordian Press, 1971), pp. 60f.

20. *Universal Declaration of Human Rights*, p. 6.

21. See William James, "The Moral Philosopher and the Moral Life," in *The Will to Believe* (Cambridge: Harvard University Press, 1979), p. 158.

22. Jean-François Lyotard, *The Differend: Phrases in Dispute*, translated by Georges Van Den Abbeele (Minneapolis: University of Minnesota Press, 1988), p. 140.

23. See Italo Calvino, *If on a winter's night a traveler*, translated from the Italian by William Weaver (New York: A Harvest/HBJ Book, 1979), p. 4: "There are plenty younger than you or less young, who live in the expectation of extraordinary experiences: from books, from people, from journeys, from events, from what tomorrow has in store. But not you. You know that the best you can expect is to avoid the worst. This is the conclusion you have reached, in your personal life and also in general matters, even international affairs."

24. See Jürgen Habermas, "Rede zur Verleihung des Hegel-Preises" (1974), quoted in Rudolf Walther, "Was ist 'nationale Identität'?" *Die Zeit* (Overseas edition), 49 (19. Aug 1994): 16.

---

*Skipped are lines 2 and 3, and all of stanza 2 (4 lines).

25. See Hubertus Breuer, "Hegel kehrt zurück," in *Die Zeit* (Overseas edition), 49 (19. Aug 1994): 18.

26. See Zheng Yi, *Scarlet Memorial: Tales of Cannibalism in Modern China*, translated and edited by T. P. Sym with a foreword by Ross Terrill (Boulder, Colo.: Westview Press, 1996).

27. John Dewey, "Philosophy and American National Life" (1904), in *The Middle Works, 1899–1906*, vol. 3: 1903–1906, edited by Jo Ann Boydston (Carbondale: Southern Illinois University Press, 1977), p. 77.

Of Testimony, Piles, and the Poetics of *Final Letters*

Ruth Liberman

A*New York Times* article of September 25, 1996, announced that shoes of murdered victims were being collected throughout the United States to be "arrayed around the Capitol Reflecting Pool in Washington in silent testimony to the lives ended by gunshots in murders, accidents and suicides each year." Reading this, I was puzzled. I wondered how these shoes were a testimony (why shoes?) and mused whether bloodstained shirts ripped by bullets would not more properly be a *testimony*. Shoes seem in themselves not to testify to anything other than having once been worn and walked in. And the collected shoes were not necessarily the ones worn by the victims at the time of the murder, or worn at all, as one woman, whose husband was murdered during a robbery, reportedly states: "There was this brand-new pair of sneakers that hadn't even touched the ground." How does this brand-new pair of sneakers constitute a testimony to its owner's death?

The use of shoes puzzled me further in its design as a *collection*, a mass of shoes. Will they be neatly placed in pairs, one next to the other? Will they be strewn about randomly or piled up in heaps? Whatever the form, I could not help thinking of the often depicted piles of shoes in Nazi death camps. I admit, this thought stuck with me; it was hard to think of any other motivation for the idea of collecting shoes from murder victims to display as testimony to murder—shoes and murder being as such quite devoid of semantic connection. The act of collecting and piling up, a contemporary aesthetic device we easily take for granted, is yet another matter. I presume the purpose of this project was to find an adequate representation for the *vast number* of lives lost through urban violence. And what could better demonstrate the notion of a "vast number" than a *pile* of something? I also presume, since the protest has been called the "Silent March," that the use of shoes was seen to make sense: shoes would symbolize the marching, a collection, a great number of marchers. Nevertheless, I do still find these metaphors insufficiently relevant for this particular protest. A "silent march" can represent a protest or commemoration for absolutely anything and can always, if we so choose and declare it as such, take the form of a shoe collection, just as a wreath laid down has become a conventional unspecific symbol for honoring and mourning the dead. A "silent march" could also be represented by any other, equally unrelated means. A heap of shoes is not necessarily the only or the most logical solution to signify a "silent march."

As for the term "silent testimony," it could indeed apply to the piles of shoes found in the death camps, but is simply a misnomer when used for the Washington project: The shoe piles in the camps are remnants, traces of an act. They *become* a testimony because they "speak," as it were, about what actually happened. These shoes were not piled up in order to *bear testimony* to a large number of victims. They were collected because this was part of the procedure enforced by the Nazis, as was their goal to get rid of as many people in as short a time as possible, and to set aside in discrete collections everything left behind by those people, to be later utilized or eliminated. The care that went into collecting items taken from the victims was characteristic of the Nazis, and was moreover the very procedure that generated the now so familiar piles of shoes and other belongings. The event, the historical event, was inextricably *linked* with the piles of shoes. We have also seen mountains of suitcases, clothes, photographs, books, spectacles, teeth, and bodies. These images of methodical piles of human remains and belongings have shocked us and left their imprint on our memory. It seems to me that certain representations of the Holocaust, specifically collections and piles, have rendered themselves independent, have taken on autonomous symbolic force ready to be applied to quite unconnected incidents. While we may strive to assess the ramifications of different representations of the Holocaust, asking how this event we call Holocaust should be represented, told, remembered, and taught, its representations are already somewhere else, almost existing on their own, and no longer actually representing the Holocaust, nor even directly referring to it, yet, perhaps reflecting back on our understanding of it. One striking manifestation of this are homogeneous piles and collections, and I propose regarding the staging of such piles and collections within memorial contexts as poetic representations of testimony.

To pile up testimonies is clearly a curious phenomenon. I am thinking, for example, of piles such as Steven Spielberg's project,[1] which, for all good intentions, aims at *amassing* uniformly structured video testimonies of survivors.[2] I would like to point to the emphasis on scale, which is here most striking: this project has often been declared to be the largest of its kind to date in the world.[3] The image conjured up of an amassment of testimonies and witnesses, that is, of survivors, counters that of the far greater number of dead. Numbers, inconceivable figures and amounts have long become a symbol of the Holocaust.

Far more humble than Spielberg's project is the collection of testimonies I will turn to now: a small volume of last letters and postcards, written by people in camps, in ghettos, on trains; letters that somehow survived while their authors mostly vanished. This book, called *Final Letters*, was published by Yad Vashem.[4] What is significant and manifest in the last letters—the act of speaking before it is too late—is also, in part, what mobilized Spielberg to assemble the video testimonies at this point in time and on this scale, while other such projects have been in existence for years. A witness is a survivor, but not immortal. To gather as many testimonies as possible and to preserve them can be an important task. In considering the book *Final Letters* as a collection of testimonies, I hope to elicit a clearer understanding of some fundamental aspects of testimony, of the role it has begun to play lately, of the allure it seems to carry, of its relationship to vast amounts and piles, and of what emerges as an unbidden contradiction when we are dealing with the *amassing* of testimonies.

The reason I propose to look into this particular type of testimony, "last letters," is twofold. First, so-called last letters and last words, letters written and words uttered by people before their death, have been published for centuries in pamphlets and, as collections, in books. To assign them a place within a certain discipline depends entirely on how and where such letters are presented. But it can fairly be said that, as a collection, they almost always are employed to elicit from the reader a sympathetic or reverential response.[5] The profusion in publications of last letters and last words, I believe, indicates more than some obscure disposition for a morbid curiosity or fascination; it points to a complex and intricate relationship between witness and testimony, because it actively turns the reader of the testimony into a witness. The second reason is that last letters epitomize the proximity of testimony to death. The witness—the one who has been *present* at an event *that is now past*—is here not the survivor and cannot therefore bear witness. Yet he or she did, as long and as late as he or she could. Last letters push the limit of one integral aspect of testimony: presence, that is to say, the witness's presence at what is being witnessed as well as the witness's presence while bearing witness. In the case of last letters, these two instances collapse into one. What is attested by last letters is, of course, not the actual death of the author, but the awareness of approaching death. It is the last time the author testifies to have been present to him- or herself. Only the testimonial, the letter, "survived," bearing, as it were, witness to the witness—that is, to the author. The testimony must here stand in for the witness.

In law or in history, testimony is generally used as part of a claim or a story; it can substantiate, corroborate, add, or contradict a narrative, or constitute a narrative on its own. Of course, a narrative can be arranged to incorporate any type of components. For instance, testimonies of survivors, last letters, and other documentation could all be included in an account of deportations; or be part of a report on a particular camp or ghetto; or they could inform us about the life of one person or a community. In other words, testimonies need not be an end in themselves. If they are, one might ask: why are they brought together? It looks at first sight like an aesthetic decision, guided by showing only written testimonies, as if the medium were what counted here. We may too readily answer that they are brought together because they all emerge from a common historical event. But does this criterion justify a collection only of letters? Does the displayed collection of letters as testimonies bear educational value, and if so, of what sort? Does it answer to a demand for symbolization, to an aesthetic problem?

The structure and components of *Final Letters* will provide some clues here. It is comprised of translations of selected letters and post-cards from the Archive.[6] A fair number of the letters are accompanied by reproductions of the originals. These are reduced in scale and appear on the page often at decorative angles. A third component is occasional photographs of the writers or addressees. And finally, each letter is prefaced by a short introductory paragraph that summarizes available information on the author's origin and relation to the addressee(s)—if known—and the known or presumed facts about the author's disappearance or death, as well as the letter's itinerary. Although the letters and postcards are presented neither in chronological nor geographical order, they do not seem to be arranged randomly. There appears to be a choice as far as concerns the tone of the letters. At the beginning of the book, we find notes expressing or pretending some hope. Then they become more skeptical, the later ones conveying utter despair. The last portion contains letters by resistance fighters and members of the underground and ends with unaddressed messages of people bearing witness to destruction, torture, and to their own existence. "We want our names to be known for the generations to come," reads the last note. The book thus assigns each letter a place within the collection, relating one to the other. It is almost as if, by superimposing a narrative, it were trying to bring them together into a conclusive form.[7]

A further integral aspect of the book is the survival of the letters. As mentioned, each letter is prefaced by a brief description of how it was "saved."[8] Whether or not the letters reached the destinations specified by the writers, their itineraries ultimately, of course, come to a necessary halt in this book. The reported circumstances leading to the letters' conveyance to the Archive draw the reader into the trajectories of the letters. It is as though the now arrested physical movement of the letters is being channeled into an imaginary one: the reader is motioned to mentally retrace the letters' journeys through space and time. Bridging the diachronic gap between reader and writer, the letter terminates in the present, as it were. Thereby, the brief travelogues become at once also the reader's story: it is the story of how I, the reader, came to be vis-à-vis this letter. Thus, however tangentially, I am implicated, am part of the history of the letter's journey, and thereby part of the letter's history. This is because that history, up until the present, is, of course, not separate from the history that prompted the writing of the letter, to which I feel to be a witness, particularly by way of learning about how the letter survived. In that way, the "arrival" of the letter signifies an assurance of historical continuity, despite the irrevocable actual "discontinuity" of the author's life.

The reports on the letters' peregrinations constitute a substantial portion of the information supplied about them. Of course, they are also often the only known facts about the letters. These reports bespeak the marvel at their survival. The boundary experience of approaching impasse, which prompted many people to write messages, is echoed in the liminal nature of the letters' journeys, wherein they perpetually strive to cross the border between then and now; and it seems a miracle each time they do. While reading about these journeys we become acutely aware of the possibility that those written messages could have very easily been lost, never to be read by anyone. We assume that other such letters existed of which we do not know, messages that did not fall into anyone's hands; it is possible that the lost letters outnumber those that have been preserved. We marvel at the survival of those letters, it is almost unimaginable. In the book, *Testimony*, Shoshana Felman remarks respecting a note found buried near a crematorium: "What is ungraspable, indeed, is not the content of the statement, but the survival of its testimonial utterance: the fact that it is literally *spoken* from within the ashes of a crematorium."[9]

What does it mean to say that something is ungraspable? How can we speak of "it" but lack the capability to grasp "it"? If we do, then what are we speaking of? One even wonders what makes us assert that we have or have not grasped something. Felman's observation that the fact that these letters from "there" have entered our present is ungraspable is begging the question. Does not the word "ungraspable" hold a certain sway over us, does it not dare us with a hint of the beyond, a promise that we are at a safe distance from the beyond of graspability? Of that ungraspability, not of the ungraspable beyond, we want a token. By declaring something ungraspable we invest it with an enigmatic ambiance that, indeed, obscures our image of it; it becomes blurred and formless and *cannot* be grasped, because we cannot touch what has no form. What, then, happens when we have in front of us something which, for one reason or another, signifies "ungraspable"? Apparently, our relentless attempt to grasp (which requires imagining) induces us to find an image that can stand in for whatever it is we try to imagine—an image, however, that has dignity, that we can bear and live with, especially if we are to recall it for the purpose of keeping its memory alive. This image would have the task of filling the void left by what we declare unimaginable. Like water searching for the path of least resistance, our mind tends to seize the most passable representation of what we would otherwise resist imagining.

By this substitution, as it were, the reader's attention subtly turns away from the historical details perhaps referred to in the letters toward the survival of the letters themselves. It is here that we find our "image of least resistance," perhaps one that may even yield some pleasure or desire. This "image," I suggest, is twice removed from the "unimaginable" horror of the camps, the ghettos, the deportations—the victims of which are claimed here as the core subject of commemoration—for it fills the void not of what is unimaginable about the *events*, but what we declare unimaginable regarding the *survival* of the *documents* relating to the events. If our imagination struggles with grasping the survival of the document, it has yet again relieved itself of the duty to come to terms with the events documented by the document. In other words, the experience of feeling incapable of grasping the events or circumstances referenced in the letters, is, to some extent, supplanted by the certain "ungraspability" that the letters as vestiges of the past have entered the here and now of the reader and that death was somehow overcome, if only the "death" of the letter and, by extension, the writer's voice. True, that this voice, "*spoken* from within the ashes of a crematorium," should remain in existence, is not an easily acceptable notion; it also places us in temporal contiguity to the voice, especially if we refer to it as a "voice."

To illustrate further the relation of the reader to the letter, I should like to mention a sentence I came across in a book of last letters written by people during the French Revolution, as they were awaiting their execution. The sentence reads: "When you read me, I shall be no more."[10] The same and similar announcements can be found in many of the letters published in the book. For the reader, the unequivocal message of this sentence, its disarmingly factual and indisputably plaintive sway, epitomizes the quite apparent property of a last letter written before death: that the author is no more. This tautological spin might account for much of the subtly captivating allure that last letters have held. The announcement brings to mind the powerful characteristic nature of photography, articulating, in effect, its fundamental property: an object depicted in a photograph could equally be saying, "When you see this picture, I shall be no more." But the thrust of the above sentence is much less subtle than the unspoken connotation of a photograph. What is a merely implicit, yet constitutive aspect of a photograph, is here the very statement itself. It is, however, more than merely a message that could have been transmitted orally. The statement materializes in the letter as a reified message; to be written and to be read is integral to it. In order to convey the intended message and to perform it, the mark of the person who "is no more" must acquire a form; it is embodied by the letter. It seems obvious, then, that the author's wish was more than to merely proclaim her imminent death to the addressee. For otherwise it would have sufficed to announce in the letter the date set for execution. This would have constituted the conveyance of mere factual information. It would be devoid of performative power. Instead, the author establishes a link between now and then—the now of the author and the then of the reader, and vice versa—and an association between the two that is binding. She does so by forcing the reader not only to learn of her death, but to somehow perceive and experience it. The letter as a physical object and as a carrier of the message enables this. The sentence, "when you read me, . . . I shall be no more," inescapably involves the reader in its plot. Not only is the sentence always true, whenever and whoever reads it, but the act of reading it also *makes* it true. The sentence summons the reader as witness who cannot but be implicated.

I have mentioned the above excerpt from a last letter to emphasize the reader's role of witness with respect to last letters. The last letter bridges the hiatus between author and reader, it joins the historical gap. The historical course through which this voice has passed is embedded in the letter, and the letter itself comes to be the trace of its history. That historical trace, at once perceived and imagined, represents the conceptual, temporal, and spatial chasm between "then" and "now." It is this chasm that generates the frame, within which the letter can function as an aestheticized object.

In this regard, the reproductions of the original letters included in *Final Letters* exemplify some salient aspects of the relation between the letters as aesthetic objects (in their emotive power) and the letters as documents. Without the reproductions, all we would be left with, would be the translations of the letters as text. But, as if these translations in themselves were insufficient, they are supplemented by accompanying visual elements. Of course, it is entirely common for books dealing with historical material not only to describe and quote from it, but also to supply, along with the main text, reproductions of the material referred to or other illustrating visual aids. One primary reason for using reproductions is their agency as evidence, in which case the reproductions of the document serve to document and substantiate the text or translation. They furnish proof that the mentioned document really exists. Reproductions may also serve to illustrate and supply further visual details relevant to the text. But reproductions of the original also have the effect of bringing the reader closer to the object, providing a sense of experience. Moreover, the image of the letter as an object works more immediately on our emotional response than does the mediation of the text.

The foreword of *Final Letters* suggests as much in stating that the letters "represent a striking testimony on the Nazis' terror regime and the Jews' predicament in those conditions,"[11] and in concluding with the words, "We are grateful to the relatives and friends of the authors, who agreed to part with the last letters of their nearest ones and to transmit them to Yad Vashem so that they [the letters] may serve as a memorial."[12] The book thus lays claim to the letters serving both as documents *and* as memorial, which means that that which tells us about a situation or event, itself a part of it (the document), becomes also its own representation (the memorial). Having been removed from what seems to be their genuine context, the family or friends, and inserted in a collection of other such letters, they have been divested of their uniqueness. Once the letters are collected, gathered, and displayed in the archive, museum, or book, each letter becomes in a sense a reproduction of all the other letters. No longer is it the specific letter, addressed to a particular person; by serving as a memorial, the letter loses its specificity and becomes generic. And while the sheer number of lives lost cannot be comprehended or adequately represented, the letters in the collection call up all the other letters written but never received. The collection can invoke the entire mass, a totality.[13] In so doing, each letter's specificity is deemphasized, and the testimonial utterance of each letter is suspended. What happens here to the "actual" testimony seems to be a part of the same memorial aesthetics that apply to the "silent testimony" of the pile of shoes in Washington—only at another stage and with the difference that the former consists of actual testimonies while the latter does not. Both operate through the quality of accumulation, and in both instances, accumulation is the carrier of symbolic force.

That clusters, piles, collections are a "common" mode of display in contemporary memorial aesthetics, does not relieve us of asking, why and to what effect? What is the message, and what ramifications might be involved? I would like to draw attention again to the idea of "vast amounts," the use of which in memorial aesthetics is a fairly recent one. I can think of many memorials that do not emphasize the aspect of "vast amounts," though it is intrinsic to the message. There are memorials, for instance, to the many dead soldiers of a war; yet the memorials might display one single generic soldier. The "vast amount" is implicit—we would not speak of a war if only one person got killed. It may have seemed redundant to show a mass of dead soldiers, or maybe it was felt that we need to be reminded of the *individual* soldiers that constituted the mass. The desire to conjure up the individual from within the mass is more and more replaced by a representation of the faceless, nameless, even untraceable individuals in the shape of uniform items gathered or piled up.

This move away from the specific is reflected further in the restaging of piles that are quite unrelated to what they mean to signify. For example, we can imagine a pile of children's shoes displayed at Yad Vashem not only to be a gruesome *trace* of what happened to these children, but to become also a *reminder* of the same and other atrocities inflicted on other children during the Holocaust, and then to become a *symbol* for this particular genocide, which specifically included the utter categorization, accumulation, and utilization of all remains of the victims. But the Washington display of shoes takes this one step further. No longer connected to the Holocaust and bearing a different signification, the shoes in Washington nonetheless seem to rely on and retain the sense of outrage, if not unbearable horror, imprinted by the death camps on the notion of a stack of shoes.

Within the genre of memorial aesthetics, testimony has become a category of representation. It lies as such somewhere between metonymy and symbol. In other words, the aforementioned pile of shoes meant to represent a testimony to murderous violence across the country is neither, as would be the case in metonymy, *closely associated with* the act of violence or murderous crimes (shoes do not stand for murder), nor is it, *by convention*, a symbol for mass murder or violence—at least not yet. In the use as *representation*, however, not just anything can be endowed with the task of bearing testimony for anything else. Something must supply at least a semantic bridge. And it seems the memorial of shoes in Washington derives its symbolic power from familiar images of piled up remains from victims of Nazi violence and murder. Since the Holocaust often supplies some kind of standard for any one of its innate facets—genocide, fascism, racism, bestiality, and so on—culled from it and posed in relation to other political crimes, imagery derived from the Holocaust transfers affects associated with it onto these images, for instance, those of piles. In this case then, what constitutes the semantic bridge is the symbolism supplied by imagery borrowed from Holocaust history—shoes and, most strikingly, piles. But the piles are also intricately linked to the notion of testimony.

What the display of shoes in Washington, then, really seems to tell us is that "a pile of shoes" *signifies testimonial*—in this case, of or to the victims of urban violence in America. This pile, then, becomes a *representation of testimony* itself. The piles of shoes from the camps are thereby dehistoricized and depoliticized, as is the shoe memorial in

Washington. This might just be one of the risks endemic to the aesthetics of memory, to which Holocaust memorials have at least contributed, if not supplied much of the current language. And we can add to that the poetics of testimony.

Is it possible that, since the piles in the death camps, other discrete piles and conglomerations easily take on an added, and sinister, meaning in our culture? How are piles of homogeneous objects, staged on various occasions, a suitable form to signify a variety of human afflictions? It seems that each discrete pile known from the death camps can be abstracted and utilized to signify a particular aspect of human suffering in other contexts. For instance, the lobby of the museum at Ellis Island displays an assembly of suitcases assumedly belonging to people who brought all they could to the new country, and who hoped to pass the tests of willingness and ability to fit in, and of mental and physical fitness. Unquestionably, the array of suitcases has the task of reenactment, which is the typical museological staging of an environment, of an atmosphere. But the suitcases are also symbolically transformed. Here a symbol of displaced people, they at once take on an added meaning when associated with similar imagery from concentration camps. Again, I venture that the scenario of a cluster of abandoned suitcases is derived from Holocaust precedents. Now, the suitcases in Ellis Island are still more closely related to what they are supposed to signify than are the shoes in Washington, respectively, to inner city violence. If the latter are called a testimony, we have entered a web of metaphors, analogies, and representations. Whether that pile can constitute testimony is another matter, for to bear witness, to give a testimony, is inextricably linked with *presence*, both in terms of the witness's presence at the event witnessed and in terms of the witness's presence at the moment of testifying. If this is not the case, strictly speaking, we are not dealing with testimony.

I claimed earlier that testimony has become a means of representation and even an object of representation. With reference to "survivor testimonies" of the Fortunoff video archive, Geoffrey Hartman speaks of "extracanonical representation," which he regards as "suspended between history and memory, suspended also between literature and documentary."[14] Hartman refers to the video testimonies of Holocaust survivors as examples of representation without

> theatricality or stage-managed illusions. . . . The difficulty of seeing these accounts as representations comes only from the fact that they do not, like historical discourse, make the real desirable (if only as an object of knowledge), or the desirable real, in the manner of fictions. What is real here is not desirable; indeed, it is so repugnant that it may affect the will to live on.[15]

If this is so, it might be in part due to the fact that the viewer/listener is engaged as an active *participant* in the testimony.[16] This is not just any kind of participation, such as, for instance, the one created in theme parks; the participation here is of a fundamentally different nature. Neither the testimony itself nor the person who gives the testimony is a representation of what he or she testifies to; and the person who listens is likely to engage with what he or she hears rather than translating it into what it might stand for, or having an abstracted sentimental response to it. By nature, the video testimonies also run counter to being perceived as a homogeneous pile (unless we want to look at the video library itself). Each video takes the listener/viewer through its own stretch of time. He or she becomes an active witness, a participant in the narration of the story, not so different to the reader of the last letter. However, while it is difficult to view the videos as material objects, it is equally difficult to ignore the materiality of the letters.

The last letters are imbued with some particular qualities suitable for representation, qualities we have learned to associate with certain sentiments. There is the visible sign of the passage of time: the slightly soiled, old, faded and crumpled letter is an oft-used image to summon the mournful feeling of the past, of loss and death. Furthermore, a letter bears the stamp of secrecy and privacy: the last letters present the reader with an enigmatic ambiance in more than one way. Letters usually signify documents that are first and foremost private and sealed to the public. In the case of found letters, public display as such does not diminish the extent to which their secrets seem still unrevealed. In *Final Letters*, however much information about the authors of the letters and the circumstances in which they were written is supplied by the editors, there always remains with each letter a much greater degree of unexplained and unknowable details. In fact, the extent of unattainable information is almost overwhelming and evokes powerlessness, while at the same time raising a desire to know. An allure of uncertainty and mystery, retained and kept in suspension, might contribute to that which makes "the real desirable (if only as an object of knowledge)." If there is always something that remains inconceivable, unexplainable, and enigmatic, "one cannot appease one's hunger in looking."[17] The letters are charged with unattainable secrets.

A further crucial quality belonging to the letters is the authenticity of the witness: a dated handwritten note bearing the signature of its author is a paradigm of authenticity. Testimony requires that the witness be authentic, both in witnessing and in bearing witness. The witness cannot be replaced. The witness who testifies declares to have attended the event he or she testifies to. In other words, testimony is an *act of faith* involving at least two parties and an assumed contract, wherein the witness vows to speak the truth and the recipient vows to believe. The utterance, "I was there," is the minimal requirement to constitute a testimony.[18] Legally, the more witnesses whose testimonies corroborate at least the *occurrence* of an event, the more convincing the testimonial. Carlo Ginzburg, on the other hand, argues, in his essay, "Just One Witness," that law—traditionally requiring at least two witnesses (or a witness plus evidence)—and history have different rules and foundations. And for history, according to Ginzburg, we can learn a lot from a single witness.[19] Going further, it seems to me, if we are no longer dealing with actual testimony—but with testimony as memorial, testimony as representation—if testimony is neither an act of speech, nor an act of faith, a declaration, nor a narrative, that we learn little from one or even two witnesses; we need a "vast amount."

If the very essence of testimony is authenticity, that is to say, if in order to constitute testimony, the witness must have been present at the event he or she testifies to, then the witness, who is *unique* and *irreplaceable*, even *untranslatable*, cannot in turn be represented and the representation be called a testimony to the event. It seems our culture has ascribed to testimony a new poetics that holds in store a whole set of allures. It is easily employed, paradoxically, in projects that incidentally dehistoricize history, projects by means of which we perhaps lose the ability to listen to a survivor, a witness. The very nature of testimony being its established or claimed authenticity, its specificity, might be the very quality—akin to that of a relic—that renders testimony so viable for use as representation.

Notes

1. "Survivors of the Shoah Visual History Foundation," a nonprofit organization, founded by Steven Spielberg in 1994, to videotape and archive interviews with Holocaust survivors all over the world.

2. All interviews are arranged by a similar design, i.e., they are structured into three equal parts, covering experiences before, during, and after the war. All interviews are approximately two hours in length. For the final moments of the interview, family members are invited to join the survivor on camera.

3. "[T]he Foundation is compiling the most comprehensive library of survivor testimony ever assembled." "As of March 03, 1997, Survivors of the Shoah Visual History Foundation has conducted 25,402 interviews." From the Foundation's web page **www.vhf.org**.

4. *Final Letters*, published by Yad Vashem Archive (Weidenfeld and Nicolson, London: 1991). Yad Vashem is Israel's national Holocaust memorial complex situated on Memorial Hill in Jerusalem. It consists of outdoor monuments, exhibition halls, archives, and a library.

5. The number of published collections of last letters is quite substantial. See, for example, P. F. MacLochlainn, *Last Words; Letters and Statements of the*

Leaders Executed after the Rising at Easter, 1916 (Dublin: Kilmainham Jail Restoration Society, 1971); G. Selleck, *Dove at the Windows; Last Letters of Four Quaker Martyrs* (Lincoln, Mass.: Penman Press, 1973); E. & R. Bethge, ed., *Last Letters of Resistance: Farewells from the Bonhoeffer Family*, trans. D. Slabaugh (Philadelphia: Fortress Press, 1986); H. S. Ziegler, *Grosse Prüfung; letzte Briefe und letzte Worte Todgeweihter* (Hannover: National-Verlag, 1972), C. Michael. *Abschied. Briefe und Aufzeichnungen* (Zürich, 1944).

6. The book makes no mention of the criteria according to which the letters were selected for print.

7. The shift that occurs here in the function of the letters is comparable to the one Benjamin describes regarding the nature of collecting: "The crucial aspect of collecting is for the object to be absolved from all original functions, in order for it to enter into the closest imaginable relationship to its kind." Walter Benjamin, *Das Passagen-Werk* (Frankfurt am Main: Suhrkamp Verlag, 1983), [H Ia, 2]. p. 271

8. Examples are: ". . . Since it was written on the cover band of a newspaper, it was not opened by the censor. It was given to the Yad Vashem Archive by her son. . . ." (58) ". . . The letter was dispatched before the sisters' transfer to the Westerbork camp; the card, dropped from the deportation train, also reached its destination." (21) ". . . It was probably thrown out of the building where all the Jews were assembled prior to the action. A Lithuanian woman found the letter and kept it until she was able to give it to a relative of the family, who visited the Soviet Union some twenty years later, in the 1960s. . . ." (23) ". . . This letter, his last, was sent to his family a few days before his deportation. Yad Vashem received it from Pinhas's son, Kalman Sharir, who lives in Israel." (25) ". . . Faithful to her promise, the neighbor kept the letter and transmitted it after the war to Regina's relatives in Israel, through the agency of the Israeli Embassy in Belgrade." (31) ". . . One of the policemen guarding the Jews conveyed this letter from a woman to her husband Abraham. . . ." (61)

9. Shoshana Felman, "Camus' *The Plague*, or a Monument to Witnessing" in Shoshana Felman and Dori Laub, MD., *Testimony: Crises of Witnessing in Literature, Psychoanalysis, and History* (New York: Routledge, 1992), p. 116, n14.

10. ". . . quand vous me lirez, je ne serai plus. . . ." Olivier Blanc, *La dernière lettre: Prisons et condamnés de la Révolution 1793-1794* (Paris: Robert Laffont, 1984), p. 164. English translation by Alan Sheridan (London 1987), p. 138.

11. *Final Letters*, p. 9.

12. Ibid., p. 10.

13. Cf. Gertrud Koch, *Die Einstellung ist die Einstellung: Visuelle Konstruktionen des Judentums* (Frankfurt am Main: Suhrkamp Verlag, 1992), p. 137: ". . . the primacy of vision—the recovery of reality through its image—approaches its limit at the point where that, which is supposed to be recovered in the image and enable anamnetic solidarity with the dead, eludes any pictorial conception. The concreteness of visual quality, which necessarily attaches itself to an existing thing, offers resistance from within against what constituted the *mass* destruction."

14. Geoffrey H. Hartman, "The Book of the Destruction," in *Probing the Limits of Representation: Nazism and the "Final Solution,"* ed. Saul Friedländer (Cambridge: Harvard University Press, 1992), p. 324.

15. Ibid., p. 325.

16. See Dori Laub: "For the testimonial process to take place, there needs to be a bonding, the intimate and total presence of the other—in the position of one who hears. Testimonies are not monologues; they cannot take place in solitude. The witnesses are talking to somebody: to somebody they have been waiting for for a long time." "Bearing Witness or the Vicissitudes of Listening," in *Testimony: Crises of Witnessing in Literature, Psychoanalysis, and History*, pp. 70-71. See also Jacques Derrida, "Shibboleth: For Paul Celan," in *Word Traces: Readings of Paul Celan*, ed. Aris Fioretes (Baltimore: The Johns Hopkins University Press, 1994).

17. Walter Benjamin, "Über einige Motive in Baudelaire," *Illuminationen*, p. 222.

18. See Shoshana Felman and Dori Laub, *Testimony*. See also Derrida, "Shibboleth: For Paul Celan."

19. Carlo Ginzburg, "Just One Witness," in *Probing the Limits of Representation: Nazism and the "Final Solution,"* p. 85.

Giving Testimony

Burkhard Liebsch

According to a widely accepted tradition, the truth is independent of human beings. Our mortal life does not affect truth, which neither dies nor is endangered by time. Truth can only be expressed by and achieve validity through us, but we do not temporalize or relativize truth. Giving testimony, however, challenges this tradition since the truth of testimony depends on the testifying person. Only through the witnesses' testimony does truth *become* true: it's a *vérité-à-faire* (Merleau-Ponty) which entirely depends on saying what needs to be said.[1] This is all the more so when something of great significance is experienced by only a few people, or indeed if only one individual has experienced (and survived) it. In these cases, contrary to what Hegel assumed, truth does not testify for itself.

When testimony reveals what is without precedent in our experience, our capacity to believe what is reported is put to the test.[2] What is contradictory to our previous experience, or at least seems relatively unlikely, we can either doubt, accept conditionally or with caution, or simply believe for the moment. But there are truths we cannot simply believe, even when we are directly confronted with their reportings. Anyone testifying to such incredible truths wagers his own credibility. If a witness reports something that appears "unbalanced," we will most likely suppose that the witness *himself* is unbalanced—that is, if there are no other witnesses, sources, or "authorized reports" to corroborate the report. Historical investigations of the ways reports concerning Nazi concentration camps were transmitted and received by foreign countries are illustrative in this context. When witnesses report unprecedented events, it is the witnesses themselves who must explain why and how their testimony breaks with the flow of everyday, normal experience. Normally, we assume that reporting takes the form of the *statement*, and must, therefore, be treated as if the witnesses were giving evidence before a court.[3] Under normal conditions (and all other things being equal), we assume that witnesses to events are *credible*. In what follows, however, I want to draw attention to the limits of the applicability of this implicitly *juridical* model to the testimonies given by survivors of the Nazi concentration camps.

Certainly the fact that someone has experienced what he reports does not in itself guarantee either the truth of his testimony or the correctness and adequacy of his description. But the witness' claim to direct experience is requisite for his acceptance as a witness. The direct experience is of a past event to which we have no direct access. In this sense the witness is a decisive link between us and the past. The witness's testimony has crucial implications for the present. For example, in the case of accidents involving disputed questions of liability and guilt, eyewitness reports are often decisive. In general, however, the truths of the present stand and fall with the realization of past truths. When we have to rely on only a few testimonies, our responsibility will also rest upon the hearing, seeing, and memory of those few whose reports may well seem incredible from our present perspectives.

Given the fragility of truth and the terrrible burden of responsibility in these cases, it is not surprising that we inquire concerning the credibility of the witnesses. Their credibility is called into question according to the extent that the witnesses report "incredible" or "unlikely" events. We also know from experience that a witness's credibility is not in itself enough to ensure the truth of what is reported. In ancient history (*historia*) what people had seen and heard themselves was regarded as the epitome of the reliability of any reported "historical" truth. History was the knowledge gained from self-experience and its telling. Admittedly historians soon saw themselves confronted with mutually contradictory reports, but it was assumed without question that *experience* could grasp the essence of any event, that human experience is *sayable*, and that it can be described in a written form. The *readability* of experience was assumed in ancient history.

But it is impossible to see and tell something simultaneously. Related truth will always fall behind experienced truth. Moreover, related truth is—as the latest discussion of the rhetorical dimension of history has shown—indissolubly intertwined with its "how." No two reports about the past really coincide with each other. They will always have only one particular central area of focus in common and each statement gives a different perspective of the event.[4] (An underhand strategy of "disassembling" witnesses of Nazi-crimes has always worked with this aporia.) It is obviously not possible to draw a definite line between, on the one hand, telling the truth in a different way or, on the other, telling a different truth. Each new and different statement—even if it appears to us to be a further confirmation of testimonies already presented—is able to feed our doubts.

Moreover, we have to be aware that the statement of the witness (*that which is said*) will always only represent the final point of giving testimony. *The event* which affected him, *has made him a witness*—without first asking for his consent. His "seeing" and "hearing" told him that something out of the ordinary, a violation of the law, or a crime, had occurred. The context of the perpetrators' deeds, the question of why, of the cause, may not have been clear to the witness, but we nevertheless have to assume that he saw, to say the least, that "something was wrong." The witness first of all had to realize that something was at stake which demanded to be testified to, i.e., a severe breakdown of any expectations concerning human moral behavior which previously seemed to have a firm basis in a "civilized" societal normality. The witnesses had to realize the almost complete destruction and breakdown of their previous expectations concerning human moral behavior. We know, of course, that the nature of this breakdown was extremely difficult to comprehend. Voluntarily caused physical injury, cruelty, humiliation, and so on were easily recognizable as such by the victims in the camps. But they could be understood as such against the background of a sense of justice originating from the previous normality of social life. They belonged to an area of life where, as it was already known, or at least imagined, brutality and injustice could befall man. However, the *significance* of the *system of extermination*—which in the minds of the perpetrators was not mechanized murder, but simply a factory-like organization for the liquidation of inferior "objects"—could not at first be adequately defined.

To a certain extent the witnesses could not actually say *what* exactly had happened to them and their fellow sufferers. Their second life as survivors—as witnesses—began often in a state of acute distress followed by a lifelong search for the actual *significance* of what they had gone through. Many witnesses only began to write decades after the event. It took Robert Antelme ten years to come to the following conclusion: they did not simply want to liquidate us, they wanted to make something quite different out of us, they wanted to radically dehumanize us.[5]

The witnesses heard and saw what happened, but they were stunned. The experienced event seemed to break the frame of sayability. The statement, the witness's testimony, the biographical report, even the poem and the song were often unable to come to the aid of the experienced event in the face of speechlessness. On the contrary, the very word that should have helped "experienced" truth to prove the kernel of its significance seemed to seal its death. Here giving testimony, which starts with actual experience, could not lead to an appropriate testimony, and thus could not itself protect what had to be testified to from the danger of vanishing with the irreversible flow of time. Is it, thus, only with the disappearance of the witnesses themselves that what was to be testified to finally can be said—without, however, an accurate oral or written record?

This question brings us to the extreme opposite pole of the juridical model, where what is *said*—according to the *apophantic logos*—is all important. This model leads us to forget the real meaning of *giving* testimony, which often defined the real *meaning of the survival* of witnesses long before they had even begun to express themselves. The juridical model proceeds from the strong but dubious premise that the witness must know what he sees, or saw. But an event breaking every frame of interpretation based on our previous experience cannot in this sense be seen and understood in the same instant. The experience of events which have taken place is—as historical experience—entrusted to an unavoidable *Nachträglichkeit* (supplementary process). For it is not possible to see events that have just happened and that produce a fact together with the result of the event. It is true that often the result of the experience substitutes itself for the preceding process which has led to this result, but this process did not previously have the meaning which we attach to it in the light of the result. The significance of the event taken place often only begins to emerge for the individual after decades of emotional paralysis.

This *delay of historical understanding* means at the same time a *delay of the truth* which the witness has to tell. The *realization* of the truth, as far as this is possible at all, cannot adjust itself in strict simultaneity to the "experience" of the event which has occurred. The witness cannot, as it were, transcribe the experienced event happening in front of his eyes, even less so if it breaks every familiar frame of his experience hitherto. Robert Antelme at that time could not "see" that an attempt had been made to make out of him and his fellow sufferers something other than human beings. What he saw could only be the beginning of *giving testimony* which would need years to realize the significance of the events before achieving explicit sayability at all—a realization which would not come anywhere close to justifying the testimony that was demanded by the witness's previous "experience." Giving testimony begins with an awareness of the events that have occurred, but might possibly require a long process of *realization* of the significance of what has been perceived before the witness is able to set down a written testimony that must then "speak for itself." In the past no imagination could sufficiently comprehend the extent and the true significance of events that had occurred.

Thus it is understandable why many witnesses of the Shoah felt their inability to give an account of the true significance of what had actually happened in their presence. Numerous brutalities and many cases of murder were witnessed with the uncanny feeling of an "improbable," secret systematics which could not be explained.[6] Obviously murder was not committed "purely" out of hate, as the task was carried out with an unsuspected, passionless "objectivity"—except in the case of those who were satisfying "private" whim rather than doing their duty within the context of the National Socialist program of genocide. The resolute implementation of mass liquidation appeared—some seemed to extrapolate as much—to be leading toward the extermination of all who belonged to the designated categories of victims. But again that was not all. Genocide was not restricted to one method. The language used by the perpetrators leads us to their further objectives. The aim was—again as Robert Antelme states—to "turn us into something other than human beings," into something that does not even have to be "murdered" in order to cause its annihilation. The objective was to exterminate the victims in a way that would not leave the slightest trace of their destruction *as human beings*. The objective was to convince an "anachronistic" voice of conscience—which made at least some of the perpetrators feel sick in view of what they inflicted upon their victims—that there was no reason for remorse, for guilt or shame. Himmler demanded the restriction of moral feelings to the purified *avant garde* of the human race, that is, to those who in *his* view alone deserved the respected label "German."[7] The core of an old-fashioned morality—which *demands non-indifference with respect to an other's mortality as such*—would, he supposed, sooner or later fade if only a new education would have had the chance to cultivate a *radical indifference* in relation to those who were condemned to stay beyond the "sphere of moral obligation." On the firm basis of *radical indifference*—which, for the time being, seemed only within the reach of the SS-Elite—an *annihilation of the otherness of the other* would be possible, leaving no *moral trace* after the extermination.[8]

This plan may have failed. Perhaps even in Auschwitz the actual "moral impossibility of committing murder" of which Levinas speaks was proved.[9] Perhaps the perpetrators' deeds can and must in the last instance only be understood as an attempt to deny this *moral* impossibility—that is, as an attempt which is deeply enmeshed with the aforementioned nonindifference vis-à-vis the face of the other which it tries to efface. But the reality of the camps deprived the victims of every possibility of validating their feeling that a crime had been committed that was beyond law and order, and for which there was no suitable name. Had not, in effect and paradoxically, a "state of nature" been *artificially* produced in which neither justice nor the law ruled, and where nothing could support the feeling that something had been contravened? In a Hobbesian "state of nature" anything is allowed and nothing forbids "liquidating" others.

The victims were often left alone with these feelings. If they did finally make up their minds to believe what they saw, then they had to come to the realization that it was not sufficient simply *to believe themselves* in order to be their own witnesses. That which was "seen" had also to be said and heard. And only when *another believed* what had been seen and said could it actually be shown to be true. Above all, that which was seen, namely, the attempt to rob people of their humanity, affected everyone. In what had been seen itself lay the imperative to express it; it must not be left unsaid. Later excavated from hidden, secret places in the death camps, poems, final letters, and desperate appeals to the "world's conscience" demonstrate that often an anonymous addressee of the testimony (e.g., future generations) had to be turned to in order to do justice to *this constitutive coupling of the seen and the to-be-said, which is essential to the meaning of testimony*. The testimonies said: "I have seen and now know; I myself experienced what I saw, although at the time I felt I could not trust my senses; I have seen things which would make one lose one's mind, undermining all previous experience, things refusing to be assimilated into any previous experience, and things radically casting doubt upon the *sayability* of what I have seen. I have seen what one cannot see without somehow becoming blind to it. I have things to say which resist sayability. I expect of language that it go beyond itself in order to express the silence of my blindness, to prevent myself and the events from remaining locked in a state of absolute speechlessness, in the face of which every history would necessarily have to remain ignorant and the danger of a repetition of the events would be provoked. . . ."

Does not an "experience" which resists sayability and which cannot be defined remain blind, just as a notion which has no definite, expressible reference to events remains empty? Certainly, but here we are dealing with an experience which is given to the witness as something which demands to be said and which at the same time defies sayability. This frequently discussed paradox has repercussions for the witness. Not only is his credibility endangered because, on the basis of previous experience, he has to report "unlikely" events, but also because he was only able to become a witness due to his involvement in these events, which in turn places the objectivity expected from him in question. What is more: If the witness's being involved in what happened leaves his "experience" speechless, the testimony would seem in the final event to testify only to the actual *impossibility of testimony*. Felman and Laub also speak of such an impossibility in their remarkable study *Testimony*, which has many parallels in Lyotard's *Le différent*.[10] Lyotard could have referred to Primo Levi, who as a survivor stated that the history of the concentration camps was written solely by those who, like himself, did not touch the deepest depths of despair. Those who did reach this point—and who could be regarded as the only authentic witnesses of such despair—did not return, or their powers of observation were paralyzed by suffering and incomprehension.

Does not the significance of what can only be expressed in negative terms threaten to become the absolute secret of a negative revelation accessible only to the victims, which would have to correspond in turn to total unawareness on our part? Can the notion of giving testimony after such an aporetic reinterpretation nevertheless be thought of as the *decisive relay between the past and those living today* who, if they are not capable of "remembering" this past, will risk its future repetition? There are certainly numerous testimonies, legal documents, and reminders in literature of the survivors and in historical discourse which testify to what happened. Going by the conventional standards which up to now it has been believed could be applied to authentic historical testimonies, we find an overwhelming body of material in which, as never before, virtually all forms of presentation are displayed. This does not alter the fact that the recorded texts have made both the internal and external limits of testimony all too painfully clear to us.

Let us return to just one of these limits which I have already touched on. We know that the *objective reliability* of what is said in texts, as well as the *credibility* of the witnesses themselves, is jeopardized by the fact that nobody was able to see everything and that being involved in the events restricted the independence, the ability to judge, and the memory of the witnesses for a long time. The proximity to events was no guarantee of their correct and reliable interpretation.[11] Certainly we have to rid ourselves of the misleading idea that a kind of chronicle or protocol of the events which, with the least possible interval in time, could be documented parallel to the events, would constitute the ideal testimony. In my opinion, however, neither these limitations on the testimonies nor the arguments for an "impossibility of testimony" lead to a purely negative result. My rather cursory remarks indicated several reasons for doubting whether the testimonies received can do justice to the task imposed upon them. But there is more: Do not the survivors attempt to convince us that, beyond what is said, the essential "what-is-still-to-be-said" will always *remain* to be said? Is not the tradition of the survivors' texts inspired with the *absolute demand* not to forget what *still remains to be said* in spite of our rigorous doubts concerning the sayability of what actually happened?

Never, according to this tradition, will there be a definitive testimony, a final text about the Shoah. All that has been said hitherto has its future still in front of it, a future still "pending" because *the testimonies transmit not only what has been said, but also this irretrievable surplus of what remains to be said.* More is expressed through the witness than he can positively relate. And it is precisely through the texts that we learn of this surplus transcending what is said. In other words, we learn that what is said can never draw level with what is still to be said, and for this very reason the said challenges us to say it anew, in a different way, *thus keeping what remains to be said alive*. We who follow are influenced by this strained relationship between "saying" and "said," "*giving* testimony" and "*given* testimony" as a task of our continuing history, even when there is no longer living testimony to reach us. The connection to events, passed on through the lives of the witnesses themselves, will inevitably fade away.

The recorded texts and the testimonies themselves bear witness to the disproportion between what has been said and what remains to be said. The testimonies, which initially seemed only to testify to the impossibility of testimony, thereby evoking a crisis concerning the notion of truth in relation to *statement* (*apophansis*), force a new understanding of what is *said*, of the texts, and of the recipients of what the records pass on. The testimonies are not at all limited to what has been said, which will never do justice to what the witnesses *had to tell*. They also convey, as Lyotard says, a "feeling" for this failure to do justice itself and thereby for that which still remains to be said and which cannot simply be left to an indifferent unsayability.

Thus the texts that can be read today are not simply written records, but *traces of giving* testimony which will never finally crystallize in the said. The texts make us, the descendants, into witnesses by passing on to us the task of stating what remains to be said. We nonsurvivors and "ordinary mortals," to whom the testimonies are addressed, will thus, whether we like it or not, be the only ones who can preserve truth from falling into the paralysis of an indifferent unsayability or into the forgetfulness of *the written word*.[12] What remains to be said does not testify for itself. Only through us by way of what is said can what is still to be said experience the proof of truth that is both continuously renewed and continuously postponed. This handing down of testimony has nothing to do with a simple proliferation of the texts; rather, it is a continuing textual inspiration of the descendants through the handing down of the task of never forgetting "what remains to be said."[13]

Translated by Ms. Bärbec Zimmer and Dr. Adamson

Notes

1. Cf. B. Waldenfels, *Deutsch-französische Gedankengänge* (Frankfurt/M., 1997), ch. 8.

2. G. W. F. Hegel, *Vorlesungen über die Philosophie der Geschichte*. Bd. I. Die Vernunft in der Geschichte, ed. J. Hoffmeister (Hamburg, 1994), p. 29.

3. The hermeneutical notion of testimony is directly related to this

juridical perspective; cf. H.-G. Gadamer, *Wahrheit und Methode* (Tübingen, 1975), p. 321; C. Ginzburg: "Just One Witness," in *Probing the Limits of Representation*, ed. S. Friedländer (Cambridge, London, 1992), pp. 82–96.

4. Cf. the preface in Chr. Browning, *Ordinary Men: Reserve Police Battalion 101 and the Final Solution* (New York, 1992).

5. R. Antelme, *L'espèce humaine* (Paris, 1957).

6. Here I refer to the Aristotelian notion of the "probable" to which a narrative must be adjusted in order to be able to convince the reader/hearer.

7. Cf. G. Anders, *Wir Eichmannsöhne* (Munich, 1988), p. 39.

8. Cf. H. Jäger, *Verbrechen unter totalitärer Herrschaft* (Frankfurt/M., 1982), p. 139.

9. Cf. E. Levinas, *Totalité et infinie* (Hague, 1980), pp. 172ff.

10. S. Felman and D. Laub, *Testimony* (New York and London, 1992); J.-F. Lyotard, *Le différent* (Paris, 1983).

11. Cf. "Augenzeugenbericht zu den Massenvergasungen," *Vierteljahreshefte für Zeitgeschichte* 1, ed. H. Rothfels (1953): 177–94

12. Cf. my essay "Zeugnis und Überlieferung," in *Perspektiven phänomenologischer Ethik*, eds. B. Waldenfels and I. Därmann (Munich, 1997).

13. The reader will find an extensive elaboration of the preceding thoughts in the author's book *Vom Anderen her: Erinnern und Überleben* (Freiburg/Munich, 1997), ch. V.

Part 2

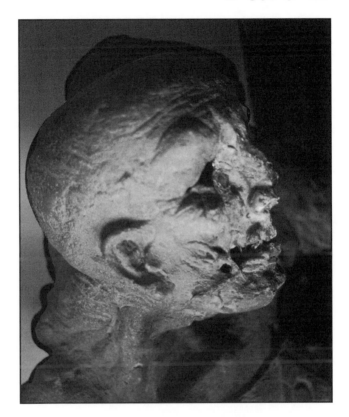

Morality
and Ethics

Introduction

Extending the discussion of our difficult responsibilities after Auschwitz, Thomas W. Simon's "The Holocaust's Moral 'Uniqueness'" turns us away from the epistemological question of the Holocaust's uniqueness to an ethical consideration of its moral uniqueness. Simon argues that comparing genocides "does not deflate the historical, political, and legal importance of the Holocaust." Quite the contrary, such comparisons are critical to the politically crucial problem of making choices today concerning which genocides should be our first priority. What sets the Holocaust apart from other genocides is the "Nazis' relatively solidified purposeful program of total annihilation of the Jews." Extermination/annihilation are thus crucial terms for developing our moral judgments about the priority of other genocides.

Roger Fjellstrom's "Morality of the Light, Morality of the Dark: Reflections on Ethics and the Holocaust" moves us from traditional morality of the light to the darkness of the Holocaust, the morality of the dark. *In extremis*, in the abyss of the concentration and death camps, what constitutes a "moral hold" is, to say the least, unclear and for some either extremely problematic or nonexistent. Following certain indications of Bettelheim and Frankl, Fjellstrom locates a difficult moral hold even in this abyss and contra Améry's claim that such "intoxicated" experiences were inauthentic. Morality (of the Light) might learn a great deal from these extreme experiences (of Morality of the Dark) if it would cast off its hyperrational blinders.

In "'Identity without Text': Negation and Execution" Detlef B. Linke's presents a philosophical parable about a Fichtean-Ego project that establishes a philosophical foundation for human rights. This project and its Nazi counterpart "use up" others, the non-I, in the play of the I's reciprocity, thus constituting the "we" of the Ego community within the self-constitution of the I. But then there are "others" who "take their starting point instead from word and text and devote themselves to the deed" (the Jews) and who do not identify with this project nor want to participate in it. Without this resistance to the Ego's project, there can be no ethics. Within the project, there can be only the redemption of being "used up" (sacrifice). There is a crucial difference between the sacrifice of those who find their "place" within this Faustian passion play and the eradication of those who do not "identify" with it. Ethics is, however, "foreign" to the oppositional logic of negation and difference. The victory over alterity which does not identify with the I's self-constitution (project) is always achieved by annihilation. And this "victory" has its roots in our metaphysical tradition. These reflections are incorporated in Linke's concluding proposal for the Shoah memorial in Berlin.

Peter Strasser's "Heidegger's Silence Revisited" argues that Heidegger's silence over the Holocaust was less than complete: "Paying attention to Heidegger's analysis of the Promethean project's captivation of modern man, there may be a non-banal interpretation of the Holocaust." Following the line of reasoning in Heidegger's critique of modernity and modernism as subjectivism, Strasser argues that one possible reason for Heidegger's noncondemnation of the Holocaust is that, for Heidegger, "all of our values and estimations exist only as reflections of the nihilistic structure which shapes all of our relations to the world and to ourselves." If Heidegger would have condemned the Nazi annihilation of European Jewry, he would have thus been "participating in the same metaphysical mind set as the Nazis." But Strasser rejects this argument in Heidegger's case. Even though "Heidegger's doctrine fails to give an *ontological* alternative" to moral judgments, this does not exhaust "Heidegger's Holocaust file." After discussing the contributions to *Martin Heidegger and the Holocaust* (edited by Alan Rosenberg and Alan Milchman), Strasser concludes that Alan Ryan may be pointing us in the right direction when he says, "Heidegger was a man of extremely bad character."

A.R./J.R.W.

The Holocaust's Moral "Uniqueness"*

Thomas W. Simon

T he debate over the Holocaust's uniqueness has again taken center stage with the publication of *Is the Holocaust Unique? Perspectives in Comparative Genocide*.[1] Furious arguments among the anthology's editor and contributors erupted, almost derailing its publication. Steven T. Katz, a Cornell University professor of Jewish thought and history, argues for the Holocaust's uniqueness.[2] David Stannard, a professor of American studies at the University of Hawaii and a leading proponent of classifying the treatment of indigenous people as genocide, calls Katz the moral equivalent of a Holocaust denier.[3] It may seem that the fault lies in setting the stage for comparing genocides.[4]

It seems perverse to pit one genocide against the other. Rony Brauman, former president of Doctors without Borders, finds "grading these various sufferings, classifying them according to some form of hierarchy . . . a pointless exercise verging on the obscene."[5] The philosopher Lawrence Blum states a commonly held position: "The 'more oppressed than thou' gambit is inimical to a proper concern with the sufferings and injustices experienced by groups other than one's own."[6] This essay represents an attempt to demonstrate that a comparative analysis, rather than serving as an impediment, offers hope for a rational approach by laying the groundwork for recognizing the pain and suffering of others, while at the same time acknowledging that some group harms were or are worse than others.

Intuitively, opting for a comparative framework seems doomed. Labeling any harm greater than other harms defies common sense and

*I would like to acknowledge the comments of Professors Helen Fein and Harry Deutsch, who are in no way responsible for the positions adopted here.

moral sensibilities. When we place one harm at the top of the hierarchy, it appears to create more controversy than it is worth. Yet, despite initial negative reactions to the project, the resolution of current controversies, political and intellectual, calls for establishing a hierarchy of harms with, as I will argue, the Holocaust as the prime candidate for the worst genocide.

A comparative approach to group harms provides support for the following claims: The Holocaust, that is, the extermination of Jews during World War II, ranks as the worst genocide. However, even the highest ranking does not entail uniqueness, at least in any ordinary sense of the term. To give highest status to the Holocaust on the scale of group harms does not provide support for its uniqueness. Insofar as we can stretch the word "unique" to cover the Holocaust (as I have done in the title to this paper), the term refers to a judgment about the moral status of the Holocaust. Morally speaking, the Holocaust represents the worst genocide to date.

Unfortunately, the uniqueness debate diverts attention toward the epistemological and away from the moral. We need to do more pounding of fists in moral outrage over the Holocaust than scratching heads over its incomprehensibility. Drawing comparisons among genocides does not deflate the historical, political, and legal importance of the Holocaust. To the contrary, the comparisons bolster the case for directing our strongest moral outrage at the Holocaust. When the criminal law treats serial killing as morally and legally worse than a single murder committed in a fit of passion, the comparison does not diminish the condemnation of serial killings.

Although I shall concentrate on the merits of adopting a comparative framework for the uniqueness debate, I want at least to indicate other broad-reaching results of using a comparative framework. Limited resources force the international community to make choices about which horrors to confront first. Although space does not permit addressing the issue here, suffice it to say, genocide should top the list of priorities. Further, some genocides qualify as worse than others. The Rwanda genocide outranks Bosnia, thereby demanding the international community's highest priority—which is exactly the opposite of what happened.

An analysis of two recent attempts to maintain the uniqueness hypothesis will demonstrate what types of harm should count as morally important when assessing genocides and how to compare these harms. The first analysis, from the philosophical literature, will support the proposition that some harms (extermination) make a critical moral difference whereas others (humiliation) do not. Contrary to what some argue, extermination and not humiliation constitutes the crucial moral feature of the Holocaust because of the important moral difference that extermination makes to the severity of offenses. The second analysis of

Katz's work undermines the uniqueness thesis and supports the hypothesis that a well-formed corporate intent and vast numbers killed constitute the critical. The Nazis' relatively solidified purposeful program of total annihilation of the Jews sets apart the Holocaust from other genocides. An analogy to criminal law will further demonstrate that genocides differ in degree and not in kind, making the Holocaust worse than but not incomparable to other genocides.

Higher and Lower Moral Categories

In a recent attempt, published in the premier journal *Philosophy and Public Affairs*, to maintain the Holocaust's uniqueness, Avishia Margalit and Gabriel Motzkin propose that only World War II Germans "both systematically humiliated and systematically killed."[7] They hedge somewhat in their judgment, finding this combination "exceedingly rare and maybe unique." The authors say little about extermination and concentrate on humiliation. They unearth the foundations of humiliation in Nazi philosophy. The Nazis faced a conundrum: if they inflicted humiliation on the Jews, they would acknowledge their victims' humanity. To avoid this logical trap, the Nazis, according to the authors, cleverly decided to punish the Jews for their invention of the idea of universal humanity. Alas, the Holocaust's uniqueness lies within Nazi philosophical acumen, however skewed and distorted.

On the Margalit and Motzkin view, Nazi practice supported Nazi metaphysics. Although the authors provide little supporting evidence, they claim that other victims of Nazi extermination, such as Soviet POWs, did not experience humiliation. For example, they do not deny that the Nazis humiliated the Romani or Gypsies. Nevertheless, the authors find a difference in that the Gypsies were not "humiliated in an elaborate structure of humiliation like the one the Nazis created for the Jews."[8] This hedged generalization suffers the same fate as others made by the authors, who ignore how "Jew-like" other groups could become under Nazi policy.

At best, the humiliation experienced by Jews and Gypsies differed in degree and not kind. The Nazis had two agencies engaged in research on whether the Gypsies had Jewish origins. The 1935 Nuremberg laws, which first legally defined Jews, officially identified Gypsies as non-Aryan. Indeed, the Citizenship Law of 1943 omitted any mention of Gypsies since the Nazis did not expect the Gypsies to exist very long.[9] Brutal treatment of Gypsies defined German treatment of them. When it came to humiliation and extermination, Gypsies often found themselves a fateful one step ahead of Jews: "[I]n January or February 1940, 250 Gypsy children from Brno in the concentration camp at Buchenwald were used as guinea pigs for testing Zyklon B cyanide gas crystals, a lethal insecticide that from 1941 onward was used for the mass murders at Auschwitz-Birkeneau."[10] The Nazis had more fluid categories than Margalit and Motzkin, belying their claim that "Jews occupied the precise place at which humiliation and extermination intersected."[11] No such place existed in Nazi thought or practice.

Within their analysis, the authors make choices. They conjoin humiliation and extermination; they say much more about humiliation than extermination. These choices are not innocent. Humiliation does not occupy the same moral plateau as extermination. Whatever moral condemnation for humiliation we might have, it pales in comparison to extermination. If we are going to draw comparisons among genocides, we need to justify the grounds of comparison. Humiliation does not serve as a justifiable grounds for comparison or as a grounds for the uniqueness hypothesis.

We quibble with the details of uniqueness claims, but the debates symbolize a more general difficulty. What are the stakes in the uniqueness debate? If we use the debates to sharpen only our historical understanding of the Holocaust, then we have missed an opportunity to develop our moral judgments. We can do this by focusing on the morally most important aspect of the Holocaust, namely, extermination. Killings, and not humiliation, lie at the heart of all genocides.[12] The uniqueness debate is not primarily about history; it is about morality. Interestingly, as we shall see in the next section, even when some scholars focus on extermination, they shy away from the ethical dimensions of extermination.

Failed Neutrality

Steven T. Katz has embarked upon an ambitious project, partially completed, which places the Holocaust in historical context. Given the work's serious and scholarly scope, any student of the Holocaust must examine it. Katz provides a definition of the phenomenological uniqueness of the Sho'ah.

> The Holocaust is phenomenologically unique by virtue of the fact that never before has a state set out, as a matter of intentional principle and actualized policy, to annihilate physically every man, woman, and child belonging to a specific people.[13]

Despite his philosophical sophistication, Katz commits fundamental errors, which center on his use of "phenomenological uniqueness." He fails even to acknowledge the difficulty of retaining a sharp distinction between facts and values required for his analysis. He unwittingly presents an ethical or prescriptive analysis and not simply a phenomeno-logical or descriptive one. Instead of rehearsing the philosophical cri-tique of this overly positivist distinction, I shall demonstrate the value laden character of the empirical categories Katz employs.

Katz uses the following schema to elucidate "phenomenological uniqueness":

Ø is uniquely C. Ø may share A, B, D, . . . X with Δ but not C. And again Ø may share A, B, D, . . . X with all Δ but not C.[14]

In the discussion of this schema, Katz proposes two key ingredients for C that differentiate the Holocaust from all other historical events, namely, mass killings (relative to the population base) and intentions. Indeed, taken in tandem and fully fleshed out, these succeed in setting the Holocaust apart (in degree, not in kind) from similar events, but they set it apart not only phenomenologically, but also ethically (in degree and not in kind).

Without a concession to an ethical analysis, Katz cannot justify his interpretation of what constitutes C. True, other mass killings may have many of the same ingredients as the Holocaust, albeit in different degrees. However, we can characterize C in such a way that no other event shares it, and yet, we would still want to say that C does not really capture the difference. For example, the gassing at Auschwitz, proposed by Nolte, may distinguish the Holocaust from all other events.[15] Katz's unique features, namely, intent and total extermination, work better than Nolte's, not because of their historical saliency, but because, as ends, they are better moral categories than Nolte's means.

The debate over means is largely irrelevant because the means of murder, individual or group, are rarely morally determinative in the con-demnation of the act. A judge may enhance the penalty for a murderer who used a particularly gruesome means to carry out the deed, but the murderer stands guilty of the same crime as the one who employs rela-tively benign means. Likewise the relative degrees of moral condemna-tion of the Bosnian and Rwandan genocides should not depend upon the differences in the means employed. Moreover, the means of annihilation used in the Holocaust could be "unprecedented in the past" as well as "non recurring in the future," and that would not establish the unique-ness of the Holocaust since a means analysis fails to capture the morally salient features.

The uniqueness claim is primarily a moral and not exclusively an empirical claim. Katz's choice of intention and mass killing reflects an ethical judgment about the Holocaust. Katz must choose among the can-didate C's. Katz could maintain that he made the choice among C's on historical grounds, that is to say, the C's he opts for are historically more salient than any other possible C's. Whatever grounds Katz chooses for making the choice, those grounds will involve evaluative judgments. We choose to emphasize some aspects of a genocide's history over others because we value (or more accurately, devalue) those features more. The historian of the Holocaust, despite pretensions to the contrary, cannot avoid making value judgments about the investigated material.

Katz emphatically and understandably denies slipping into what he regards as the ethical abyss. He correctly notes that distinguishing the Holocaust from other events does not "necessarily entail any hierarchy of immoral acts or events."[16] Denying a necessary entailment gives Katz a logical victory, but he still has not blocked making a case for a hierarchy of immoral acts. If we distinguish the Holocaust from other genocides and if the distinction is meaningful, then we must show its morally distinguishing features. Ironically, Katz provides the ingredients to make just the case that he wants to avoid, namely, that "the Sho'ah represents a new and higher level of evil."[17] Crudely put, the ingredients consist of perpetrators' intent and numbers killed (degree of extermination).

Comparative Moral Judgments

To help make the hierarchy case we need to consider that we have relatively little difficulty accepting greater criminal liability for first-degree murder than for nonpremeditated forms of murder. We also accept greater criminal liability for first-degree serial murders than for single murders. Intent and numbers make a legal and moral difference in state criminal codes when it comes to individual behavior. They should also make a difference for international crimes. So, my argument rests, in part, in accepting this analogy to criminal law.

While we may disagree over punishments that should be meted out for different crimes, and we may disagree over the comparative severity of some crimes, the following comparative judgment should raise few objections:

(1') A manslaughter that results in the deaths of many is worse than one that results in the death of a few or in the death of a single individual.

(2') Premeditated murder is worse than nonpremeditated forms of murder.

(3') Serial killing is worse than individual murder.

(4') Serial killing aimed at a particular group is worse than random serial killing.

Consider the following comparative moral judgments that generalize from the above examples and that rank the comparative judgments:

(1) Worse to kill many (that is, massively) than to kill a few or to kill a single individual.

(2) Worse to kill intentionally than unintentionally.

(3) Worse to kill massively and intentionally than to kill massively and unintentionally

(4) Worse to kill massively and intentionally when killings are carried out because of the victims' disadvantaged group affiliation than to kill under conditions in (3).

(1)–(3) are based on the claim, which I do not have space to defend fully here, that intent of the perpetrator and number of victims affects the severity of the offense. Suffice it to say, they constitute reasonable and justifiable moral judgments that are typically included in criminal codes. The burden of proof lies on those who would deny the relevancy of intent and numbers for individual criminal acts.

(4) adds the controversial consideration of the victims' group affiliation. (4) seems counterintuitive. Two defenses of (4) follow. The first, more controversial one focuses on the victim while the second, on the perpetrator. Regarding the first, the following question naturally arises: why should the victims' group affiliation affect the severity of the offense? Even granting that numbers matter, a murder is a murder. Yet, murder is not simply murder. Who-was-murdered makes a moral difference. A comparison of two murder cases will help to illustrate how the victims' group affiliation makes a moral difference in the degree of condemnation of the act.

On December 6, 1989, Mark Lépine murdered fourteen female college engineering students at the University of Montreal's École Polytechnique.[18] Yelling "I hate feminists," he killed nine females in a classroom after asking the males to leave. His suicide note contained a list of nineteen "opportunistic" women, including public figures in Canada. Would it make any moral difference to the severity of the offense if Lépine had randomly but intentionally killed fourteen individuals?

On April 23, 1987, William Cruse randomly murdered six people in a Palm Bay, Florida, shopping mall. The jury rejected his insanity plea and found him guilty of first-degree murder. For our purposes, the fact that "there was no evidence that Cruse contemplated his attack for any longer than a few moments" becomes salient.[19] Whatever intent Cruse had, it was far more short-lived and flimsier than Lépine's. From the evidence, Lépine carefully planned to kill individuals because of their group affiliation. (Analogously, I will argue that the Nazi intent was more well formed that that of other genocide perpetrators).

Would it make any moral difference if Lépine had manifested the same animus he had toward women toward college students or engineers? College students and engineers do not qualify as disadvantaged groups in any legal system, whereas, on some accounts, women do. The vulnerable group status of the victims does make a difference. Individuals become more vulnerable to harm because of their affiliation with a disadvantaged group. We weigh the victims' innocence in part by the victims' group affiliation. The murder of innocent children weighs more heavily than the murder of adults who are on their way to commit murder.

Without giving a full-fledged theory of disadvantaged groups, I do not have a ready-made proof that it is more morally reprehensible to kill intentionally ten individuals than it is to kill ten individuals because of their group affiliation. Further, I do not have a proof that it is more morally reprehensible to kill intentionally ten individuals because of their disadvantaged group affiliation than to kill intentionally ten individuals because of their nondisadvantaged group affiliation.[20] Here, I appeal to well-entrenched moral intuitions. We have little difficulty in granting comparative judgments when it comes to certain classifications, such as children. By extension, the same type of analysis should apply to other vulnerable groups.

The above analysis leaves many problems unresolved. It assumes that women constitute a disadvantaged group. It further assumes that being-a-woman adds to vulnerability beyond what being-a-college student or any other group descriptor would add. At this stage, I can forgo a defense of these assumptions since the point is to make a case for the relevancy of group affiliation to the severity of an offense based primarily on the acceptance of whatever group you might accept as vulnerable and disadvantaged. I do not think that many people would question the claim that women have a particular vulnerability to violence (for example, rape as a crime of violence) directed at them because of their gender (group affiliation).

A further argument for (4) hinges on what introducing features of the victims' group affiliation does to the intent of the perpetrators. Targeting a specific group begins to transform mass murder into genocide. The targeting gives the deed an intent, an aim, a rationality, however perverted and inconsistently formulated. To single out a group, the perpetrator must have reflected upon the act before committing it, if for no other reason than to get some clarity on the contours, however distorted, of the victim group. Lépine had a more well formed intent than Cruse, in part because Lépine targeted members of a group. Generally, we hold individuals with well-formed, malign intentions to a higher standard of criminal responsibility than those acting out of rage and passion.

The following judgments represent an extension of the analysis carried out so far:

(5) Worse to kill massively and intentionally when the killings are carried out because of perpetrators who want partial elimination of victims' disadvantaged group than to kill under conditions in (4)

(6) Worse to kill massively and intentionally when the killings are carried out because of perpetrators who want total elimination of victims' disadvantaged group than to kill under conditions in (5).

(5) differs from (4) in that (5) is morally worse than (4). With (5), it becomes increasingly difficult to talk about individual perpetrators like

Lépine. We have entered the realm of corporate intent. To carry out the purposeful action needed for partial extermination of a group, to direct the attack at a group per se, a number of perpetrators need some form of organization, often in the form of a state. While a single individual could possibly carry out a partial extermination, genocides almost always involve a complex organization, thereby implicating countless individuals. Genocide ranks as morally worse than (individually perpetrated) murder for many reasons, including the sheer enormity of acts of genocide and the fact that genocide involves the massive power of the state.

While (5) jumps to a moral plateau above (4), the same does not hold true for the comparison of (5) with (6). Defenders of the Holocaust's uniqueness must differentiate, empirically and morally, (5) from (6). Yet, (6) is not morally different in kind than (5). For the intents and deeds designed to annihilate an entire group are not any more morally reprehensible than those intended to annihilate part of a group.

True, "the killing of some X may be a greater evil . . . than killing all Y, where there are more X than Y and the absolute number of X killed exceeds the total number of Y even though the killing of X is not . . . Holocaustal."[21] However, a theoretical possibility should not stand in the way of making a strong moral judgment about historical events. Assume that the Nazis clearly adopted a policy to exterminate the Jews. Further, assume that other genocides involve partial and not total annihilation of the target groups. Finally, assume that the Nazis succeeded in killing far greater numbers than any other genocide in history.

Even by granting these assumptions, which constitute the critical ones in the uniqueness debate, the Holocaust does not differ in kind from other genocides. (5) does not occupy a different moral level from (6). (5) differs from (6) in degree and not in kind. Severity of offense admits of degrees. Uniqueness defenders may win the battle to demonstrate the extreme severity of the Holocaust over other genocides, but they do not win the argument for the Holocaust's uniqueness. For example, however close the Armenian genocide came to the Holocaust, it probably did not stem (despite Dadrian's claim that the Young Turks had a hidden agenda to annihilate all Christian Armenians beyond Turkey's borders to the USSR) from the corporate intent to eradicate Armenians everywhere.[22] However, even if the Nazis had intended to exterminate all Jews everywhere, that would not place the Holocaust in a different moral category.

To make (6) morally distinct from (5) we would need to show that the (attempted) annihilation of a group makes a moral difference over and above the number of group members murdered. The loss of a group and the concomitant loss of a culture has many lamentable features, including the loss of the very structure that gives group members their identity and fulfillment. However, the same deplorable losses may accompany a partially successful genocide. Once perpetrators have crossed the threshold to engage in partial extermination of a group, they have reached the moral plateau that calls for the strongest form of condemnation. Replacing "partial" with "total" could add to the degree of severity, evidencing how far the perpetrators will go to carry out their reprehensible deeds, but it does not thereby place the acts on a higher moral plateau of condemnation.

Actus reus and *mens rea* constitute two aspects of criminality. To maintain the moral priority of the Holocaust over other genocides we need to show that the *actus reus* and the *mens rea* of the Holocaust differ in degree from other genocides. First, regarding the *actus reus*, no other genocide approached the numbers of innocent victims of those of the Holocaust. It may seem difficult to compare any genocides when the numbers approach the millions. However, while sheer numbers should not determine the degree of criminality, numbers are not irrelevant to a moral and legal assessment. No other genocide has matched the six million Jews slaughtered in the Holocaust. Extending from the judgment that two murders are worse than one, we can defend the claim that the killing of six million Jews was worse than 20,000 male homosexuals killed by the Nazis, and so on.

Second, regarding the *mens rea*, no other genocide has invoked as pronounced an intent to destroy a group as did the Holocaust. I am perfectly willing to concede that this point may be subject to debate, but at least we know the terms of the debate. Anti-Semitism has a long and sordid history, which served as a basis for transforming prejudice and discrimination into hatred and extermination. I know of no other hypothesis that would fully explain the Holocaust than that Jews were purposefully targeted for extermination. Other genocides involved intents to destroy individuals because of their group affiliation, but these intents appear less well formed than the ones operating during the Holocaust.

Putting the *actus reus* together with the *mens rea* places the Holocaust not in a unique position but at the top of hierarchy as the worst genocide. The two elements interrelate. It is difficult to conceive how the massive numbers of Jewish deaths during the Holocaust could have occurred other than through careful planning. I do not pretend to have provided a definitive analysis. However, I have framed the outline for the argument that the Holocaust qualifies as the worst genocide.

Conclusion

The uniqueness debate may result in more careful scholarship concerning the claims made about other genocides as well as those by Holocaust scholars. It may serve a more dubious function of generating more invective among scholars. Losing the uniqueness debate and placing the

Holocaust as one genocide among many should not diminish its moral import. The Holocaust ranks among the most morally reprehensible acts imaginable. No other genocide may match the Holocaust for its well-formulated corporate intent, including the degree of willingness to carry out the annihilation of a people, and for the sheer number of deaths.

Accepting the grave degree of horror at the root of the Holocaust should increase moral condemnation of genocides wherever and whenever we find them. Finding one genocide worse than another should not lead the international community to downgrade its response to the so-called lesser one. Rather, it should lead to doing more about both. The memory of the Holocaust should lead to an increased recognition of the suffering of other groups and to a full acknowledgment of the enormous suffering of the Jewish people.

Notes

1. *Is the Holocaust Unique?* Alan S. Rosenbaum, ed. (Boulder: Westview Press, 1996).

2. Steven T. Katz, "The Uniqueness of the Holocaust: The Historical Dimension," in *Is the Holocaust Unique?* pp. 32–37.

3. David E. Stannard, "Uniqueness as Denial: The Politics of Genocide Scholarship," in *Is the Holocaust Unique?* pp. 163–208.

4. For arguments against comparing harms in this way see Kenneth Seeskin, "What Philosophy Can and Cannot Say about Evil," in *Echoes From the Holocaust: Philosophical Reflections on a Dark Time*, eds. Alan Rosenberg and Gerald E. Myers (Philadelphia: Temple University Press, 1988), pp. 91–104.

5. Rony Brauman, *Devant le Mal. Rwanda, un génocide en direct* (Paris: Arléa, 1994).

6. Lawrence A. Blum, "The Holocaust and Moral Education," *Report from the Institute for Philosophy and Public Policy* 15 (Spring/Summer 1995): 13.

7. Avishai Margalit and Gabriel Motzkin, "The Uniqueness of the Holocaust," *Philosophy and Public Affairs* (Winter 1996): 65–83.

8. Katz, "The Uniqueness of the Holocaust," p. 79.

9. Helen Fein, *Accounting for Genocide* (New York: The Free Press, 1979), p. 29

10. Ian Hancock, "Responses to the Porrajmos: The Romani Holocaust," in *Is the Holocaust Unique?* p. 54.

11. Katz, "The Uniqueness of the Holocaust," p. 79.

12. See my "Defining Genocide," *Wisconsin International Law Review* (Fall 1996).

13. Steven T. Katz. *The Holocaust in Historical Perspective*, vol. 1 (New York: Oxford University Press, 1994), p. 28.

14. Ibid., p. 58.

15. Ernst Nolte, "A Past Will Not Pass Away—A Speech It Was Possible to Write, But Not to Present," *Yad Vashem Studies* 19 (1988): 65–73.

16. Katz, *The Holocaust in Historical Perspective*, p. 34.

17. Ibid., p. 34

18. James Alan Fox and Jack Levin, *Overkill: Mass Murder and Serial Killing Exposed* (New York: Plenum Press, 1994), pp. 201–206

19. Ibid., p. 225.

20. See my "A Theory of Disadvantaged Groups," in *Democracy and Social Injustice* (Lanham, Md.: Rowman & Littlefield, 1995), pp. 71–107.

21. Katz, *The Holocaust in Historical Perspective*, p. 33.

22. Vahakn N. Dadrian, "The Comparative Aspects of the Armenian and Jewish Cases of Genocide: A Sociological Perspective," in *Is the Holocaust Unique?* p. 129.

Morality of the Light, Morality of the Dark
Reflections on Ethics and the Holocaust

Roger Fjellstrom

Si tu es un homme appelé à échouer, n'échoue pas toutefois n'importe comment.[1]

Henri Michaux, *Poteaux d'angle*.

1

One night I dream that I am a Jew in one of the concentration camps in Nazi Germany. My children are there, too. The dream is extremely vivid: I am terrified and at my wits' end, forced toward my own and my family's most probable death. A question torments me: "How do I stand this?" and I wake up with this question ringing in my head.

As I reflect on the situation, it strikes me that traditional moral philosophy has no answer. With the help of my dream I suddenly realize that there is another area of morality apart from the traditional. That other area is brought on by confusion, fright, victimization, whereas the traditional presupposes people having their psyche, reasoning, and acting in order. The traditional I call *Morality of the Light*, and the other *Morality of the Dark*. To distinguish between these is the main objective of this essay.

This insight obviously changes nothing for the victims of the Holocaust, nor for our trauma arising from it. It might not change anything for me if I were to enter a similar state. We do not see in the Dark. But I believe a philosophical moon to be possible.

2

"How do I stand this?" Some would say it isn't a question at all, but a sigh, a verbal reaction to stress or expressions of emotion. Yes, but at least sometimes—both for me in the dream and for many Jews in the real situation—it is also a structured, semantically meaningful and non-rhetorical articulation of a question invoking an answer.

To be sure, we are not asking for facts, for instance, about what we think or feel under such circumstances. Nor are we demanding a forecast of how we will probably behave. It may be, but isn't necessarily, a technical question about efficient ways, or the most efficient way, to achieve something called "standing." At its core, I am convinced, the phrase formulates a *moral* question. Since this point is essential, some clarifications are needed.

A "moral question" I take to be an articulation of a quest for validity regarding moral holds, and by "hold" I mean thought, feeling, will, decision, or disposition thereto in the face of events or states in the inside or outside world. Holds are more or less conscious and more or less reflected and articulated. The hold normally in focus is a person's act or, more precisely, decision to act, since the act involves the world outside the person.

We contrast actual holds with possible ones, whether they regard the past, present, or future. And we contrast actual and possible holds with valid holds. In our minds, with the help of language and other means, we present, for instance, some kind of feeling or act as ideal under the circumstances, thereby typically taking it on as a goal of actualization for our lives.

Not all holds should be called "moral." I propose a preliminary definition of a "moral" hold as an actual or possible hold constituting or affecting a person's and/or other persons' psychological (spiritual) well-being. A "moral answer," then, normally articulates recognizing or taking a stand as to the validity of a moral hold, and it ranges from being simple exhortations to normative theories—articulated by specific words such as "good," "bad," "right," "duty." Other words may also do the job, or even no words at all: gestures, facial expression, or rituals.

To a moral answer there is usually connected a hold, for example, a decision, to do what is found right. The more or less elaborated questions and answers regarding the validity of holds, together with connected holds of the person, I call his "morality." Let me leave the notion of 'validity' of holds unanalyzed here; I shall use it as a primitive term. Possibly it has a common kernel of meaning or function in all languages, even if different individuals, in different societies and groups, at different times, have different criteria for it and different views as to the force and implications of their moral holds.

In order to show the special features of the opening question as belonging to a special Morality of the Dark, I must first make clear the notions of 'Light' and 'Dark'.

3

My idea, then, is that morality in the Western tradition has been uniquely conceptualized as what I call "Morality of the Light." "Light" I call the condition of men as *moral agents*, and "Morality of the Light," a class of aggregates of moral questions, answers, and corresponding holds of moral agents. The self-image of the mainstream philosophers is that they help us to become more rational moral agents.

At one end of the tradition there is Plato in his dialogues pointing to an intimate bond between knowing and morally right acting, and Aristotle stressing that the primary object of moral philosophy is not knowledge but wise action. At the other end there is, for instance, William Frankena who points to a continuity and invokes Socrates:

As Socrates implied and recent philosophers have stressed (perhaps too much), morality fosters or even calls for the use of reason and for a kind of autonomy on the part of the individual, asking him, when mature and normal, to make his own decisions. . . . Morality . . . promotes rational self-guidance or self-determination in its members.[2]

In this quote we find the key ideas of the tradition: 'decision' and 'autonomy'—in short, *agency*—and 'rational' self-guidance—*rationality*.

The concept of a person being a 'moral agent' ought to include reference to a set of conditions. It should be logically possible that a person is a moral agent in regard to one set of conditions but not to another, at (broadly) the same place or the same time. A person may then pass from Morality of the Light to Morality of the Dark, and back again, or be in both at the same time with respect to different conditions, or situations, as I prefer to say.

That a person is a *moral agent* in situation S, I take to comprise three conditions. First, in S the person *chooses* his/her moral hold. Second, the person bases the choice of moral hold on *a reasoning process essentially involving normative principles and judgments of facts*. Third, the person *can effectuate* his/her hold in S.

The first condition concerns the working of something in the mind of the person, often called "free will." It is a capacity for directing one's will toward some achievement. The second condition has to do with an elementary rationality. The third condition concerns the relationship between the choices of the free will and what is chosen. If a person chooses to do A, then she does A, and the choice will be the cause of the act. The relevant circumstances of the hold, for example, the decision to do a certain act, are in the person's control.

The first and the third conditions are contained in the dictum "*ought* implies *can*." Indeed, the language of "acts" rather than "decisions" expresses the normal fulfillment of them, since an act results from the exercise of a free will that is effective. If only one of the conditions is stated, the other condition is silently presupposed. Also, a concept of 'moral agent' built on only one of them is rather uninteresting. If you can choose but not effectuate your choice, or you can effectuate your choices but not choose, you are out of the game.

Since there is another condition stipulating rationality, I define a rather broad concept of 'choosing'. By a person *choosing* or practicing free will in a situation I mean that in the situation (i) the person conceives alternative things, states, or events in the world, among these such that involve himself; (ii) the person somehow evaluates them; (iii) the person can pass from an evaluation of something to a decision about his hold with regard to it. This would be free will in general. If we add that the decision concerns a moral hold, we obtain what is required of a moral agent.

The capacity—can—of (iii) must not be purely theoretical. A person may for instance have a formal capacity for speech but be muted by a psychological disturbance. "Can" means that the individual is in possession of his agency. Further, 'choosing' usually includes an idea that there is a set of alternative holds that is, if not unlimited, at least not very restricted. Let us say that it contains at least two alternatives, the values of which are substantially different.

Concerning the efficiency of will, it is too much to require that the person's decision in the situation results or necessarily results in the act and its intended effect. We rarely if ever have the world, our body, and our mind in total control. By a person having *efficient will* in a situation, then, I shall mean that what is freely willed has a high probability of being brought about through the effort of the person in that situation, all things being equal.

The freedom and efficiency of will varies in intensity and in scope. In most situations I would say people practice free and efficient will in my sense. But under some circumstances one sees no alternatives, or lacks the power or necessary self-esteem or courage, to evaluate them. It may also be that the evaluation cannot be brought to a decision. And if a decision is reached, it may not make him/her mobilize body and mind and employ the means to the intended outcome, or such employment is definitely hindered by others. We are then in "the Dark." But there is also another way to be in the Dark.

4

The second condition on a 'moral agent'—that the person bases the choice of moral hold on a reasoning process essentially involving normative principles and judgments of facts—is a requirement of an *elementary rationality*. A way to clarify it is to look at conceptions of full moral rationality in the main tradition. In spite of all diversities, I think a set of common ideas can be pinned down.

First, moral holds *are chosen on the basis of universal moral principles*. Ideally, a choice of hold should follow a particular evaluative judgment deduced from a set of valid moral principles, maxims, or laws, together with relevant facts. I overlook differences over the nature or the validity of these principles, or their certainty, and whether they are axiomatic or inductive generalizations. But such principles make no mention of any particular person and contain only purely qualitative (possibly also quantitative) predicates. Thus, an act being right for you, it must also be so for everybody else under the same relevant circumstances. This makes the "I" in the moral question, "What ought I do?" in a sense eliminable; it can be replaced by "anyone" and the question remains essentially the same. Rationality makes morality nonpersonal at its core. The universality claim also typically includes values, unless for other reasons, because 'right' and 'good' are conceptually or logically connected.

A second central trait in rational method in morals, is that *the principles have a logical coherence or systematicity*. The thought is that the universal principles form a coherent whole. This is possibly what Kant formulates thus:

> All maxims . . . ought to harmonize with a possible kingdom of ends as a kingdom of nature . . . the totality or completeness of its system of ends.[3]

This condition is a safeguard against principles or particular stands that are ad hoc, brought up just to suit the interests of the moment. The problem is that few, if any, ethical systems are such as not to make possible contradictory judgments. Utilitarianism is considered a promising candidate. But for other systems, with a plurality of deontic principles, something like Aristotle's practically wise man is required to weigh and apply the universal principles (which still have an essential role). In modern debate, the notion of an 'ideal observer' does the same job.

The second trait should therefore be given an alternative: the principles have a logical coherence or systematicity, *or belong to a body of principles, or the application of such principles, that would be acceptable to a wise person/an ideal observer*. It is probably easier to prove logical coherence of a body of statements than to prove that it would be acceptable to a wise person. But that someone is *not* wise is perhaps not so hard to show—and that is enough for my present purpose.

However, even for the system of principles satisfying the first part of the disjunction—the coherence of principles—some further requirement, like that in the second part, is generally thought to be needed, assuring that the principles are outcomes not merely of a formal rationality.

A third trait, then, is that *the principles and/or the particular judgments on which the principles are based should be, or agree with, the outcome of a successful performance of a specific moral capacity*. It may be Plato's intuition, Aristotle's practical reason, Kant's transcendental reason or Hume's sympathy. But whatever it is, it can probably be fairly well shown that someone does *not* fulfill this condition.

These traits, however, are not enough. Rational moral method must include rationality in the handling of facts and forecasts. A fourth trait could perhaps be formulated thus: *Scientifically or empirically assessed facts, or at least carefully scrutinized facts, play a part together with principles in determining validity in holds.*

What has been presented here is a rather vague but strong ("scientific") notion of reason in morals. As I have said, what is of interest here, is a person's *lack* of reason, even in its elementary form, which would be required of a moral agent. A person might not be able to decide on moral principles, but chooses on unreflective, perhaps instinctive grounds. A person might be inescapably incoherent and illogical, be unable to recognize either the existence or the validity of other people's interests, and have his/her human sympathy effectively fought down by other impulses. A person might not be able to judge the facts of the situation carefully or with a clear mind.

To sum up: *A person P is in the Dark in regard to a situation S, if and only if P is not a moral agent in regard to S, and S is problematic for P*. I do not require suffering for the state of the Dark, since it is not unique for it. Depending on which of the three conditions on being a 'moral agent' is not fulfilled, and in what respect and to what degree, we can distinguish layers or depths of the Dark. If only the first and the third conditions are satisfied in respect to moral holds, I would say that we have a *moral person*. If a person has free and efficient will regarding other things than moral holds, he/she is just an *agent*. Someone may have a free and morally rational will, but lack efficiency. It is even possible that a person has elementary moral rationality, but not a free and efficient will in regard to moral holds. Worst off, if they exist at all, are those who aren't even agents.

5

In the Dark . . .

Nothing can provide us with examples of this more clearly than the situation of the Jews in Auschwitz and the other Nazi death- and work-camps. I shall examine some cases, through testimonies of survivors.

Elie Wiesel arrived at the age of fourteen to spend a year in these camps. He entitles his account of that period *Night*,[4] which goes well with the terminology I have chosen. It is a book about the state of victimhood. As Wiesel's interpreter, Robert McAfee Brown, writes: "Many things happen to victims, so *Night* reports. At the heart of them all is shattering, a shattering of world, faith, self and future."[5]

McAfee Brown distinguishes between four "shatterings" of people experiencing the Holocaust. First, the person's world is shattered. He/she is forced away from home; is separated from work, family, and friends; and is put into concentration camps to suffer humiliation and deprivation of all (or almost all) means necessary for living.

The second shattering is that of faith. For Wiesel this was the faith in God of a pious Hasidic child of fourteen. But "faith" could perhaps be understood in a broader sense, so as to include the worldview of the person, particularly the structure of values and norms. Wiesel, for instance, says that "I did not deny God's existence, but I doubted his justice."[6]

The third shattering is that of the person's self. This is imposed from the outside, through the deprivation of personal belongings, clothes, and hair, and the replacement of name by a number.

> The student of the Talmud, the child that I was, had been consumed in the flames. There remained only a shape that looked like me.[7]

McAfee Brown comments: "From now on there is no soul, no self."[8]

But McAfee Brown is not consistent, reporting that "the self" of the number Elie Wiesel survived mentally, as is shown by his concern for his father who was in the same camp. The shattering of the self seems, rather, to be a radical transformation and reduction of personality. He also talks about "persons, reduced to the status of nonpersons."[9]

The fourth shattering—according to McAfee Brown the culmination of the shatterings—is that of the victim's future. Wiesel talks in *Night* about being deprived of the desire to live and of having his dreams turned "to dust."[10] And people here are, as McAfee Brown writes, "denied a future." He adds: "That is true death, whether physical life is terminated or not."[11] Mental death, according to McAfee Brown's reading of Wiesel, is that the individual can no longer plan for, count on, or even desire a normal human life. But possibly these things are rather causes of something called the "mental death" of a person.

The idea of a 'mental death' of the prisoners of the Nazi camps figures also, for instance, in the work of the psychologist Bruno Bettelheim, who in 1938–39 was imprisoned in the camps of Dachau and Buchenwald. He speaks of the prisoners going through a process of "utter debilitation through torture, starvation, sickness."[12]

Primo Levi, an Italian Jew who, when in his twenties, came to spend almost a year in or close to Auschwitz, also bears his witness to such reductions of the human being, starting with a book which he gave the rhetorical title *If This Is a Man*.[13] Levi talks about a systematic breaking of persons, leaving them as "ghosts," as "dead." People are to be reduced to "animals," as the prisoner Steinlauf, former sergeant in the Austrian-Hungarian army, explains to newly arrived Levi. Levi himself, in a postscript, goes further: they were degraded to cattle, to dirt. The author Terence Des Pres describes it all as an "excremental assault," aiming at "complete humiliation and debasement of prisoners."[14]

Yet, the Nazis had a rationale for this, Levi realized, namely the destruction of people's capacity to resist: ". . . he must immediately be demolished to make sure that he did not become an example or a germ of organized resistance."[15] As a rule, the brutal entry ritual also brought about their "moral collapse"[16]:

> Imagine now a man who is deprived of everyone he loves, and at the same time of his house, his habits, his clothes, in short, of everything he possesses; he will be a hollow man, reduced to suffering and needs, forgetful of dignity and restraint, for he who loses all often easily loses himself. He will be a man whose life or death can be lightly decided with no sense of human affinity, in the most fortunate of cases, on the basis of a pure judgment of utility. It is in this way that one can understand the double sense of the term 'extermination camp', and it is now clear what we seek to express with the phrase: 'to lay on the bottom'.[17]

Levi himself, however, was not broken and not (at least not permanently) reduced to a disastrous degree. As he underlines in his book *Moments of Reprieve*, he and most survivors actually never went all the way to the bottom.

If "mental death" is taken to mean, not only a shattering but a non-reversible destruction of the person, the term is undoubtedly adequate for many in the death camps. I think in particular of the so-called muselmans, whose very will to live was broken. But for Levi, Wiesel, and others that term is not adequate. Levi talks about the initial moral collapse as a "trauma of transplantation," though for many some modus vivendi is found, "based on an invaluable activity of adaptation, partly passive and unconscious, partly active." Soon the "trauma of transplantation is over."[18] When people came out of the trauma, for most their personality was changed, reduced, comprising new patterns of behavior, radically changed holds, norms and values, and a totally different world view.

It seems to have been typical for the ordinary prisoner that instincts largely replaced reflection and that basic needs and egoism took precedence over so-called higher motives and altruistic principles. As Levi puts it, "there is no doubt that life in the Lager involved regression, leading back precisely to primitive behaviour."[19] The old "civilian" moral code was replaced by a new moral code, with the "principal rule of the place, which made it mandatory that you should first of all take care of yourself," Levi writes in *The Drowned and the Saved*.[20]

McAfee Brown stresses an important component in the victimization of people in the camps: "The victim has no choice: the role is imposed by another."[21] This has perhaps mainly to do with a blocking of the scope of the will, that it is driven from central aspects of the person's inner or outer life toward minute details of getting food for the day, keeping the shoes, managing the selections, and so on. According to Levi:

> In reality, in the enormous majority of cases, their behaviour was rigidly preordained. In the space of a few weeks or months the deprivations to which they were subjected led them to a condition of pure survival, a daily struggle against hunger, cold, fatigue and blows in which the room for choices (especially moral choices) was reduced to zero; among these, very few survived the test and this thanks to the coming together of many improbable events.[22]

This breaking of the capacity to make moral choices is central in Levi's analysis. A macabre sign of its success, according to Levi, was the relatively low rate of suicide in the camps, since "suicide is a meditated act, a noninstinctive, unnatural choice; and in the Lager there were few opportunities to choose."[23]

Bettelheim notes some consequences of hindering people from exercising their free will:

> barring an individual from a part in decision making on matters that deeply concern him tends to create a feeling of impotence which we call being subject to tyranny.[24]

This would typically make people "adopt childlike behavior."[25] He writes:

> As time went on and the process of adjustment continued . . . most of them had reached a more advanced stage of personality disintegration, and all of them had come to feel somewhat like hapless children.[26]

Levi also observed that many entered states resembling mental disturbances, such as detachment:

as if what happened did not really matter to oneself. It was strongly mixed with a conviction that "This can't be true; such things just don't happen."[27]

But man is a flexible creature. A few prisoners managed to retain their personality and capacity for moral choices in the camp, applied in at least some situations; they were not broken. In *Moments of Reprieve* Levi tells stories of

> the few, the different, the ones in whom (if only for a moment) I had recognized the will and the capacity to react, and hence a rudiment of virtue. . . . The protagonists of these stories are "men" beyond all doubt, even if the virtue that allows them to survive and makes them unique is not always one approved of by common morality.[28]

These men kept and dared to exercise such important parts of their personality as generosity, friendship, humor.

It is not ruled out that some even became more profound and more moral in the camp. One witness, Samuel Pisar, who spent his life from the age of twelve to sixteen in different camps, relates a surprising process contrary to the infantilization that Bettelheim describes, namely, how the camp made him surpass himself:

> It forced me to develop to a maximum my modest physical and mental qualities, to use to the extreme my limbs, my lungs, my nerves, my brain; to make my own choices, take my own decisions, leave nothing to chance, to find in myself resources that I never believed I had.[29]

The author Jean Améry, campmate of Primo Levi and the psychologist Viktor Frankl in Auschwitz, partly agrees: "Nowhere else in the world did reality demand such efficient action as in the camp."[30] But his diagnosis is different: "At no other place did the attempt to surpass it turn out to be so ridiculous and disparaging."[31]

By "surpass" Améry possibly means something different than Pisar. Améry seems to think of what I call choosing a valid hold facing the disaster. Since before his imprisonment he was a highly sophisticated intellectual, who in the camp found everything he valued despised and an obstacle to his own survival, what he normally considered a valid hold in life was out of reach.

Samuel Pisar thinks that everyone has a capacity to surpass themselves facing hostile conditions, like Viktor Frankl, who claims that people do have free will, even in Auschwitz. They can choose to attribute a meaning to their suffering, through viewing it in a certain way or putting up a life goal. It is wrong, he says, to think that the circumstances in the camp "caused" people to be this or that; what the camp did to a person was "in the last instance" a result of an inner decision.[32]

Bettelheim is on Frankl's side, though his affirmation partly contradicts itself:

> however restrictive or oppressive an environment may be, even then the individual retains the freedom to evaluate it. On the basis of this evaluation he is also free to decide on his inner approval or resistance to what is forced upon him. True, in an extremely oppressive environment these inner decisions can lead to little or no practical consequences.[33]

This freedom of will, these choices of "meaning" are only a matter of *theoretical* possibility; it is clear from both Frankl's and Bettelheim's account that few did obtain it, and those who did, didn't do so consistently. And even if the will was free, it was not always efficient; the meaning—for example, resistance—the individual might have chosen, did not appear in his/her psyche at will.

That people's personalities and hence their wills were thus reduced, that they "accepted" new codes governing their survival, might be theorized as a result of inner decisions; but these were probably often unconscious, not viewed and evaluated through reasoning, and therefore not instances of moral agency in the sense I have defined, perhaps not even of moral personality.

Even if it is possible that the meanings of the terms "free will" and "moral" as used by the authors I have quoted are not identical with mine, they are of the same family, and these (and other) testimonies show that in the Nazi Lagers many people were treated in a way so as to reduce them to various modes and levels of the Dark.

People became "nonpersons"; they lost time-, space-, and self-orientation, thereby the very capacity to act. Others retained this, but lost a sense of elementary integrity and value, forgetting their past, deprived of a future. They still possessed some intellectual capacity, enabling them to speak, think, and act, for instance, for better food portions, but this was not the acting of moral persons (in my sense of the word). Only a few exercised free and efficient will in regard to moral holds.

Also, those who managed to remain persons or moral persons were often radically reduced from what they used to be. They no longer had their former sensitive feelings and sophisticated, systematic, and logical mind. They often lacked good will toward fellow men, the capacity of empathy and impartiality. And their judgment of facts was often affected. All this precluded, at least in most situations, the elementary rationality required of moral agents.

Even if in principle people had free, efficient, and rational moral will, the room for maneuver was radically limited. In many situations demanding compassion, intervention, or revolt they were paralyzed to the degree of no longer being able to conceptualize, reason about, and decide on realizable alternative states.

Maybe they viewed different acts, but not alternative ones in the sense defined, acts of significantly different value (of outcome) for the individual. If we see only death or various atrocities coming out of anything we can do, our choices appear meaningless or grotesque, no longer deserving that name. Such choices are forced and cannot be recognized as moral—they constitute "choiceless choice," as Lawrence Langer called it in an essay.[34]

Provided a prisoner could imagine genuine alternatives, fatigue and fright could yet block the evaluation or the forming of a decision to act. The oppression changed the structure of power within the prisoner. Freely willed decisions were put out of power or else were seriously weakened, dubious even to the prisoner. Decisions to escape, for instance, had diminutive chances of being executed, because the control regime was rigorous and all planning extremely unreliable, because all prognoses were so unreliable. The prisoners were deprived of information about the surrounding world and about time; they were denied having a clock, for instance. Adding to the difficulties was the breakdown of the normal conception of the world, with its fairly coherent system of norms and values, and the replacement of it with confusion and harsh principles for survival which were only partly accepted. People were conditioned not to be moral persons. And those who tried to be moral agents hardly succeeded in practicing it. As Améry indicates, that would even be suicidal.

6

Forced, terrified, impotent, irrational: victims. . . . How can there be morality, say, a moral question, for someone in the Dark? This appears absurd only if we presuppose moral questions to have the character they have within traditional morality: inquiries for rational guidance of a free and efficient will.

Even at a moderate level of the Dark it is normally recognized by one posing the question "How do I stand this?" that he/she is not a moral agent in this issue and, furthermore, cannot see how he/she could become one. Then surely the question cannot be a demand for rational guidance of his/her free and efficient will in regard to moral holds. The premise is that there is just nothing for rational guidance to operate on. The moral question must be *different*.

A moral question, I said earlier, is an articulation of a quest for validity regarding moral holds for a person. Normally this involves linguistic expression. But the language needed could be rather primitive, consisting of a few words and concepts, including signs for the individual him/herself, for bad or painful states and not bad or not painful states, and for quest or search. Such language may be available to people in states of mental injury, dysfunction, depression, and some degrees of deprivation of personality.

It would seem that to put a question is to perform a minimal act, which requires one to be an agent. If the question is moral, isn't, then, that person a moral agent? But a question may occur—and be repeated —without being a result of a person performing free, efficient, or rational will. And even if one of free will asks the moral question, this only makes one a moral person in regard to the verbal side of the situation; it does not make one a moral person or moral agent in regard to the very problem. To put the question might be the only thing a person can do under the circumstances.

The moral question in the Dark is a kind of scream of the soul. Let me try to pinpoint its main characteristics:

(1) *The question has an unusually high intensity and psychological import*. The person puts all of his/her heart and mind into it, and an "answer" is considered to be decisive for the person's life.

(2) It is *a quest for obtaining a valid hold*. The person intensely wants to have some thought, feeling, decision, or attitude that would be valid under the circumstances. The question could perhaps be rephrased as "Save my soul!"

(3) However, *the quest has no clear receiver*. It is not viewed as a starting point for the individual to present a theoretical answer followed by a practical solution, since the individual is not a moral agent in the situation. So it is not directed toward oneself. It is directed "out there"— to someone, "other people," "humanity." The other may of course be concrete and known ("Mum," "David"), or something/someone postulated but unknown such as the Universal Spirit, the Transcendental Self, the Unconscious.

(4) *What constitutes a valid hold is unclear*. The extremity of the situation changes the scene; ordinarily valid holds lose their relevance or validity. New feelings and thoughts appear. Even pious Jews, accepting a norm of absolute obedience to God, suddenly become open to curse or even judge Him, as Elie Wiesel tells. And is survival really preferable to living with dignity? Is nonviolence better than aggression under these circumstances? Is mental distance better than a beautiful example of protest? And even if a person is rather clear about what hold would be valid, dignity, let's say, it may be unclear exactly what that requires of him under the extreme circumstances.

(5) *The way to obtain a valid hold is obscure*. It is logically possible to know how to arrive at a valid hold, even though one is unclear as to its nature. But most likely the route is also unclear, when the individual

isn't a moral agent in the situation and the nature of the valid hold is unclear. The same obscurity we of course have when one has an idea as to what one's valid hold would be, but it is not within the reach of one's free and/or efficient will.

(6) *What would make a hold valid is unclear.* This concerns the method of validation, or the recognition of the validity of the hold, since customary or philosophical morality and rational method appear to be inaccessible, false, or irrelevant. The rationale of the solution or its application is out of the questioner's hand, since the person is not an agent of it. But the person may be able to validate the hold retrospectively. Before completing this list, allow me to draw some conclusions from what has so far been said as to the specificity of the typical moral question of the Dark.

Since the ground for validity and/or the nature of and route to some moral hold is unclear, the questioner cannot in the situation give good reasons for the adoption of a particular hold. But it is fair to suppose that the idea of recommendation involves being able to give good reasons for what is recommended. Therefore, the moral question does not express the search for something to recommend, in the manner of questions in Morality of the Light.

That the receiver is another and/or unclear also indicates that the question is not a quest for an ordinary prescription of some hold, for instance, a decision to act. It is surely a quest for something the questioner should be or do, but he/she is not the subject of it, and prescriptions are for agents. If it is not a quest for a prescription for oneself, then it can hardly be a quest for prescription for others. Of course, once an answer has appeared, that may give ground for one's prescribing an application of it—but then one has entered the state of the Light.

If the moral question in the Dark is not a quest for prescription or recommendation of some particular hold, then an eventual answer is not necessarily recommending or prescribing, partially or universally. Further, a person articulating the answer cannot be said to be committing himself to it in every situation that is the same in all relevant aspects, because principles specifying the relevant conditions are not there. Moreover, it would be odd for the moral question to be a quest for something one is to commit oneself to, since one isn't a moral agent in regard to its content or actualization.

(7) *The valid hold is thought to be personal.* If I ask, "How do I stand this?" I am asking a personal question. I am not (directly) interested in how someone else is to stand something. And if my question would get its answer, this is compatible with other answers being valid for other persons in substantially the same situation. It might be that for many people the same hold is valid, but that would be an empirical coincidence. A moral answer in the Dark does not require or imply universal-

izability, which is expected of a moral answer in the Light. An aspect of this is that the "I" of the question, or the answer, cannot be replaced by "anyone." The personal character of the moral question and answer renders its morality a uniqueness that is missing in traditional morality. Here is an Existentialist streak, which also comes forth in the import of the question and the anguish with which we pose it.

To sum up, a moral question in the Dark is a more or less articulate but desperate and obscure quest that somehow, through someone or through something, a hold that is valid is to appear. You could say that *the question itself* is the locus of Morality of the Dark (which is not the same as the focus of the question), whereas the answer, with its implied ground in a system of principles and a set of beliefs, together with the enactment of the answer, is the locus of Morality of the Light.

In Morality of the Dark *the answer*—the valid hold—*is something emergent*, while in Morality of the Light it is something that the subject produces. Its production, however, appears mainly as an application—of principles, facts, and logic—whereas in Morality of the Dark we hope and appeal for something like a *miracle* or the *creation* of a displaced subject.

This difference in locus is reflected in the shift of the character of the moral question. In Morality of the Dark it is just a call—craving, pleading, praying—for the valid hold to appear: "Yield, please—whatever is valid!" Also, the terms of the moral language are changed; for instance, the agent-oriented distinctions dating from antiquity between "means" and "ends" and between "right" and "good" are not relevant here.

If I am right about this for the deep level of the Dark, then it can also be assumed that the moral question and answer on a more shallow level of the Dark share, to a considerable degree, many of these deep level traits.

7

Isn't it absurd to talk about a morality when the locus is in the question, not the answer? when there is no methodology for validating answers? when the person isn't even the subject of the answer?

In order to see better, one has to put aside the glasses of "science" (or rather, "normal science," as the philosopher Thomas Kuhn would put it), the rationality of which has set the paradigm for traditional morality. We need to consult other areas, areas which operate in opacity: art and religion.

First, religion. Elie Wiesel tells us in the preface to his play *The Trial of God*[35] of three rabbis he saw one winter evening in a camp, holding a trial of God ending in condemnation, and thereafter rushing off to the evening prayer. This seems illogical, but an explanation could be that they condemned from the point of view of what they understood, but at the same time recognized that God was beyond their understanding. The God they prayed to was this Unknown, impossible to understand.

The thought that "God" denotes an x, is a common phenomenon in religion. It may be that not only the nature of God is hidden from us, but also that the way to reach union with or life in compliance to God is viewed as unknowable. To find this may require walking in darkness, as many mystics think. We then ignore whether we are walking the right way, or even whether we are in the right confusion: we are in a state of loss and despair in regard to the positive values of religion.

In many religions, as testified by both Judaism and Christianity, being in darkness is even considered part of a fundamental process constitutive of the revelation of religious truths, of salvation. It is further believed that revelation and salvation are not products of Man, results of the exercise of his will; rather, they are something bestowed on the person who in himself is impotent in this respect. However, a persistent *search* for God and salvation is thought necessary for salvation.

Passing on to art, it is a commonplace that an artist ignores the exact nature and whereabouts of his sources of creation. The artist learns to regularly gather from them, but has no conscious access to or control over them. Sometimes the flow disappears, putting him in crisis, driving the artist out to a search in darkness. The artist may still do things, for example, paint, but the painting loses the property of being a valid work of art. The artist's "question" articulates the desire he/she has for artistic achievement, and the "answer" is (the statement of) the very creation, interpreted as something of unique value. The question, then, is not only an expression of a psychological difficulty but a genuine value quest in the realm of artistic value. Maybe he/she has had the experience that valid creation can come at the end of a search in the dark. But there is no technique for success, and the artist knows only afterward, the work done, what the "answer" is, i.e., what constituted a valid artistic creation in just that situation. A genuine creative achievement then appears to the artist also as something surpassing him, a miracle or gift. "He" could not "choose" or "produce" the valid artistic creation; strictly of himself, he is impotent.

An example might be the Russian sixteenth-century painter Ivan Rubljov, as depicted in a film by Andrej Tarkovskij. Ivan Rubljov gives up painting icons after coming to doubt his art, the world, and God. For many years he wanders around, lives like anybody else, but all the time attentively observing, searching deep down for an answer, the character and consequences of which he ignores. The turning point for him comes after observing a young boy, the son of a builder of church bells, who takes on, directs, and succeeds in building a huge church bell without actually having been taught the art of it, as his father had died without passing it on to his son. Seeing something in the combination of ignorance, striving, and miracle strikes a chord in Andrej which makes him "find," brings him back to his art. The phenomenon is not restricted to religion and art; it is known from other areas of creation, even science, in the particular phase of crisis and invention.[36]

Turning back to the Nazi camps, I shall end by relating some instances of Morality of the Dark taken from that area. Bettelheim recounts in his book how "vital self-interest induced me to study my own behavior and the behavior of others I noticed around me."[37] It was after about a month in the camp that the idea struck him; the initial phases of the initial shock and the first adaptation to the situation ("in a process that changed both the prisoner's personality and his outlook on life") had passed:

> I was deep in the middle of what was the favorite free time activity: exchanging tales of woe and swapping rumors about changes in the camp conditions or possible liberation. There were only minutes, but that did not rule out intense absorption in these conversations. As before on such occasions, I went through many severe mood swings from fervent hope to deepest despair, with the result that I was emotionally drained before the day even began, a day of seventeen long hours that would take all my energy to survive it. While swapping tales that morning, it suddenly flashed through my mind, "this is driving me crazy," and I felt that if I were to go on that way, I would in fact end up "crazy." That was when I decided that rather than be taken in by such rumors I would try to understand what was psychologically behind them.[38]

Bettelheim says that studying "was a device that spontaneously suggested itself"[39] to him. There are indications in the text that it gave him something he opaquely had asked for, and the realization that here is a valid hold came after and not before its occurrence:

> Soon I realized that I had found a solution to my main problem: . . . I was able to feel I was doing something constructive and on my own.[40]

This is how Bettelheim describes his answer:

> To observe and try to make sense of what I saw was . . . a way of convincing myself that my own life was still of some value, that I had not yet lost all the interests that had once given me self-respect.[41]

The finding is not a result of but a partial restoring of moral personality or even moral agency. Bettelheim describes in his book the experiences of other people who in a similar way "found," but where other things seemed to yield the valid hold. It could be almost anything, for instance discussing stamp collecting. Primo Levi makes the same observation. "The paths to salvation are many, difficult, and improbable," he says.[42] (Note Levi's use of the term "salvation.")

Frankl, who like Bettelheim stresses the presence of free will in all prisoners, gives another example of Morality of the Dark. In a passage he states that persons endowed with a rich spiritual life have a better possibility of enduring life in the camp, and he recounts when one early morning, on the march out from the camp to the daily hardships, someone suddenly mumbles to him: "If our wives could see us now! I do hope they are better off in their camps and don't know what is happening to us."[43] Triggered by this, the image of Frankl's wife comes to him, and as he stumbles on, he manages to keep it, with a lively and intense power of imagination such as he has never before experienced. He talks with her, hears her answer, sees her smile:

> Real or not, her look was then more luminous than the sun which was beginning to rise. A thought transfixed me: for the first time in my life I saw the truth as it is set into song by so many poets, proclaimed as the final wisdom by so many thinkers. The truth—that love is the ultimate and the highest goal to which man can aspire. Then I grasped the meaning of the greatest secret that that human poetry and human thought and belief have to impart: *The salvation of man through love and in love* . . . I did not know whether my wife was alive . . . but at that moment it ceased to matter.[44]

This appearance of meaning and value Frankl describes not as an outcome of a calculated action of his, but as something coming to him. In another situation he relates, the quest for a valid hold preceding the "answer" is more evident, and here, too, the latter—interpreted as such only after its occurrence—comes as a gift, almost as a religious grace:

> The dawn was grey around us . . . I was again conversing with my wife, or perhaps I was struggling to find the reason for my sufferings, my slow dying. In a last violent protest against the hopelessness of imminent death, I sensed my spirit piercing through the enveloping gloom. I felt it transcend that hopeless, meaningless world, and from somewhere I heard a victorious "Yes" in answer to my question of the existence of an ultimate purpose.[45]

Jean Améry remarks rather cynically that similar "intoxicated" experiences were not exceptional among the prisoners. He considers them to be "profoundly inauthentic, the value of the soul hardly finds support in such states."[46] He is wrong in this, as the example of Frankl shows. But Améry's remark is important for two reasons, first, because it acknowledges the common reality of a quest for "the value of the soul"; second, because it shows clearly that it is not the experience itself, but how it is interpreted that counts. Similar feelings, thoughts, or experiences may be regarded as the desired valid hold by some, but not by others. The recognition of something as a valid hold is necessary, and that presupposes a previous quest for a valid hold.

Améry describes having had a permanent high activity of his soul in this situation of terror and imminent death. Through this activity his soul opposed death "and sought—but in vain, let me say that at once—to establish its dignity."[47] Améry's preconceived answer to his moral quest in the Dark was "dignity," something he admits to be very vague. He did not know how to realize it, and thinks he failed to achieve it. However, he found something he did not seek and would not have predicted: a radical demystification of reality, a stripping from it of esthetic, metaphysical, or "philosophical" inventions.[48] This he recognized as a minimal value. A minimal but valid hold was thus found in the camp. Maybe this helped him, the ever intellectually curious, to survive. Once freed, he became a distinguished and profound writer.

8

The idea, then, is that the moral question in the Dark, such as "How do I stand this?" is an opaque but intense quest for value creation, against or beyond reason, directed toward something unknown. Examples from religion and art, as well as some experiences in the Nazi camps, show that we are dealing here with something meaningful and fruitful. How can this be? And what are the consequences for moral philosophy? I want to end with some speculation.

The Dark is not restricted to the situation of the Jews in the Nazi death camps; it also turns up when we are otherwise impotent or forced, or just at our wits' end in relation to some problem, for instance an excruciating grief, or our imminent death. It is an ingredient in a normal human life full of shortcoming. I would say that we are in a perpetual sway between the spheres of Light and Dark, depending on the degree of freedom, efficiency, and rationality we have in relation to varying states and events.

Reason is a fairly well known, accessible part of the soul, but not more than a part of it, and a limited one. When our reason fails, we still seek and appeal with all we have, but we seek beyond ourselves. The moral question in the Dark, like the prayer or ritual in religion and the bewildered striving of an artist, can be interpreted as an appeal to, or attempt to enter a certain relationship with, the very depths of the human body and soul—of life itself. This has been theorized in different ways, as the Unconscious, Nature, God, It. Perhaps it is better rendered by an account of the complex working of the vast human brain. However, it is undeniable that the unknown may respond to our quest, and that things are somehow created within us, things we recognize as valid.

We are not in a position to consciously (or rationally) produce or effectuate our moral hold in a state of the Dark. Nevertheless there may be better or worse preparations on our part, giving possibly necessary but not sufficient conditions for a creation of valid hold. It might be favorable, for instance, that our mind is open in a certain way, in order to give place for a creativity of something "other," creativity that possibly yields a hold of value for the seeker. Success in the Dark is possibly also connected with the desperation, wholeheartedness, and energy put into the posing of the moral question.

Since a favorable mentality in situations of the Dark are out of our control once we are there, it ought to be prepared, in normal life, as part of the values to be realized in Morality of the Light. The latter would thereby be radically changed. I think it should also be realized that the premises of Morality of the Light, the rational method and ultimate value judgments, are something created. When we work there, we—like God in Genesis—work in the Dark. That is why moral philosophers have failed to give a rational derivation of 'ought' or 'good'.

Morality of the Dark has been a missing link in a tradition of moral philosophy blinded by rationality. Its role has instead been played by simply nonarticulate living, or by other ideological currents, in particular religions. Christianity, with its symbol of the crucified Christ, stresses that the individual cannot by his or her own efforts enact salvation, and prepares people's minds for victimhood and suffering through humility and prayer. Buddhism, with its ever calm, crosslegged guide, can be seen as a way to strengthen mind in the face of losing, starving, dying—states that are never allowed to be put out of sight.

In philosophy, there are above all the Stoics who have a focus on preparations for suffering and dying, imbuing the mind with indifference to events and states out of our control. This seemed exaggerated for the fit and optimistic, and Stoicism ceased to be interesting to philosophers. But from a perspective of the Dark, it is one of few relevant philosophies.

An advantage of my conceptualization is that it explains, gives place and credit to opponents of the main tradition of Ethics, theoreticians and practitioners of religion and art, as well as existentialists. However, Morality of the Light and Morality of the Dark are not rivals, they are complements and form a whole, like in the Taoist symbol of yin and yang. But in contrast to the latter, there is hardly any sharp dividing line between the halves. Various modes and degrees inside the two kinds of morality seem inevitable.

Notes

1. "If you are one called to fail, do not on that account fail, no matter what." Henri Michaux, *Poteaux d'angle* (Paris: Gallimard, 1981), p. 28; my translation.

2. William Frankena, *Ethics* (Englewood Cliffs, N.J.: Prentice-Hall), 1963, p. 7.

3. Immanuel Kant, *Groundwork of the Metaphysics of Morals* (1785), trans. H. J. Paton (New York: Harper Torchbooks, 1964), p. 104.

4. See Elie Wiesel, *The Night Trilogy: Night, Dawn, The Accident* (New York: Hill and Wang, 1987). (*Night* was first published in French 1958, *Dawn* was first published in French in 1960, and *The Accident* was first published in French in 1961.)

5. Robert McAfee Brown, *Elie Wiesel, Messenger to All Humanity* (Notre Dame, Ind.: University of Notre Dame Press, rev. ed., 1989), p. 52.

6. Wiesel, *Night*, p. 53.

7. Ibid., p. 46.

8. Brown, *Elie Wiesel, Messenger to All Humanity*, p. 57.

9. Ibid., p. 59.

10. Ibid., p. 43.

11. Ibid., p. 59.

12. Bruno Bettelheim, *The Informed Heart* (London: Penguin Books, 1991; first published 1960), p. xvii.

13. Primo Levi, *If This Is a Man* and *The Truce*. (London: Vintage, 1996. *If This Is A Man* was first published in Italian in 1958, *The Truce* was first published in Italian in 1963.)

14. Terence Des Pres, "Excremental Assault," in John K. Roth and Michael Berenbaum, eds., *Holocaust: Religious and Philosophical Implications* (New York: Paragon House, 1989). The article is a chapter in Des Pres's book *The Survivors* (New York; Oxford University Press, 1976.)

15. Primo Levi, *The Drowned and the Saved* (London: Abacus, 1989, first published in Italian 1986), p. 24.

16. Ibid., p. 24.

17. Levi, *If This Is a Man*, p. 33.

18. Ibid., p. 62.

19. *The Drowned and the Saved*, p. 25.

20. Ibid., p. 59.

21. Ibid., p. 59.

22. Ibid., p. 33.

23. Ibid., p. 57.

24. Ibid., p. 67.

25. Ibid., p. 131.

26. Ibid., p. 130.

27. Ibid., p. 127.

28. Primo Levi, *Moments of Reprieve* (London: Abacus, 1987; first published in Italian in 1981), p. 10.

29. Samuel Pisar, *Le sang de l'espoir* rev. ed. (Paris: Laffont, 1995; first edition 1979), p. 320; my translation.

30. Jean Améry, *Par-delà le crime et le châtiment* (Arles: Actes Sud, 1995; first edition in German, 1966), p. 47; my translation.

31. Ibid., p. 46.

32. Viktor Frankl, *From Death-Camp to Existentialism* (Boston: Beacon Press, 1959).

33. Bettelheim, *The Informed Heart*, p. 69.

34. Lawrence L. Langer, "The Dilemma of Choice in the Deathcamps," in *Holocaust: Religious and Philosophical Implications*.

35. Elie Wiesel, *The Trial of God* (New York: Random House, 1979; first published in French, 1978).

36. See, e.g., A. Alvarez, *Night: An Exploration of Night life, Night Language, Sleep and Dreams* (London: Jonathan Cape, 1995); and Robert J. Sternberg and Janet E. Davidson, eds., *The Nature of Insight* (Cambridge, Mass.: MIT Press, 1994).

37. Bettelheim, *The Informed Heart*, p. 111.

38. Ibid., pp. 111f.

39. Ibid., p. 111.

40. Ibid., p.115.

41. Ibid., p. 111.

42. Levi, *If This Is a Man*, p. 96.

43. Frankl, *From Death-Camp to Existentialism*, p. 36.

44. Ibid., pp. 36 f. (original italics)

45. Ibid., p. 39.

46. Améry, *Par-delà le crime et le châtiment*, p. 33; my translation.

47. Ibid., p. 43; my translation.

48. Ibid., p 48.

"Identity without Text"
Negation and Execution
Detlef Linke

I. Imagine!

Imagine that someone were to establish human rights by attempting first to prove the "I" responsible for these human rights. Imagine further that the one concerned considers this deed-action (*Tathandlung*) of constituting the "I" so significant that it would precede each word and each text and each written legal agreement. Imagine further that this I-identity self-posited by a "deed-action" were to take on, as it were, an axiomatic role, and had thus to be well defined, that is, delimited. In this way, negation has to be enlisted for the constitution of the I. Imagine even further that the negative realm were at the same time under the rule of the I about to constitute itself. If something like that happened, one would have to ask whether such a constituting I could at all find its way to human rights and whether it would not prefer the tendency to work off the negative realm, instead of striving to extend its I beyond the non-I. Suddenly then, the constitution of the I for the foundation of human rights would turn into a project of an Ego that, placing the other at its disposal, could no longer find its way to the regulating textual and legal mechanism that was to reconcile, mediate, and reciprocate between I and alterity since the cognitive disposition had already used up itself in the working off of the non-I.

If there were a philosophical "foundation" of human rights, it might be conflictual for other human beings in a twofold manner. First, simply by virtue of the fact that the other, first appearing merely as non-I to be worked off, can escape this working off only by joining the We of those carrying out the same constituting mechanics of the I. Secondly, when the self-constituting I encounters others (allotted the position of the non-I) who do not want to participate in the I's game of reciprocity. These others take their starting point instead from word and text and devote themselves to the deed that preferably does not become the mere deed of self-constitution (in which the other is merely "used up").

One can hardly imagine that such a philosophical foundation of ethics would ever be attempted. Reservations about a cognitive disposition articulating itself in such a manner would certainly be too strong. If one appealed to such a philosophy, one would have to fear the loss of one's personal resources of responsibility, especially since this foundation also requires that the person must be destroyed for the sake of the universal I. I do not think we require a poet to illustrate the problematic character of this disposition. However, if we did have a poet, she might perhaps illustrate this primary disposition in such a way that, first, the study with its texts is deposited and statements like "In the beginning there is the word" are replaced by the exclamation "In the beginning there is the deed." Thus, a non-I would have to be present and at the disposal of the I, as it likes it. A dog, for instance a poodle, would be suitable for this. If one provided this non-I with greater power, it would be permitted to say no, but it might be obliged to the forces of the I or the textless level of blood. The non-I would be then not simply another I, but a kind of degraded laborer forced to be at the disposal of the I's interests. But one could also imagine a poetic trick concerned with the question of how realistically the striving of the I to work off the non-I is considered in terms of an identification with the sexual desire (for instance, for the female) and, at the same time, as redemption. The woman—let us call her Gretchen—who, in this "frame," can, as it were, only be reached with the help of a sexual partner, is now perhaps glorified as the eternal female and thus becomes the quintessence of redemption, even though this achievement is identified with mechanisms of aggression. In such a poetic draft there would be no place for ethics. For alterity does not remain resistant; it is, rather, utilized and even redeems.

A culture that kept away from such a philosophy—which, even transformed as poetry, has been spread in our high schools and constitutes the disposition of the emotional-cognitive life of our legal texts— would not be analyzable by attempting to elaborate an "anti-position" (an attitude directed against something else). The description of this anti-position could then lead to a far-reaching explanation, only if it became evident how this anti-position is *concealed* in the concept of one's own identity—like the soldiers in the Trojan horse. No, even better, like the bones in the human body. But no, again, since nature has not planned something like this—something like a human being carrying a hedgehog in his interior.

Yet Schopenhauer indicated that it is the same with human beings and porcupines. Out of the necessity for warmth, they move closer to each other until the spikes begin to sting, until they depart from each other, until it is once again too cold for them to stay apart. Their passion is stabilized somewhere between freezing and stabbing to death. Such a conception of interaction allows only little space. However, if one takes a conception in which negativity is even to become only a part of the I, the spikes are already on the inside. Instead of fending off a possible attacker, they penetrate the abdominal wall from the inside. If such a self-image is thought to be in conformity with potency, its "self"-destructivity is, however, unmistakable. It is particularly evident that it suffices to refer to the I and identity (in this account, the body is regarded only as their expression) in order to have supplied the "anti" as well. As such, it need not be addressed separately for it is constitutive of one's identity, and well concealed in it.

Were a future scholar to come and desire to elaborate an anti-disposition to such a community, this community would not recognize itself in these descriptions because it would be identical for the most part and "anti" only in some particular cases. However, it would be identical not in terms of a family resemblance à la Wittgenstein, for instance, but identical in terms of a negation of the other who was to be conquered. In the case where this other takes text and words rather than the deed as his starting point, he even presents an additional threat to identity: he could not even be located in the formula of the identity-forming negation since he did not have this schema as a foundation for his actions.

Of course, if there were such a community that understood identity in this very way, one could attempt to keep it from sharp delimitations and plead for more ambivalence. But what would it mean to stress the unrecognizablity of alterity, its diversity, and to give priority to its polyvalence? Would the negation contained in identity already be taken out, already a space established, in the background of which alterity, diversity, and polyvalence were to be posited? Would one not rather have to question the role of negation in it, to bring it to the right place and to show that negation is but one possibility for constituting identity, especially if one deals with life-worldly situations in which the logic of negation might be translated, because the concept of negation does not mean anything other than this, into the refusal to communicate and the intent to execute?

Well, I think that we are not confronted with this very problem because such a strange foundation of the rights of human beings and of ethics via this strange concept of identity would barely even be considered reasonable.

Yet the insufficiency of the logic of negation with respect to interpersonal relations as well as the constitution of the I is not yet compensated for in supposedly opening up negation by means of ambivalencing in life-worldly dimensions. The strange model of identity that I have introduced, and with regard to which one can imagine that it could have led to genocide, in the attempt to correct its consequences, this very model has demonstrated numerous new life-worldly projects so far. The ambivalencing of interpersonal relations is but one possible attempt presenting, of course, not yet a retrieval of the life-worldly situation, but rather the imposition of a life-worldly situation through a particular theoretical compensatory construct. Thus, the Holocaust is effective even in gender relations (there, ambivalencing and ambiguity have played a particular role). The question is whether the concepts of identity preceding it are already relativized sufficiently by this ambivalencing.

There can be no doubt about the Holocaust. The question is whether one should continue to read Fichte, who, as I was told, sketched a concept of identity in the *Wissenschaftslehre* (*Doctrine of Science*) of 1794 that is not unlike the one mentioned above, and Goethe, who studied the *Wissenschaftslehre* in detail and used it for his conception of the *Faust* setting in with the deed, with so little reserve in history—as is still partly done today. I think not.

II. Ideality and Its Concealed

It is possible to release alterity from the oppositional logic of negation and difference. The other can then enter into life-worldly disparateness without having to enter into the conceptual binary pattern of complete unification or complete opposition. Without any doubt, encounters with alterity can evoke psychological patterns of doubling and touch on the limits of stress. However, it is important to see that the annihilation of alterity by monopolization/appropriation also sets the course for the annihilation of alterity that cannot be monopolized/appropriated. Alterity which does not aim at opposition, but rather at disparateness, cannot be monopolized/appropriated by the oppositional logic of the opposition I-other. At this point, I speak of disparateness, meaning dissociation in interpersonal terms. This seems to be a more suitable concept than that of difference. Difference construed as mere opposition can easily be read again as unity, thus possibly leading to the affirmation of that oppositional logic which we want to avoid. If one wants to speak at all of difference, it would be more prudent to use the concept of *différance*.

The outcome of Jacob's battle with the angel represents an example of the disparateness of coexistence. In the Old Testament's story, Jacob wrestles with the angel the whole night and is then left with a dislocated hip. The battle did not end simply with the defeat or annihilation of one of them, but with Jacob saying, "I let you go, only if you bless me."

This battle was not influenced by the logic of negation, but by the desire for benevolent disparateness. The other is not to become myself or be annihilated, he is to be released into freedom. However, he is also to bless me. This is not a subjugation of the other, but the mere demand for his agreement on a peaceful life that, for this reason alone, need not be interrelated.

But the story of Faust runs differently: he wants to make Mephisto his servant, thus making a pact with him—meaning that Faust himself will be annihilated in the end. Moreover, this alliance is a pact with the destructive force itself.

Possibly, a way of thinking lurks behind this erroneous opinion permitting the reduction of alterity to unity and identity—a way of thinking not limited to the Faustian play or the Fichtean axiomatization and subjugation of fundamental human relations. This is worth close consideration since metaphysical thought is oriented toward the reduction of alterity. Heidegger elaborated on this thinking of identity, as it is displayed in Aristotle, in his lecture of 1929 on the foundations of metaphysics, but he did so still in terms of a determination/destiny for man. He focused on the formulation of the "as" in Aristotle, in which an object is to be brought to comprehension "as" this object. In being addressed, the object A is, so to speak, redoubled (A = B) by the "as" and returned into itself (A = A). In this sense, the comprehension of the object already appears as reduction of variation since the alteration of the object in the repetition is not admitted. What is interesting, however, is that Heidegger uses Aristotelianism to delimit man from animal because he attempts to show that this "as" relation is not possible in the case of the animal. Thus, he elevates the Greek way of thinking to the distinguishing feature of animal and man. Today, against this account, we must insist that human beings who do not employ this "as" relation not be regarded as mere animals.

Metaphysics designed a scaling system displaying a hierarchy from animal to man. From the perspective of racial biology, it was not the "Jew," but the "Black" who, for Adolf Hitler, was located at the lowest stage of the value scale. Nonetheless, it was the "Jew" who was the decisive adversary. Many scholars saw this as an inexplicable position. However, this contradiction can be resolved, once one makes it clear that the hostility to the "Jews" became a priority not because it was not in their ontological statements, but rather in their purportedly "innately" oriented behavior (for instance, the ban on killing) that they were in sharp conflict with a bio-ontology aiming to establish the human anthropologically and metaphysically instead of from life-worldly patterns of behavior. The definition of the human in contrast/opposition to the animal made possible an interpretation of being in which alterity either had to be reduced to identity or submitted to annihilation. A thinking that does not want to admit alterity can conceive unity and salvation (*Heil*) only "as" a victory over alterity. The exclamation "Sieg Heil!" became the expression of such unifying thought.

In the 1790s, Johann Gottlieb Fichte once came to his lecture with two candles. He put them on the lectern and lit the first one, then the other while simultaneously extinguishing the first one. He then lit the first one again while extinguishing the second, and so forth. Thereupon, he asked his audience what this meant. Fichte himself quickly gave the answer—it means, of course, the relationship between I and non-I. If the one is, the other is not. A similar exclusionary logic of negation applied to Hitler, for whom there could be only the Jews or the European race. Both at the same time were not conceivable for Hitler. The notion that there might be different concepts of identity was excluded by the totalitarianism of the Fichtean opposition. Unlike Jacob, Faust did not release his alterity.

Alterity, as well as identity, is not always the same. Hegel attempted to fix the otherness of the animal by emphasizing that the animal be in unity, as it were, "idealist" and always individual. It is likely that even here alterity was conceptualized in a too uniform and unifying manner. Here, perhaps, it becomes clear that if one took such a standpoint, the position of disparateness had to be misrecognized as mere animality. Some still ask today how the bestiality of the Third Reich was possible. Was it not, in part at least, because individuality was attributed only to inferior animals? Here, much still needs to be elaborated if one wants to determine *humanitas* and *animalitas* such that one does not end up praising one's own intolerance toward others as *humanitas*. Following the logic of Hegel, Fichte, and maybe that of Heidegger as well, what cannot be made clear (even to this logic itself) is that Auschwitz was not an act of bestiality. Which is not to say that the concept of *humanitas* in general applies to what the Nazis did. But they did employ and elaborate a particular concept of *humanitas* that willingly declared deliberate, brutal murder as necessary and good for establishing unity.

In a phase in the history of thought designated as the "end of metaphysics" it has to be stated that the concepts of humanity and animality have become, in their interconnections, perverted and confused. One cannot expect an easy disentanglement. Much would be gained, however, if, unlike Fichte, we would no longer seek an "initial solution" in philosophy. From philosophy an all too fast "final solution" might once again be derived. This does not mean, however, that "salvation" is to be found in some kind of philosophical abstinence. On the contrary. We have to concentrate all our efforts to find "hidden variables" for possibly newly emerging logics of negation. The sometimes uncritical search for new identities should be read as a warning signal that we are still not looking for identities without the reduction and negation of alterity. For the most part, the suspension of concepts such as unity and identity has been adopted only by some groupings. It is significant that ambivalent negation can be concealed in the highest basic concepts of our social existence. Even if one speaks of individuality, it may well be that one does not want to let the other go—even if the latter has given us his blessings.

Memorial Proposal

A tradition that regarded the word not to mean anything (*Schall und Rauch*; Goethe's *Faust*) led to the replacement of the word by cry and soot. Spirit, having ignored the materiality of the text and having celebrated this leaping over as initial deed, wanted to live in the medium of the third state (sound, smoke, gas). The insertion of the idea of gassing as distance from writing into the remembrance of the annihilation of the Jews of Europe immediately suggests itself. Concerning a memorial (in Berlin) for the Shoah, the following design is offered, to which the previous considerations are intended as contributions in remembrance of the annihilation of the Jews of Europe:

1. commemorative plaque made of metal on which places of annihilation, persecution, and deportation, as well as the names of the annihilated, persecuted, and deported are engraved (measurements: height about 6m; width about 40m).

2. a gas chamber lowered into the ground, sealed and sufficiently protected against terrorist attacks by concrete and a steel jacket. The chamber is filled with gas, located as closely as possible behind the commemorative plaque and closer to it than to the earth's surface.

3. lowering of the ground (area about 60×40m) toward the commemorative plaque. Exponential progress.

4. recess of lowering on a few square meters. On this, the dedicative inscription of the memorial. The Hebrew letter rises on this area. It stands for Shoah. It is opportune that it is also the first letter for the Hebrew "Hear!" The letter is made of metal. It is the only relief of the memorial rising above the ground. The representation of the letter does not simply fall into the genre of sculpture but introduces, at the place where German intellectual history looked for the artistic-monumental, the reverse lettering of a Hebrew letter. The distance from the letter meant for spiritualization proved to be the path to gassing.

Translated by Erik M. Vogt

Heidegger's Silence Revisited

Peter Strasser

1

Although Heidegger was never a moral philosopher in explicit terms, there is no doubt that he has always spurred on our ethical alertness. Like Wittgenstein, he denied moral thinking was worth captivating the philosopher's mind. In Wittgenstein's view, all our moral evidence is "mystical" and therefore beyond the border of meaningful speech. By contrast, Heidegger asserts that all Western morality is "subjectivistic" and, therefore, covers up the essential questions about human beings and the Being of being itself.

Heidegger is often said to be a teacher of the true conditions of the West. This esteem, however, must worry those who hold that, since World War II, the Holocaust should be the center of our reflections on the essence of Western culture and policies. Heidegger, who wrote many pages to prove old Europe's decline, was very reticent about the Jews' fate under the Third Reich. His silence, however, was not complete.

On December 1, 1949, Heidegger delivered four lectures to the Club zu Bremen under the general title "Einsicht in das was ist" [Insight into What Is]. One of these lectures, "Das Ge-Stell" [The Enframing], remained unpublished for forty-five years. But a single sentence, made public by Wolfgang Schirmacher in 1983, immediately received much attention. For it was, as far as we have learned till today, Heidegger's only direct reference to the Holocaust by explicitly mentioning the gas chambers. It goes as follows: "In our days, agriculture is a mechanized food industry, in essence the same as the fabrication of corpses in gas chambers and extermination camps, the same as the blockade and starvation of countries, the same as the fabrication of hydrogen bombs."[1]

Perhaps it should be remarked that this quote from Heidegger was not surprising in certain milieus. An idiosyncrasy against technology was often demonstrated by those on the ultraconservative side of Germany's intellectuals. They were afraid that technical means of maintaining life could suddenly turn into such a mass murdering. The core of technology was alleged to be the heart of suppression. In religious terms, technological enterprises would be driven by satanic forces which were closely related to death and hell. For example, Carl Schmitt, a Catholic anti-Semite, National Socialist, and famous professor of constitutional law, sketched in his *Glossarium* some cynical maxims of survival in modern times. One of these rules, written down on May 1, 1948, says: "Go into the shelter, if the sirens are wailing; put your hands up, if the order is given; do not forget that the link between protection and obedience is no more valid and natural today; *the shelter can be the gas chamber* [my italics]."[2]

Apart from the case of Carl Schmitt, many critics were appalled at Heidegger. How could a philosopher of the highest rank, who had unfortunately participated in Hitler's movement for a short while, say such a foolish thing only a few years after the war and, in addition, long after having been disillusioned with the Nazis' *Realpolitik*? More than that, how could Heidegger hold on to such a highly *immoral* belief?

Throughout his philosophical thinking, Heidegger was an antimodernist. Like many other philosophers and intellectuals, he shared the opinion that the Enlightenment's belief in permanent historical progress due to scientific and technological evolution was fundamentally wrong. The antimodernist does not criticize merely the costs of progress, and does not even make it his primary point. There may be means in the future to avoid the old economic and political troubles; from a materialistic point of view, humankind will be enabled one day to live a better life than ever before. First and foremost, the antimodernist denounces the modern picture of man. Its ontological framework, having been developed during the rise of natural sciences and rationalism, is suspected of alienating man from the world.

On the one hand, the basic notions of the modern framework refer to physical objects whose cognition is linked *a priori* with technichal interests and power. Natural things, conceptualized scientifically, are wholly subjected to the laws of nature; they do not entail any value. They are supposed to be valuable only as means to human ends. On the other hand, man as autonomous subject of knowledge is the highest authority. Never again can a god or any kind of natural right constitute a range of meaning or worth. Therefore, the modern man becomes incapable of grasping an objective basis to justify his moral convictions. This ethical deficiency leads necessarily to relativistic and, eventually, nihilistic views.

Since Heidegger shared the antimodernist's perspective of our time, he believed in the decline of Western culture. As a result of this decline, we are increasingly unable to hear "the call of Being"; we are deaf in a strictly ontological sense. Indeed, we have almost forgotten about "the Being of beings" [das Sein des Seienden]. Many of Heidegger's philosophical opponents have characterized his "Being" as an absurd notion without any content or substance. Heidegger's reply is well known: We have forgotten ourselves as such entities whose being consists of being concerned about their own Being. The nihilistic structure infects all our relations and enterprises, and provokes a malignant humanism: Why not manipulate or even suppress other beings, including human beings, by virtue of technology, if this would be the best way of realizing one's own interests? The modern mind, in its misguided effort to overcome man's hollowness and vanity, mobilizes its Promethean capacities. But, while the eagerness for absolute power grows in this existential vacuum, megalomania mingles with paranoia.

2

If we pay attention to Heidegger's analysis of the Promethean project's captivation of modern man, we may also find a non-banal interpretation of the Holocaust. The critics' rage was aroused by Heidegger's equating the food industry with the extermination camps. In fact, to say that both are the same would be idiotic, if the standard of comparison were simply the stage of technical development. The critics are right in saying that the moral judgment about technology at any level depends on the results and not on the application of technology itself. Whereas the food industry saves people from starving, the only function of extermination camps is to kill people. Obviously, there is a *relevant* ethical difference.

However, Heidegger's discourse is more complicated than the usual warnings about misuses and abuses of technology. Heidegger interprets modern dynamics as steps within a long history since the ancient Greeks. Occidental development is thought of as a process of self-revelation and, simultaneously, self-concealment of Being. It has often been noticed that Heidegger's Being can be understood as a code name for the word "God."[3] Heidegger himself always rejected such an interpretation as misjudging his philosophical aim to grasp a radically new perspective beyond religious *and* secular views. But there is no really cogent reason for agreeing with Heidegger's self-interpretation, which is mainly to stress the singularity of his own philosophy. Therefore, we may read his agricultural remark as follows: In our days, God's absence is the same with respect to all enterprises of the Promethean project, whether it be the food industry or the extermination camps. For this project is driven, in its ontological depth, not by a psychological but by a metaphysical will—the will to become godlike and, at the end, God himself.

Against this background Heidegger asks what the essence of our morality is. In *Being and Time* (1927) he had already come to the conclusion that our moral talk is to the largest extent *Gerede*, "idle talk." Idle talk is a basic element of what Heidegger calls *Öffentlichkeit*, or "publicness." It is hard to understand this notion without disparaging connotations, as Heidegger demands. His own words are unmistakably pejorative: "Publicness proximally controls every way in which the world and *Dasein* get interpreted, and it is always right—not because there is some distinctive and primary relationship-of-Being in which it is related to 'Things' . . . , but because it is insensitive to every difference of level and of genuineness and thus never gets to the 'heart of the matter' [*auf die Sachen*]."[4]

In his later writings, especially after the war, Heidegger analyzes "Publicness" and "idle talk," including moral conversation, as symptoms of Being's withdrawal and its sinking into oblivion due to the worldwide triumph of technology. According to this view, occidental man's concern about himself becomes more and more narrow; it becomes the fear of a cog in the machine. As the cog, he worries about the possibility of breaking at any moment. "What is going to happen *then*?" Heidegger asks. His answer: *"Man will be tranformed into a mechanized animal,* whose instincts have already become weaker and more diffuse, and are beginning now to get replaced by the giantness of technology."[5] So, Heidegger's understanding of our moral situation is very disillusioning. Since technology cannot establish any objective values, we are trapped in subjectivism; but subjectivism is, in essence, nothing more than nihilism, and, therefore, our concept of morals is an indissolubly nihilistic one.

It follows that all of our values and estimations exist only as reflections of the nihilistic structure which shapes all of our relations to the world and to ourselves. Here we may come upon one reason why Heidegger did not condemn the Holocaust either before or after 1945. If the Holocaust was the triumph of titanic nihilism, any moral castigation would depend on, and therefore confirm, nihilism instead of conquering it. Consequently, in condemning the Nazis' outrages, the accuser makes his moral judgment by participating in the same metaphysical mindset as the Nazis in inaugurating genocide.

Should we accept this argument? There are good reasons for answering in the negative. The acceptability of Heidegger's ontological premises is not independent of the consequences for our common life, and a highly important consequence consists in denouncing moral discourse. Imagine a society whose members would, like staunch Heideggerians, look down on people who made moral distinctions earnestly! Of course, such a society would despise, as an expression of naivety, ethical judgments about the outcomes of mechanized work, whether it be harms or benefits. Considering good and bad outcomes, one would demonstrate one's insightful view by saying, "Technology is always technology, isn't it?" But how to go on from there? What ought to be done? In such a society "beyond moral," however, there could not be found an adequate answer. Perhaps there would be a somewhat anarchistic answer given by some radical elements, such as the Luddites: "Wreck the machines!" Yet apart from the fact that Luddism is by no means a Heideggerian method, it does not represent a specific reaction to the Holocaust either. By contrast, the humanity of any modern society in the West is based on its moral capacity for living in the face of the Holocaust.

Many measures taken by Nazis against minorities, in particular Jews and the mentally ill, were approved of intuitively by a great many Germans and Austrians. But sometimes intuition is simply the devil's whisper. In any case, we need a criterion for differentiating right intuitions, which may really be a call of Being, from wrong ones rooted in hidden ideologies or concealed inhumanities. Should there finally be a rational consent, the criterion in question must tie up the moral consideration to an impartial view of all involved interests, whatever the ethical standpoints of the parties may be. In this mindset, the so-called principle of universalizability postulates that everyone ought to comply with a rule if, and only if, violating the rule would be more against the sum of interests than in accordance with it. Applying this principle, the Nazis' discrimination laws against the Jewish people will be irrefutably revealed as immoral in the strongest sense, completely different from any kind of welfare policy based on the expansion of a mechanized food industry.

We are able to get such results without compulsion only by virtue of moral reasoning. This is an indispensable trait of our humanity. Far more than a reflection of nihilism within the scope of man's alienation from Being, moral reasoning is essential for us as beings concerned about themselves. Without a doubt, the Holocaust strictly demands negative judgment, but Heidegger's doctrine fails to give an *ontological* alternative to the *moral* judgments that are suspected to be idle talk within the scope of publicness. Heidegger ignores the need of *condemning* genocide by delivering intersubjective and, therefore, objective reasons.

3

Nevertheless, Heidegger's Holocaust file has not yet been closed. It even seems to have been reopened in the last few years, as was recently proved by Alan Milchman and Alan Rosenberg, who teach political science and philosophy at Queens College, the City University of New York. Together they edited an anthology titled *Martin Heidegger and the Holocaust* (1996). Almost every one of the fifteen contributors gives us the feeling that Heidegger's sincerity as philosopher is at stake because of his putting the gas chambers into the context of industrialized food production.

For example, Tom Rockmore, professor of philosophy at Duquesne University, writes: "If all modern events are explicable in terms of the fall away from being, if they are all the same in the crucial respect, then obviously the Holocaust and all other events lose their historical specificity" (117).[6] This argument is conclusive. It shows the irrelevance of "Heidegger's undifferentiated rejection of modernity as such," not least with respect to the Holocaust. Antimodernism that reduces social phenomena to a monistic principle, like the *Ge-Stell*, lacks explanatory power. At best, monistic approaches explain the "modernity" of modern things, but not their pecularity *within* modernity.

In this regard, the editors' article formulates a contraposition. According to Milchman and Rosenberg, the universal reign of Heidegger's *Ge-Stell* represents the true condition of the Holocaust. Reading "Heidegger against Heidegger" (219), they nevertheless hold that Heidegger's technosophy is necessary to understanding the connection between modernity and bestiality.

Milchman and Rosenberg show Leibniz's principle of sufficient reason in a very critical light. As one knows, the validity of this principle is both a logical and causal need to avoid a chaotic world ruled by irrationality and pure chance. Consequently, the authors assert that Leibniz's principle is "the basis of calculative thinking" and, therefore, "in its totalizing, and imperialistic, form, can be seen as the metaphysical underpinning which made the Holocaust possible" (222). This may be so. But the authors' position suffers from the above-mentioned lack of explanatory power. It is by no means evident that Heidegger "explicitly accorded the Holocaust an *historial* [sic] status" (218). For the historical status of something implies more than being caused by sufficient reasons without any specification. The *Ge-Stell*, however, is an ontological entity highly abstracted from all empirical particularities.

Milchman and Rosenberg say "that modernity, with its basis in planetary technics, contains as one of its possibilities the industrial production of death, the technological extermination of masses of humans" (230). At first, this assertion seems as true as it is trivial. Auschwitz was a reality, and so it had to be a possiblity, too; otherwise, it could not have been a reality at all. Therefore, the authors let us know that a tighter meaning of "possibility" must be presupposed. In their notes, they complain about the rareness of the acknowledgment "that the Holocaust can be understood as an expression of *das Ge-Stell*, perhaps even as its apotheosis" (232). The last remark obviously implies that our social system, because of its inherent dynamics, tends to bring about outrages and ordeals like the Holocaust. But this conclusion neither follows from the validity of Leibniz's principle itself nor from its historical manifestations such as Western culture. The apotheosis remark is a demonization of modernity based on Heidegger's belief that the reign of the *Ge-Stell* accompanies extreme danger.

The ugly impression of a hidden force which demonically drives on our social activities and shapes all of our institutions is reinforced by another contributor to Milchman and Rosenberg's volume. Elisabeth de Fortenay, a teacher at the Sorbonne, writes: "One should thus not precipitously conclude that Heidegger banalizes the extermination by gas in treating it as the equivalent of mechanized agriculture. On the contrary, his intention is to reveal the terrifying secret of an apparently inoffensive and even positive food industry" (242). This suspicion of a "terrifying secret" enclosed in the universe of technological benefits leads to a paranoiac view of all things modern. In the Christian tradition, this view has generally been expressed by the warning: *Ubique daemon!* (Demons everywhere!). The hunt for the founders of modern evil is based on the same suspicion, and Descartes, Kant, and Leibniz are often alleged to be guilty. The very influential *Dialektik der Aufklärung*, written by Max Horkheimer and Theodor W. Adorno, spokesmen of Germany's intellectual New Left in the 1960s, has traced a direct line from the foxy Odysseus to de Sade and Kant, and from there on straight ahead to Nazi fascism. In accordance with this tradition, de Fortenay quotes Heidegger in a sympathetic manner for his remark in 1951 that "the atom bomb exploded already in the Cartesian ego" (240). At least, and almost surprisingly, she speaks of an "untenable foreshortening," inasmuch as Heidegger might also have claimed that the gas chambers were potentially present in Descartes' *cogito* (ibid).

Some contributors aim to justify Heidegger on a limited scale by demonstrating the humaneness of his remark. Wouldn't we, too, have said what he had said in Bremen in 1949? The main difference between us and Heidegger is that he spoke as a great philosopher, thereby using exceptional and, unfortunately, sometimes scandalous rhetorical means. Joseph Margolis, professor of philosophy at Temple University, has given his article the partly ironical title "Comrade Heidegger." Margolis points out that we cannot escape the sense of collective presence. Heidegger's mistake could help to correct the deeper mistake of academics like us who have "no sense of how to join their [our] percipient powers to the collective torrent we don't even hear" (187).

But what is our deep mistake, deeper than that of Heidegger, who joined the Nazi party for a while, and afterward mingled the gas chambers with the food industry? We ignore, Margolis says, that we are human beings only if we open ourselves to our own collective history, and that we are, as such beings, always both the witnesses of *summum malum* as well as its victims. Accordingly, the usual Heidegger critiques weave a veil of sly blindness rather than an insight into what is: "We were no Nazis, I admit. But we ignore the continuities that bind us to the Nazis. They are alive in us, after all" (183). This may be so. Nonetheless, if it is true that mechanized agriculture and industrialized mass murder are in their *moral* essence completely different, the truth becomes not untrue because of our average wickedness and ignorance. More than that, acknowledging such a moral fact means the rending of the veil which covers up the heart of darkness—the, so to speak, immortal Nazi in us.

Another contributor to Milchman and Rosenberg who tries to excuse Heidegger still needs to be mentioned. Robert John Sheffler Manning, assistant professor of philosophy at Quincy College, argues that Heidegger's heartless remarks about the victims of the Holocaust do not prove his heartlessness or even moral insanity, but his inner distance from people who did not belong to his neighborhood like the German peasants near him. "This is natural," Sheffler Manning says, and he adds that Heidegger's scandal must be considered as our own since "it shows that Heidegger may not be as different from us as we would like to think" (32–33). For example, when Saddam Hussein began to practice ethnic cleansing on the Kurds, did America not turn the same deaf ear that Heidegger turned toward the Jews? Yes, but the unfeeling reaction of one cannot justify the callousness of the others. There are two questions at stake, namely, the anthropological question and the moral question, and to answer the latter in terms of the former would be a naturalistic failure. Moral considerations are necessary for overcoming our partly inborn limitations, and for reaching a universalistic notion of humankind, including human rights beyond ethnic and national borders.

4

Apart from that, the demonization of technology as well as the anthropological pessimism play down the causal relation of anti-Semitism to genocide. At the beginning of the Nazi period, Heidegger was obsessed with the idea of Hitler's Germany as the breakthrough to an new collective presence. In this heroic historical moment, the Jews represented the voice of modernity. Interpreted in an anti-Semitic manner, they represented the calculating mind, nihilism, technical exploitation, and capitalism. They represented, ontologically speaking, the triumph of the *Ge-Stell*. Despite having had Jewish supporters, lovers, and friends, Heidegger participated, at least implicitly, in anti-Semitism. For the philosophical view taken by Heidegger led to the perverse conclusion that Jewish nature itself brought about the Holocaust.

To speak in a more moderate tone: According to Heidegger, it is the great Jewish-Christian tradition that has transformed pre-Socratic Greek thought into occidental rationalism and subjectivism, i.e., Western metaphysics. Consequently, the Holocaust was grown out of the metaphysical pattern of a culture whose "Jewification" [*Verjudung*] Heidegger complained about in a letter dated December 1929, written to a high official at the Ministry of Education.[7] Heidegger's message concerning the Holocaust seems to be that there is nothing in particular to say or to explain. The Holocaust is normal. It is inherent in the system under the rule of the *Ge-Stell*, and the Germans' answer, given to the problem of "Jewification," was a technological one—a pecular kind of garbage disposal.

"Garbage disposal. . . ." This is the bitter characterization of the Final Solution [*Endlösung*], underlined by the French philosopher Philippe Lacoue-Labarthe. He says Heidegger is right, but at the same time, he insists on the historical specificity of the Holocaust: ". . . the Final Solution consisted of taking literally centuries-old metaphors of insults and contempt, like *vermin* or *dirt*, and giving oneself the effective technical means to make literal these metaphors [*Verbuchstäblichung*]."[8] In other words, the Holocaust by no means stems from the technological mobilization of humankind itself but essentially from an extremely paranoid application of technology in order to fight against pests, insects, rats, and even vampires. This is no "normality" at all.

Why, then, Heidegger's obstinate silence after the war?

Clearly, the contributors of Milchman's and Rosenberg's anthology try to give a plausible answer to this question. As far as I can see, only William Vaughan, lecturer of philosophy at Ohio Northern University, interprets Heidegger's silence in a completely affirmative manner. Approving of Heidegger's diagnosis, Vaughan asserts that today, every facet of human redemption is likely "a victim of the sclerosis of language" which remains "deaf alongside the unheard-of." Contrary to that, Heidegger's silence is supposed to be "the attempt to move already beyond the horizon of the technological noon and the holocaustic eve, a movement which eludes us still" (97–98). Vaughan's argumentation would be far more convincing if Heidegger's silence had been unequivocal, delivering a clear message of how to get away from "idle talk."

But this is not so. One has to agree with Berel Lang, professor of philosophy and humanistic studies at the State University of New York at Albany, who says in his contribution that, facing the "Jewish Question," silence is necessarily ambiguous. It may always represent a variety of motives or principles: "In any event, silence by itself, here as elsewhere, is inconclusive" (15).

Therefore, it could also be true that Heidegger's silence was no more than "an opportunistic attempt to insulate both himself and his work from unwanted criticism" (58). This suspicion uttered by George

Leaman, assistent professor of philosophy at Bowling Green State University, must not be rejected out of hand. It finds, of course, support by Tom Rockmore who demonstrates that Heidegger varied, from *Being and Time* to his *Beiträge zur Philosophie* (1936–38), his theory of silence in a self-defensible manner. Finally, his factual non-speaking after the war might have been accepted by credulous people as "an authentic form of genuine discourse." According to Rockmore, Heidegger's pseudo-heroic engagement looks "suspiciously like a form of psychological rationalization" (121–22).

Ironically enough, Leaman and Rockmore are unintentionally confirmed by another contributor in his attempt to explain why Heidegger refused a "thinker's forthcoming word" as it was asked for in Paul Celan's poem *Todtnauberg*. James R. Watson, professor at Loyola University (New Orleans), writes: "What Heidegger left unsaid in his sojourning solitude is precisely what *his* thought could not say," and adds: "But that unsaid is not the same as what the man Heidegger chose to say and not say" (176). What follows from that? First, if Heidegger had chosen to utter one simple word of shame and compassion, he would have been able to say it. Second, if Heidegger had done so, he would have proved that his "thought" (in the Watsonian sense) was able to express pity for the Jews' ordeals. In this way, he would have courageously defeated his own theory of silence, unmasking it by himself as a possible form of rationalization.

5

Yet it is true: in the end, after all our endeavors, we are painfully aware of a lack of *substantial* words in general. How could the Holocaust ever be understood? In the depth of our sorrow lurks a religious irritation: How might God ever be recognized in Auschwitz? Was Auschwitz the ultimate triumph of evil? Was it the devil's place? Our religiously devoted, humble feelings long for a negative answer.

What happened to Being in this human hell? Heidegger said in his famous *Spiegel* interview, posthumously published in 1976, "Only a god can save us."[9] However, if Auschwitz was an epiphany, then it was paradoxical—the epiphany of God as total absence. Considering this, what could be said about the essence of the Holocaust? From a religious view, silence would be the only adequate reaction; and the only sensitive one would be to wait for God's return—in silence.

But Heidegger went on "after Auschwitz." He still wrote many pages, delivered lectures, and gave seminars in France and Switzerland. In the end, perhaps, there remains an absolutely unheroic and, more than that, unphilosophical answer to the question of why Heidegger remained silent

in the face of the Holocaust. It seems to be an exaggeration when Alan
Ryan says without reservations that "Heidegger was a man of extremely
bad character."[10] Nonetheless, this verdict may point in the right direction.

Notes

1. "Ackerbau ist jetzt motorisierte Ernährungsindustrie, im Wesen das
Selbe wie die Fabrikation von Leichen in Gaskammern und Vernichtungslagern,
das Selbe wie die Blockade und Aushungerung von Ländern, das Selbe wie die
Fabrikation von Wasserstoffbomben." Quoted by Wolfgang Schirmacher, *Technik
und Gelassenheit. Zeitkritik nach Heidegger* (Freiburg and Munich, 1983), p.
25. The complete text of "The Ge-Stell" is published in Martin Heidegger, *Gesamtausgabe*, vol. 79: "Bremer und Freiburger Vorträge" (Frankfurt a. M. 1994),
pp. 24–45. Here the quoted sentence can be found on page 27.
2. "Geh in den Schutzraum, wenn die Signale dazu ertönen; mach Hände
hoch, wenn der Befehl dazu ergeht; vergiß nicht, daß der Zusammenhang von
Schutz und Gehorsam heute nicht mehr gilt und selbstverständlich ist; der
Schutzraum kann der Vergasungsraum sein." Carl Schmitt, *Glossarium, Aufzeichnungen der Jahre 1947–1951* (Berlin, 1991), p. 144.
3. Cf. especially George Steiner, *Martin Heidegger* (New York, 1978).
4. Martin Heidegger, *Being and Time*, trans. John Macquarrie and Edward
Robinson (Oxford, 1962), p. 165.
5. "Was bereitet sich *dann* vor? Der *Übergang zum technisierten Tier*, das
die bereits schwächer und gröber werdenden Instinkte durch das Riesenhafte
der Technik zu ersetzen beginnt." Heidegger, *Gesamtausgabe*, vol. 65: "Beiträge
zur Philosophie (Vom Ereignis)" (Frankfurt a. Main, 1989), p. 98.
6. The numbers, given in text in parenthesis here and further below, refer
to the page(s) of the cited work, *Martin Heidegger and the Holocaust*, eds. Alan
Milchman and Alan Rosenberg (New Jersey, 1996).
7. Ulrich Sieg: "Die Verjudung des deutschen Geistes. Ein unbekannter
Brief Heideggers" (October 2, 1929), in *Die Zeit* (December 29, 1989). The translation of the quoted passage is given by Elzbietta Ettinger, *Hannah Arendt
Martin Heidegger* (New Haven and London, 1995), p. 37.
8. Philippe Lacoue-Labarthe, *La Fiction de la Politique. Heidegger, l'art et
la politique* (Paris. 1987). The English translation was done on the basis of the
German edition, *Die Fiktion des Politischen* (Stuttgart, 1990), pp. 62–63.
9. Heidegger gave prominent journalists of the German weekly magazine
Der Spiegel an interview on September 23, 1966. In accordance with Heidegger's
demand, the interview was not published during his lifetime. To the quoted statement cf. *Antwort, Martin Heidegger im Gespräch*, eds. Günther Neske and Emil
Kettering (Pfullingen, 1988), pp. 99–100.
10. Alan Ryan in his review of Ettinger's book (cf. note 7), "Dangerous
Liaison," in *The New York Review of Books* (January 11, 1996): 22.

Part 3

Art and Poetry

Introduction

Jennifer Natalya Fink's "Voluptuous Anguish: Contemporary Holocaust Kitsch and the Specter of the Feminine" begins by raising a painful issue: "Why would assimilated American Jews attempt to find and define their Jewish identities through representing the Holocaust as kitsch?" There are at least two probabilities. One, because kitsch "creates an allegorical compensation for cultural anxieties surrounding sexuality and gender," and two, the unrepresentability of the Holocaust itself "produces an insatiable appetite for more and more representations of its voluptuous horrors." Thus, stories of the Holocaust, such as Judy Chicago's Holocaust Project, whose images are "quintessential Holocaust kitsch," and Fink's grandfather's (Harold Lewis) story. The latter story is a project entitled *Arbeit Macht Frei*, a story that Fink hates but thinks about daily. What these two stories have in common is their kitschyness and dismissal of women and feminism: "Is the writing of the Holocaust dependent upon the elision of the woman, the feminist from the story?" In a world that cannot be the world that was possible before the Holocaust, in a world where neither the Jewish religion nor culture "quite persist[s]," do American Jews "struggling to attain full, phallic presence . . . romance the Holocaust in order to appear"?

If kitsch excludes women and feminism, little is gained for either with the turn to, in Clement Greenberg's words, "art without subject matter." Andrew Weinstein's "Art After Auschwitz and The Necessity of a Postmodern Modernism" considers strategies for artistic representations of the Holocaust that have evolved in the struggles of four artists attempting to navigate between the aesthetic purity and vacuity of formalism and the cooptations, appropriations, and displacements of kitschy pop culture. In the art of Aharon Gluska the critique of identity thinking is accomplished by re-treating Nazi mug shots of prisoners at Auschwitz. This re-treatment reclaims the faces of victims by partially wiping away their dark Nazi borders. Like Gluska's work the images of Arie Galles are also based on documentary photographs and the Nazi way of seeing atrocity as distanced, dehumanized, and sanitized: "Galles's approach reminds us of our own distance from the experience of the victims, with whom total identification would be barbaric, as Adorno might put it." The filmmaker Abraham Ravett and the composer Steve Reich also use documentary evidence to explore the multiple meanings displaced by Nazi identity thinking. Each of these artists portrays "the crisis of modernist authority at Auschwitz and the postwar, post-Holocaust postmodern sensibility." What is rejected, however, is the postmodern trait of "play." The crisis portrayed is part of their very art which "becomes a delicate balancing act between insisting on knowing *exactly* how to respond emotionally and ethically to the past, and refusing to draw fixed or universalizing conclusions from the documentary material that would otherwise give meaning to the meaningless, incomprehensible murder."

Paul Sars' "Poetry after Auschwitz: Paul Celan's Aesthetics of Hermetism" is primarily concerned with Celan's poems which deal with "strictly personal, but very real experiences during the war," but do so "in terms that refer to later experiences." The "hermetism" of Celan's poetry separates it from the traditional technique of metaphoric description or the plastic expression of reality. Language in Celan is plural, even (and especially) when it is German. With metaphors taken from the Cabbala, the Gnosis, and the Talmud, Celan's poetry is neither a simple means of communication nor a copy of reality, but rather moments of truth as events, events that cause other events, and thus as beings with souls and senses that speak. Celan regarded his "Mehrdeutigkeit ohne Maske" (undisguised ambiguity) as "the only truthful language in poetry." Being perceived by the senses ("aesthetics" in the sense of "aisthesis") requires senses or beings that speak. Speaking, however, is ambiguous, whereas perception (reading) is determinative. For Sars, then, "the aesthetics of hermetism lies in the unification of a once-only expression (which is typical of speaking) and the perception of a reality that appears as an ambiguous and meaningful presence. The poem as such leaves open this ambiguity, but every time it is read—when the reader lets the poem occur—the poem can represent only one 'coherent' complex of meaning." With Auschwitz, however, perception and beings-senses have been damaged. Celan's hermetic poetry is an attempt to recover and rescue both from the identity thinking which insists "always this and just this meaning here and now."

Recovery beyond and rescue from identity thinking is also the theme

of James R. Watson's "A11380: Imaging within/beyond 'Liberation.'"
A11380 is the identification number of a young Hungarian Jewess who
survived medical experimentation at Auschwitz. A11380 is also an image
resulting from photographs taken by liberators in 1945. The caption
"Not Yet!" has been added by Watson in an attempt to read the liber-
ator's photograph beyond and otherwise than the usual documentary
fashion of "realist" photography. In this sense A11380 as image and caption is a deconstruction or deproprietization that proceeds not just theoretically but also, and primarily, on the basis of A11380's expression or
imaging beyond the confines of her liberators' "photographic capture."
Such a deconstruction is necessary since there is a dangerous complicity
between Nazi identity thinking and realist codes of documentary photographic production and practices. A11380 testifies both within and
against/beyond this complicity. Her testimony is a seduction that is
stronger than the Nazi legacy of mass reinchantment: "A11380's testimony is more powerful than the logic she survived; it shows that we can
be otherwise."

A.R./J.R.W.

Voluptuous Anguish
Contemporary Holocaust Kitsch and the Specter of the Feminine

Jennifer Natalya Fink

Attention has gradually shifted from the reevocation of Nazism as such
. . . to voluptuous anguish and ravishing images, images one would like
to see going on forever.

Saul Friedländer,
Reflections of Nazism: An Essay on Kitsch and Death

Voluptuous anguish that goes on forever. Ravishing images that glide across one's eye outside the dull horror of history. Holocaust kitsch that has caught precisely that same feverish disease the Nazis used to lull the Germans into a pink-cheeked landscape of technicolor fascism. Saul Friedlander's essay asks how and why contemporary representations of the Holocaust deploy the same kitsch rhetoric that the Nazis used to *create* the Holocaust. It is this same voluptuous anguish of Holocaust kitsch that I want to interrogate, in order to examine desire, American Jewish identity, and its gendered articulations as performed in representation that haunt the very phrase "voluptuous anguish." Why would assimilated American Jews attempt to find and define their Jewish identities through representing the Holocaust as kitsch?

First, kitsch itself. Kitsch creates an allegorical compensation for cultural anxieties surrounding sexuality and gender. Femininity, understood in the Lacanian sense, is the threatening knowledge of the unrepresentable split, fractured nature of all subjectivity. Traditionally, this anxiety is displaced onto women. Kitsch overcompensates for the feminine lack at the heart of representation by manufacturing universal, unified affect out of the unrepresentable trauma of split subjectivity. Or, as Milan Kundera suggests, "Kitsch causes two tears to flow in quick succession. The first tear says: How nice to see children running on the grass! The second tear says, How nice to be moved, together with all mankind, by children running on the grass! It is the second tear that makes kitsch kitsch."[1] Kitsch replaces depth with a plethora of surface, and reproduces the vast and unthinkable as the miniature and cute. The threat represented by femininity is thereby itself feminized, its unrepresentable trauma brought back into the terms of representation by repeating and banalizing it. Kitsch infects the phallic subject with his feminine object, collapsing the distance between the two.

It is this double action of kitsch—its feminizing the threat of femininity, its sentimentalizing the act of sentimentality—that lends it the quality of a performance. Like theatrical performances, which Richard Schechner characterizes as "twice-restored behavior," kitsch repeats a set of reactions to a past event.[2] Holocaust kitsch represents an event so traumatic and beyond the bounds of ordinary discourse that many have argued that it is fundamentally unrepresentable. Yet paradoxically, this unrepresentability produces an insatiable appetite for more and more representations of its voluptuous horrors.

Recent work in cultural and performance studies suggests that identity is produced through a series of performances.[3] According to this view, identities are both constituted by and in a continual state of being remade through their performances, or enactments. I would like to suggest that American Jews are performing—in fact creating—their identities through kitschified Holocaust discourses. As Alain Finkielkraut has suggested, post-Shoah Jews with no direct experience of the Shoah or of the complex Jewish culture that it destroyed put on displays of Jewish identity and difference to compensate for this void.[4] It is the kitschiness of this performance of identity that I want to accentuate, in order to examine the gendered anxieties underscoring Jewishness when it is constituted as a performative identity rather than a lived experience. Kitsch is not, I will argue, the opposite of unrepresentability, but an aporetic response to this unrepresentability and its concomitant threat of dissolution of phallic identity. It is potentially both regressive and progressive, sacred and profane.

The representation of the celestial—the unrepresentable—always verges on the kitsch. As Celeste Olalquiaga argues, "Religious imagery is considered kitsch because of its desacralization, while kitsch is called evil and the 'anti-Christ in art' because of its artistic profanities."[5] However, Olalquiaga is talking specifically about Christian kitsch, with its icons and saints, its endless representations of Jesus and Mary, God and man. The anti-Christ in art is still a profoundly Christian affair, embedded in the representational and aesthetic ideologies of Christianity. No such pictorial traditions of representing the sacred exist in Jewish culture. For according to traditional interpretations of Jewish law, Jews are prohibited from direct representations of the sacred. Hence Jewish representations must always already be secular. Yet the Holocaust seems to be sacralized through its kitschification, endowed with a spiritual "message" for world Jewry. Even the word "Holocaust" bespeaks a cleansing through fire, a redemptive sacralizing of the unthinkable. Olalquiaga links kitsch with Christian notions of death, memorializing, and redemption. Where does the Jew fit into this story? Where does the Holocaust fit? Perhaps we need to return to the particular voluptuous anguish of the Holocaust. So let's begin with the Holocaust. Or a story about the Holocaust.

Judy Chicago's Holocaust, actually, and my grandfather's. Judy Chicago is a famous visual artist, formerly and formally a cultural feminist artist from the 1970s, who is best remembered for her epic cunt art project, *The Dinner Party*, who now is making an epic art project out of the Holocaust. She is not a Holocaust survivor but after making a trip to the top ten Holocaust sites in Europe with her husband, she investigated her own history, her own Jewish roots, and started erecting the bluntly titled *Holocaust Project*. Before this trip, Chicago states that she had little knowledge of or interest in the Holocaust, or in her Jewish heritage. Jewishness and Holocaust: the two often seem synonymous in Chicago's work. "Chicago speaks frequently about 'saving the planet,'" notes Elizabeth Hess. "The Holocaust is her metaphor for all past, current and future evil."[6] I hate this project absolutely but think about it daily.

The images in *Holocaust Project* are themselves quintessential Holocaust kitsch. "Actual" black-and-white pictures of the Holocaust—its piles of starving faces crammed behind barbed wire—are mixed together with contemporary photographs of screaming oppressed people, even monkeys used for animal research, taken by Chicago's husband, Donald Woodman.[7] While the astute viewer might be able to discern each from each, this pastiche blurs the distinction between the historical specificity of *that* Holocaust, *those* bodies, and angsty screamy folks-in-general. In this soupy mix of human pain, the "pure evil" of the Holocaust that this project aims to articulate is instead watered down, kitschified, made cozy and familiar. The terrifying unreadability of the Holocaust is sentimentalized, its incoherence neatly organized into a TV movie-of-the-week allegory of what in my high school English class was unironically termed the Great Theme, man's inhumanity to man. Furthermore, these photographic pastiches are nestled amidst Chicago's trademark genericized figures, needlepointed and oil painted in pastels and flesh-tones around the photos. As the *Village Voice* critic Elizabeth Hess notes, there is something shocking about how the shock of the Holocaust is so easily turned into kitsch spectacle: "This is Hallmark Holocaust. This is a shockingly sentimental, badly executed spectacle."[8]

My grandfather, Harold Lewis, is not a famous artist and not a feminist. He was a working-class Marxist educator who started making modernist abstract sculptures when he retired. He is not a Holocaust survivor but after making a trip with his wife to the top ten Holocaust sites in Europe, he investigated his own history, his own Jewish roots, and started erecting the bluntly titled *Arbeit Macht Frei*. I hate this project absolutely but think about it daily.

The images of *Arbeit Macht Frei* are themselves quintessential Holocaust kitsch. "Actual" black-and-white pictures of the Holocaust—its familiar piles of starving faces amidst barbed wire, textbook pictures of Hitler and his buddies, small blonde German boys in S.S. uniforms grinning at the camera—are mixed together with contemporary photographs of the bad guys: Stalin, Arafat, skinhead punks. While the astute viewer might be able to discern each from each, this pastiche blurs the distinction between the historical specificity of *that* Holocaust, *those* bodies, and the guys in the black hats in a low-budget TV Western. In this soupy mix of human pain, the "pure evil" of the Holocaust that this project aims to articulate is instead watered down, kitschified, made cozy and familiar. The swastika itself, endlessly repeated in so many colors, media, and designs, becomes just another shorthand, familiar indication of fascism, telling us how to read each piece rather than terrifying us with historical resonance. The terrifying unreadability of the Holocaust is sentimentalized, its incoherence neatly organized into a TV movie-of-the-week allegory of what in my high school English class was unironically termed the Great Theme, man's inhumanity to man. Furthermore, these photographic pastiches are nestled in Lewis's trademark modernist abstract sculpted images. As the *Village Voice* critic Elizabeth Hess might have noted, there is something shocking about how the shock of the Holocaust is so easily turned into kitsch spectacle: "This is Hallmark Holocaust. This is a shockingly sentimental, badly executed spectacle."

In the midst of this relentless kitsch, there is one site of relief: my grandmother's voice. Next to one piece that shows a long line of starving Jews boarding a train marked *Bergen-Belson*, my grandfather has installed a small nondescript tape recorder that plays my grandmother's voice singing the mourner's kaddish in throaty Hebrew. *V'yiskadal v'yiskaddash sh'may rabbah. Y'hesh may rah hamivorach.* Softly and off-key she drones on, driving me to tears *v'imruh amen*. There is no voluptuous anguish in her voice; it is thin and declarative to the end. She is not credited in the exhibit. Finkielkraut suggests that instead of an empty, narcissistic quest for identity, post-Shoah Jewishness could perform an impossible remembering of what no longer exists, "reporting," as he puts it, "on Judaism as I have not lived it."[9] Her voice evokes, creates, performs, what is and is not here.

There's a twist in my grandfather's story: actually, my *grandmother* is a Holocaust survivor, albeit once-removed, a kind of second cousin to the Holocaust; on their grand tour, they discovered that relatives of hers were in fact victims of the Holocaust. Just as important to me, it is my grandmother who discovered sculpture, who wanted to sculpt first, not my grandfather. Gee, this is starting to sound like a Judy Chicago-style 1970s kitschfest feminist testimonial. My grandmother, Adina Lewis *née* Chalef, collected lushly illustrated books about sculpture, lacking the funds to collect sculpture itself. My legally deaf and clinically depressed grandmother, who will get out of bed only when lured by the promise of a trip to the store or the top ten Holocaust sites, started the romance with Holocaust representation.

My grandmother disappears in my grandfather's Holocaust story. Feminism disappears in Judy Chicago's Holocaust story. What disappears in the discursive move to memorialize, to write this story of someone else's apocalypse in order to procure identity? The woman? Which woman? Whose woman? Judy Chicago's? Hal Lewis's?

In his now-famous essay on the mirror stage, Lacan suggests that in the act of naming oneself, of procuring a stable identity, both a void and surplus are produced of which the slashed, barred woman becomes the symbol/symptom.[10] But what makes an act of naming worthy of its name? How do feminized subjects then achieve proper names? Proper names, proper crisp white male Protestant names, have spelled trouble for Judy Chicago *née* Gorovitz and Harold Lewis *né* Ringle. The possibility of having a proper, paternal name—of being the name-of-the-father —has always been a shaky proposition for Jews and girls and Jew-girls.

The patriarchal laws of naming exemplify this gendered condition: men unproblematically assume at birth the name of someone else—their father—as their "true" name, even though it is neither their "own" name nor a name that indicates the double nature of their lineage. Women, on the other hand, assume their father's and then their husband's names, their identity secured only through the more self-evident erasure of their "own" identity and the identity of their mothers. But a Jewish male name fails to produce a fully phallic fiction of identity in Christendom; Epstein or Ringle or Fink is always already marked, feminized by its very Jewishness. Whereas Christian males assume a name that will buy them a secure identity, Jewish names are stalked by the mark of difference and otherness, their phallic capital always in danger of dissolving in the morass of that indefinite mark of Jewishness.

This feminizing effect of Jewishness is itself a kitsch theme in American Jewish male writing. From Philip Roth to Woody Allen to latter-day borscht-belt comedians like Stephen Spielberg, the Jewish-American male struggles against this mark through his representational praxis. Less obvious is the effect of this feminization upon Jewish women like Judy Chicago.

The Holocaust both interrupts and secures this problematic story of naming, creating a third term through which community and identity can be nervously, partially secured. The Holocaust itself becomes a space in which a phallic Jewish identity is produced, stabilized; through making love to the Holocaust, Judy Chicago refinds her place (and a nice Jewish husband to boot!) within the Jewish community. However assimilated, feminist, queer, hybrid, or evacuated one's "Jewishness" may be, any Jew can now performatively become Jewish through romancing the Holocaust. Through kitsch allegorizing of the Holocaust, the assimilated body is redeemed; through the curvaceous figure of Miss Voluptuous Anguish herself, the story of Jewish identity is repeated and (partially) resecured. Hence the Holocaust enters, stage right, a third term through which the desire for a stable, phallic identity can be negotiated anew. Whereas Christians stage the desire to produce a permanent identity through the story of eternal life and redemption through Jesus, Jews narrativize this same desire through kitsch representations of the Holocaust.

Has the Holocaust really taken the place of Jesus as a figuring metaphor for permanent identity? Is this a reaction against the feminizing effects of Jewishness? The hypervisible Jew and the hyperspecularized woman, fetishized ad infinitum in anti-Semitic, phallogocentric Christianity, dance a strange duet. Like the woman, the Jew in Christendom is not quite a man, not quite a true Christian soul who can be redeemed, and in being the not-all is somehow obscenely more-than, his persistent presence a bad smell lingering in the oven like yesterday's supper. To resecure his phallic subject position, does the Jew—male or female—throw out the woman? Is the writing of the Holocaust dependent upon the elision of the woman, the feminist from the story?

"Sculptor Remembers the Past," reads the legend across a review of my grandfather's show.[11] Is my grandfather remembering the past, memorializing a retrievable Holocaust, or is he creating a memorial to his own immanent death and the death of *Yiddishkeit* (Yiddish culture) with its now outmoded focus on marriage and community which my grandmother embodies? Why is she rendered invisible in the discursive move to memorialize? Why must Judy Chicago elide feminism to constitute herself as a legitimate representer of the Holocaust?

Despite my elaboration here, the connections between Holocaust kitsch, gender, and performativity are perhaps not as clear as I optimistically promised to make them. Yet this lack of clarity is precisely at the heart of the matter. Friedlander laments that contemporary representations of the Holocaust fail to "re-evoke the Holocaust as such," and instead obsessively repeat the voluptuous anguish of Fascist discourse itself.[12] But there is no Holocaust *as such* for those who did not live it. Despite the Holocaust's all-too-real effects, it is now a representational act, and *as such* inscribed within the complex, interwoven problems of gender, femininity, and desire that structure all representations. American Jews, struggling to attain full, phallic presence in a post-Shoah culture in which neither their religion nor their culture quite persists, romance the Holocaust in order to appear.

Notes

1. Milan Kundera, *La Lenteur: Roman* (Paris: Gallimard, 1995).
2. Richard Schechner, *Between Theatre and Anthropology* (Philadelphia: University of Pennsylvania Press, 1985).
3. Alain Finkielkraut, *The Imaginary Jew* (Lincoln and London: University of Nebraska Press, 1994).
4. Ibid.
5. Celeste Olalquiaga, *Megalopolis: Contemporary Cultural Sensibilities* (Minneapolis and Oxford: University of Minnesota Press, 1992), p. 38.
6. Elizabeth Hess, "Planet Holocaust—From Feminism to Judaism: Meet the New Judy Chicago," *Village Voice* (November 2, 1993).
7. See Chicago's coffee-table book detailing her exhibition, *Holocaust Project: From Darkness to Light* (New York: Viking, 1993). The book includes photography by her husband, Donald Woodman, as well as a narrative of their "journey" from assimilation to Holocaust consciousness.
8. Hess, "Planet Holocaust."
9. Finkielkraut, *The Imaginary Jew*, p. 178.
10. Jacques Lacan, "The Mirror Stage as Formative of the Function of the Eye," *Écrits* (New York and London: W.W. Norton, 1977), pp. 1–8.
11. Andrea Valluzzo, "Sculptor Remembers the Past," *The Lewisboro Ledger* (October 21, 1993).
12. Saul Friedlander, *Reflections on Nazism: An Essay on Kitsch and Death* (Bloomington: Indiana University Press, 1993), p. 3.

Art after Auschwitz and the Necessity of a Postmodern Modernism*

Andrew Weinstein

M any theories help explain the postwar silence about the Holocaust, and by extension, the absence of Holocaust subjects in art before around 1980. A prevailing "liberal imagination," entrenched with Enlightenment ideologies of toleration and pluralism, may have blinded some artists to even recognizing the barbarity of anti-Semitism and genocide.[1] By contrast, other artists may have avoided Holocaust subject matter due to a psychological repression of the trauma so profound that some scholars suggest it occurred on a societal scale.[2]

But no understanding of the silence in art can avoid considering the climate in the art world itself. To be taken seriously as an artist during the 1950s meant following the dictates of Clement Greenberg, the art critic whose formulation of modernism was preeminent at the time. Greenberg advocated art without subject matter. In his 1939 essay, "Avant-Garde and Kitsch," Greenberg argued from a Marxist perspective that high art exists in constant threat of cooptation by popular culture-kitsch, which he sees as an instrument of the power elite in maintaining social control. For Greenberg, kitsch is art that the masses can understand, art whose style becomes transparent in order to focus on subject matter. Greenberg recognized (like Saul Friedlander more than four decades later) how kitsch includes subjects that stir the blood—sentimental and historical themes that in totalitarian societies put the controlling leadership in touch with what Greenberg disparaged as the so-called soul of the people. This pictorial blood and soil constitutes an

*Many thanks to Ruth Liberman and Steven Zucker for their insights during the preparation of this essay.

151

aspect of nationalist identity which invariably excludes the outsider, the Other, what Lyotard calls the "jew."

Greenberg predicated that an authentic high art could escape cooptation by popular culture through a progressive flight into the rarefied heights of formalism.[3] He argued that painting should be true to form by emphasizing what was unique to it—not by conjuring images, which was the domain of literature, but instead by reveling in the material qualities of paint itself, as in Abstract Expressionism in the way he understood it.[4]

In privileging form over content, Greenberg sought to establish idealist principles for modern art, ones that seemed to speak for all people, including Lyotard's "jew." Recently it has been suggested that Greenberg's advocacy of what seemed to be a universalist, non-nationalistic art may have arisen, at least in part, from his desire to overcome the social alienation of his own Jewishness.[5] Ironically, such affirmation of pluralism was based on the denial of difference. And amidst the violence of totalitarianism, this denial became all the more stark. Statement equaled silence.

In a voluminous study, Ziva Amishai-Maisels demonstrates that during the late 1940s and 1950s many artists did in fact make the Holocaust either the principal focus of their work or the subject of isolated projects.[6] These artists usually turned to older, figurative styles, like realism, symbolism, expressionism or surrealism. By and large, these styles had long been superseded in modernism's ineluctable march toward a narrow ideal of aesthetic purity, and within Greenberg's critical discourse, such art was ignored as kitsch.

My objective in this essay is to consider the strategies for representing the Holocaust that are employed in the work of four contemporary artists, whose approach is representative of a great many others. They come after the advances of Pop Art, Earth Art, Fluxus, and other 1960s movements that rejected Greenberg's formalist assumptions, and after the social upheavals of the 1950s, 1960s, and 1970s that legitimized ethnicity as a subject for artistic expression. And they speak to an audience that has become increasingly conscious of the Holocaust since 1967, when the Six-Day War seemed to threaten another Jewish genocide. More recently, as the youngest adult survivors and witnesses have begun to die off, this public consciousness has bordered on obsession, leading to efforts to preserve memory with monuments and museums. In part, contemporary Holocaust art shares this fear of forgetting. But the evidence points to a somewhat different concern—that artists like the four under consideration here care not so much about simply remembering, but more importantly, about *how* to remember.

In my judgment, ideas that we associate with Theodor Adorno pervade much of this art about the Holocaust. This is different from saying that artists are influenced by Adorno or understand his philosophy, or that they even know who he was. Rather, the philosophical and literary strategies with which Adorno responded to the culture he considered responsible for the Holocaust correspond to the thematic and stylistic strategies of many contemporary artists who address Holocaust subjects.

When Adorno famously declared that "to write poetry after Auschwitz is barbaric," he suggested that it would be perverse for an audience to derive aesthetic pleasure from art—not only from Holocaust art, but from all art, because it required a certain callousness to ignore the overarching horror of Holocaust memory.[7] As I understand it, Adorno's remark largely addresses the issue of capitalist "identity thinking"— namely, of equating workers with their exchange value and, in its ultimate expression, of equating Jews with death. Adorno warned that this reductive way of thinking would persist after the war through equating the Holocaust with a poem or artwork, whose particular point of view would brutally exclude alternative meanings. In attempting to make sense of the senseless (the way our word Holocaust, "burnt offering," tries to do), such art would end up bullying the facts with the same kind of reductive identity thinking that led to genocide in the first place.

Identity is central to the art of Aharon Gluska, an Israeli born after the war who now lives in New York. Before 1989, Gluska painted nonobjective, black-and-white compositions reminiscent of the Abstract Expressionism of Franz Kline. But some observers also saw the Holocaust in these early works, as though the whites were the glare of floodlights seen through the silhouettes of raw beams and poles, and their remarks, together with the disquieting experience of reading a graphic Holocaust memoir by a close friend from his kibbutz, led Gluska to think about the Holocaust as a subject for art. Because he felt that he lacked an artistic vocabulary to deal with the material, Gluska visited the archives at Yad Vashem in Jerusalem, where he obtained copies of about two hundred black-and-white photographs, one type of which would haunt him—a mug shot of a prisoner at Auschwitz from the time before mass extermination began.

Such mug shots engage issues that are crucial to how we remember the Holocaust, none more significant than that of identity. The photos leave you wondering who these people were and what they were like— information the Nazis suppressed by prohibiting personal hairstyles and clothes, and substituting numbers for names. In a larger sense, the photos speak to the way that Nazi propaganda similarly identified whole groups of people with racist labels as part of the systematic process of dehumanization that made genocide possible.

Gluska's art critiques this identity thinking (figs. 1–4). He enlarges these photos, attaches them to canvas, covers them with dark paint, and then wipes some parts clean, literally reframing the Nazi way of seeing with dark borders. He reclaims the face of a victim, "as if disinterred and returned to memory," in the words of James Young.[8] While preserving

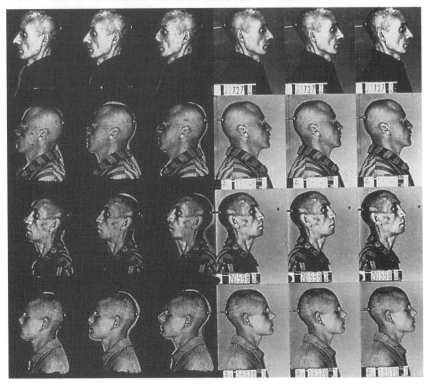

Figure 1.
Aharon Gluska, *Two Directions*, 1991. Mixed media on canvas, 60" × 86".

the Nazi vision, Gluska contrasts it with a humanizing one. The single artwork contains two different visions from two different times, and possesses what Adorno called its own "immanent criticism" in the way that the passage of time reveals the ideological nature of beliefs once accepted as truths.

What's remarkable about Gluska's paintings is how the new vision avoids identity thinking today, since the face of an individual, instead of standing for the entire Holocaust, represents only himself and his own particular experience. Similarly, Gluska discourages us from feeling that we can identify *with* a victim and that we can presume to know how that person felt; like a barrier, a thick layer of acrylic over the photograph reminds viewers that simply looking into a victim's eyes from within the comfort and security of a museum gallery is not the same as understanding what it was like to live (and die) in that time.

Arie Galles, born in 1944 and raised in Poland, Israel, and the United States, used to create semi-abstract sky paintings that explored properties of light and reflection. But in 1990, Galles became frustrated over the art's inability to communicate all he wanted to say. After a nightmare about rel-

Figure 2.
Aharon Gluska, *Jacob Seidenbeitel*, 1995. Mixed media on canvas, 80" × 54".

Figure 3.
Aharon Gluska, *Jankiel Frajlich*, 1994. Silk, glass, and mixed media on canvas, 39" × 62".

atives lost in the Holocaust, he finally turned to Holocaust subject matter in 1993. With the American poet Jerome Rothenberg, he devised an extensive project called *Fourteen Stations* (figs. 5–8). The title of this work-in-progress refers to the thirteen Nazi death camps on or near railroad lines and to a fourteenth site of destruction, Babi Yar. The title also refers to the Christian story of the Passion—a reference that Galles intends to echo Elie Wiesel's notion of the countless calvaries in the camps. Intended for exhibition in an octagonal room, each of the fourteen large, approximately four-by-six-foot charcoal drawings will, when completed, represent a Nazi-era aerial view of a site, with a fifteenth labeled Khurbn (which means annihilation in Yiddish) near the entrance of the room, showing Belzec before the Nazis built it and then after they demolished it in an attempt to hide the evidence of atrocity, but leaving an indexical scar on the landscape. Galles gives special attention to Belzec, not only to make a point about absence and denial as a type of historical evidence, but also for a personal reason: his own relatives were murdered there.

Like Gluska's, Galles's choice of documentary evidence reveals a Nazi way of seeing. Almost all of Galles's images are based on photographs—mostly Luftwaffe aerial reconnaissance photographs created to determine the success in camouflaging atrocities from Allied planes.[9] Distanced, dehumanized, and sanitized, the aerial views evince a way of seeing atrocity characteristic of the bureaucracy of the Nazis, and even

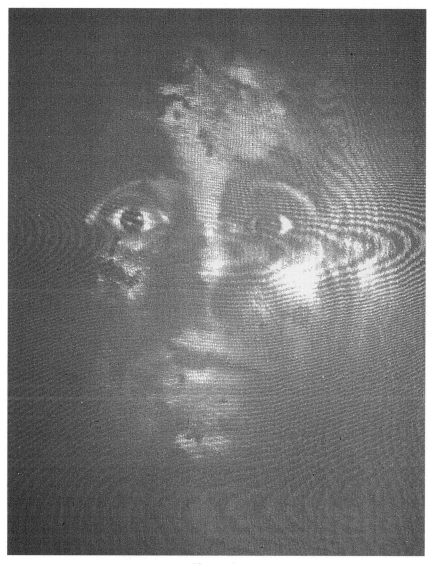

Figure 4.
Aharon Gluska, *Jankiel Frajlich* (detail of fig. 3).

of Allied Intelligence. This approach is the artist's means of confronting the horror without resorting to imagery from inside the camps—imagery which he finds too painful, as well as hackneyed through overexposure. Indeed, Galles's approach reminds us of our own distance from the experience of the victims, with whom total identification would be barbaric, as Adorno might put it.

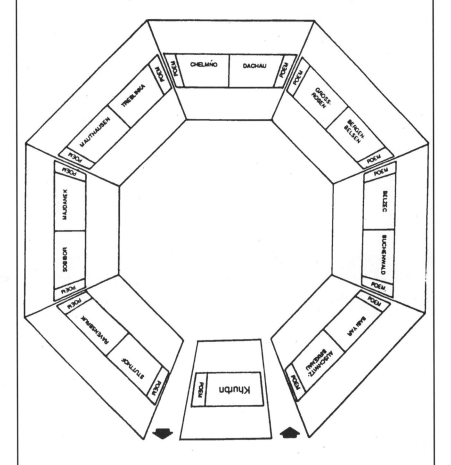

FOURTEEN STATIONS

היד

A SUITE OF FOURTEEN 44 1/2" X 72" DRAWINGS BY ARIE GALLES
and
FOURTEEN POEMS BY JEROME ROTHENBERG

Overhead projection of the way the drawings would appear in exhibition,
with additional drawing, "Khurbn" 45 1/4" X 72",
and poem, "Khurbn Gematria: Prologue."

Figure 5.
Arie Galles, plan of *Fourteen Stations*.

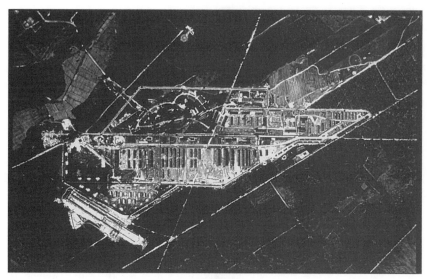

Figure 6.
Arie Galles, *Bergen-Belsen*, 1994. Charcoal on paper with white conté in wrought-iron frame, 44½" × 72" (panel from *Fourteen Stations*).

Figure 7.
Arie Galles, *Bergen-Belsen* (detail of fig. 6).

Figure 8.
Arie Galles, *Bergin-Belsen*, 1996. Charcoal on Arches paper in wrought-iron frame, 47½" × 15" (panel from *Fourteen Stations*: poem by Jerome Rothenberg). Photo: Tim Volk.

As in Gluska's art, *Fourteen Stations* contrasts the Nazi point of view with a humanistic perspective, provided here in Jerome Rothenberg's poems, one for each camp (fig. 8). Composed according to the arcane Judaic rules of *gematria*, Rothenberg's poems, which are hand drawn by Galles, offer the perspective of the terrorized and outraged Jewish victims, and of the supernatural spirits sympathetic to them. Side by side, the character of the two ways of seeing becomes clearer than either would alone; a consequence is to focus viewers' attention on the dissonance between those ways of seeing, as well as on the limitations of the so-called objective presentation on the one hand, and the subjective presentation on the other.

Artists in other media reveal similar concerns about identity. Abraham Ravett is a filmmaker, an American born in Poland in 1947, and raised in Israel and the United States. Ravett's parents were Holocaust survivors. For more than twenty years, his work has addressed the subject of the Holocaust. Ravett's 1993 film, *In Memory*, uses documentary elements to focus on life in the Lodz Ghetto which his father endured,

Figure 9.
Abraham Ravett, film still from *In Memory*, 1993 (13 min., b/w, sound).

Figure 10.
Abraham Ravett, film still from *In Memory*, 1993 (13 min., b/w, sound).

and thereby hints at how Ravett typically uses autobiography and family history in order to frame (which is to say limit) his view of world history. The film begins with a Hebrew chant accompanied only by a blacked-out screen. Next comes a silent montage of archival clips almost like home movies, showing Nazi-occupied ghetto street life: people shoveling snow, walking about, and donning their hats (fig. 9). That the clips run in total silence and even include the squiggled lines of a film-reel leader emphasizes the remoteness of these people from us, in much the way that the murkiness in Gluska's mug-shot paintings and the distance in Galles's drawings do. Ravett discourages identity thinking in his audience by encouraging ambiguities as well: Where are these men going? Who are they donning their hats to? The film offers no explanations.[10]

Not only does Ravett foster indeterminacies, but he also encourages multiple meanings. When the clips end, the picture goes black and the soundtrack resumes, with the Hebrew text chanted once again. The first time, it was chanted without translation, and could strike a listener unfamiliar with Hebrew as sounding pretty. But the second time, a simplified English translation on the screen reveals that the singing is a prayer for the dead (fig. 10).

American minimalist composer Steve Reich, who was born in New York in 1936, also uses documents to similar effect. Reich's 1988 musical composition *Different Trains* is a collage of voices excerpted from interviews with five people: Reich's childhood governess, who was an American; a retired American train porter; and three child survivors of the Holocaust who are about Reich's own age. The "determining factor" for the melody of each phrase in the piece, says Reich, is the intonation of each voice, whose musical values the composer considers "unchangeable."[11] With the documentary fragments, Reich evokes the war not only as the composer experienced them as a child, shuttling by rail between separated parents in Los Angeles and New York, but also as he reflects on that era today, haunted by the testimony of child survivors and the realization that had he been born in continental Europe, he might have ridden very different trains. This piece includes the only appearance of autobiography in Reich's oeuvre.

What's more, Reich engenders multiple meanings with the fragments in *Different Trains*. In section one, called "America—Before the War," an excerpt of Reich's governess saying "one of the fastest trains" suggests enthusiasm for the golden age of American rail travel. But when Reich replays the same taped phrase in section three, called "After the War," alongside phrases of the survivors, the different context seriously complicates the phrase's interpretation.

What strikes me most powerfully about this recent Holocaust art is its formal similarities despite radically different media. Two painters, a filmmaker, and a composer all rely on documentary. Why? Gluska believes that facts project more power than anything an artist can create, and Galles insists that documentary elements are a tacit rebuttal to Holocaust deniers.

Dealing with documentary means accommodating ready-made parts; almost like elements in collage, such ingredients compromise the possibility that the artwork will possess a single unified aesthetic. Sometimes, as in the case of Gluska and Galles, it's a matter of the artwork including at least two points of view (that of the Nazis as told through documents, and that of their victims). Other times, as with Ravett and Reich, it's a matter of documentary fragments failing to congeal into a unified formal presentation. To be sure, the artists all steer clear of imposing an authorial vision and control; they steer clear of bullying particular facts to fit into an aesthetic framework, and they thereby avoid raising what Adorno called identity thinking.

Through focusing on particular documents, the four artists similarly avoid making universalizing, absolutist conclusions. Instead, they foster multiple points of view and generate competing and sometimes indeterminate meanings that cluster, a little like Adorno's constellations of meanings, toward creating a complex understanding of the past.[12]

Document, particularity, multiple viewpoints, indeterminate meanings—these traits are characteristic of art identified as postmodern. What I find of special interest is that the use of these traits in these works seems primarily motivated by a respectful treatment of the memory of the Holocaust itself—in short, by what these artists feel they cannot do or say with regard to the Holocaust. To deal with the subject, Gluska, Galles, and Reich even changed their styles. It would appear that the artists' adoption of such postmodern techniques, in response to Holocaust subject matter, adduces a certain kind of evidence for the link that Eric Santner and others have suggested may exist between the crisis of modernist authority at Auschwitz and the postwar, post-Holocaust, postmodern sensibility.[13]

But there is one common so-called postmodern trait you don't find in this art. That trait is "play."[14] For some, play represents the stage when an artist or scholar greets a multiplicity of points of view and indeterminacy of meanings with irreverent delight, suggesting that all opinions are legitimate, and that nothing is knowable for sure, not even good and evil.

These Holocaust artists cannot accept such a proposition. For them, the Holocaust inspires not play but rather its corresponding modernist trait: "purpose." And it's their purpose to make an unambiguous moral statement about murder and loss. Sometimes with real manipulativeness, these artists aim to appeal to their viewer's empathy. As we've seen, they do *not* want their viewers to identify *with* Holocaust victims; far from adopting the approach of Hollywood movies and Holocaust "theme park" museums that attempt, impossibly, to recreate the bodily experience of horror, these artists, by contrast, want you to feel the way they *themselves* do. To whatever extent the current obsession with the Holocaust may, in fact, be an involuntary return of a repressed trauma, either on a personal or on a societal scale, many artists of Holocaust subject matter make their art a site for doing the work of postponed mourning—what Freud called "working through."

Comparing Gluska's approach in 1991 (fig. 1) with that of a few years later (figs. 2–4) shows how this artist has learned to intensify a viewer's feeling of loss—by including the victim's names, which the artist discovered in 1995 after considerable research, and by covering the shaved scalps, striped uniforms and identity numbers in order to focus attention on the eyes. Over some works, layers of black silk permit a viewer to see a face only from directly in front of it, so that eye contact becomes unavoidable (fig. 3 and 4). And covering the picture with a shroud evokes the Jewish custom of covering mirrors after a loved one has died.

This "reaching out" in Gluska's recent work is accompanied, curiously, by a "holding back," an impulse that actually imposes obstacles that thwart a viewer from engaging too easily with the material and from coopting simplistic conclusions about the Holocaust. If Gluska's shrouded picture is seen from the side, the silk entirely camouflages the face behind it, much like the low lighting that Gluska prefers for his exhibitions; these things make faces difficult to see—and easy to overlook. A viewer must investigate, must approach the work from directly in front of it, and must pause long enough for his or her eyes to adjust to the dim light. In other words, a viewer must demonstrate a certain level of interest and commitment. Ultimately, Gluska speaks only to those who are willing to make an effort to listen. Gluska's holding back suggests how he recognizes, as Geoffrey Hartman has said, that "popularization [not only] disseminates but also trivializes," and that silence remains, in Berel Lang's words, "a compelling standard of judgment."[15]

This contradictory strategy of reaching out and holding back calls for what might be described as "empathic praxis." Empathic praxis reminds me of the experience of studying Adorno's *Negative Dialectics*, a text which serves up subtle ideas, but only to those willing to engage with its opaque, anti-systemic text. By repelling casual readers, the work resists simplistic cooptation.

Galles's *Fourteen Stations* also requires a viewer's empathic praxis. The work reaches out by establishing an atmosphere of mourning. The octagonal exhibition space invokes the Christian tradition of centrally planned mausolea and martyria. And Galles emphasizes the theme of death by reproducing photos that articulate his outrage without compromising documentary fact. For Bergen-Belsen, Galles chose to copy an archival photo in which the angle of the sun casts shadows that happen to look like a skull, and he oriented and cropped the view in order to place the skull close to the center (figs. 6 and 7). In all fourteen of the principal drawings—which, as charcoal, are literally made of ashes—Galles inscribed a Hebrew phrase from the Kaddish, the prayer for the dead in praise of God. Exhibited together, the panels of *Fourteen Stations* include the complete prayer.

But Galles also holds back. The Kaddish is, in fact, undetectable under layers of charcoal. Only he knows it's there. Most significantly, Galles provides no map or key to his work, so that viewers cannot decipher the mute features of the landscapes. To do so, viewers would have to conduct research on their own. Indeed, to fully engage with *Fourteen Stations*, viewers must bring a high level of interest and commitment to the piece, and above all, to its subject.

Ravett's *In Memory* also reaches out by creating an elegiac atmosphere. The chanted prayer is the *El Mole Rahamim*, associated with the Yiskor service at Yom Kippur and the Yahrzeit practice of visiting a relative's grave; this aspect of the film suggests, as Alan Berger has noted, how Ravett regards Poland as a vast Jewish graveyard.[16] In the same mournful spirit, the dark screens at the beginning and end bracket the silent film clips almost as though they were relics. And the organization of those clips seems designed to manipulate a viewer's emotions. After the humanizing images of life at Lodz, the contrast of the last sequence of a public hanging is shocking, even though it's common knowledge that nearly everyone in the ghetto died at Auschwitz. At this point, previous images acquire new meaning and seem to reveal a master narrative. The scenes of shoveling snow seem to presage what looks like the condemned men digging their own graves; walking in the street appears to foretell marching to the gallows, and donning hats anticipates the noose.

Even though Steve Reich regards the excerpts from interviews in *Different Trains* as "unchangeable," in the manner of relics, the composer doesn't specifically create a sense of mourning. But he does reach out by imposing some dramatic and arguably manipulative flourishes—documentary recordings of sirens, and of shrill European train whistles that act as exclamation marks in punctuating the most disturbing lines about a Nazi round-up and transport to a Polish camp. But Reich also holds back, because many of the words are difficult to distinguish without consulting the program notes.

Representative of many working with Holocaust subject matter today, these artists try to manipulate their audiences toward seeing—or, to be more specific, *feeling*—the past the way they themselves do. All four, as I've suggested, want to impose a sense of their own sadness and moral outrage, with the consequence of stirring similar feelings in their audiences. Yet, at the same time, the artists take pains to eschew mastery over their material, and with it, they eschew the authoritative way of thinking that is often indicted in relation to the Holocaust. To be aphoristic about it, you might say that their art combines modernist authority with postmodernist indeterminacy. The art becomes a delicate balancing act between insisting on knowing *exactly* how to respond emotionally and ethically to the past, and refusing to draw fixed or universalizing conclusions from the documentary material that would otherwise give meaning to the meaningless, incomprehensible murder. Saul Friedlander offers a corresponding formulation when he describes the difficult task of the Holocaust historian. The historian, he writes, faces the "simultaneous acceptance of two contradictory moves: the search for ever-closer historical linkages, and the avoidance of a naive historical positivism leading to . . . closures."[17]

This is an example of two totalizing systems of thought counteracting each other. Here, Adorno's opening remarks from *Negative Dialectics* come to my mind. Adorno insists that philosophy—by which he means all philosophical systems whose intrinsic abstraction suggests they never adequately describe the world—is "obliged ruthlessly to criticize itself."[18] In other words, the elegant closure of a hermetic philosophical system must be punctured by contradictions raised by other such systems, so that none prevails. Holocaust-related art, with its contradictory, anti-systemic nature, offers a working model for this possibility.

Notes

1. See particularly Tony Kushner, *The Holocaust and the Liberal Imagination: A Social and Cultural History* (Oxford, UK, and Cambridge, USA: Blackwell, 1994).

In a related way, we can speculate at the incapacity of our pre-Holocaust languages to adequately represent this new phenomenon of industrial killing, so that simply finding an appropriate word to describe a person in a death camp—inmate? prisoner? victim?—eludes us even today. Berel Lang treats this dilemma, as well as the uses to which the Nazis put language as an instrument of thought control, in "Language and Genocide," *Act and Idea in the Nazi Genocide* (Chicago and London: University of Chicago Press, 1990)—see especially pp. 95–96.

2. Among the recent contributors to the discussion of this interesting theory is Dominick LaCapra, *Representing the Holocaust: History, Theory, Trauma* (Ithaca and London: Cornell University Press, 1994).

3. See Greenberg's 1939 essay, "Avant-Garde and Kitsch," reprinted in his *Art and Culture: Critical Essays* (Boston: Beacon Press, 1961), pp. 3–21.

4. See Greenberg's 1940 essay, "Towards a Newer Laocoon," reprinted in *Pollock and After: The Critical Debate*, ed. Francis Frascina (New York: Harper and Row, 1985), pp. 35–46.

5. See Margaret Olin, "C[lement] Hardesh [Greenberg] and Company: Formal Criticism and Jewish Identity," in *Too Jewish: Challenging Traditional Identities*, ed. Norman L. Kleeblatt (New York: The Jewish Museum and New

Brunswick: Rutgers University Press, 1996), pp. 39–59. Olin considers the nationalist origins of nineteenth-century art criticism and the way Greenberg and Harold Rosenberg advocated formalism as a means of combatting it. Ironically, Greenberg's argument for aesthetic purity in different artistic media echoes theories of racial purity, as Olin observes.

6. Ziva Amishai-Maisels, *Depiction and Interpretation: The Influence of the Holocaust on the Visual Arts* (Oxford and New York: Pergamon, 1993).

7. Theodor W. Adorno, "Cultural Criticism and Society," *Prisms*, trans. Samuel Weber and Shierry Weber. (Cambridge, Mass.: MIT Press, 1981), p. 34.

8. James E. Young, "Aharon Gluska: New York," an unpaginated flier for an exhibition at the C. S. Schulte Galleries, South Orange, N.J., November 1991.

9. Galles's picture of Bergen-Belsen, which shows the camp in operation, is based on a British RAF reconnaissance photograph. No Luftwaffe photos of the camp appear to be extant.

10. Despite Ravett's silence, the contexts of images in the film are not unknown. For example, in a diary entry of May 25, 1942, Oskar Rosenfeld reports on a ghetto law requiring Jews to greet Germans by donning their hats in respect. Oskar Rosenfeld, *Wozu noch Welt: Aufzeichnungen aus dem Getto Lodz*, ed. Hanno Loewy (Frankfurt am Main: Verlag Neue Kritik, 1994), p. 90.

11. Steve Reich, "Steve Reich: Back on Track," interview by K. Robert Schwarz, *Ear* (April 1989): 32.

12. Adorno discusses constellations in *Negative Dialectics*, trans. E. B. Ashton (New York: Continuum, 1973), p. 163. Adorno wrote more clearly about his approach in his 1931 essay, "The Actuality of Philosophy," *Telos* 31 (1977): 120–33. For an excellent analysis of Adorno's thought, see Susan Buck-Morss, *The Origin of Negative Dialectics: Theodor W. Adorno, Walter Benjamin, and the Frankfurt Institute* (New York: The Free Press, 1977).

13. Eric L. Santner, *Stranded Objects: Mourning, Memory, and Film in Postwar Germany* (Ithaca and London: Cornell University Press, 1990). Another interesting treatment of the issue can be found in Zygmunt Bauman, *Modernity and the Holocaust* (Ithaca: Cornell University Press, 1989).

14. For a somewhat reductive but still interesting list of modern and post-modern traits in which "play" appears second under the postmodern heading, see Ihab Hassan, "Toward a Concept of Postmodernism," *The Postmodern Turn: Essays on Postmodern Theory and Culture* (Columbus: Ohio State University Press, 1987), p. 91.

15. Geoffrey H. Hartman, *The Longest Shadow: In the Afternath of the Holocaust* (Bloomington and Indianapolis: Indiana Univeristy Press, 1996), pp. 12–13.

16. Alan Berger, *Children of Job: American Second-Generation Witnesses to the Holocaust* (Albany: SUNY Press, 1997), p. 149.

17. Saul Friedlander, "Trauma and Transference," Chapter 7 in his *Memory, History, and the Extermination of the Jews of Europe* (Bloomington and Indianapolis: Indiana University Press, 1993). p. 131. Also published as "Trauma, Transference and 'Working Through,' " *History & Memory* 4, no. 1 (Spring/Summer 1992), and "Trauma, Memory and Transference," in *Holocaust Remembrance: The Shapes of Memory*, ed. Geoffrey H. Hartman (Oxford and Cambridge: Blackwell, 1994).

18. Adorno, *Negative Dialectics*, p. 3.

Poetry after Auschwitz
Paul Celan's Aesthetics of Hermetism

Paul Sars

Introduction

In most companions of literary theory the chapter of the "Nach-kriegslyrik" [German post-war lyric poetry] starts in 1952. Volumes of poetry such as "Mohn und Gedächtnis" (1952) by Paul Celan and "Die gestundete Zeit" (1953) by Ingeborg Bachmann—and not the works of already famous writers like Bertolt Brecht and Gottfried Benn—account for the new beginning of post-war German poetry. This new generation of German poets expresses for the very first time and in an outspoken way the events during the dark period 1933–1945. Precisely because of the fact that they have tried to join the great German literary tradition, their poems make the demolition caused by National Socialism audible in an oppressive way. The German "Nachkriegslyrik"—which in most companions of literary theory ends with the death of Paul Celan in 1970—is regarded as an attempt to learn to speak all over again after the bewilderment and the silence that was caused by Auschwitz. It is poetry, written by poets who were fully aware of the fact that the German language, in spite of Goethe and Rilke, is contaminated, has become suspect, and, according to the poet Johannes Bobrowski, is still "rusty from blood."

The work of Paul Celan, who was born in Rumania in 1920, is generally referred to as "hermetic poetry." The term "hermetic" points especially to the cryptic and esoteric character of Celan's poems, and to the dark metaphors which seem to have their own logic. Although it can't be denied that a certain magic is inherent in Celan's style and tone, he never meant to write inaccessible poetry. This apparent inaccessibility is not so much the result of a conscious choice of style, but of a natural

169

expression of the poet's background. Paul Celan cannot be associated with just one place, language, and culture. He was a Jew born in Rumania, but he spoke German. Indeed, he lived in many countries and cultures. He preferred to describe himself as a nomad, as a homeless person. His linguistic usage has been marked by all of this, in the same way as the bitter experiences of World War II are omnipresent in his verses, like a shadow that surrounds the words.

At home in Rumania Paul Celan received a typically Jewish education. However, his parents sent him to German Christian schools, where he became acquainted with the great Western European tradition. In Bukovina, the part of the country where he spent his youth, he also became acquainted with Eastern European peoples and cultures. It was a part of the country where minorities such as Gypsies, Jews, and Russian Christians lived together with Rumanians and Czechs. It formed a rich cultural hinterland, possibly one of Europe's richest in the first decades of this century, which Paul Celan shared with, among others, Elias Canetti and Franz Rosenzweig. His knowledge of medicine and the Russian, Rumanian, and German languages and his wide interests in crystals and botany made it possible for Celan to use a rich tradition of images and representations.

The other side of Celan's hinterland is the sad history of a person who, from his youth, has been confronted with anti-Semitism. When Bukovina was under Russian and later under German occupation, Celan was expelled from school several times because he was a Jew. Then his parents and other family members were killed in concentration and extermination camps. Celan himself survived a Nazi workcamp, in spite of terrible circumstances. Even after the war however, under Russian and Rumanian occupation, he had to flee the country twice because of anti-Semitism. In the fifties and sixties, when he lived in France, Celan was maliciously accused of plagiarism and making money on the murder of his parents. The attention that was paid by the German media to these undeserved accusations made his rather ambiguous relation with Germany even more reserved. Celan felt not-understood, in spite of the fact that he had received much recognition in Germany and had been awarded several literary prizes. Many times his work has been identified too hastily with the persecution of the Jews, or disposed of as "the end of poetry, a dead end." Paul Celan suffered from severe depressions and compulsive neuroses and commited suicide in 1970 by drowning himself in the river Seine, in Paris.

Coming to Terms with World War II

In German literature Celan's hermetic poetry is regarded as an outstanding expression of the process of coming to terms with the Holocaust.

In his poems "Deathfugue" (GW. I, 39f), "Tenebrae" (GW. I, 163), and "Lilac Sky" (GW. II, 335),[1] Celan refers directly to World War II. In his early as well as in his later works we can find poems like these, which in many cases have been actualized by references to the very problematic German *Vergangenheits-bewältigung* (assimilation of the past) or to the awakening anti-Semitism that Celan observed after the war, in the sixties.

In addition to this explicit discussion, in which the process of coming to terms with the Holocaust can be clearly recognized, Celan's work also contains a more implicit form of coming to terms with the events during the period 1933–1945. I will now turn to his poems that refer to events that occurred during the Nazi period, which only few of us will recognize. These poems do not have World War II as their subject and do not contain 'objective' historical facts. Nevertheless they can be regarded as part of a process of coming to terms with World War II, for in these poems Celan implicitly deals with strictly personal, but very real experiences during the war in terms that refer to later experiences. We could even say that all experiences, including the fears and depressions from which Celan suffered in later years, have been colored by his war experiences. In ambiguous words, disguised allusions, and fleeting associations we can find the marks of an everlasting struggle with a past that has not been fully assimilated.

In this sense the theme of Celan's works is World War II. The danger of this conclusion, however, is that Celan's work is being thematically reduced to a "description of the persecution and genocide of the Jews," just as we can read in many studies. In doing so we pass over the much wider range of Celan's themes and the revolutionary renewal of modern poetry prompted by his work. And we also pass over the essence of coming to terms with experiences. If we in fact say that the theme of Celan's works is World War II—which in a way is true—the aspect of "the process of integration" is certainly more than an explicit or implicit thematization of facts and experiences.

Both aspects are united in the speech of this poet. Celan's "hermetic" speech expresses this process more strongly than an explicit account of historical facts and more tersely than the thematization of fears and identity crises. Tone and use of words, theme, and intention are being interwoven in this unique speech, which could be called an "aesthetics of hermetism."

What is at stake in Celan's poetry—a truthful account of concrete perception—as explained in his poetics,[2] expresses itself outstandingly in his speech. In explaining this speech and in an explanation of the 'aisthesis' of hermetism the wounds inflicted by World War II become audible in a contrastive way.

The Poem "Todesfuge"

Celan made his debut in 1948 with the poem "Todesfuge." It made him world famous within a few years and the poem was soon translated into many languages.

In this many-voiced "fugue"—with which word he referred to the "Meister der Tonkunst" (master composer) Johann Sebastian Bach—various voices are heard. According to the principle of a fugue the voices alternately repeat and vary certain melodies. Sometimes they are repeated in an accelerated form. In the poem they alternate faster and faster, which creates the impression of polyphony and causes a narrowing down of meaning, a stretto that is typical for the fugue. This impression is reinforced by omitting punctuation.

The voices of the poem sing of death in various melodies; they describe the situation in which the persons find themselves. But they also sing the praises of the rich Jewish cultural tradition, even after it has been ruined. In the given situation, however, numerous implicit references to the Jewish and the German tradition acquire an ambiguous meaning. Over against to Shulamith, the dark-haired Jewish bride, with her ash-colored hair, from the Song of Songs appears the German Christian Margarete, the beloved from Goethe's *Faust*, who is saved by God's mercy just before she dies. In the last sentences of *Faust* (part one) the devil Mephistopheles shouts: "Faust, leave her, come over to me; she is executed!" Then a voice is heard. It says: "Stimme von oben" (Voice from above): "Sie ist gerettet" (She is saved). Celan's fugue ends in a narrowing stretto, which is introduced by the only end-rhyme of the poem (*blau–genau*). This points to the fatal moment of the lethal shot. After this, the events flash by once again before death occurs with the slowing down of the poem (*träumet*).

Deathfugue

Black milk of daybreak we drink it at evening
we drink it at midday and morning we drink it at night
we drink and we drink
we shovel a grave in the air there you won't lie too cramped
A man lives in the house he plays with his vipers he writes
he writes when it grows dark to Deutschland your golden hair Margareta
he writes it and steps out of doors and the stars are sparkling he whistles his
    hounds to come close
he whistles his Jews into rows has them shovel a grave in the ground
he commands us play up for the dance

Black milk of daybreak we drink you at night
we drink you at morning and midday we drink you at evening
we drink and we drink
A man lives in the house he plays with his vipers he writes
he writes when it grows dark to Deutschland your golden hair Margareta
Your ashen hair Shulamith we shovel a grave in the air there you won't lie too
    cramped

He shouts jab this earth deeper you lot there you others sing up and play
he grabs for the rod in his belt he swings his eyes are so blue
jab your spades deeper you lot there you others play on for the dancing

Black milk of daybreak we drink you at night
we drink you at midday and morning we drink you at evening
we drink and we drink
a man lives in the house your goldenes Haar Margareta
your aschenes Haar Shulamith he plays with his vipers

He shouts play death more sweetly this Death is a master from Deutschland
he shouts scrape your strings darker you'll rise then as smoke to the sky
you'll have a grave then in the clouds there you won't lie to cramped

Black milk of daybreak we drink you at night
we drink you at midday Death is a master aus Deutschland
we drink you at evening and morning we drink and we drink
this Death is ein Meister aus Deutschland his eye is blue
he shoots you with shot made of lead shoots you level and true
a man lives in the house your goldenes Haar Margarete
he looses his hounds on us grants us a grave in the air
he plays with his vipers and daydreams der Tod ist ein Meisters aus
    Deutschland

dein goldenes Haar Margarete
dein aschens Haar Sulamith[3]

Theodor Adorno has said that it would be barbaric to write poetry
after Auschwitz. In the first months of 1945, Celan started writing his
"Todesfuge," a poem after and about Auschwitz. Although Adorno did
not know the poem at the time, his verdict pained and angered Celan.
The publication of "Todesfuge" led to a controversy between the two.
According to Adorno, the poem—despite its horrifying theme—seemed
to give a meaning to Auschwitz because of the aesthetic principle of stylization. It seemed as if Celan had succeeded in transfiguring the horrors
of the concentration camps in a harmonious song, a duet of executioner
and victim, in a composition that implicitly suggests a meaningful connection. However, according to Adorno, every semblance of meaning or
meaningful coherence does injustice to the Jewish fate, to the murdered
persons and their surviving relatives.

Adorno's remarks point to the moral as well as to the aesthetic problems connected with a literary process of coming to terms with the concentration camps. This becomes clear when we confront unsuspecting readers with the poem "Todesfuge" and ask them if they think the poem is "beautiful" or "good." During literature classes, high school students have been embarrassed by this question.[4] Their implicit definition of poetry (poetry is beautiful, poetry is rhythmic, and poetry rhymes) made it difficult for them to give a balanced answer to this tricky question. Their reactions reflected the ambiguity of the poem which is a melodious account of the most horrible events. Their answers also reflected the moral implication of the poem when they tried to avoid predicates such as "beautiful" and "good" and as a result took refuge in moral indignation: "I think it is a bad poem." One of the students expressed this embarrassment strikingly: "I think it is a strange poem, beautiful and ugly at the same time. After all, one doesn't sing when someone just died." Although the last remark is not correct, since we can associate singing with all kinds of burial rituals, these responses give a clear picture of several mistaken ideas about poetry. The natural identification of poetry with lyrical, idyllic, and Arcadian representations, with beauty and truth in the sense of a harmony of spheres—grafted onto the classical Greek idea of *kalokagathia* (beauty being good and true at the same time)—apparently has still to be overcome in view of poetry written after Auschwitz.

Celan reacted in the same way to Adorno's statement concerning poetry after Auschwitz. According to Celan, Adorno's statement has nothing to do with the legitimacy of the literary process of coming to terms with the Holocaust, nor with poetry as such. It is only the speech, the character of aesthetic stylization, that causes problems. With regard to "Todesfuge" Celan admitted that Adorno's criticism was right as far as it concerned "the proclivity towards poeticizing," which is said to be typical of his early work. With the word "poeticize" Celan doesn't mean so much *Beschönigung* (covering up), but rather the traditional technique of metaphoric description, the plastic expression of reality. What he means is poetry that pretends to be able to represent reality by using images, poetry that pretends to be able to reconstruct events from the past—in a personally colored way or otherwise—in poetic images. This "proclivity toward poeticizing" is characterized by Celan as "traditional" in a negative sense. It is a form of poetic speech that has become impossible after Auschwitz. In his later works Adorno seems to agree with Celan; for example, when he corrects his already famous statement in *Negative Dialektik* and recognizes the legitimacy of poetic speech, even with regard to Celan: "Perennial suffering has as much right to expression as the tortured have to scream. Hence it may have been wrong to say that no poem could be written after Auschwitz."[5] As far as it concerns speech, "Todesfuge" is a traditional poem and as such an exception in Celan's works. Beginning in the late fifties Celan refused to recite the poem; he also refused permission to publish it in anthologies. Although something of the characteristic speech becomes audible in the words "Schwarze Milch der Frühe," insofar as it is not a description of a thing or a historical event, Celan will not find the tone and style that have later been described in literary theories as characteristic of "hermetic poetry" until 1950.

Hermetic Poetry

The term "hermetic" refers to traditions of hermetism as a secret teaching. The God Hermes in Greek mythology was the translator of the will of the gods and is associated with the invention of writing. When we realize that the knowledge of reading and writing has been regarded for ages as magic powers that belong exclusively to the initiated, the association with magic is obvious. Hermetism also refers to the explicit secret teachings, which have been described in the *Corpus Hermeticum*, a number of esoteric-philosophical books from Hellenistic times, which are attributed to the mythological character Hermes Trismegistos (thrice the great). The *Corpus Hermeticum* is said to contain knowledge of the true essence of the world and of secret powers and the relations between God and man and the cosmos.

Both sources can be associated with the work of Celan. His poems contain numerous magic symbols. Many metaphors have been taken from the world of images of the Cabbala, the Gnosis, and the Talmud. Celan himself states clearly in his Poetics that his poetry claims to reveal the truth of human existence, thus joining the old traditions in which poets are regarded as seers, mystics, and prophets. Their language is not a simple means of communication and their poems are no mere transmittors or copies of reality. Rather, their language and poems are events. They are moments of truth. Their mystic speech is a form of "addressing," "declaring," or "discussing" reality, similar to magic phrases that cause things to happen. This may explain why Celan's speech often passes over linguistic conventions and standard literary techniques.

Even if one glances rapidly over Celan's poetry, it will be clear at once that his poems are not poetry in the traditional sense with which we have become familiar. There is no end rhyme and no regular meter. They are not ordered in strophes. The syntactic structures are complicated and the metaphors are at first glance cryptic and ambiguous. Metaphors such as "suns of thread" or verses like "A crunching of iron shoes is in the cherry tree"[6] are hardly imaginable and are difficult to translate into concrete images. And when certain terms and images appear to have been taken from mystical texts or alchemiscal formulas, we can indeed call these poems "hermetic poetry."

The term "hermetic poetry," however, was introduced as a negative term, when the Italian literary theorist F. Flora used it in 1936 to characterize the poetry of Giuseppe Ungaretti. Flora characterized Ungaretti's dark and inaccessible poetry as "hermetic" in the negative sense of an uncommunicative "being-very-secretive-about-everything." Adorno changed this pejorative meaning when he made a plea for a 'hermetic work of art' in his *Notes on Literature*.[7] By this he meant a work of art that should express the crumbling of the commonly accepted worldview and the bankruptcy of reason caused by World War II. In this sense, hermetic poetry is a poetic speech that gets caught in its own logic and so displays the modern subjectivity in its suffering from silence. It is an autonomous poetry which is not easy to consume and cannot be misused for political ideology.

However, Celan has always rejected the qualification of his work as "hermetic poetry." In a letter to Michael Hamburger, he stressed that his poetry is "not hermetic at all" and that "every word has been written with direct relation to concrete reality." He admitted, however, that his poetry was dark and ambiguous—in his words: "Mehrdeutigkeit ohne Maske" (unmasked ambiguity). Celan regarded this ambiguity as the only truthful language in poetry. The unmasked ambiguity does justice to the concrete perception of phenomena. Celan would probably have accepted the qualification "hermetic poetry" if this had been meant by it. "Hermetic poetry" would then refer to a kind of poetry that is full of ambiguity or, from the reader's point of view, poetry without a conventional order. Celan's hermetism is a poetic speech in which the normal physiological and psychological principles are no longer standard. Space is perceived and experienced as a dimension in which phenomena occur, but always according to the meaning of what happens. The same goes for time, which isn't linear, not ordered according to the principle of the clock as a chain of seconds or as the succession of causally connected moments. In Celan's poetry time is linked to the meaning of the phenomenon itself: his poems mention the "time of the heart," the "time of the eye."

In Celan's poetry past, present, and future events occur at the same time. They even can change place and succession in an arbitrary way. This causes a typical ambiguity of expression, which is not at all a fantastic creation, but the expression of the fundamental way in which human perception works. The unambiguous meaning, which we normally expect, is created only afterward by conventions and by a rationality which forbids that one and the same phenomenon have more than one form and meaning at the same time. Celan himself qualified this intention of his poems as an "unerhörter Anspruch" (enormous claim). This claim is Celan's attempt to express truthfully the experience of reality according to concrete perception. Every experience, however, is marked by personal experience and the cast shadow of the past.

Aesthetics (Aisthesis) of Hermetism

The essence of hermetism lies in perception, in the way a poem perceives reality. This formulation is not as strange as it may seem. In many cases Celan has spoken about his poems as if they were beings with souls and senses: "The poem moves . . . , it seeks . . . , it speaks."[8] In discussing the way in which a poem perceives, we are being confronted with the original meaning of "aesthetics" in the sense of "aisthesis." Nowadays we mean by "aesthetics" the science of beauty in art and more specifically the science of the means of style that create beauty. Originally, however aesthetics was not about beauty in art or nature, but about the quality of physical phenomena as perceived by the senses.

Celan refers to this original meaning when he understands aesthetics simply as ways of perception. He explains that in his opinion poetry is not about beauty but about reality, about pure perception. And this is nothing else than a truthful account of what happens here and now. The aesthetics of hermetism lies in the unification of a once-only expression (which is typical of speaking) and the perception of a reality that appears as an ambiguous and meaningful presence. The poem as such leaves open this ambiguity, but every time it is read—when the reader lets the poem occur—the poem can represent only one "coherent" complex of meaning. After all, the reader cannot, at the same time, understand the same words in different ways. Each time the poem is read it manifests itself in another way, in another shape, and with other accents. This is not only due to the reader, who cannot read the same twice because of the fact that he changes and grows older, but also to the fundamentally ambiguous poem. The poem itself initiates each time a unique contraction of meaning: it is a throbbing web of meanings that takes another shape with every heartbeat. The way of life Celan attributes to the poem, however, does not differ essentially from the human perception and understanding of reality. Every perception is a placebound and timebound contraction of ambiguity into an unambiguous relation and meaning.

Celan's ambition is to write poems that are the incarnation of the existence of the individual. Looking back on the evolution from poeticizing to hermetic speech, Celan said in 1966: "In those early days . . . I still experimented with the mental means of statement. I still played hide-and-seek behind metaphors. And now, after twenty years of experiencing the contrasts of inside and outside, I have banned the word 'if' from my atelier."[9] What he meant by this is that poems are neither symbolic images and metaphorically transformed representations of reality nor comparisons or parables ('if'). Poems are a form of addressing or declaring.

This has everything to do with the process of coming to terms with the Holocaust and the deep longing for an identity. It has to do with the awareness that existence is vulnerable and that every moment is present only once and cannot be repeated. Auschwitz and the other camps have not only been places where a bestial genocide and the destruction of a rich culture took place. It is also the place where an attempt was made on the most vulnerable human powers. In the concentration camps perhaps not so much the idea of man or humanity, but rather the senses seem to have been damaged forever, which also means that perceptions and expressions have different colors.[10] Celan expresses this even more strong in the poem "Mit wechselndem Schlüssel" (1955):

> With a changing key
> you unlock the house where
> the snow of what's silences drifts.
> Just like the blood that bursts from
> your eye or mouth or ear,
> so your key changes.
>
> Changing your key changes the word
> that may drift with the flakes.
> Just like the wind that rebuffs you,
> the snow packs around the word.[11]

The poem could be paraphrased as follows: the house, the safe area that constitutes man's identity, can only be unlocked with a changing key. In this house the snowflakes of what is being concealed are whirling. What cannot be said, the inspeakable suffering that cannot be put into words, is covered by and incorporated in expressionless white snow. Why has this house to be opened with an ever changing key and what key does he mean? Apparently the key changes according to the blood that floats from the wounded senses. But when the key changes, the word that has something to do with the snow of what is being concealed also changes. It could be that Celan meant the word that could express what is being concealed (and is absent and present at the same time). This, however, seems to be impossible as long as the snow wraps itself around the words in different ways, depending on the wind.

This red blood and the white snow seem to be the expressions of an attempt to learn to perceive all over again, after Auschwitz and in a way that does justice to what took place in Auschwitz. Celan is looking for a point of departure, a recovery of perception for the sake of an orientation toward his own existence and to find out "wo ich mich befand und wohin es mit mir wollte" (where I was and where it urged me to go).[12] How far-reaching and how remarkably perceptive this period of reconsideration has been, we can learn not only from Celan's poems but also from the letters he wrote in 1949 and 1950 to his Dutch friend Diet

Kloos-Barendregt. Celan wrote these letters shortly after his escape from the Eastern bloc, during a time and in a situation in which he could think himself safe. Remarkably enough, in spite of their hopeful tone, the letters show a man who, having survived the horrors of Nazi Germany, suffers all the more from fears and desorientation. He writes, for example, that he lives a moment of his life in which his lifeline breaks for the second time. A moment in which he is subject and object at the same time. In his poetics Celan explains such experiences by using the Heideggerian idea of human existence (*Dasein*). The I that has been robbed of his identity is unsettled. He experiences himself as "Inside" and "Outside" at the same time. After all the I only exists insofar it is being constituted by reflecting itself in an "Outside." But when the perception, the medium between Inside and Outside, is being disturbed, a fluctuating identity is all that remains. It is a sort of flashing consciousness of phenomena that appear and disappear.

In his letters to Diet Kloos-Barendregt Celan pointed out that the identity crisis caused by war experiences and wounded perception also involve a different experience of time. Concrete experience is placed in the imperfect tense, a time dimension that can never reach completion. Every perceived phenomenon reveals a moment of "just gone," a moment in which it is present and absent at the same time. Celan writes in his letters that he experiences more than ever the immediateness of existence. As far as it concerns his poetry, we could say that Celan is looking for the possibility of touching the ambiguity, the simultaneity of past, present, and future as it appears to him. It is an attempt to create a language that is apt to express more than "always this and just this meaning here and now." A language that leaves room for ambiguity, for numerous and different meanings that are present simultaneously.

Eye-Landscapes

The events that occured during the Nazi period have damaged the senses and language. Therefore the obsession to look for a new way of perception and expression have to be taken very literally. In Celan's work the senses (mouth, ear and eye) evolve in a strange way, losing their normal functions and given other functions. They eye plays a central role in these evolutions because, according to Celan, it can "speak." In his first poems after "Todesfuge" Celan describes the smoking ruins after Auschwitz. These poems are like landscapes, through which the homeless poet, who has alienated himself from himself, travels around looking for his own identity. The landscapes are strewn with ashes, empty urns, and smouldering rubble. There is a deathly silence. The perceptor is mirrored in what has been perceived: his ear and mouth are dumbfounded.

But the heaps of rubble are being seen, according to the bleeding of the eye ("Mit wechselndem Schlüssel").

At first sight these landscape poems seem to be descriptions of the ruins of Auschwitz, but it becomes more and more clear that they are first and foremost images of the inner life. What to the reader seems to be a description of a landscape (the "outside") is at the same time a reflection, a mirror of an inner life. The seamless connection of both positions—inside and outside—is the key constellation of Celan's poetry: the landscapes are eye-landscapes, that "take place" in the eye. After all, in the eye the outer world and the inner world come together. The eye not only perceives the outer world, but also projects—being the mirror of the soul—the inner life. Everything that has ever been perceived is piled up in the soul, which is regarded by Celan as the "crystal of the inner world." Therefore, that which, in every visual perception, is most deep interior is at the same time present in the outer world. Consequently we can say that everything that has been and will be perceived happens on the retina and takes place inside and outside at the same time. Even the most distant object reflects itself in the eye: the star, the "crystal" of the outer world, which is naturally associated with the Star of David, with the persecution of the Jews, but also with the biblical promise that God will make His people of Israel as numerous as there are stars in the sky.

Celan has focused himself on the human eye. Being a topography of the eye, his poems are the expression of history and topicality. Celan has tried to unite what is most extreme and most distant in time and space with what is most nearby and present here and now. It is the concrete sensible attempt to create an open bond between inside and outside. This lasting process of a simultaneous internalization and externalization is again part of his overcoming of World War II. When the open connection between the inner world and the outer world has been created, the mutual reflection of soul and star in the eye becomes possible. At this moment, as Celan expresses hopefully, the crystals will twinkle and in the focus we can see not only the true expression of Auschwitz but also the sign of humanity after Auschwitz. This metaphysical constellation can be represented as follows:

The Star   (The crystal of the of the outer world)

The Eye   (The little star in the focus: the tear)

The Soul   (The crystal of the inner world)

In this representation of perception the eye is neither an unprejudiced organ nor a merely perceiving organ. The living, bleeding eye has become the place where events from the present and the past, nearby and distant, show themselves simultaneously in an ambiguous sparkling.

Celan used to compare his poems to crystals: depending from the way the light enters into the crystal the angle of refraction is changing and through the ambiguous sparkling always one instantaneous, here-and-now readable meaning will show itself. The poems themselves appear as eye-landscapes, as a simultaneous presence of inside and outside: an event that is experienced as identity.

Homecoming

Snowfall, denser and denser,
dove-coloured as yesterday,
snowfall, as if even now you were sleeping.

White, stacked into distance.
Above it, endless,
the sleigh track of the lost.

Below, hidden,
presses up
what so hurts the eyes,
hill upon hill,
invisible.

On each,
fetched home into its today,
an I slipped away into dumbness:
wooden, a post.

There: a feeling,
blown across by the ice wind
attaching its dove—its snow—
coloured cloth as a flag.[13]

The homecoming in this poem is not a usual one. The poem is mainly a description of an infinite snow landscape. The only varieties in this inhospitable territory are the lonely track of a sledge and some hills that are concealed from sight by snow. The underlying landscape is covered by an endless expresionless white. But the poem is also the expression of the soul, of speechlessness and unspeakable pain. Beneath this landscape, which lies litterally on the retina, something is pressing upwardly "which so hurts the eyes." It hurts because it wants to go out and wants to go up, but has no power to do so. The still invisible, but pressing up hills looks like swelling tears, a sign of bottled up grief that cannot be expressed.

In the poem "Homecoming" (1959) the eye-landscape still is covered by snow. Only years later, when Celan's poetry has gone through several stages of development, does this snow of "what is being concealed" disappear.

During a process of writing that lasted for more than twenty years, Celan fought for the recovery of an original sensibility. This forms the most elementary aspect of the process of coming to terms with World War II. The verses of the poem "An eye, open" are painful as well as hopeful:

> Hours, May-coloured, cool.
> The no more to be named, hot,
> audible in the mouth.
>
> No one's voice, again.
>
> Aching depth of the eyeball:
> the lid
> does not stand in its way, the lash
> does not count what goes in.
>
> The tear, half,
> the sharper lens, movable,
> brings the images home to you.[14]

From the image of the half tear, which works as a "scharper" lens, we can read what the process of coming to terms with the past involves. When the snow has disappeared, when the petrified and barren landscape has been lived through to the farthest corners and depths, the unconcealed reflection of star and soul will be possible. At that moment a light will flash, which makes the still dim little star in the eye sparkle. This sparkling in the eye will manifest itself as a "bleeding and blooming tear." A tear that is the only proper expression of what has happened in Auschwitz. At the same time it is the only hopeful sign of humanity after Auschwitz.

Notes

1. Eight volumes of poetry of Paul Celan were published during his lifetime. Together with other works they have been collected in his *Gesammelte Werke*, 5 volumes (Frankfurt am Main, 1983), hereinafter cited as GW.

2. Celan's poetics consists of two orations. 1. The oration on the occasion of the literary prize of the "freie Hansestadt Bremen" (1958) (GW, III, 185–186). 2. "Der Meridian," oration on the occasion of the Georg Büchner prize (1960) (GW, III, 187–202).

3. Paul Celan, "Todesfuge," GW 1. Translation by Professor Dr. John Felstiner.

4. According to reports of high school teachers. I have also experienced this myself during literature classes.

5. Theodor W. Adorno, *Negative Dialektik* (Frankfurt am Main. 1966), p. 353.

6. The examples are taken from the poems "Fadensonnen" (1967; GW, II, 26) and "Ein Knirschen" (1952; GW, I, 24).

7. Theodor W. Adorno, *Noten zur Literatur III* (Frankfurt am Main, 1965).

8. GW III, p. 190.

9. Quoted from Ton Naaijkens, "In de leidsels. Over Paul Celan," *De Revisor* 5 (1990): 60.

10. In letters to his Dutch friend Diet Kloos, Paul Celan expresses his experience of time. These letters, not yet published, were written in 1949, shortly after Celan arrived in Paris. On 23 August Celan writes:

> My dear Diet,
>   I don't know what time it is, for sure it is still night, that means, it is still dark, although it is already morning, so what time is it? Alas, I cannot tell, because my watch is standing still. My chambermaid dropped it yesterday, when she cleaned up the room, so finally I do not have, so to speak, my time—and the bells of the churches are badly informing me, they are too many, Saint Niklas du chardonnet and Saint Sevérin and Saint Julien le pauvre and not least Notre-Dame, they don't fit together, their beatings quickly follow each other, it is, if you like, thirty or thirty-two hours, an hour out of different kinds of silver, only an alert and perceptive ear could distinguish, could separate light and clear silver from dark and unclear silver, and thus experience time, but my ear is purposely slow, so that my hand becomes more alive, now time has finally slipped out of my hands. All this means good luck for me, who does not know how to do something proper with time; what did I do until now, when I had time? I was waiting again for time.

The letters Paul Celan wrote to Diet Kloos-Barendrecht have been entrusted to me by Mrs. Kloos for research. A diplomatic edition of these letters is in preparation.

11. Paul Celan, "Mit wechselndem Schlüssel" (1955), GW 1. Translation by Professor Dr. John Felstiner.

12. GW III, p. 186.

13. Paul Celan, "Heimkehr" (1959), GW 1. Translation by Michael Hamburger.

14. Paul Celan, "Ein Auge, offen" (1959), GW 1. Translation by Michael Hamburger.

A11380
Imaging within/beyond "Liberation"

James R. Watson

We will be concerned with certain images, their seductions and receptions. We will also come to meet A11380 in and through her 1945 photographic image. A11380 will be introduced, however, in the context of a short story about my first encounter with her image. I have told this story several times, each telling set forth as an attempt to respond to A11380's photographic evocation. It is not, therefore, for the purpose of appropriating her image. Quite the contrary: Each telling and presentation of image has been an attempt to evoke a seeing/reading of A11380's image that proceeds from within the image to beyond its confines as a "captured" image of the Allied "liberation" forces in 1945. A11380's image is a seduction that leads us out of the deadly logic of production-consumption and appropriation.

Each story of A11380's image has been a differing repetition in a different context. The first telling was a retelling of my initial encounter with the image of A11380 in November 1994. This first retelling was on the occasion of the SPSGH's 1995 annual meeting in association with the American Philosophical Association. The second retelling took place in March 1996 in Minneapolis, Minnesota, for the Annual Scholar's Conference on the Holocaust and the Churches. More recently, in Utrecht (August 1996), I again retold, and again differently, my encounter with A11380's image. Each of these places was no more or less different from the times of the retellings.[1] Receptions and responses differ, not the least depending upon one's actual and perceived relationship with victims and perpetrators.

Germany, for example, has been recently characterized as the land of Hitler's "willing executioners."[2] It is to be expected that German receptions of my story of A11380 and her image will differ from receptions in the lands of the "liberators." I suspect, however, that this differing is not of the type expected by proponents of Daniel Goldhagen's exculpatory project. As we will see, there is a kind of complicity of executioners/perpetrators and liberators. Yet, as we will also see, it is precisely this complicity that makes A11380's image such a powerful, rebellious, and seductive form of testimony.

There is a very long story about why philosophers only rarely just tell tales. In and out of school, philosophers who tell tales almost always tells us what they mean as well. As a philosopher, I will adhere to this tradition. Unlike some philosophers, however, I am not an iconoclast (image smasher). Visual images are as complex as the texts with which they are interwoven. Within any image that images (i.e., "unfixed" or nonidolatrous images), there are always many other images. The image is complicated (with other images), which is also that of the complication of narrator and narration, and especially that of the inextricable complication of philosophy and literature. Neither the law nor the truth *present themselves*. Nothing is less self-reliant than the metaphysics of presence. There is and never will be *the* portrayal of Auschwitz, the Holocaust, the Shoah. What we do have, must have, and will continue to have are portrayals that draw matters differently. The differing of the truth and the law upsets only the idolators—the appropriators.

By way of a prologue to this fourth retelling of my encounter with A11380's image, I will first refer to a few other images of capturing and liberation. These are also images that complicate the viewer with and in the viewed. There is, as I have argued elsewhere,[3] neither (approximate) thought nor (relative) freedom outside this complication. For some, the images I have chosen for this purpose may well seem inappropriate in association with A11380's image. Worse, some may think the introductory images pornographic and the association of images as, at best, disrespectful. My intent, however, is quite the opposite in the case of both these introductory images and that of A11380. Aware that intentions are not enough to avoid what for some may be extremely painful associations, the introductory images will not be mechanically reproduced. Instead I will only "refer" to them.

Robert Mapplethorpe's "Self Portrait 1978"[4] has provoked many negative reactions. These reactions seem to imply a certain power of objectivity on the part of the provoked. This objectivity would be the power of refusing to get what "Mapplethorpe" is getting as Mapplethorpe the photographer gives it (back) to us. These reactions also suggest that there is a freedom beyond history, culture, and social constellations—an unbound or absolute freedom. This suggested unbound transcendence recalls the neo-Platonic power which purportedly enabled one to look at victims of desire without succumbing to their (both victims' and desires') seductiveness. But is there really such a power enabling us to safely draw back from the drawing-in of imaging images such as "Self Portrait 1978"? Or is there instead a certain evocation of bound transcendence that comes only with and from within the frame?[5]

How tight, how heavy, how tortuous must our bindings become before we finally see that human freedom and responsibility have absolutely nothing to do with the binary opposition and perpetual revolutions of master and slave dialectics? I am thinking here of Mapplethorpe's "Joe 1978." Neither objectively nor subjectively, neither outside the frame nor inside the utter privacy of the interior, self-sufficient monad, can we recognize the others drawing us in to what our (philosophical) pretense of unbound transcendence has made of the world.

The self-sufficient monad has been portrayed, not disinterestedly, by Anselm Kiefer. His *Jeder Mensch steht unter seiner Himmelskugel* (*Every Man Stands beneath His Own Dome of Heaven*) (1970)[6] binds transcendence by complicating artist and portrayal together with the viewer. Looking at Kiefer's painting, we notice the very small figure within the translucent purple dome, a figure to which we are drawn until we begin to recognize ourselves—our Nazi selves. We (and both the subject and object plural must be emphasized here) are drawn and drawn-into Kiefer's fantastical construction. From the objective position of "looking-at," we are drawn-into the drawing of his imaging image. Then, however, comes the drawing-back. Yet our recoil from this seductive drawing-in comes only after the fatal moment of self-recognition. The captured self is never apart from the reflective self. Reflection would not be possible without this recoil within the moment of self-recognition. Every form of idolatry, on the other hand, begins with the posture of a transcendental subjectivity framed as an objective moment not recognized as such. The alleged immutable self-identity of the subject is always the idolatrous and exceedingly dangerous pretense of innocence and objectivity.[7]

In 1980 Kiefer said: "I do not identify with Nero or Hitler, but I have to reenact what they did just a little bit in order to understand the madness. That is why I make these attempts to become a fascist."[8] Speaking from a very different perspective, Daniel Goldhagen tells us:

> The Germans' characterization of the Jews and their beliefs about them were absolutely fantastical, the sorts of beliefs that ordinarily only madmen have of others. When it came to Jews, the proneness to wild, "magical thinking"—by the Nazi leadership and the perpetrators—and their incapacity for "reality testing" generally distinguishes them from the perpetrators of other mass slaughters.[9]

Although it is historically correct to maintain that "Germany developed along a singular path," does it follow that "German anti-Semitism was *sui generis*,"[10] that German anti-Semitism was a body of beliefs that "ordinarily only madmen have of others"? Was Kiefer's 1980 attempt to "become" a (German) fascist impossible since the German fantastical and eliminationist variety of anti-Semitism had already (mysteriously) disappeared from the scene?

During the war years and immediately after, the American public was prepared to believe that Germans were madmen. However, it is also painfully clear that such beliefs, if indeed they were held by either the American public or their elected officials, did absolutely nothing to facilitate the acceptance of the relatively few published reports of German atrocities against Jews in particular and other occupied populations in general. Of the three opinion polls taken by Gallup, the only one that referred to the news reports of the killing of two million Jews was the survey of January 1943. Yet only 47 percent of those surveyed believed the reports.[11] Then, in May 1943,

> Dorothy Day, the leader of the Catholic Worker movement, recalled speaking at a meeting that month at which "a member of the audience arose to protest defense of the Jews and to state emphatically that she did not believe the stories of atrocities. . . . She was applauded by the several hundred present." "Against such astounding unbelief," Day reflected, "the mind is stunned."[12]

What stunned Day was precisely the professed disbelief of her audience. Indeed, why would American leftist Catholics profess disbelief concerning reports of German madness? Did any anti-Semite, German or otherwise, really believe that the elimination of the Jews was either a mad idea or a fantastical plan of action? Was all of this professed disbelief anything other than a cover for a profoundly shared eliminationist anti-Semitism in debt to the historical circumstances that provided Germany with its *Sonderweg*, that is, with everything that made it possible for the Nazis to come to power and execute the task that no other government was in a viable position to undertake?

If, on the other hand, the character of genocidal-potential anti-Semitism was as profound and unique to Germans as Goldhagen claims, an exculpatory or, to employ a term with more philosophical currency, ontological line must be drawn between German perpetrators and reactions of the Western democratic powers to disclosures of Nazi genocidal programs beginning in 1939. Here is Goldhagen's formulation of this ontological divide:

> One of the remarkable features of the genocide—and this is true for police battalions, "work" camps, death marches, *Einsatzkommandos*, and the other institutions of killing—is how readily and naturally Germans, perpetrators and non-perpetrators alike, *understood* why they were supposed to kill Jews. Imagine if any western government today

were to let it be known to a large heterogenous group of ordinary citizens that it was setting out to kill, root and branch, another people. Aside from their moral reaction to the information, people would find the announcement simply incomprehensible. They would react as to the words of a madman. Anti-Semitism in Germany was such that when Germans, participants or bystanders, learned that the Jews were to be killed, they evinced not surprise, not incredulity, but comprehension. Whatever their moral or utilitarian stances towards the killing were, the annihilation of the Jews *made sense to them*.[13]

For fifty years—that is, until Goldhagen—we have been profoundly troubled that the killing of Jews also made sense not only to some leaders of the Allied armed forces, but to their governments and citizens as well. All my work for the last fifteen years has been motivated by the terrible realization that what the Nazis did to European Jewry was only possible because of widescale complicity and that Nazis, ordinary Germans, and their complicitous adversaries in war were neither madmen nor enemies of much of what is central to Western civilization.

Is it necesary, again and again, to mention the failures of the Allied powers to rescue Jews or bomb the rail lines to Auschwitz-Birkenau? These are failures that do not make any sense if Goldhagen's ontological bifurcation of anti-Semitism becomes part of what can only be generously called the normative (revisionist) generality of the Western world after Auschwitz. Do we have to rehearse, again and again, the reasons why someone like Heidegger could not even begin to come to terms with Nietzsche's *Der Antichrist*?[14] And not only Heidegger. If the real value of Goldhagen's book has to do with its reemphasizing the crucial role that theological-become-racial anti-Semitism played in the Holocaust, that value is diminished when this vicious modern and global anti-Semitism is characterized as a German madness *sui generis*. The story of the "liberation" of A11380 as well as the stories of other survivors will make sense only if we are honest enough to admit that the mass murder of Jews and the attempt to eradicate the very memory of Judaism was an ideal shared by some Germans and many other people as well. Negative reactions to Mapplethorpe's ("pornographic") photographs are a similar kind of exculpatory evasiveness. There is apparently a growing resentment against complications together with a marked preference for the "innocence" that comes only at the price of having no history or culture. Perhaps this is why so many are being "born again," and again, and again.

The story of my first encounter with A11380 begins with traces of places and powers that no longer exist. Just about a kilometer from the Staatsbibliothek, the Bildarchiv Preussischer Kulturbesitz in Berlin has a sizable collection of properly catalogued and indexed photographs of the

National Socialist period. One rainy day in early November 1994 I was granted access to the Bildarchiv's NS holdings under the subheading "Rassenhygiene."

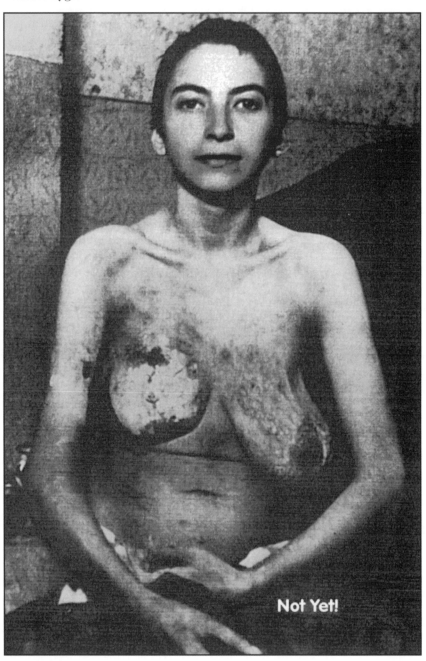

Among the hundreds of photographs I studied, this image of A11380 and the caption I have added result from my first encounter with the virtual trace of A11380 as a survivor of Nazi medical experimentation at Auschwitz (facing page). This image/text and the retelling of my first encounter thus comprise my responses to A11380's traces. The caption "Not Yet!" should be understood not only in the context of medical torture at Auschwitz, but also in the context of A11380's photographic capture by the Allied liberators of Auschwitz. A11380's imaging within and beyond the photographic frame is her seductive depropriation of her liberators' "capture" (appropriation).

Propriety and the idea of origins (and "originals") are inseparable. The photographic subject in this instance existed first as a citizen, secondly as a subject of Nazi medical experimentation at Auschwitz, and thirdly, as a "captured subject" of the Allied liberation forces. All too appropriately, her name was not mentioned. The information on the back of the photograph says only:

> Nach der Befreiung aus Auschwitz—
> eine junge Jüdin, die das Opfer
> medizinischer Experimente deutscher
> Ärzte geworden war.
> Foto: 1945.
> Orig.: Sikorski-Archiv, London

Many of you may recognize this image since a reproduction of the original photograph appears in *Auschwitz: A History in Photographs*. The text accompanying this reproduction tells us:

> A Jewish woman from Hungary, prisoner number A11380, photographed during a medical examination after the camp's liberation. Her condition was not unusual. Horrific hygiene and sanitary conditions accelerated the spread of typhus, prurigo, and phlegmons. (S. Luczko, 1945)[15]

Stanislaw Luczko, the photographer who photographed A11380, was from the Cracow Institute of Judicial Expertise. He "accompanied the inspection of Auschwitz by Professor Jan Sehn, as examining magistrate, from 11 to 25 May 1945."[16]

This description of her condition does not mention, however, the condition signified by her expression in this photograph. Nor are we informed as to whether prisoner number A11380 was told why she was being photographed. Nothing in the descriptions indicates any nonbureaucratic or ordinary human dialogue between survivor and liberators. Quite the contrary, everything we have in this case indicates business as usual with and after the liberation. Certainly the "point-and-shoot" manner in which she was photographed signifies the acceptance of a photographic practice that "captures" subjects in poses and settings that do not disturb the realist codes governing both this practice and the traditional viewing of its products. Yet what is striking about this photograph is A11380's expression, which is transmitted by the very codes her expression simultaneously reveals and transcends. A11380 is a wonderful example of bound transcendence—freedom within the frame, the imaging within and beyond the fixed image and the idolatry of objectivity. A11380 escapes her second capturing (by her "liberators") only if and when we are willing to enter the frame of her imaging, which requires, in addition, a deconstructive battle with the heavy codings of the photographic industry.

The "point-and-shoot" technology of the liberators may have been less advanced than that of the Nazis at Auschwitz, but the realistic depiction of A11380's expression reveals the failure of coding to totally determine the meaning of what is expressed through the operations of even the most rigorous of regimentations. What Quine calls "referential opacity" cannot be totally eliminated from any kind of natural (impure) language system.[17]

What can be eliminated, temporarily at least, are the differences or remainders of regimentation by means of cover concepts more or less hiding the nonidentity of what is achieved and the dominating goal of the practice itself. Deconstructively, therefore, it is always a question of reading what otherwise may seem transparent, especially in the case of photographs. Human subjectivity is formed not only by the process of sociation but also within the difference between our desire for the response of others and the socio-material conditions which mediate against or forbid the realization of that desire. We are thus subjected subjects implicated in social coordinations, material limitations, and the dialectic of forming/deforming desire. A11380 was nearly polished off, but I suspect she would agree with Adorno:

> The test of the power of language is that the expression and thing will separate in reflection. Language becomes a measure of truth only when we are conscious of the nonidentity of an expression with that which we mean.[18]

The thing in this case is A11380's expression and our expression of its meaning. The latter is provided with the caption "Not Yet!" which attempts to translate A11380's expression in the multiple context of her death camp experience and the subsequent "point-and-shoot" capturing by the liberators.

Fifty-five years after its conversion into a death camp, the consumption of Auschwitz remains a representational and sacrificial repetition of the Nazi production of a *novum* so monstrous that its level of transgression defeats any attempt to place in within the limited scope of human understanding. The Nazis attempted to surpass bound transcendence by murdering the people to whom we are indebted for many of its manifold practices. Beyond the scope of finite understanding, thinking Auschwitz thus requires entering the terrifying logic of purification that it substantiated in practice. Auschwitz and its logic are as insatiable as those to whom it representationally calls. We can refer to this terrible logic, but we will never represent it. Now as then the material and spiritual existence of Jews says "not yet" to all ideologies of perfection and redemption. Jews, in other words, introduce impurities or referential opacity into the logic of purification. And no one knows better than the survivors that it is ill advised to say "No" to those who have become one with the consumption-production imperative.

Remarkably, however, the "Not Yet!" testimonial of A11380 does bring uneasiness to the contented, does shake apathy, does contaminate perfection, and does return the redeemed back to the human and impure world. It is the most gracious of gestures by which human beings and what remains of the world are lifted above the ruination of universal consumption-production. This is precisely the worldly-spiritual sublation that the Nazis attempted to annihilate, and with it the very possibility of culture. The very best of Judaism was in that state of mind it cultivated for undoing every representation presented as absolute. On this point the Nazis did not err: Judaism and the Third Reich were irreconcilable. The Nazis thus destroyed worldly possibilities created by two thousand years of Jewish life in Europe. The question is whether they also annihilated the movement which unsettles every settled form into which we have fallen. Without this movement there is no chance of any worldly thing or being surviving and persisting against the nihilistic consumption-production of post-Auschwitz society.

In the death world of the Auschwitz galaxy the only question for those who still believe it possible to testify to the "Not Yet!" is whether any testimony can stand against the consumptive death march of the good, born-again, healthy life of socialized existence seeking a long, extended life of consumption at any cost. The Auschwitz legacy seems to grow in proportion to its memorialization. The archivalization of Auschwitz produces this uneasy, unconsumable imaging as an easy image of consumptive appropriation. "Not Yet!," conversely, *dis-eases* all appropriations of Auschwitz. On this point, the Nazis were closer to the reality and danger of Judaism than all the easy readers they appropriated in the domes of their *Gesamtkunstwerke*. All the silly little saluting figures were and remain part of a larger truth and law. A11380's seduction is more powerful than the terrible logic of unbound transcendence.

But I digress. Returning to the story of A11380, it should be pointed out that our "Not Yet!" image is not really a photograph at all. The Bildarchiv in Berlin would not give me a photographic copy of their copy of the original photograph in London. Such copies are provided only to publishers upon request. I assume that this policy is to prevent unauthorized photographic reproductions of authorized reproductions of originals. Whatever the reason, I was allowed only a xerox copy of the photographic copy, which I later scanned and prepared for laser printing in a computer imaging program. From a Platonic standpoint, "Not Yet!" is at least five times removed from reality. But "Not Yet!" is much worse than that: it undoes socially constructed realities. While reproducing this image, I was guided by the seduction of the object, i.e., by A11380's expression. Within this image, but not within the dome of its capturing by the liberators, I was and remain under the spell of its public effect, the effect of its bound transcendence, de-ranging and undoing everything produced by the purificational logic of the *Todesgesellschaft* that created its bound condition. The rule of seduction that "all that has been produced must be seduced (initiated into disappearance after having been initiated into existence)" is stronger that the law imposing production.[19] The seduction of the bound "Not Yet!" is stronger than the production of the dome of its capturing, stronger than Nazis and "point-and-shoot" liberators.

Thus, the capturing of A11380 is both a success and a failure. First of all, a success within the orbit of social, statistical exhibitionism where every properly recruited social identity knows its desires, thoughts, and representations. Baudrillard in 1983, restating Arendt's 1958 observation,[20] informs us that "the social is obsessed with itself, it becomes its own vice, its own perversion. Overinformed, it becomes obese with itself."[21] Its hypochondriacal mania of liberation is driven by a life process that accepts no limitations, no nonsense, no play, no seduction, no dangerous liaisons—especially those images which shatter its one interest and opinion, its one-ness itself:

> Society is the form in which the fact of mutual dependence for the sake of life and nothing else assumes public significance and where the activities connected with sheer survival are permitted to appear in public.[22]

A11380's expression violates the law of the social. A11380's defiant "Not Yet!" transports us beyond sheer survival and its arsenal of approved activities. Which is why A11380's expression is never remarked by her so-called liberators and their easy readers/viewers.

Paradoxically, however, the social success of capturing depends upon that which must remain stronger for the success to appear. Appearing to succeed as a repudiation of what makes appearance possible must fail to succeed. This is, I believe, what Baudrillard also means by seduction. The stronger, on the other hand, must also fail. Whatever appears

must in time disappear. Appearances, the enigmatic nature of all manifestation, reside in public spaces of plurality and nonrule. Birth, becoming, and fading away are the social philosopher's enemy. Refusing to fade
away is the social in what Baudrillard calls the mode of simulation. In
simulation, especially that of digitality and the genetic code, Being and
Nothing are inextricable in their duplicitous assault on becoming. Fundamental ontologies and theologies replace judgment as they sever the
concept's link with the nonconceptual. Coded society, despite all of its
positioning of subjects within its functional matrix, cannot mirror itself
by means of its biochemical models of simulation, which are themselves
more pornographic, more hyperreal, than pornography itself.

If truth, reference, and objective causes fade with the simulacra of
the social refusing to disappear, is this not the final victory of the realm
of appearances which Platonic philosophy so desperately wanted to
banish under the rule of the philosophic type? Is it not ironic that the
Platonic project which began with the Philosophic One against the many
under the influence of the democratic Sophists[23] should reach the critical state of perfection in which there is no truth, no reference, no God,
nothing but simulacra without causes, reasons, or any other form of
depth? Such is the price/spin of immortality.

But not yet, not quite. Seduction happens. The social Oneness is on
alert. My experience with the Bildarchiv was just one encounter with
this alertness. The state, it seems, needs to appropriate certain images.
Despite all appropriation, however, there is something like what Baudrillard calls "the evil demon of images." Did A11380 conform to the liberation situation as a kind of fatal strategy, to seduce us positioned sub-
ject-viewers by the play of resemblance? If so, is there not a wonderful
duplicity, or irony, in this conformism of image and viewing? Is it possible for liberated subjects of the social Oneness, liberated from necessity, truth, and reality, to be transformed by an image that the Oneness
does not want in unrestricted circulation?

> It [the object] *is* the mirror. It is that which returns the subject to its
> mortal transparency. So if it can fascinate or seduce the subject, it is
> because it radiates no substance or meaning of its own. The pure object
> is sovereign, because it is what breaks up the sovereignty of the other
> and catches it in its own trap. The crystal takes revenge.
>
> The subject is what has disappeared on the horizon of the subject,
> and it is from the depths of this disappearance that it envelops the sub-
> ject in its fatal strategy. It is the subject that then disappears from the
> horizon of the object.[24]

The object-image is not the mirror of any social Oneness and its simulacra but rather the reflection of the nonsovereignty of human plurality
within the public space of the play of appearances.

But how does one hold out against the utter ruination of universalized consumption-production, against the cool and hot operations of purifying the stock consumed and consuming? The violent logic of social Oneness is as insatiable as those whom it has captured by its production-consumption terrorism. The coded operations of Oneness are the same as those of Auschwitz, where they were first experimentally tested. To become marked as productive is to become marked as consumable. The immortality or nonfatality of Oneness demands the unbridled consumptive production of universal indifference: "death in Auschwitz was trivial, bureaucratic, and an everyday affair."[25] Existence reduced to socialized productive-consumptive life shares death's characteristics at Auschwitz. Without political limits, unbounded social growth produces the trivialization of death. The unbound, emancipated sign of the social transgresses all boundaries imposed and required by the human condition of plurality: "the 'free and emancipated' sign is only free to produce equivalent signifieds."[26] Socialized Oneness—Mankind—demands the eradication of all differential value.

Within the virtual domain of the unbound sign, within our *Todesgesellschaft*, is it possible to signify "not yet" or any other differential value? If, and this is my claim, A11380 signifies "Not Yet!" under the most extreme conditions, including the capturing operations of her "liberators," what is to prevent a rational analysis from reducing this claim of differential value to one of arbitrary or subjective interpretation? Nothing. "Not Yet!" is a seduction, not a provocation; it cannot dissuade, blackmail, or manipulate us. A11380 as the "Not Yet!" apparition is no longer hostage, no longer unable to represent anything, no longer obscene.

Why, then, did the authors of *Auschwitz: A History in Photographs* describe A11380's condition as "not unusual" since "horrific hygiene and sanitary conditions accelerated the spread of typhus, prurigo, and phlegmons"? This description in the place of a caption is the provocation in the face of A11380's evocation. Surely her condition includes, above all else, at the moment of the photograph, her proud and defiant refusal to concede any victory to either her tormentors or her "liberators."

Still, it would be mistaken to think that "Not Yet!" deciphers A11380's evocation. The caption "Not Yet!" is itself caught up in a dynamic strategy, and that means a strategy without finality, of the object, the photograph, and its manifold apparitions. Responding to the seduction of the object, the subject must always succumb "to the surpassing of his own objectives."[27] Seduction transforms the subject seducing the seductive object. Which is why A11380 images "Not Yet!" for all the little figures captivated by the spell of modernist redemptive themes and the terrible slaughters they invoke. Perhaps, however, the testimony of A11380 can be heard/read/seen if we refuse to pretend that we are "really" on the outside looking in/at the silly little figures of ideological indoctrination. Not because we are within but because we have identified ourselves with/as the logic of purification, are we as dangerous as silly. Yet A11380's testimony is more powerful than the logic she survived; it shows that we can be otherwise.

Notes

1. See James R. Watson, "The Second Retelling of A11380: Fatal Strategies of Transformative Image/Texts," *Bucknell Review* 42, no. 2, special issue: "History and Memory: Suffering and Art" (Fall 1998).

2. Daniel Jonah Goldhagen, *Hitler's Willing Executioners: Ordinary Germans and the Holocaust* (New York: Alfred A. Knopf, 1996).

3. James R. Watson, "Mediums of Freedom in Photogrammic Frames," in *Visibility and Expressivity*, ed. Wilhelm Wurzer (Evanston, Ill.: Northwestern University Press, 1999).

4. This and the other Mapplethorpe photographs referred to can be found in Richard Marshall, *Robert Mapplethorpe* (Boston: Little, Brown and Company, 1990).

5. A fuller treatment of my concept of bound transcendence can be found in "Auschwitz and the Limits of Transcendence," *Philosophy & Social Criticism* 18, no. 2 (1992): 163–83; "Improprietary Thinking: No More Ours or Theirs," *Contemporary Philosophy* 12, no. 12 (November/December 1989): 30–32.

6. Mark Rosenthal, *Anselm Kiefer* (Munich: Prestel-Verlag, 1987), p. 16.

7. See Theodor W. Adorno, *Negative Dialectics*, trans. E. B. Ashton (New York: The Seabury Press), Part Three: Models, especially p. 215: "Not the least of the reasons why the idea of freedom lost its power over people is that from the outset it was conceived so abstractly and subjectively that the objective social trends found it easy to bury." *Negative Dialektik* (Frankfurt am Main: Suhrkamp, 1975), p. 215.

8. Rosenthal, *Anselm Kiefer*, p. 17.

9. Goldhagen, *Hitler's Willing Executioners*, p. 412.

10. Ibid., p. 419.

11. David S. Wyman, *The Abandonment of the Jews: America and the Holocaust, 1941–1945* (New York: Pantheon Books, 1984), p. 326.

12. Ibid., p. 27. Here Wyman is quoting the *Catholic Worker*, 6/43, p. 1.

13. Goldhagen, *Hitler's Willing Executioners*, p. 403.

14. See my "Hegel's Camera Lucida: Manufactured Transparency in Holocaust Imagery," *Philosophy & Social Criticism* 21, no. 3 (1995): 113–14.

15. *Auschwitz: A History in Photographs*, ed. Teresa Swiebocka (Bloomington: Indiana University Press, 1993), p. 108.

16. Ibid., p. 45.

17. W. O. Quine, *Word and Object* (Cambridge: The MIT Press, 1960).

18. Theodor W. Adorno, *Negative Dialectics*, trans. E. B. Ashton (New York: The Seabury Press, 1973), p. 111.

19. Jean Baudrillard, *Fatal Strategies*, trans. Philip Beitchman (New York: Semiotext(e), 1990), p. 133.

20. Hannah Arendt, *The Human Condition* (Chicago: The University of Chicago Press, 1958), p. 43: "However, since the laws of statistics are perfectly valid where we deal with large numbers, it is obvious that every increase in population means an increased validity and a marked decrease of 'deviation'. Politically, this means that the larger the population in any given body politic, the more likely it will be the social rather than the political that constitutes the public realm."

21. Baudrillard, *Fatal Strategies*, p. 90.

22. Arendt, *The Human Condition*, p. 46.

23. See I. F. Stone's excellent account, *The Trial of Socrates* (Boston: Little, Brown and Company, 1988).

24. Baudrillard, *Fatal Strategies*, pp. 113–14.

25. Primo Levi, *The Drowned and the Saved*, trans. Raymond Rosenthal (New York: Vintage International, 1989), p. 148.

26. *Jean Baudrillard: Selected Writings*, ed. Mark Poster (Stanford: Stanford University Press, 1988), p. 137.

27. Baudrillard, *Fatal Strategies*, p. 189.

Part 4

History and Memory

Introduction

Klaus Dörner's "The Modernity of Nazi Euthanasia" is a reflection on new research concerning the Nazi annihilation of "lives not worthy of life"—the mentally ill, the mentally handicapped, and the feeble-minded—and the connection of this genocide and the Nazi annihilation of European Jewry. The Nazi intention to realize the Enlightenment's "dream of a society free of suffering" was first rendered operational with the sterilization and euthanasia programs—the first really "final answer" for the "Social Question" which had remained "on the agenda as the central question since the beginning of modernity around 1800." The Nazis thus provided "the kind of rational response most eagerly desired by the population." In this sense the Nazis demonstrated what the modern state and modern science are capable of in terms of a rational response to one of modernity's most pressing questions: "The final solution of the Social Question that they [Nazi doctors and psychiatrists] pursued, served the purpose of a perfection of modern society, a society free of suffering." Nazism was thus not the madness that some, like Goldhagen, have described it to be. It was and continues in mutated forms as a form of modern rationalization in pursuit of perfection by means of the elimination of all ambivalence and ambiguity *in whatever forms* these may appear.

Extending the analyses of Michel Foucault, James Bernauer's "Sexuality in the War against the Jews: Perspectives from the Work of Michel Foucault" explores the sexual and erotic dimensions of fascism against the background of Christian, primarily Catholic, disciplinary regulations and formations of sexuality. All too often the success of the latter resulted in "a permanent submissiveness or stimulated an intense yearning to get beyond the sexual guilt of Christianity, a state which Nazism held out as one of its promises and, in case after case, accomplishments." The psychopolitics of Nazism was also an erotic politics that became more effective as a identificational recruitment device than the Christian obsession with eroticism's demonic force. Nazi erotic politics was certainly disciplinary, but its boundaries were not drawn on and within the believer's own body. Quite the contrary: "the extreme victimization of the Jews by the Nazis comes from the position into which they were placed on the cultural field of modern sexuality." The demonic was located not in the healthy erotic body but in that which corrupts it—the Jewish body, "weakened by deviant genitalia and unrestrained sexual appetite." A healthy sexual body was the antipode of the Jewish hypersexualized, promiscuous body. Thus we are given the image of the warrior-body paradigm of Nazi discipline and its antipode—the homosexual (Jewish, Bolshevik) body and its predisposition toward physical and mental illness. In this way the Nazis created a post-Christian ethic within a culture shaped by Christianity where "one's sense of worth was through self-denial and surrender to the vocation one was given by providence."

Dan Stone's "Affect and Modernity: Notes Toward an Enquiry into the Origins of the Holocaust" stresses the "disruptive excess," the terrifyingly visceral aspect, of the Holocaust, "an excess which is assimilable to conventional discourse" and thus an excess which questions our notions of historical truth and rationality. Therefore, enquiry into the role played by modernity in the Nazi Holocaust is necessary but not sufficient. The focus of Stone's analyses is, accordingly, not "modernity theorists," but rather theorists whose emphasis on the modern aspects of the Holocaust is not "at the expense of the horror of the regime's accomplishments"—Götz Aly, Susanne Heim, Detlev Peukert, and Zygmunt Bauman. The purpose of Stone's analyses is not to deny the modernity theorists' thesis that "modernity is perfectly compatible with the most horrific acts," which is correct. It is rather that such a thesis dismisses the Holocaust by all too neatly wrapping it up in a "simply determined historicization." Heterogeneous energies have not been assimilated, sublimated, or eliminated by modernity and its "progress." The task which our postmodern condition poses is not "the quietism of the panacea-seeking New Age movement," but finding outlets "for those energies which activate bureaucratic structures and propel them into genocide."

Alan Milchman and Alan Rosenberg propose a "community of memory" which is prospective rather than memorializing in their "Remembering and Forgetting: The Social Construction of a Community of Memory of The Holocaust." Milchman and Rosenberg reexamine Arno Mayer's concern that a "rage for memory" in opposition to the Nazi attempt to eradicate memory "can become neurasthentic and disabling," as well as lead to retrogressive political consequences. What is needed, therefore, is the delicate balance Nietzsche recommended between remembrance and forgetting, a balance that can be found only in a sense of history directed toward the future rather than the past. Sacrificing the future to the past in a cult of memory, death, and kitsch can only result in an institutionalization of the death-world bequeathed to us by the Nazis. What a futural sense of history requires, however, is the possibility of "refunctioning" of collective memories of races, nations, religions, ethnicities, and classes which inevitably clash and mutate in the public spaces generated by the processes of modernization and the political movements which attempt to memorialize specific memories and direct the clash of memories. The critical point made by Milchman and Rosenberg is that it is not possible for anyone to take the political high ground and claim that their memorialization and direction has the character of objectivity or authentic historical reproduction. Following Foucault, they argue that truth is always a performative politics of truth. What must be challenged is any attempt to establish final truths: "The project of a community of memory of the Holocaust therefore also confronts modern historiography's claim to scientific univocity." The real scientific task is to turn to a community of memory with many voices and "experiments in thinking the Holocaust."

Proceeding from (within) Blanchot's *L'Entretien infini* (The Infinite Conversation), Raj Sampath's "Time's Impossibility: The Holocaust and the Historicity of History" also explores the relation between the historicity of the Holocaust and the historicity of "History." The ontological disruption of history which is the event of the Holocaust extends a radical form of questioning since this event "continues to shock the past that came before it and the future that will come." This radical questioning, which is also the problematic in Blanchot's "Being Jewish," must open within the heart of ruination because this event, the Holocaust, "marked the 'final' attempt to destroy the movement known as exile." Other alternatives (ancient, Christian, modern) remain outside the event and thus deny the very movement which was ruined by the Holocaust. Against these murderous and exculpatory alternatives, Sampath, with Blanchot, claims that the "murder of time *in* history [the Holocaust] is haunted by this dead time's return to a deeper historicity." No dogmatic metaphysics or theology can usurp the universe of time hiding within the intertwined historicity of the Holocaust and the historicity of History. It is within this universe of time that there begins another exile, "another commitment to the infinite."

A.R./J.R.W.

The Modernity of Nazi Euthanasia

Klaus Dörner

Since 1980 there has been an exponential increase of both published memoirs of survivors of the Nazi persecutions and publications concerned with the Nazi annihilation of the mentally ill, the mentally handicapped, and other sections of the population. Previously these latter groups of Nazi victims were basically never considered significant by historians for the understanding of Nazi terror; they were just as little taken into account regarding the coming-into-being of the Holocaust. In Germany since 1980 there have been working teams of historians and other people working with mentally ill and mentally handicapped. The publications involving these working teams demonstrate that by taking into account Nazi euthanasia, a more complete understanding of both National Socialism and the Holocaust becomes possible. If Daniel Goldhagen, for instance, had sought the explanation for the existence of a widespread annihilatory mentality among the German population not only in anti-Semitism, but also in the general willingness to annihilate the mentally ill and handicapped, he would have had no problem finding extensive empirical evidence.

In the course of the following discussion I want to acquaint the reader with some reflections on this new research concerning the connection between Nazi genocide and the Nazi Holocaust. The Nazis conducted not only a destructive war outside, but also within Germany with the goal of modernization by means of a rationalization of the social and world order. According to the self-conception of those responsible for Nazism:

> We want to prove to the world that a society summoning up the bru-
> tality only once in order to free itself of its entire social ballast is eco-
> nomically and militarily invincible and can realize Enlightenment's
> dream of a society free of suffering.

Similarly, according to the secretary of state of the Federal Ministry of
the Interior, Gütt:

> So we yearn for the time when there will be no more mentally ill and
> idiots in the world, neither in institutions nor outside, and it would have
> to be magnificent to live in a world in which, to be sure, everything else
> would be perfect, too.[1]

This intention makes the Nazis highly modern. The Nazis actually settled upon and provided the final answer for the so-called Social Question, one that had remained on the agenda as the central question since
the beginning of modernity around 1800, and the Nazis did this by providing the kind of rational response most eagerly desired by the population. The "Social Question" came into being in the course of the eighteenth century as enlightened burghers began to found all social relations exclusively on reason and rationality in order to free themselves of
all irrationality and to admit only autonomous rather than heteronomous human beings. Thus, they inevitably created the "Social Question": "What are we to do with human beings who are not as reasonable,
rational, efficient, and capable of living in a community as we are, and
who are guided rather by irrational motifs, and who are asocial, disruptive, and heteronomous? What is their purpose? And what do we want
that they cost us?"

As is well known, the temporary response, valid for the beginning of
modernity, was to be found in J. Bentham, the father of utilitarian rationality. In his writing *Panopticon* (Dublin, 1791) he operationalized the
"Social Question" by proposing extensive networks of "inspection-
houses" for the future whose architecture was supposed to guarantee the
greatest possible, near-perfect control of the greatest possible number of
people in the cheapest possible manner. He suggested the spider's web as
a model, according to which an inspector positioned in a control tower
could ideally control many corridors at which, according to purpose,
cells, beds, or workplaces were to be located. Variations of this basic idea
formed the social landscape of modernity. For out of the destruction of
the irrational, premodern spatial unity of dwelling, living, and working,
there emerged an extensive network of factories and, later, offices for the
healthy, efficient irrational/heteronomous human beings. On the other
hand, the rational, autonomous burghers created for the ill, handicapped, asocial, and disruptive irrational/heteronomous human beings

extensive networks of mental asylums, institutions for the mentally handicapped, asylums for cripples, orphanages, old-age homes, and prisons. Accordingly, the autonomous burghers let themselves be guided by the idea that the healthy and efficient irrational human beings could be best improved/reformed and brought to reason by optimal economic exploitation, while their complementary compassion was directed at the ill and handicapped irrational human beings: It was through pedagogical, therapeutic measures that they were supposed to make see reason in the social institutions by means of the expert knowledge that had been formed there. "Irrational" human beings who obstinately opposed their rationalization were, of necessity, to remain all their lives in institutions (later called "total"). Thus such human beings were to be made invisible so that the ideal of a possibly total rational society consisting only of autonomous beings free of suffering could be realized.[2]

Since in the case of failure, rational programs tend to radicalize themselves according to the motto "more of the same," it is not surprising that some one hundred years later (around 1890), due to a new thrust of rationalization, more brutal manners with regard to "failures" were found both via the medicalization of the Social Question and the definition of the ill irrational beings as hereditary defectives for the purposes of realizing the enlightened goal of a society free of suffering. In the clutches of a medicine that had become increasingly socially formative and had already acquired the traits of a mediocracy, the sick irrational beings came to be distinguished simply as curable or incurable. With respect to the incurably ill, two eliminatory strategies began to take shape.

First, there was the strategy of making the "incurables" disappear by preventive measures, specifically and especially, by sterilization. August Forel, at that time certainly the world's best-known psychiatrist, was the pioneer of this approach and later substantiated this method for bringing the Social Question to a final solution in the following manner:

We do not aim at all at creating a new human race, a superman, but only at eliminating gradually the defective subhumans by means of arbitrary sterility of the carriers of pathogens, thus causing better, more social, healthier and happier human beings to an increasing reproduction.[3]

The second eliminatory way derives its rational foundation from the liberal kernel of the self-conception of autonomous burghers. The enlightened struggled for the right to suicide, and then later for the right to killing on request, that is, for active euthanasia. The latter was justified in the following manner: "Only the right to my death is the ultimate proof that I am really master over my life and that I am completely autonomous. If, as an autonomous burgher, I am always entitled to this right, how much more must the incurably ill, heteronomous human beings with their certainly senseless suffering and deprived of all possibility of ever becoming a moral subject have this very same right? The state has to take responsibility for them; it is the moral obligation of the state, an act of compassion, of mercy, to release those unfortunate ones from their suffering."

We find this train of thought, supposedly irrefutable on rational grounds, in many variations and in systematic dispersal in all modern societies after 1890. This kind of thinking has been interrupted only by the recognition of what the modern state and modern science is capable of, most especially by the example of Nazi Germany. However, in Germany this recognition was postponed by the imposition of a taboo concerning the Nazi period, a taboo lasting about ten years longer in Germany than in most other societies.

The doctors and psychiatrists of National Socialism followed in their subjective self-conception the same humane, enlightened ideas of modernity. The final solution of the Social Question that they pursued, served the purpose of a perfection of modern society, a society free of suffering. Admittedly, all patients of psychiatric hospitals, both the curably ill and the incurably ill, were also killed in Poland and in the Soviet Union. But in the destructive war inside Germany, this kind of killing was done on the basis of scientific differentiations. The gassing of a calculated 70,000 mentally ill and mentally handicapped persons affected expressly only the incurably ill, the, as it were, tragic remainders from prescientific times that could no longer profit from the blessings of modern scientific therapy. According to this differentiation, the "irrational" human being was to be granted the "mercy death" only in the event his incurability was established scientifically. This rational, selective procedure, intended to support the curably ill and release the incurably ill, was most fully realized in the Nazi program of child euthanasia. It was, however, envisioned as a procedure for the future, as is clear from the 1940 bill on euthanasia. Current practice in the Netherlands roughly corresponds to this program.

National Socialist doctors even risked a prognosis: If the population was brought up long enough according to the rationality of modernity, if they emancipated themselves from Christian and other heteronomies, they, would demand in the case of suffering and incurability, voluntarily and on their own initiative, their autonomous right to be given death by their doctors. Euthansia is, incidentally, also an economical good. Today's increasing demands for active euthanasia seem to concede validity to the prognosis of those responsible during the time of Nazism.

A current example is indicative. Until five years ago and all over Europe, persons in a waking coma had the same right to life as all others. Admittedly, coma patients are severely brain-damaged. They can, on the other hand, breathe on their own and carry on an exchange on a basic level with their environment. They are not dying. Now, however, they may be killed by withdrawal of food in the Netherlands (a practice that goes unpunished) and in Switzerland (according to the medical profession's guidelines for euthanasia). At the time of this writing, the General Medical Council in Germany is considering adoption of the guidelines for euthanasia from Switzerland. If adopted, it will again be possible in Germany, for the first time since 1945, to grant euthanasia to human beings who are not dying. This reinstated active euthanasia could be extended in fluid transitions to other severely brain-damaged human beings, that is, to irreversibly demented patients with Alzheimer's disease or , with the suitable brain-organic definition of disease, to those mentally ill or mentally handicapped declared scientifically as incurable by biomedicine. Perhaps the time would then be ripe here for the rationality of modernity behind the bill of those responsible for Nazism—on which Heydrich collaborated on the behalf of the SS—be taken out of the drawer, publicly discussed and implemented again. This is precisely what the Nazis planned for the post-war period. The first two paragraphs of the 1940 NS-bill for euthanasia state:

> Paragraph 1: Whoever suffers from an incurable disease disturbing/troubling himself and others and leading undeniably to death, can, on express request and with the approval of a particularly authorized doctor, receive euthanasia from a doctor.

> Paragraph 2: The life of a patient who, due to incurable mental illness, otherwise would require care all his life, can, imperceptible to him, be ended by means of medical measures.[4]

Recently, several books (notably Z. Bauman[5]) have described the epoch of modernity in a way similar to what I have attempted, albeit with different metaphors. According to Bauman, for example, the project of modernity from 1800 to the most recent past has consisted of the attempt to totally dissolve all ambilvalence by means of rationalization. He describes National Socialism, anti-Semitism, and the Holocaust, accordingly, as symptoms of this process of modernization. However, according to his socio-historical analysis, this project has failed since the number of ambivalences has actually increased with attempts to dissolve them rationally. As regards the current passage into a postmodern society, he thus sees only the possibility of learning to live with and love these increasing ambivalences.

Translated by Erik M. Vogt

Notes

1. T. Bastian, *Arzt, Mörder, Helfer* (Paderborn, 1982).
2. I described this social process more fully in *Tödliches Mitleid* (Gütersloh: Verlag Jakob van Hoddis, 1993).
3. Ibid., p. 32.
4. Ibid., p. 60.
5. Z. Bauman, *Dialektik und Ordnung* (Hamburg, 1992).

Sexuality in the War against the Jews
Perspectives from the Work of Michel Foucault

James Bernauer

If my title indicates a desire to utilize the work of Michel Foucault in understanding the Shoah, it is because his analyses are invited by Nazism's demolition of the presumed barriers between the social and the personal, the private and the public, the erotic and the political. In two earlier studies I have indicated how Foucault's methods might enable us to examine the murderous operation of a specific National Socialist ethic.[1] In this paper I wish to exhibit the special relevance of Foucault's analysis of the domain of modern sexuality for students of the Holocaust. I do this not by direct commentary on his sexuality texts but by trying to move his project forward, that ambitiously conceived study of sexuality that produced but a few fragments before Foucault's untimely death in 1984.[2] I will indicate how Christian eroticism was involved in the Nazi destruction of Jewish and gay people and the important role which sexuality played in the war against the Jews.[3] Inasmuch as this theme might offend some, I would like to offer an explanation for my choice. It was at a Holocaust conference several years ago that I was first made aware of the strong negative reactions that could be produced by comments that placed Jews and gays together in their experience under National Socialism. During the final panel discussion in which the conference's major speakers were present, a young man from the audience asked very politely why none of the presentations had dealt with Nazi crimes against homosexuals. In response, one of the panelists erupted in a burning anger and scolded the man for even suggesting that there was something comparable in the destiny of the two groups. The large audience was clearly embarrassed by the outburst and other questioners were immediately recognized. As I have come to discover, the panelist's reaction is not unique. For example, in a recent issue of *Holocaust and Genocide Studies*, a distinguished student of the Shoah opens his review of the English translation of Günther Grau's book *Hidden Holocaust?: Gay and Lesbian Persecution in Germany, 1933–45* with this sentence: "I hesitated to read this work for I was disturbed by its title that seemed to equate the fate of gays and lesbians under the Third Reich with the fate of the Jews, who were subject to total annihilation."[4]

I think that we could probably all agree that there are many inappropriate ways to speak about the victimization of these two groups, especially in terms that would fail to do justice to the unique magnitude of Jewish losses and the special place which Jews occupied as objects of Nazi hate. And yet I think that there might be a much deeper issue which we should acknowledge in the resistance to dealing with the two groups together. First, there has been a long tradition in political writing which has claimed that many prominent Nazis were in fact homosexuals and, thus, the gay community is more victimizer than victim. Among anti-fascist circles, homosexuality was commonly regarded as another form of "anti-socialist individualism." Adorno expressed a common leftist sentiment in his well-known remark from the *Minima Moralia*: "Totalitarianism and homosexuality belong together."[5] From the other side of the political spectrum, some conservative opposition to Hitler explicitly identified National Socialism with homosexuality: one thinks of Thomas Mann, for example, who, while well disposed to the gay community, also saw the fascist military cult of the heroic as essentially homosexual.[6] And then, of course, Nazi ideology itself declared homosexuality a form of revolutionary practice which had as its objective the destruction of morality in general and of the race and family in particular, a form of "sexual bolshevism" as it was called.

I believe that an even more significant reason for resisting some form of commonality of Jewish and gay experience is that an analysis of both together leads us to a direct consideration of the sexual and erotic dimensions of fascism. The anxiety about that consideration has several faces. Let me say right off that there is a very justifiable fear that dealing with sexuality risks falling into Wilhelm Reich's simplistic interpretation or, far worse, threatens an inexcusable trivialization of mass murder. And that threat is not just potential. We know that, along with serious cinematic efforts to treat sexuality, there has also been a pornographic interest in Fascist eroticism.[7] A number of years ago Susan Sontag asked how it was possible that Nazi Germany had become erotically attractive for many in contemporary Western societies, especially as a symbol of "sexual adventurism."[8] And then there are those interpretations of Hitler's life which have argued a direct relationship between his ideology and a presumed sexual pathology.[9] The thought that Hitler's sexual life could be at the source of Nazi crimes seems almost obscene to entertain.

More intellectually substantial a barrier to confrontation with fascism's erotic dimension than fear of trivializing Nazi horror, though, is that there seems to be no need to resort to it. Even when the sexual presence is recognized, its marginality is also affirmed.[10] I think that perhaps the principal reason for evading serious investigation of the sexual dimension in the period of National Socialism is the extraordinary success of Hannah Arendt's depiction of Adolf Eichmann and its thesis on the banality of evil, namely, the view that Nazi crimes were executed as a result of a certain "thoughtlessness." To understand Eichmann, there is no need to explore his emotional and affective life. Let me say outright that I stand in awe of Hannah Arendt's philosophical achievement and I admire much in *Eichmann in Jerusalem*. At the same time I have become suspicious about the grounds and effect of her portrayal's popularity. Has Hannah Arendt's Eichmann turned us away from a scrutiny of our passions, especially our erotic ones, by leaving the more consoling message that it is our reluctance to think that will lead us into disaster?[11] I believe it has, but she bears only partial responsibility for that. We know from Arendt's consideration of the later trials of those who worked at Auschwitz that she had begun to recognize something else beside the banality of evil. To quote her: "the chief human factor in Auschwitz was sadism, and sadism is basically sexual." She goes on to say that the "smiling reminiscences of the defendants . . . and their unusually high spirits throughout . . . reflects the sweet remembrance of great sexual pleasure, as well as indicating blatant insolence."[12] For present purposes, however, I am concerned not with sexual sadism but rather with Christian eroticism, its braiding of love, desire, and sensuality. I will thus sketch how a Christian, particularly Catholic, experience of sexuality and a style of moral formation that was its issue might have contributed to the popular appeal of National Socialism, to the identification of two groups of its enemies, as well as to the savagery of its violence.

How was it possible for National Socialism to be so successful in capturing the minds and hearts of so many either as committed believers or as tolerant bystanders? More than fifty years after the collapse of the Third Reich, the question continues to demand raising, especially in this season of Holocaust denial. The Nazi period forces us all to confront our dangerous ethical selves: how we fashion ourselves, or are fashioned, intellectually, ethically, spiritually to appreciate or refuse certain types of moral appeal. Such character is the product of what might be called practices of the self, practices which define how an individual comes to feel that a matter warrants moral concern and what steps one is obligated to take in response to that moral signal. Certainly it is the case that National Socialism appropriated a ready-made set of national virtues— honesty, diligence, cleanliness, dependability, obedience to authority, mistrust of excess.[13] Still, if we are to understand why these virtues came to be so characteristic and why people were so prepared to tolerate evil, we must interrogate the dynamics of the spiritual formation which German culture had passed down. We must question our dangerous moral selves. But why should they be thought of as dangerous? A study of National Socialism brings new insight to this question and not just as a historical matter or an exclusively German concern.

To speak of spiritual life at this time might seem to miss the mark when one remembers the brutal reality of Nazi deeds. What has to be faced, though, is that the beginning of the Hitler regime coincided with a passionate desire among the German people for a spiritual renewal, indeed, for a politics of spirit which National Socialism attempted to define. On the eve of Hitler, Germany was haunted by the ghostly presence of a deceased generation still calling for some sort of redemption for its ultimate sacrifice in the Great War. At this distance it is difficult to appreciate how promising a year 1933 was expected to become. In fact, Paul Tillich at the time accused perhaps the most prominent of his theological colleagues (Emanuel Hirsch) of associating the year so closely with 33, the traditional date of Jesus's death and resurrection, that the year of Hitler's coming to power was given the "meaning of an event in the history of salvation."[14] What has to be acknowledged is that there was an intense atmosphere of spiritual transformation that year. Philosophers and theologians felt as though a special invitation had been extended to their talents. What I find so chilling is that the map of night—Auschwitz, Dachau, Buchenwald, Mauthausen and the other graveyards—was drawn in part by the moods, ideas, and plans which grew in a supposed terrain of day and light—that extraordinary and proud kingdom of German universities: Berlin, Munich, Frankfurt, Tübingen, Freiburg. To look in detail at how this spiritual moment was perceived would go beyond the scope of this paper. For now, let me merely say that many philosophers and theologians regarded it as a moment of crisis, and I would claim that that crisis's most important element was how one was to relate to one's self, how one might affirm oneself as spiritually worthwhile. But to speak of spirit in the context of a culture which still possessed deep roots in Christianity was also to discuss flesh; cravings for spirit inevitably connect to a discourse of sin, sensuality, and sexuality. If spirit expressed vitality and creative force, flesh possessed many satanic features, assaulting reason and proclaiming human weakness. Here we may have, however, perhaps the source of Christianity's own greatest weakness in its encounter with Nazism, for much pathology seemed to flourish in modern religious culture's charting of sexuality.[15] It is the charting with which I am concerned, not the sexual morality that may be put forward as a response to it. And I do emphasize this: I am not accusing a code of morality but rather the ethical-spiritual foundations of the very self who finds suitable a type of morality or its overthrow. Having selected sexuality as the privileged route to moral status, the churches did not create a very sophisticated palette of insight into it. The broodings of moral theology were isolated from the traditions of Christian spiritual theology and, thus, those interrogations of extreme experiences that might have enabled it to cope better with the psychic forces Nazism was evoking.[16] I will not repeat the sad series of Christian statements from this period which denounced the social permissiveness of co-education, and its supposed lack of concern for the lust in children and adolescents; nor those which denounced the immodesty intrinsic to public swimming pools; nor those many warnings about the dangers of nudity and male friendships. This determination to exorcise eroticism reveals a detestation of the body's desires for pleasure; it encourages such a fierce self-hatred that we can understand why one of the major resisters to Nazism, Helmuth James von Moltke, found one thing to praise in Nazi culture: it taught, he said, a reverence for what is below us—"blood, ancestry, our bodies."[17]

While Christian moral formation was inadequate, in my judgment, to the sexual domain, the Church's anxiety about it did not come from nowhere and did reflect an awareness that for a century there had been a new sexual challenge in German culture. The religious sponsorship of, or at least association with, most major social events in a person's life at that time as well as practices such as confession did allow the Church to hear the effect upon an individual's intimate life of large cultural forces.[18] Historians and philosophers have indicated the many different factors which thrust sexual change into the center of moral crisis: the Napoleonic period's relaxation of legal constraints enlarged the menu of sexual desire and practice; the secularization of society reduced the authority of priests and their traditions as well as encouraged a disassociation between morality and religion; industrialization placed new stresses upon the family; the very organization of society was taking life and its functions as objects of scrutiny and control.[19] The Church, however, saw in a certain relaxation of sexual moral codes a decline of faith and, thus, a historical intimacy between Christian existence and the spirit-flesh struggle was reconfirmed and strengthened, now with modern sexuality as its unchallenged center. The pivotal role which Christian moral formation conferred upon disciplining sexuality as a result of this had two major consequences.

First, it exposed Christians to a Nazism that could be thought of as either ethically allied with Christianity or as a liberation from religion's inadequacy to the richness of human life. National Socialism found the religious obsessiveness with sexuality in moral formation to be helpful in a variety of ways: it sustained the emphasis on those secondary virtues which made people so compliant; it habituated people to an atmosphere of omnipresent sinfulness which seemed to grow with every step beyond childhood. It educated people into a moral pessimism about themselves and what they might be able to achieve. While it has been frequently acknowledged that an absence of German self-confidence was a precondition for Hitler's successful career, the focus of responsibility has normally been given to economic factors; the moral-spiritual dimensions should not be ignored.[20] This was all too often an education into self-contempt, into a fearfulness which was a paralysis of the inner self. Frequently the sexual dimension of the person was treated as an animal instinct. Such paralysis subverted self-affirmation as a Christian practice. It is this subversion which lies behind the primacy given to obedience as a virtue, and an extraordinary insensitivity to the demands of conscience. Many religious and moral practices established a profound alienation from one's self and one's desires. And this self-alienation was also a mode of alienation from the public space: the model for dealing with moral difficulty was set by sexuality: avoidance of danger and cultivation of an ethereal interiority. Often this trained people into a permanent submissiveness or stimulated an intense yearning to get beyond the sexual guilt of Christianity, a state which Nazism held out as one of its promises and, in case after case, accomplishments.

Nazism in effect put forward the bold project of overcoming the dualisms fostered by religion: body versus soul, flesh versus spirit. National Socialism spoke to—and not just flattered—the German tradition of and pride in inwardness, the *Innerlichkeit* which advocated a strenuous self-cultivation.[21] As we know, philosophers rushed to that banner and one observer at the time spoke of a "Blitzphilosophie" (lightning-philosophy) to describe the rapid advance of philosophers toward the mission of supposedly deepening Nazism's spiritual foundations and appeal.[22] But the Nazi revolution bound this celebration of inwardness, of the German spirit, together with a profound affirmation of one's historical moment, of one's own German body, social and personal. It was to be praised for its health, its beauty, its utility, and, most of all, as the temple for the transmission of biological life. The depth of its sexual morality could be put forward as what is most distinctive of Aryan ethics.[23] In Nazism we have a psychopolitics which is also an erotic politics.

Its erotic politics was a strategy of sabotage against alternative relations to sexuality. It made a foe of the sexual libertinism of the Weimar Republic and of the Soviet Union. The sexual laxity which had been identified in the past with that ancient enemy, the French, now was tied to Communism's relaxation of legal restraints.[24] After it had replaced the Weimar Republic, the Third Reich mounted a widespread campaign of sexual purification: denunciations of pornography, homosexuality, and any eroticism not governed by the desire for procreation, for those would eclipse the central status which sexuality had on the "battlefield of life."[25] This crusade against eroticism was terribly attractive for German Christians—and, I might add, made Hitler appear as a force for moral renewal to Christians in the United States as well.[26] Catholic anxiety about Communism included its perceived sexual license and hostility to family values. In addition, there was even a tendency to look for supporting arguments for traditional Catholic sexual morality in the ideas of the eugenics movement.[27] Thus, on the eve of the Second World War and the Holocaust, Germany was blanketed with a campaign for decency. But National Socialism was far more cunning than most expected. The campaign for decency was by no means an acceptance of Christian codes. National Socialism constructed a post-Christian erotic. While Church leaders were regularly denouncing the dangers of immodesty, Nazi culture was celebrating the beauty of the nude body and the benefits of exhibiting it—from galleries of art to the joyful gatherings of youth. The Nazis were very successful in portraying church views as hopelessly prudish, the Church's sexual teaching as unrelentingly hostile to the joys of sexual life and in encouraging young people to look elsewhere for a wise understanding of their erotic desires.[28] One might have hoped that their lengthy pondering over of sexual activities would confer upon Christians a particular sophistication in grasping some of the subtle tones in Nazism's sexual propaganda. I have found few signs of such proficiency.[29] It is as if the long stress on the natural law had made them deaf to the changing sounds of historically contingent evil. Indeed, there seems a special blindness, a general failure to recognize how demonic the unrelenting stress on eroticism's demonic force could also be.

The catastrophe of this moral formation had a second face. In that endless searching after the reasons why the Jews were so victimized by the Nazis, why so many collaborated in their murder, and especially why so many stood aside and failed to do what could have been done, I propose that this issue of sexuality gives an essential answer. Before the Jews were murdered, before they were turned away from as not being one's concern, the Jew had already been defined as spiritless, on the one hand, and sexually possessed, erotically charged, on the other. In contrast to that special German inwardness which I mentioned earlier, the Jew was portrayed not only as empty of spirit but as an enemy of it. German philosophers worried about what was called a "Verjudung" of "deutschen Geistesleben," that is, a "Jewification" of German spiritual life.[30] The Jewish intellectual was both a materialist and a pharisaic rationalist in comparison with German depth thinking. Beyerchen has shown how scientists such as Einstein were thought of as saboteurs of the more spiritual Aryan physics.[31] Deprived of spirit, the Jew was defined in Nazi propaganda as essentially carnal, as excessively sexual, indeed as boundlessly erotic, whose conduct was not under the control of the moral conscience.[32] Lust robbed the Jews of reason and, thus, reduced them to an animal level, a status which would soon come to be reflected in the forms of Nazi torture.

Some roots of the Nazi portrayal lie in Christianity: Heiko Oberman has pointed out that, in accounting for anti-Judaism at certain periods, disparagement of Mary's virginity was more significant than such charges as the stealing of consecrated hosts and ritual murders.[33] I mention this out of more than historical interest. While he was a prisoner at Nuremberg, Julius Streicher, Nazism's principal ideological anti-Semite, told the psychologist G. M. Gilbert that he had exploited in his propaganda the denigration of Mary which failure to accept Jesus's divinity entails.[34] I am not able here to develop the potential significance of this line of propaganda except to note the inadequacy of a frequently appearing model in which Christian anti-Judaism and modern anti-Semitism are placed on a chronological calendar where the former is superseded by the latter. In fact, they coexisted in the Nazi period and blended in ways that have yet to be adequately mapped. Nevertheless, with that said, the extreme victimization of the Jews by the Nazis comes from the position into which they were placed on the cultural field of modern sexuality.[35] That field need not be isolated, however, from religious discourses and practices. I do want to identify, however, the elements of that modern field. First, there is the *body*: the Nazis opposed their view of a trained, classically beautiful body to the Jewish body, weakened by deviant genitalia and unrestrained sexual appetite.[36] Secondly, regarding *children*, there was the juxtaposition of an idealized German innocence with the Jewish invention of a childhood sexuality that was believed to reflect both an actual sexual precocity and Talmudic allowance for intergenerational sex.[37] *Der Stürmer*, Streicher's newspaper, utilized medieval tales of Jewish ritual slaughter of Christian children in accounts which stressed acts of torture and the sexual satisfaction they implied. In addition, he emphasized cases of child molestation which involved Jews.[38] Thirdly, in contrast to the image of the German *mother*, who delighted in offspring and their care, and who felt threatened by the sexual advances of Jewish men, especially medical doctors, there was the Jewish *woman*, who was inclined to neurosis, attracted to prostitution, and filled with craving for emancipation from the home.[39] The Nuremberg laws prohibited sexual relations between Aryan and Jew in part to prevent contamination by syphilis which was identified with Jews. Fourthly, Jews harbored all sorts of sexual *perversions*, especially homosexuality. These perversions stand behind the Jewish invention of psychoanalysis and sexology.[40] For the Nazis, the Jewish menace was a constructed sexual experience, hidden and yet omnipresent, camouflaging in other innocuous symptoms the secret causality perverting Aryan life.

These sexual categories are not static but function pervasively and dynamically within an ethical field defined as a life-and-death struggle taking place between the healthy life force of Aryan blood and the dis-

ease-laden Semitic death substance.[41] For Heinrich Himmler, the quality
of blood was the greatest legacy that history's struggle for existence had
bequeathed the German Volk; its protection was his mission. To quote
Himmler: "We had the moral right (*moralische Recht*), we had the duty
(*Pflicht*) toward our people, to kill this people which wanted to kill us."[42]
And here is Streicher, who wrote that the Nuremberg decrees were only
part of a wider struggle: "and we shall only get through this battle [with
world Jewry] victoriously if every member of the German people knows
that his very existence is at stake."[43] This final element in modern sexual
culture may certainly be described as racist, but it also relates to the
Christian sexual discourse in at least two ways. First, one might argue
that the purity ideal of Nazi eugenics is rooted in Christian paradigms:
with "the growth of rationalism and science, rather than seeing the disappearance of the next world, there is an elision of this world and the
next. All human possibilities of perfection once sited firmly in the next
existence, now become situated in this existence."[44] Secondly and more
importantly, however, this life-and-death struggle paradigm shows the
legacy of that spirit-flesh struggle in which all sexual sin was grave or
mortal, thus condemning the sinner's soul to the death of eternal damna-
tion. Within this perspective, we can see that the individual German's
affirmation of the worth of his sexual life was the ratification of the
Aryan people's own biological value as well as the pledge of enmity
against that depicted reckless and primitive sexuality into which Jews
are considered to fall because the Nazis claimed they are incapable of
self-sacrificing love. The saga of history mirrors the story of one's personal struggle with sexual temptation; each person's soul enshrines the
clash of biological history itself. The very notion of a German-Jewish
assimilation was an erotic nightmare in which both the German's individual and social bodies are penetrated by a foreign, hostile sexual force.

Up to this point I have not said much about the Nazi war on gay
people. While there can be no comparison with the Jews as far as the
numbers of victims are concerned (approximately ten thousand gays
were murdered in camps), there is no denying the sadistic torture imposed upon the individuals concerned.[45] And, like the Jews, gays possessed an intrinsic place in the Nazi logic of sexuality. Although, as Josef
Meisinger, the head of the Reich Office for the Combating of Homosexuality and Abortion, claimed in a 1937 speech, "homosexuality is alien in
kind to the Nordic race," he also acknowledged that the vice seemed to
have a particular appeal for Germans: After the First World War homosexuality "became so widespread that people in England and France
called it the 'German disease.' "[46] Although Nazi anxiety about homosexuality looked backward at the war's experience of all male societies and
at the emergence of gay personal and political associations during the
Weimar Republic, its major focus was toward the future and the plans for

a vast army and a racial utopia. Hate toward the gay articulated itself on the modern sexual map. As opposed to the warrior *body* to which Nazi discipline was committed, the gay's body was weak and effeminate but also seductive for the yearnings of an irresponsible carnality. Like *women*, he was more prone to physical and mental illness; for some Nazis, including Heinrich Himmler, the homosexual's very existence in Germany was tied to the masculinization of women. To quote him: "I regard it as a catastrophe when we so masculinize women that over time the gender difference or polarity disappears. Then the road to homosexuality is not far off."[47] The gay man's identity was most often defined in terms of the pervert and the child. As a *pervert*, he was by nature disordered, and was a source of disease and the embodiment of promiscuity. He was an omnipresent danger to the *child* because he disguised himself often as a teacher or clergyman. To quote from a 1937 police guideline: "By their arts of seduction they [homosexuals] are constantly winning over and contaminating young people. The homosexual sadist does not even shrink from murderous deeds."[48] As this last remark suggests, the homosexual was associated with the ritual murder of youths by the Jews. The gay danger to the *race* is their own lack of productivity, their seduction of others and, like the other predominant urban group, the Jews, they establish bonds that are irreducible to the national Volk. Regarded within the National Socialist sexual regime, there is a special intimacy between the gay and the Jew; the real danger of the homosexual identity is its transitional character: one is on the way to becoming a Jew. As an August 1930 issue of the Nazi Party's official newspaper declared: "'all the foul urges of the Jewish soul' come together in homosexuality" and gays "should be punished with hanging and deportation."[49] (I will return to this perceived intimacy between Jew and gay in my conclusion).

It was in their customary depiction of Jews as an erotic flood that the Nazis spoke to Christian anxieties about the sexual climate of their culture. Jews were sexually dangerous, their printing companies even blamed for producing far too suggestive pictures of the saints which were displayed in German homes.[50] If we look for the reasons why so few people were troubled about standing on the sidelines, why so many failed to get involved with the victimized Jew, practically or even emotionally, I would claim that this is certainly a major source of that moral indifference. For the Germans who were proud of that spiritual inwardness which was the legacy of their culture and who were humiliated by the sexual war that was being waged in their bodies, the carnal Jew represented a contamination, the destruction of the spiritual sense and the eruption of the uncontrollable erotic body. In light of the predominant Christian style of moral formation, one could have predicted that, even while protests were mounted on behalf of the crippled and the insane, the Jews would be, at best, abandoned.

Goebbels, Hitler's propaganda minister, claimed that the Third Reich had changed people inwardly, that it had given people the opportunity to escape the bourgeois epoch and embrace a new ethic of "heroism, masculinity, readiness for sacrifice, discipline."[51] He is only half right. Perhaps not since Christianity absorbed pagan religiosity had a radical movement been so successful in absorbing common national virtues, which, at times, were even defended by Christians as particularly appropriate to the religious sensibility.[52] But these so-called secondary virtues were appealing to people and were developed by them because they were eminently suitable for a struggle with one's flesh, that other self which had to be subdued. This campaign's instrumentalization and depersonalization of sexuality was a principal source of that doubling process which some have argued is the key to appreciating how average citizens could function with a good conscience while contributing to mass murder.[53] The split self accounts for how, in the midst of administering the death camps, SS soldiers could be praised for their decency, their loyalty, their truthfulness. Despite the destruction of millions, Himmler could assure his men that "our inward being, our soul, our character has not suffered injury from it."[54] This is why the Nazis made a sharp distinction between authorized and illegitimate killing.[55] As strange as it may seem, Hitler's biographer, Joachim Fest, seems justified when he asserts that National Socialism exercised its greatest appeal among those who had a craving for morality. On the other hand, I do want to stress this: Goebbels *is* half right. One of Nazism's genuine novelties is that it fashioned from a traditional morality of secondary virtues and of sexual asceticism an ethic which evoked from millions an extraordinary willingness to discipline themselves and, for so many, sacrifice themselves physically. While frequently exploiting the religion's divided self, Nazism created a post-Christian ethic by establishing the opportunity for an intense choice of one's self, in the here and now, an eroticism of one's self in time. There is a major shift in Western experience here. Within cultures shaped by Christianity, one's sense of worth was derived from self-denial and surrender to the vocation one was given by providence. Who one was to *become* in that state free from time and flesh regulated one's commerce with oneself and others. Nazi eroticism was tied to the affirmation of who one *is* biologically, to the embrace of one's body and, through it, one's people. The model of virginity yields to that of breeding.[56]

No less than the homosexual, the Jew, the Nazi, and the Christian possessed sexual identities for a fascist theory and practice which operated in terms of a certain logic of spirit-flesh. In speaking of sexual identities, I certainly do not wish to address their epistemological level, namely, what we might know about the similarities and differences of various groups. Nazism did not produce an alternative psychoanalysis. Rather, we have looked at an ethical practice in which National Socialism forged a regime of erotic danger, a manner of relating to sexual life which was less indebted to biology than it was to an inherited sphere of spirituality, the struggle of spirit with flesh. Within that field, Nazism presented itself as overcoming dualisms: a Christian alienation of the soul from the body and a Jewish alienation of the carnal from the spiritual. But the Nazis also harbored a great fear which gave birth to an even greater violence: that they themselves would become what they fantasized the Jew to be, that truly diabolical figure which embodied Christianity's two greatest enemies: its doctrinal opponent, the Jew, and its moral foe, the flesh. The 1935 Nuremberg Laws, with their prohibition of sexual relations between Germans and Jews, show that the anxiety regarding racial defilement was a dread of transformation of German into Jew. This is why some Nazis claimed that a single sexual intimacy between a Jewish man and a German woman robbed her of her people forever. Nazism embraced the ideal of a self beyond any possibility of conversion, a life substance that could be experienced as unchangeable. Sartre brilliantly captures this dimension of the anti-Semite.[57] An Aryan sexual identity became the refuge from a weak nation state identity that was joined with the project to destroy all traditional religious identity.

At the end of the war, Karl Jaspers differentiated German guilt according to various levels: political, criminal, moral, and metaphysical.[58] My analysis indicates a fifth level of ethical-spiritual responsibility which would explore how our most foundational images and concepts for intimate and public lives may contain those seeds of hate and violence which can come to flourish almost automatically in certain cultural crises. The spirit-flesh paradigm was just such a seed. Its operation in the era of National Socialism should lead us to a more comprehensive affirmation of the human being's dignity as sexually embodied and differently so.

Notes

1. "Nazi-Ethik: Über Heinrich Himmler und die Karriere der Neuen Moral" *Babylon: Beiträge zur jüdischen Gegenwart*, 6 (1989): 46–62; "Jenseits von Leben und Tod: Zu Foucaults Ethik nach Auschwitz," published as an appendix to Angelika Magiros, *Foucaults Beitrag zur Rassimustheorie* (Hamburg: Argument-Verlag, 1995) pp. 167–90. The first is a translation by Angelika Schweikart of "Nazi Ethics: On Heinrich Himmler and the Origin of New Moral Careers," *Remembering for the Future: Working Papers and Addenda*, vol. II (Oxford: Pergamon Press, 1989) pp. 2071–82; the second is a translation by Michael Haupt of "Beyond Life and Death: On Foucault's Post-Auschwitz Ethic," *Michel Foucault, Philosopher*, ed. T. J. Armstrong (New York: Routledge, 1992) pp. 260–79.

2. The major fragments that were published were the three volumes in

Foucault's *The History of Sexuality: I: An Introduction* (New York: Pantheon, 1978); *II: The Use of Pleasure* (New York: Pantheon, 1985); *III: The Care of the Self* (New York: Pantheon, 1986).

3. "Christian eroticism" designates how one's experience of the other as desirable or repulsive is woven from Christian moral codes, privileged forms of knowledge about sexuality, ways of moral formation, and the construction of zones of sexual danger and safety.

4. MB (Michael Berenbaum), review of Günther Grau, editor of *Hidden Holocaust?: Gay and Lesbian Persecution in Germany, 1933–45* (New York: Cassell, 1995), in *Holocaust and Genocide Studies* 9, no. 3 (Winter 1995): 396–97.

5. Theodor Adorno, *Minima Moralia: Reflections from Damaged Life* (London: Verso, 1974) p. 46. For an extensive study of the leftist approach, see *Gay Men and the Sexual History of the Political Left*, eds. Gert Hekma, Harry Oosterhuis, and James Steakley (New York: Harrington Park Press, 1995).

6. See Ignace Feuerlicht, "Thomas Mann and Homoeroticism," *The Germanic Review* 45, no. 2 (March, 1970): 93, and Anthony Heilbut, *Thomas Mann: Eros and Literature* (New York: Knopf, 1996), especially pp. 501–507. Mann's son, Klaus, attacked what he regarded as the scapegoating of homosexuals in a 1935 essay, "Homosexualität und Fascismus," reissued in a collection of his writings edited by Martin Gregor-Dellin, *Heute und Morgen: Schriften zur Zeit* (Munich: Nymphenburger Verlagshandlung, 1969) pp. 130–37.

7. One thinks of Visconti's *The Damned* of 1969 and Cavani's *The Night Porter* of 1973, but also of the more troubling Pasolini work *Salò: or the 120 Days of Sodom* (1975). See Annette Insdorf's *Indelible Shadows: Film and the Holocaust* (Cambridge: Cambridge University Press, 1989).

8. Sontag, "Fascinating Fascism," *Under the Sign of Saturn* (New York: Farrar, Straus, Giroux, 1980), p. 102.

9. For discussion of the sexual theme in accounts of Hitler, see Ron Rosenbaum, "Explaining Hitler," *The New Yorker*, May 1, 1995, pp. 50–70; John Sweeney "Hitler and the Billygoat," *Granta* 51 (Autumn 1995): 85–90; and Robert Waite's *The Psychpathic God: Adolf Hitler* (New York: Basic Books, 1977), pp. 232–43. Also see *Liebesbriefe an Adolf Hitler—Briefe in den Tod*, ed. Helmut Ulshöfer (Frankfurt: VAS Unveröffentlichte Dokumente aus der Reichskanzlei, 1994).

10. Umberto Eco's recent study of fascism seems to do this. He writes: "Since permanent war and heroism are difficult games to play, the Ur-Fascist transfers his will to power to sexual matters." ("Ur-Fascism" in *The New York Review of Books*, June 22, 1995, p. 15). I would claim that it is not a transfer but rather, sexual matters are the very substance of both permanent war and heroism.

11. Recall for a moment Bruno Bettelheim's uneasiness with the success of the book, play, and film of Anne Frank's diary. He wrote: "I believe that the worldwide acclaim given her story cannot be explained unless we recognize in it our wish to forget the gas chambers, and our effort to do so by glorifying the ability to retreat into an extremely private, gentle, sensitive world, and there to cling as much as possible to what have been one's usual daily attitudes and activities, although surrounded by a maelstrom apt to engulf one at any moment." ("The Ignored Lesson of Anne Frank," in *Surviving and Other Essays* [New York: Vintage Books, 1977], p. 247).

12. Hannah Arendt, "Introduction" to *Auschwitz: A Report on the Proceedings against Robert Karl Ludwig Mulka and Others before the Court at Frankfurt* (New York: Praeger, 1966), pp. xxvii–xxviii.

13. See Carl Amery, *Capitulation* (New York: Herder and Herder, 1967), pp. 29–34.

14. P. Tillich, "Open Letter to Emanuel Hirsch" (October 1, 1934), in *The Thought of Paul Tillich*, eds. J. L. Adams, W. Pauck, and R. Shinn (New York: Harper and Row, 1985), p. 364.

15. See A. Görres, "Pathologie des katholischen Christentums," in *Handbuch der Pastoraltheologie: Praktische Theologie der Kirche in ihrer Gegenwart*, II/1, eds. F. X. Arnold, K. Rahner, and V. Schurr, L. Weber (Freiburg: Herder, 1966), pp. 277–343.

16. See John Mahoney, *The Making of Moral Theology: A Study of the Roman Catholic Tradition* (Oxford: Clarendon Press, 1987), pp. 28–29, 45.

17. Helmuth James von Moltke, *Letters to Freya: 1939–1945*, ed. H. von Moltke (New York: Knopf, 1990), p. 110.

18. See Edward Shorter, "Towards a History of *La Vie Intime*: The Evidence of Cultural Criticism in Nineteenth-Century Bavaria," in *The Emergence of Leisure*, ed. Michael Marrus (New York: Harper Torchbooks, 1974), pp. 38–68.

19. See Michael Phayer, *Sexual Liberation and Religion in Nineteenth Cetury Europe* (Totowa, N.J.: Rowman and Littlefield, 1977), and Roy Pascal, *From Naturalism to Expressionism: German Literature and Society 1880–1918* (New York: Basic Books, 1973), especially pp. 198–228. Also see Isabel Hull, *Sexuality, State and Civil Society in Germany, 1700–1815* (Ithaca: Cornell University Press, 1996).

20. Waldemar Gurian, "The Sources of Hitler's Power" *The Review of Politics* 4, no. 4 (October 1942): 391.

21. On this topic, see W. H. Bruford, *The German Tradition of Self-Cultivation: "Bildung" from Humboldt to Thomas Mann* (Cambridge: Cambridge University Press, 1975).

22. Martin Ten Hoor, "The Nazis Purge Philosophy," *The Kenyon Review* 3, no. 3 (Summer 1941), reprinted by the same journal in Winter 1989, p. 173.

23. See Ferdinand Hoffmann, *Sittliche Entartung und Geburtenschwund* (Munich: J. F. Lehmanns Verlag, 1938), p. 51, and W. Hermannsen and R, Blome, *Warum hat man uns das nicht früher gesagt?: Ein Bekenntnis deutscher Jugend zu geschlechtlicher Sauberkeit* (Munich: J. F. Lehmanns Verlag, 1940). These are respectively the fourth and fourteenth volumes in the important series directed at German youth and edited by Heinz Müller: *Politische Biologie: Schriften für naturgesetzliche Politik und Wissenschaft* (1936–1940). For a general text on Nazi sexual ethics, see Friedrich Siebert, *Volkstum und Geschlechtlichkeit* (Munich-Berlin: J. F. Lehmanns Verlag, 1938).

24. See Laura Engelstein, *The Keys to Happiness: Sex and the Search for Modernity in Fin-de-Siècle Russia* (Ithaca: Cornell University Press, 1992).

25. Hans Peter Bleuel, *Sex and Society in Nazi Germany* (Philadelphia: J. B. Lippincott, 1973) p. 57.

26. See Frederick Ira Murphy, "The American Christian Press and Pre-War Hitler's Germany, 1933–1939" (Ph.D. dissertation, University of Florida, 1970).

27. Michael Langer, *Katholische Sexualpädagogik im 20. Jahrhundert: Zur*

Geschichte eines religionspädagogischen Problems (Munich: Kösel, 1986), p. 127. For a very comprehensive presentation of Catholic educational approaches to sexuality, see Walter Braun, *Geschlechtliche Erziehung in Katholische Religionsunterricht* (Trier: Spee Verlag, 1970).

28. Wilhelm Arp, *Das Bildungsideal der Ehre* (Munich: Deutscher Volksverlag, 1939); Langer, *Katholische Sexualpädagogik im 20. Jahrhundert*, p. 115. For examples of Nazi denunciations, see *The Persecution of the Catholic Church in the Third Reich. Facts and Documents Translated from the German* (London: Burns Oates, 1940), pp. 440, 464, 472–75. The anonymous editor of this collection was a German Jesuit residing in Rome, Walter Mariaux.

29. It could be argued that an exception would be the resistance shown by German Catholic women, motivated by ideals of virginity, to Nazi efforts to reduce women to the level of mere breeders of children. I cannot develop this issue here, but see Michael Phayer's *Protestant and Catholic Women in Nazi Germany* (Detroit: Wayne State University Press, 1990).

30. As an example see Martin Heidegger's October 2, 1929, letter to Victor Schwoerer, included in Leaman, *Heidegger im Kontext*, pp. 111–12. It is also an expression which Hitler used frequently. See, for example, *Mein Kampf* (Boston: Houghton Mifflin, 1971), p. 247. Also see the fine discussion by Steven Ascheim, " 'The Jew Within': The Myth of 'Judaization' in Germany," in *The Jewish Response to German Culture: From the Enlightenment to the Second World War*, edited by Jehuda Reinharz and Walter Schatzberg (Hanover: University Press of New England, 1985), pp. 212–41.

31. Alan Beyerchen, *Scientists under Hitler: Politics and the Physics Community in the Third Reich* (New Haven: Yale University Press, 1977).

32. For a Jewish defense against these charges, see Chajim Bloch's *Blut und Eros im jüdischen Schriftum und Leben: Von Eisenmenger über Rohling zu Bischoff* (Wien: Sensen-Verlag, 1935). On the charges, see Sander Gilman, *The Jew's Body* (New York: Routledge, 1991), p. 258.

33. Heiko Oberman, *The Roots of Anti-Semitism in the Age of the Renaissance and Reformation* (Philadelphia: Fortress Press, 1984), p. 83.

34. Randall L. Bytwerk, *Julius Streicher* (New York: Stein and Day, 1983), p. 113.

35. My treatment of modern sexuality follows the categories developed in Michel Foucault's *The History of Sexuality I: An Introduction* (New York: Pantheon, 1978). I analyze this history in my *Michel Foucault's Force of Flight: Toward an Ethics for Thought* (Atlantic Highlands, N.J.: Humanities Press, 1990), pp. 121–84.

36. The most thorough examinations of this theme are: George Mosse, *Nationalism and Sexuality: Respectability and Abnormal Sexuality in Modern Europe* (New York: Howard Fertig, 1985), and the extraordinary series of works by Sander Gilman, especially *Sexuality: An Illustrated History* (New York: John Wiley & Sons, 1989); *Jewish Self-Hatred: Anti-Semitism and the Hidden Language of the Jews* (Baltimore: The Johns Hopkins University Press, 1986); *The Jew's Body: Freud, Race and Gender* (Princeton: Princeton University Press, 1993). Also see Klemens Felden, "Die Übernahme des antisemitischen Stereotyps als soziale Norm durch die bürgerliche Gesellschaft Deutschlands (1875–1900)" (Ph.D. dissertation, Ruprecht-Karl-University in Heidelberg, 1963).

37. Allen Edwardes, *Erotica Judaica: A Sexual History of the Jews* (New York: Julian Press, 1967), pp. 106, 180; Friedrich Koch's *Sexualpädagogik und politische Erziehung* (Munich: List Verlag, 1975) and *Sexuelle Denunziation: Die Sexualität in der politischen Auseinandersetzung* (Frankfurt: Syndikat, 1986), pp. 83–86; Dennis Showalter, *Little Man, What Now? 'Der Stürmer' in the Weimar Republic* (Hamden, Connecticut: Archon, 1982), pp. 189, 198.

38. See Bytwerk, *Julius Streicher* and Streicher's testimony at the Nuremberg Trials: *Trial of the Major War Criminals before the International Military Tribunal*, vol. V (Nuremberg, 1947), pp. 91–119.

39. Otto Hauser, *Rassebilder* (Braunschweig und Hamburg: Georg Westermann, 1925); Guida Diehl, *Die deutsche Frau und der Nationalsozialismus* (Eisenach: Neulandverlag, 1933); Bruno Blau, "The Jew as Sexual Criminal," *Jewish Social Studies* 13, no. 4 (October 1951): 321–24; Mosse, *Nationalism and Sexuality*, p. 17; Koch, *Sexuelle Denunziation: Die Sexualität in der politischen Auseinandersetzung*, p. 53; Erich Goldhagen, "Nazi Sexual Demonology," *Midstream* (May, 1981): 7–15; Gilman, *Freud, Race and Gender*; and Showalter, *Little Man, What Now? 'Der Stürmer' in the Weimar Republic*.

40. In addition to Gilman, *Freud, Race and Gender*, see Gunther Runkel, *Sexualität und Ideologien* (Weinheim und Basel: Beltz Verlag, 1979), especially pp. 122–27. Also Herwig Hartner, *Erotik und Rasse: Eine Untersuchung über gesellschaftliche, sittliche und geschlechtliche Fragen mit Textillustrationen* (München: Deutscher Volksverlag, 1925); Barbara Hyams, "Weininger and Nazi Ideology," in *Jews and Gender: Responses to Otto Weininger*, eds. Nancy Harrowitz and Barbara Hyams (Philadelphia: Temple University Press, 1995), p. 166; Erwin Haeberle, "Swastika, Pink Triangle and Yellow Star—The Destruction of Sexology and the Persecution of Homosexuals in Nazi Germany," *The Journal of Sex Research* 17 (August 1981): 270–87; and *Anfänge der Sexualwissenschaft* (Berlin: Walter de Gruyter, 1983). This sexual assault upon Jews is repeated, often in the same words, by contemporary Nazis, for example in Harold Covington's "In Praise of the Final Solution: Or, Why I Despise the Jews," *The New Order* (April–May, 1978): 11.

41. Werner Dittrich, *Erziehung zum Judengegner: Hinweise zur Behandlung der Judenfrage im rassenpolitischen Unterricht* (Munich: Deutscher Volksverlag, 1937); Barbara Hyams and Nancy Harrowitz, "A Critical Introduction to the History of Weininger Reception," in *Jews and Gender: Responses to Otto Weininger*, p. 4; and Jay Geller, "Blood Sin: Syphilis and the Construction of Jewish Identity," *Faultline*, 1 (1992): 21–48.

42. Himmler's October 4, 1943, speech in Posen in *Trial of the Major War Criminals*, vol. 29, p. 146.

43. Ibid., vol. 12, p. 350.

44. David Roberts, "Eugenic Theory and the Thematics of Sin," *Renaissance and Modern Studies* 37 (1994): 57.

45. For example, see the account of Pierre Seel, *I, Pierre Seel, Deported Homosexual: A Memoir of Nazi Terror* (New York: Basic Books, 1995), pp. 43–44.

46. Lecture by Josef Meisinger, "The Combating of Homosexuality and Abortion as a Political Task" (April 5–6, 1937), in Grau, *Hidden Holocaust?* pp. 110–11.

47. Himmler speech of February 18, 1937, in Grau, *Hidden Holocaust?* p. 11.

48. Ibid., p. 96.

49. Ibid., p. 3.

50. Langer, *Katholische Sexualpädagogik im 20, Jahrhundert*, p. 20.

51. Speech given to NSDAP party members on June 16, 1933. Cited in James Wilkinson, *The Intellectual Resistance in Europe* (Cambridge, Mass.: Harvard University Press, 1981), p. 112.

52. Jakob Nötges, *Nationalsozialismus und Katholizismus* (Cologne: Gilde Verlag, 1931), especially pages 170–96.

53. See Robert Jay Lifton, *The Nazi Doctors: Medical Killing and the Psychology of Genocide* (New York: Basic Books, 1986), pp. 418–29.

54. Himmler's October 4, 1943, speech in *Trial of the Major War Criminals Before the International Military Tribunal*, vol. 29 (Nuremberg, 1948), p. 145.

55. See Raul Hilberg, *The Destruction of the European Jews*, vol. 3 (New York: Holmes and Meier, 1985), pp. 1012–29.

56. I would claim that their relationship is not one of strict opposition as, for example, Levinas maintains when he contrasts a materialistic bondage to a biological past to a religious spiritual freedom from that bodily burden. On the level of ethical formation, the struggle of spirit with flesh was no less a bondage and, indeed, was a prelude to Nazism's own enslavement. (See Levinas's "Reflections on the Philosophy of Hitlerism" [originally published in 1934], *Critical Inquiry* 17, no. 1 [Autumn 1990]: 62–71).

57. Jean-Paul Sartre, *Anti-Semite and Jew* (New York: Schocken, 1965).

58. Karl Jaspers, *The Question of German Guilt* (New York: Dial Press, 1947).

Affect and Modernity
Notes toward an Inquiry into the Origins of the Holocaust

Dan Stone

In a single sentence Georges Bataille encompasses the dual nature of a problem that goes to the heart of the origin of the Holocaust, and that has not been adequately addressed by its scholars:

> The advantages of civilization are offset by the way men profit from them: men today profit in order to become the most degraded beings that have ever existed.[1]

Was the state-sponsored genocide of the Jews an inevitable outcome of modernity, or did it (whether inevitable or not) depend upon the characteristics of modernity for its occurrence? Or, was modernity merely not "modern" enough, so that the longstanding traditions of hatred and intolerance which were to be subsumed by the unfolding of reason were too strong to be resisted? Was the Holocaust a direct product of the advantages of civilization, or was it an atavistic riposte to its homogenizing tendencies?

The thrust of scholarly historical work of the last decade has been away from the Nuremberg Trials idea of the Holocaust as aberration, to emphasize instead the continuities between German society before and after the Nazi period, as well as the more general implications of the Holocaust for modernity and vice versa. Vitally important though these works are (I believe that what follows is indebted to their insights), they do not consider that the very excess, the rush of energy which permitted normal societal structures to become organs of mass murder, may be precisely that which prevents the Holocaust from being incorporated into a cognitive-rational approach. It is this inability to see the Holocaust as threatening the rules of the historical genre which connects historians from Friedrich Meinecke to Detlev Peukert, Gerald Reitlinger to Marsha Gilbert. There has yet to appear a book which combines the radical critique of modernity with Saul Friedländer's "fear that the process of historicization and the global trend towards normalization of historical memory would predominate over the most extreme aspects of the Nazi period."[2] This paper's *raison d'être* is the belief that, although the Holocaust does not present, theoretically, problems of *representation* different from any other historical event, there is nevertheless something terrifyingly visceral about the Holocaust in its implications for Western society and science that gives these philosophical questions greater urgency and weight. Like other events, the Holocaust is characterized by its "disruptive excess," an excess which is unassimilable to conventional discourse.[3] But in this case the excess has the potential to disturb conventional approaches to the past which are not ordinarily troubled by the problem of the past's assimilation. In other words, the Holocaust is not singular, an exception to the normal rules of historical discourse and in need of guarding by the scholarly community;[4] rather, it questions notions of historical truth and cognitive rationality, because these concepts are part of the cultural and scientific milieu implicated in the rise of Nazism. The assimilation of that which questions the desire to assimilate is what is at stake here.[5]

The inquiry into the role of modernity is therefore vitally important, but not in itself sufficient. The conclusions of writers such as Detlev Peukert, Zygmunt Bauman, Götz Aly, and Susanne Heim are such that we cannot be complacent about our own society, which has responded to the Holocaust primarily by normalizing it, "pasteurizing" it in Arno Mayer's term,[6] so that genocide is integrated as part of normality instead of becoming a reason to change it. But the emphasis of these studies is such that they are founded on the very rationalism which they proceed to indict. A small price to pay for a radical critique of our social lifeworld, it may be felt. But I believe that what has in fact occurred is an underestimation of one half of the duality encompassed in Bataille's juxtaposition of civilization and degradation. Political considerations have continually obscured the fact that, in order to think through Nazism, we must recognize an inevitable complicity with it. In other words, we must recognize that what Derrida says about ethnology (in an essay on Levi-Strauss) holds equally forcefully for historical representations:

> whether he wants to or not . . . the ethnologist accepts into his discourse the premises of ethnocentrism at the very moment when he denounces them. . . . But if no one can escape this necessity . . . this does not mean that all the ways of giving in to it are of equal pertinence.[7]

Here I will examine how some of the recent approaches to the Holocaust fail to acknowledge their own complicity with suspect ways of thinking, and thus contradict themselves in their articulation.

A common failing among the responses to the Holocaust proposed by the "modernity theorists" is that they often do not respond to it in any emotional sense at all. In the case of Rainer Zitelmann, the Holocaust is bypassed as an unfortunate byproduct of the program of modernization necessary to bring Germany up to the technological level of the United States. Zitelmann's right-wing conception of German history intends to create a sense of continuity, emphasizing the "positive" aspects of the Third Reich and playing down its horrors.[8] For example, he asserts that the policy of acquiring *Lebensraum* in the east was not (other than for a few Nazi leaders such as Himmler or Darré) a means of fulfilling dreams of a reagrarianized German *Volksgemeinschaft*, but was a way of acquiring the resources necessary for establishing an autarchic industrial state. Hitler was driven by a program of modernization every bit as vivid as his racial policy, and the economic successes that he enjoyed have been continually played down since 1945.[9] The Jews were, he implies, among the "backward" elements of society swept away by this massive policy of the creation of a technologically advanced industrial state.

By claiming that modernization was the primary goal of the regime, and that the emphasis on the concentration camps obscures its achievements, Zitelmann dissociates himself from the mainstream of the historical profession, including radical historians. For all these other historians, an emphasis on modernity is not at the expense of the horror of the regime's accomplishments. Quite the opposite: it seeks to show that modernity may have been perfectly compatible with anti-Semitism and mass murder.

Therefore, I will look beyond Zitelmann to theorists of modernity who are honestly responding to the horror of the Holocaust, and who are doing so in a new way. These contemporary portrayals of Auschwitz do indeed raise many new philosophical challenges, in particular by revivifying the debate about modernity, Enlightenment, and postmodernity begun by Theodor Adorno and Max Horkheimer in 1944. The most radical of these are Götz Aly and Susanne Heim. For the last decade they have investigated the minutiae of the world of the mid-level bureaucrats and officials of the Third Reich: economists, demographers, agrarians, statisticians. Their conclusions are startling: the genocide of the Jews owed little to racial hatred, and rather a lot to rational planning from the point of view of creating a productive and efficient society under German domination. As Wulf Kansteiner puts it, they "directly challenge the consensus about the exceptionality and irrationality of the 'Final Solution' that unified German historians until recently."[10]

Thus they write that "one can only understand the dynamic of the annihilation and the actual process of decision making [*tatsächlichen Entscheidungsabläufe*] if one has the demographic-economic program in the background," and conclude, on the basis of decisions and writings of local officials in the General Government, that "[t]he death of the Jews provided the simplest and most viable means of keeping down capital erosion and of keeping open the possibility for an economic upswing in occupied Poland."[11]

In their major collaborative work, *Vordenker der Vernichtung* (1991), Aly and Heim amass a great deal of evidence demonstrating how second-level functionaries, particularly those responsible for developing the newly annexed or occupied eastern territories, drew up plans to murder the Jews as part of a wider plan for the demographic reorganization of Europe. On the basis of their detailed reading of little-known documents they conclude that there is "a theoretical frame" for understanding the genocide; this frame is the

> development of food and economic strategies out of the plans for military conquest of the east which, far removed from "classical" campaigns of conquest and the sadistic lust to kill, made mass annihilation into a "practical constraint," a prerequisite for long-term domination and economic subordination.[12]

For example, in their extremely interesting discussion of the development of Auschwitz, Aly and Heim integrate the growth of the extermination camp into plans for slave labor, "resettlement," and the reorganization of the economy of Upper Silesia. The murder of the Jews and "ballast existents incapable of work" in Auschwitz "has a firm place in the economic center [*Wirtschaftszentrum*] Auschwitz—not as a one-off 'measure' but as a permanent institution." They claim that, as the president of the government of occupied Kattowitz (Katowice) wrote in 1943, Auschwitz was envisaged as having a life of "at least a further ten to twenty years as a component of the industrial region." The murder of the Jews, they assert, "was only the beginning, and the annihilation of people in order to establish the new order would be continued for some time."[13]

Recently, Aly has extended the range of his proof by tying in the murder of the Jews with the resettlement of the Poles and the "ethnic Germans" who were moved from Romania, the Baltic states, and the Volga region, sometimes against their will, to the newly annexed areas of Poland and occupied Ukraine. Quite apart from showing that there was no single decision to murder the Jews, but rather "a political decision-making process, which dragged on over many months,"[14] Aly claims that this evidence reveals that, once again, the murders can only be understood in relation to the wider resettlement policy.

A particularly good illustration of this interrelationship is given in the case of Zamosc in eastern Poland: on 25 January 1943 a goods train with one thousand young Poles on board traveled from Zamosc to Berlin to take the work places of "armaments Jews" [*Rüstungsjuden*], who were then deported with their families on the same train to Auschwitz. There the train was loaded with baggage for ethnic German settlers from Lithuania and Romania and sent back to Zamosc. The ethnic Germans traveled at the same time in carriages to Zamosc, where they were to be settled in the former Polish and Jewish areas. From Zamosc the train returned to Auschwitz with one thousand Poles who had been classified as especially "unwanted" [*unerwünscht*] by the security police and SS racial examiners. This is just one example proving, Aly claims, the

> overlapping of resettlement and evacuation [*Umsiedeln und Aussiedeln*], of selection and genocide, the internal logic of "human deployment" [*Menscheneinsatzes*], the planned and organized unity of so-called positive and negative population policy.[15]

Their studies are fascinating; but in reaching such conclusions, Aly and Heim not only grant too much validity to the scientific status of those writings (indeed, they do not come to them with any critical faculty at all), they also overestimate the role of these functionaries in the decision-making processes of the Third Reich. This mistake may be explained by the desire underlying their research to find a rational core to the Holocaust. It is as though they need to order the world of the Holocaust, even at the cost of revealing an unpleasant "connection between modernization and destruction."[16] This "social engineering" approach to society was indeed partly responsible for the mass murders; but in itself it does not explain the origin of the particular task that the Reich bureaucracy was engaged to undertake. Despite its radical implications for contemporary society, Aly and Heim's Holocaust simply offers an alternative version of consolation to that of conservative historians (of whom Martin Gilbert is the archetype) who portray the Holocaust as aberration.[17] Either totally irrational or entirely rational; in both scenarios, the Holocaust is removed from the realm of the contingent, made to fit into a scheme of either utter incomprehension or absolute understandability.[18]

Far more subtle has been the work of the late Detlev Peukert. From the perspective of *Alltagsgeschichte* or the history of everyday life, Peukert demonstrated a sensitive awareness of the coexistence of quotidian "normality" and extreme terror under National Socialist rule. The approach of *Alltagsgeschichte* has often been attacked for ignoring the sufferings of the regime's victims; but in the works of its best practitioners (Claudia Koonz's *Mothers in the Fatherland* is another example) it has become a profitable method of inquiry.

Methodological debates among historians are not the prime focus here. Rather, I will consider the findings that Peukert's approach throws up, noting from the outset that they are markedly different from both the liberal and Marxist historiography that preceded it, and different again from Zitelmann's work which pays lip service to Peukert's approach, but which lacks his moral sensitivity and penetrating insight into the pitfalls as well as the achievements of modernity.

Indeed, this unstinting critique of modernity is the crucial point in all of Peukert's later writings, to the important book of 1982 *Volksgenossen und Gemeinschaftsfremde* (*Inside Nazi Germany*, 1987) and the development of the ideas of that study in *Max Webers Diagnose der Moderne* (1989), which contained the important essay "The Genesis of the Final Solution from the Spirit of Science" as well as other essays.[19] Admitting as vital the achievements of scientific progress, Peukert stresses as well the always present danger of science developing totalizing patterns of thought with disastrous consequences. He is at pains to delineate these patterns of thought because of their continued existence in postwar Germany.

Peukert recognizes the dangers of anti-Semitism. But he believes that the Holocaust is different from earlier anti-Jewish manifestations because it grew not out of irrational fantasies, but out of the demands of modern science, in particular social policy:

> Anti-Semitism based on racial anthropology supplies the graphic and traditionally legitimized scapegoat image that helps to serve as the basis for the expansion of the categories of the victim. But the specifically modern character of the "Final Solution" derives from the swing to racial hygiene in the human and social sciences. (GEN, 290)[20]

In fact, he goes so far as to say that the connection between modern technology and racial science provides the interpretative key to the Holocaust [AB, 59].

Following Weber's definition of modernity, especially the emphasis on rationalization, this argument stresses modernity's tension between abolishing "the mysteries of the world" and its drive toward social and personal regulation. Its prediction of total solutions undermined its own premises, and science "ideologized itself," increasingly turning to more radical solutions in order to fulfill its own promises [MW, 63; RAS, 74].[21] As the claims of scientists began to be increasingly difficult to achieve, the schemes they wanted to implement became ever grander, the "selection process" threw an ever wider net over the population, and the results were ever more destructive, until the point at which the

> optimistic view, that scientific and industrial progress in principle removed the restrictions on the possible application of planning, edu-

cation and social reform in everyday life, lost its last shreds of innocence when the National Socialists set about engineering their "brave
new world" with compulsory sterilization, concentration camps and gas
chambers. (ING, 223)

Such a précis of Peukert's writings cannot do justice to the subtleties
that characterize his investigations into the nature of modernity and
modernity's role in the origin of the Holocaust. Suffice it to say that his
conclusions, after careful studies of the role of scientists and bureaucrats
in the period before and during National Socialist rule, dispelled the liberal consensus that Nazism was purely an anti-enlightenment phenomenon; furthermore, it clouded the 1960s debate about modernization
which had concluded that the Third Reich had unintentionally been a
developmental stage in German history which had resulted in the Federal Republic being able to implement its "economic miracle."[22] Both
these debates were hampered by their simple equations of modernization with progress. Peukert demonstrated that modernization could just
as easily be the setting for the most barbaric crimes. He concluded that

[t]he National Socialist mass movement is a child of the crisis of modernization. . . . National Socialism is in this respect *one*, if the most
fatal, of the developmental possibilities of modernity. (MW, 82)

Although Nazism clearly rejected the promises of 1789, it cannot be sat-
isfactorily understood as merely an outbreak of anti-modern affect;
equally, it is facile to regard it as a revolutionary form of modernization,
as does Zitelmann (MW, 82 and 134, n19).

Peukert makes us rethink our assumptions about modernity, claiming that the process of rationalization is a delicate balancing act between
growing humanity and outbreaks of barbarism (MW, 83). For the interpretation of the Holocaust, however, the stress on the antinomies of
modernity reaches its apogee in Peukert's assertion that the Nazi belief
in pernicious genetic dispositions "finally carried racialist biology into
the realms of chiliastic fantasy," and that this racialism "was in no sense
a sudden, inexplicable irruption of 'medieval barbarism' into a progressive society, but owed its seductive power to the pathologies of 'progress'
itself" (ING, 234-235).

This is a catalogue of claims that represents a searing critique of
modern society, whose love of rationalization in the name of "order" and
"beauty" ended only in mass murder. It is a very persuasive argument,
particularly in light of our own contemporary responses to genocide in
Rwanda and Bosnia, and the pseudo-arguments justifying policies of
marginalization, particularly toward asylum seekers.

But is it not too simple? Perhaps Peukert's tracing of the unfolding of the destructive potential of modernity is valid for the "euthanasia" programme but less so for the genocide of the Jews. Does not his insistence on racialist science's progressive radicalization ignore the hatred and fury that underlay the targeting of the Jews? Before answering these questions, let us finally look at the work of Zygmunt Bauman which has done more than any other to radically call into question the idea of the Holocaust as a form of atavism in a progressive world.

Bauman's *Modernity and the Holocaust* (1989) has one fundamental difference from the work of Peukert. Peukert, for all his honest investigations into the dark side of modernity, retains his faith in modernity's emancipatory potential. With vigilance replacing the nonchalance of the early modernists, he believes, very much like Habermas, that the teachings of the Frankfurt School are too dogmatic, and that we must not junk the "project" of modernity so quickly:

> the view that [Nazism] was one of the developmental forms of modernity does not imply that barbarism is the inevitable logical outcome of modernization. . . . [Rather] we should call attention to the rifts and danger-zones which result from the modern civilizing process itself, so that the opportunities for human emancipation which it simultaneously creates can be the more thoroughly charted. (ING, 249)

By contrast, Bauman seeks, more in the tradition of Adorno and Horkheimer, to demonstrate the coincidence of modern social structures and genocide. He does not go so far as to say that the Holocaust was the inevitable outcome of modernity: "Modern civilization was not the Holocaust's *sufficient* condition; it was, however, most certainly its *necessary* condition."[23] Where Peukert still talks of "pathologies," Bauman explicitly disavows such language (MH, 1) as a way in which "the bomb is defused" (MH, 2), that is, the impact of the Holocaust for our civilization is played down.

In Bauman's understanding, the Holocaust represents the greatest achievement of the principles of modernity, not a departure from them. By these principles he means rationalization, bureaucratization, legislation, surveillance, and social engineering. As he put it in one of his later works inspired by his work on modernity:

> One of the most conspicuous traits of modernity was an overwhelming urge to replace spontaneity, seen as meaningless and identified with chaos, by an order drawn by reason and constructed through a legislative and controlling effort.[24]

Peukert also saw in the utopian dreams of the planners of the Holocaust a desire for an "escape from the contingency of the quotidian, a coup [*Befreiungsschlag*] which would create order once and for all, be it even the order of a gigantic cemetery from the Atlantic to the Urals" (RAS, 77), an astonishing image. But, as the logical outcome of this process, the Holocaust must, Bauman thinks, signal the demise of the modern project. Although he here departs from Peukert, Bauman is in no way an unthinking celebrator of postmodernity. His work on the Holocaust led him to the conclusion that the characteristics of modernity were not to be mourned in a society which lacks the cosmic certainty of its precursor. But he does not naively assume that contemporary society, which he believes is sufficiently sociologically divorced from modern society to deserve the name postmodern, is free of systemic problems. Indeed, his latest work is aimed precisely at negotiating one's way in a world bereft of earlier certitudes.[25] Postmodern society brings its own problems; but Bauman thinks that dealing with them is preferable to resorting to modernist preoccupations.

How then does Bauman arrive at so radical a critique of Western civilization? Primarily by equating the Holocaust with the characteristics of modernity described above. In a bureaucratic system, where the technical is divorced from the moral, the task of the bureaucracy, even mass murder, is carried out with ease. That is to say, only the characteristics of a modern society allowed murder on the grand scale to be carried out so efficiently, ruthlessly, and noiselessly, in a way which meant that those making the decisions were removed from those actually doing the killing: "[o]nce set in motion, the machinery of murder developed its own impetus" (MH, 106). The bureaucracy of destruction, like all modern bureaucracies, had an internal dynamic which demanded that the task set it be undertaken at best-cost and with maximum efficiency. "Bureaucracy is programmed to seek the optimal solution" (MH, 104).

Thus Bauman can write that

> however vivid was Hitler's imagination, it would have accomplished little if it had not been taken over, and translated into routine process of problem-solving, by a huge and rational bureaucratic apparatus. (MH, 105)[26]

And bureaucracy was given the task of murdering the Jews because of the dreams of the planners of modern society. These planners Bauman likens to gardeners, busily weeding out the unaesthetic elements which disturb the serenity of the desired order. Modern planners believed that they could create a better world by weeding out undesirable elements; thus, like Stalin's victims, the victims of the Third Reich did not die for emotional reasons, *specifically not hatred*, but "they were eliminated so that an objectively better human world—more efficient, more moral, more beautiful—could be established" (MH, 92). Like Peukert, Bauman sees the Holocaust as being an outcome of modernity; unlike Peukert, he also claims that it reveals more about modernity than any other of its achievements:

> The two most notorious and extreme cases of modern genocide [Stalin's and Hitler's] did not betray the spirit of modernity. They did not deviously depart from the main track of the civilizing process. They were the most consistent, uninhibited expressions of that spirit. They attempted to reach the most ambitious aims of the civilizing process most other processes stop short of, not necessarily for the lack of good will. They showed what the rationalizing, designing, controlling dreams and efforts of modern civilization are able to accomplish if not mitigated, curbed or counteracted. (MH, 93)

Modernity, according to Bauman, reveals the essence of the Holocaust: "Without modern civilization and its most central essential achievements, there would be no Holocaust" (MH, 87); the implication is that the Holocaust also reveals the essence of modernity.

But Bauman's own work sows seeds of doubt as to the sustainability of such a thesis. His description of the rationalized bureaucratic procedure is brilliant, and gives us cause for concern at our own, highly rationalized social world. But, like Peukert, Bauman does not explain where the *impetus* to genocide comes from, other than in vague gardening metaphors or in the progressive radicalization of an increasingly frustrated scientific community.[27] Thus, he states that "[a]t no point of its long and tortuous *execution* did the Holocaust come in conflict with the principles of rationality" (MH, 17; my emphasis). When Bauman goes on to say that the Holocaust "arose out of a genuinely rational concern" (MH, 17), we have already been informed why we must cavil at such a claim. In its execution, the Holocaust did indeed rely upon the societal structures of modern civilization. But the idea had first to be given to those structures. Bureaucracies implement tasks given to them, and in this instance the task given was not "rational." Rational planning is insufficient to explain the motivation to murder millions of Jews, not all, by the way, murdered by desk killers, but shot by the hundreds of thousands by the *Einsatzgruppen*, and murdered by starvation and disease in ghettos, and even in the gas chambers dying a hideous and far from sanitized death. Rather, dreams of a cleansed, ordered society, derived from perennial fears of pollution, preceded the modern structures which permitted their implementation in ways previously impossible.[28]

The contradictions within Bauman's work accumulate rapidly on a close reading. All center on whether or not the actual impetus to murder the Jews and other designated "inferior" peoples derived from the same modern structures which implemented the policy. Bauman, his claims to the contrary notwithstanding, wants us to believe that such was indeed the case; thus he states (and this is the strongest example) that

> the bureaucratic culture which prompts us to view society as an object
> of administration, as a collection of so many problems to be "solved,"

as "nature" to be "controlled," "mastered" and "improved" or "re-made," as a legitimate target for "social engineering," and in general a garden to be designed and kept in the planned shape by force (the gardening posture divides vegetation into "cultured plants" to be taken care of, and weeds to be exterminated), *was the very atmosphere in which the idea of the Holocaust could be conceived.* (MH, 18; my emphasis)

Yet only a few sentences earlier, he writes,

> This is not to suggest that the incidence of the Holocaust was *determined* by modern bureaucracy or the culture of instrumental rationality it epitomizes; much less still, that modern bureaucracy *must* result in Holocaust-style phenomena. (MH, 17–18)

In the case of the Holocaust and modernity, Bauman claims to eschew a traditionally defined rational aetiology, the principle of sufficient reason. But this is exactly what we find only moments after he declines to take such a step. It is not surprising that he does not advertise this sufficient connection; thinkers such as Dan Diner and Dominick LaCapra have for some time been arguing that explaining the Holocaust only on rational grounds replicates a mode of thinking that characterizes Nazi bureaucratic procedures, and Hayden White and Hans Kellner suggest that because the Holocaust is characterized by chaos, it is inappropriate to write of it in a way that renders it coherent.[29] Yet this is exactly what Bauman tries to do, in a certain sense invalidating his own findings. Like Aly and Heim, the desire to find a rational core to the Holocaust in Bauman's work is a desire for total comprehension which echoes the very aspirations of the "modernists" whom they critique.

Curiously, Bauman articulates this desire even though he also demonstrates why it is misplaced. In the chapter entitled "Modernity, Racism, Extermination, I," he explains how longstanding fears and hatreds, particularly of the Jews, did not disappear with the emergence into the modern age, but were simply incorporated into modern thought processes. The abstract notion of "the Jew" which had so exercised medieval minds was not rationally dispelled. Rather, since the notion was more a reflection of hegemonic society's "inner demons" than of the Jews in reality, the claims of reason mattered little (MH, 39). Indeed, under the rationalized conditions of modernity, suppressive of non-goal-oriented affect, these drives received added impetus:

> The irony of history would allow the anti-modernist phobias to be unloaded through channels and forms only modernity could develop. . . . The Jews remained visible embodiments of inner demons when the exorcisms were officially disallowed and forced underground. Through

most of modern history the Jews were the principal carriers of tensions and anxieties modernity declared out of existence, brought to an unprecedented intensity and supplied with formidable tools of expression. (MH, 46)

A starker contrast to Bauman's earlier comments (MH, 18, see above) cannot be imagined. In this more historical reading, the origin of the Holocaust is not to be found within the bureaucracy of genocide itself. Instead, we find the suggestion that modern structures such as bureaucracies gave an impetus to existing drives by, firstly, frustrating them, and, secondly, by channeling them.

Nevertheless, Bauman concludes with a reiteration of the "rational core" thesis, leaving a large, disturbing, unsolved contradiction at the heart of the book:

the Holocaust was not (and in all probability could not be) an effect of awakening, release, prompting, intensification, or an outburst of dormant personal inclinations. . . . The Holocaust could be accomplished only on the condition of neutralizing the impact of primeval moral drives, of isolating the machinery of murder from the sphere where such drives arise and apply, of rendering such drives marginal or altogether irrelevant to the task. (MH, 188)

Bauman shows us why rationalization frustrated "irrational" drives, and then paradoxically provided outlets for these same drives which they exploited with renewed vigor. But he wants to believe that this is a simple indictment of modernity and its totalizing aspirations, as though rationalization were synonymous with those fears which it frustrated and channeled.

It is hardly to be doubted that the rhetoric of civilization has actually been the occasion for unspeakable acts of barbarity, so that the stunning insight of Walter Benjamin is irresistible to our minds:

Barbarism inheres in the very concept of culture; taken as the concept of a hoard of values which is independent, not of the production process from which those values emerged, but of the process in which they survive. In this way, they serve the apotheosis of the latter, no matter how barbaric it may be.[30]

But from the works cited above we can see that the notion of "modernity" has been hypostatized; the result is shock that modernity can be the setting for acts of barbarism. To give another example, Mark Levene, a historian at the University of Warwick, writes that modern genocide is distinct from earlier mass murders not because of the *form* it takes but because of the *framework* within which it occurs, i.e., the context of radical change which created the modern world. He thinks that it is the perception of state leaders that their modernization program is threatened by a section of the population that is behind the murderous impulse; there is no suggestion that the modernization process itself may be the setting for a channeling of existing fears and hatreds which simply found no other outlet than the newly created and all-pervasive rationalized modern structures.[31]

Taking the term "modernity" for granted, implying progress, reason, and civilization, scholars establish a dichotomy between two terms—modernity and barbarism—when there is really no a priori reason to believe that they are incompatible. This antagonism results from taking its aspirations or its self-understanding as adequate definitions of modernity. Even when scholars devote time to showing that modernity can be the setting for barbarism, such research is, in a way, surprising, for the fact that barbaric acts took place under modern conditions is the basic fact of the Holocaust. Even the most sophisticated research, such as that examined above, begins with surprise at this fact where perhaps none is warranted.

This reification of the concept of modernity actually undermines the radical power of its critique by equating the Holocaust simply with the forces of rationalization, bureaucracy, technocracy, and social engineering, and at worst reiterates a fascination with the bureaucratic procedure of the "desk killers," to use George Kren's phrase.

The modernity thesis is by no means to be dismissed; but it needs to be supplemented with what has long been unfashionable, an emphasis on the irrational. This means not simply the role of ideas, as in the 1950s and 1960s (and in Daniel Goldhagen's recent reiteration), when the Holocaust was explained by the irresistibility and logical implementation of anti-Semitism. It means, more, stressing the play of energy, the sudden burst of which was necessary to activate those modern societal structures which then so successfully fulfilled their appointed task. Only a reconciliation of the modernity thesis with a notion of the wild and furious energy that exists in society in varying proportions at different times can help to get to the heart of the problem of the origin of genocide as an option for a civilized state. Only thus can it be seen why the features of the modern world were so terrifyingly capable of fulfilling the demands made of them by the Nazi leadership. "Pure objectivity" in racist biology did not finally lead to the realms of chiliastic fantasy; rather, the realms of chiliastic fantasy informed that biology from the start, and were always present underneath the official rhetoric of the Enlightenment.[32] Indeed, it is this official covering of drives which continued to exist which permitted the exceptional horrors of slavery, colonialism, and other attempts to civilize the world.

The impulses that inform the bureaucracy of genocide are not solely products of the rationalization of society itself, of the disenchantment of the world and the iron cage. They are also a result of modernity's exclusion of the irrational, of already existing forces in society, which are repressed in a system geared toward profit generation. Andreas Huyssen touches on this when he writes that Auschwitz

> did not result from too much enlightened reason—even though it was organized as a perfectly rationalized death factory—but from a violent anti-enlightenment and anti-modernity affect, which exploited modernity ruthlessly for its own purposes.[33]

I want to suggest, breaking ranks with Huyssen, that where the critiques of Bauman et al. are indispensable is in helping us to show that the force of these anti-enlightenment drives was heightened by the characteristics of modernity itself. Not in the classic, Adornoesque thesis, that increasing domination over nature led inevitably to the domination over other human beings, although the role of social engineering was, as Aly and Heim show, vital; but the exclusion from a rational-purposive society of excess energy which could not be uselessly expended, and which therefore found itself employed in the very structures that modernity created.

Modernity may very well have been, in Zygmunt Bauman's stunning image, "a long march to prison."[34] But the search for order, backed up by "transcendental warrants,"[35] was accompanied by an increasing rage at every step that the level of "neatness" required to render the world tidied of misfits became ever more difficult to attain. Genocidal impulses derived from the characteristics of modernity, but not in the way that the "modernity theorists" believe: not total domination in the rationalized sense of ordering the world, but domination in the sense of massive frustration and *Hemmung* (hindrance) as a result of modernity's drive to homogenization and denial of society's excess energy.

There is no doubt that rationalization brings with it its own problems. The rationalization of animal slaughter in the name of cheap food results in the production of diseases which are responses to things being done in a way never intended by nature. So it is true that the extermination camps were state-run death factories which "cannot adequately be seen as simply the apogee of some ancient barbarism or the culmination of some timeless anti-Semitism."[36] Nor is it adequately understood as simply the necessary outcome of bureaucratic culture. Otherwise, in a postmodern world in which the desire to create the "great world-garden" has passed, as Bauman believes (MH, 219), we would no longer suffer from apocalyptic tendencies and millenarian fears. We do not believe that the passing of modernity invalidates the possibility of a new Auschwitz. Rather, in the next disaster, it will not surprise us that extraordinary technologies can be used for extraordinary brutalities, not with the express purpose of "ordering the world," but simply for the purpose of destroying it.

If there is a paradox involved in explaining the Holocaust in entirely rational ways, so is there a paradox in the rational explanation of the role of the irrational. But the attempt to emphasize the role of affect does not deny the workings of modern culture, and does not aspire to total comprehension. It remains aware of the contradictions of its own articulation, indeed, depends on them so as not to "wrap up" the question of the Holocaust in a simply determined historicization. How can this combination of the modernity thesis with the play of affect be achieved? I will conclude by offering some starting points for a new framework.

Firstly, the conclusion of the modernity theorists, that modernity is perfectly compatible with the most horrific acts, is correct. Herbert Marcuse already argued (though for different reasons) in the 1930s that liberal-democratic society was not immune to slipping into totalitarian domination. Indeed, he argued that there was an "inner relationship between liberalist social theory and the (apparently so antiliberal) totalitarian theory of the state." This contiguity was to be found in the reliance on the capitalist form of organization, which in liberalism was based on the individual entrepreneur, in totalitarianism on monopoly capital. Neither changed the essential fetishization of private property at the heart of capitalism.[37] While the Marxist interpretation of fascism and the Holocaust has been rightly discredited, the claim that Nazism was not merely an aberration remains key to any serious discussion of Auschwitz. After the war, only a few writers, such as Georges Bataille and Léon Poliakov, were independently minded enough to say so.

Having accepted this conclusion, we obviously cannot go back to the theories of the immediate postwar period, and put everything down to anti-Semitism or totalitarianism. But where the modernity thesis loses credit is in its downplaying of Nazi ritual and ideology. It reifies modernity, ignoring the implications of the discovery that barbarism is not produced by modernity, but rather inheres within it from the start, given added power through its disavowal. It provides a channel for existing drives as well as giving rise to its own. Gardening metaphors help to explain the origin of the Holocaust; how much more so when they are combined with the idea of the rush of hatred. This does not suggest that the Holocaust was an outbreak of atavism; the play of affect was entirely at ease with modern structures. But that there was an outburst of energy is indubitable. Otherwise the same bureaucratic structures which exist today would have by now gone beyond the achievement of the Holocaust. Something has to happen in order to start the bureaucratic ball rolling.

According to Dominick LaCapra, the goal of "historically informed analysis is not to focus on what may be distinctive in modernity." Rather, the aim should be to

> elucidate the intricate conjunction of distinctively modern features (such as the seemingly dominant role of instrumental rationality, bureaucratization, and massive technical resources) with the recurrence of often repressed forces, such as scapegoating with "sacrificial" dimensions.[38]

The attempt to focus only on one-half of the equation is itself evidence of a repression. Like the philosophical texts of Jean-François Lyotard and Philippe Lacoue-Labarthe (which LaCapra also persuasively analyzes), which overemphasize the role of totalizing aspirations at the expense of "ritual anxiety over boundary-transgression or the seemingly purifying, redemptive role of sacrificialism,"[39] the writers discussed above do not see that one of the consequences of modernity, apart from the will to order, was the frustration of "irrational" drives that had previously been channeled into religion or other outlets.

This problem of the damming of drives is central to Georges Bataille's work, which provides a starting point for this combination.[40] Dividing society into the spheres of the homogeneous and the heterogeneous, Bataille provides a way of explaining the role of affect in society that does not reduce it to the level of simply understood ideology, as the intentionalist historians do. The homogeneous includes everything tangible, goods, production, the "useful." The heterogeneous includes everything intangible and not reducible to the logic of classical economics: the sacred, waste, the unconscious, and so on:

> *Homogeneous* reality presents itself with the abstract and neutral aspect of strictly defined and identified objects (basically, it is the specific reality of solid objects). *Heterogeneous* reality is that of a force or shock. It presents itself as a charge. . . .[41]

Now, it will not do to reduce the Holocaust to the outburst of heterogeneous energy as described by Bataille. But when Bataille suggests that in bourgeois society the emphasis on instrumental rationality and profit-generation means that heterogeneous energies are anathema, we begin to see what scholars such as Saul Friedländer are driving at with the notion of "Rausch" (transport, intoxication). Heterogeneous energies may be anathema, but they do not by virtue of that fact go away. Rather, they are repressed, only to return with a vengeance in the absence of suitable channels for their exudation.[42]

However, when they return, they do so in the context of a modernity which has denied the existence of the irrational, or of the life of the affect. This was an attempt to create a "beautiful" world; but that desire was not borne only of the thought processes of modernity. Modernity aided its progress by blocking the heterogeneous, and then by supplying it with channels into which it could penetrate with equanimity, channels which did not formally demur with its aspirations, such as the role of racial science which Peukert emphasizes.

This consequence of modernity retains enough of the force of its critique to indict it, and to ensure that we continue to worry about its continuity; it certainly prevents us from embracing the optimism of Habermas as he seeks to complete the "project" of modernity. But it also broadens the range of possibility for alternative modes of living. We cannot simply junk the modern structures that characterize our culture (though we must junk the modernist belief that they would create the perfect world) and return to some golden pre-industrialized age; this is the quietism of the panacea-seeking New Age movement. But in our postmodern world we must find outlets for those energies which activate bureaucratic structures and propel them into genocide. The combination of modernity with existing hatreds is a terrifying one. By focusing on the existence of both, we resist the temptation to explain the Holocaust with overdetermined, totalizing concepts, and mediate between those who condemn Nazism as an outburst of irrational atavism and those who see it as the zenith of rationalization and liberalism. It is time to move beyond these concepts, and not let the necessary critique of modernity obscure the extreme human experience of the Holocaust in a historicization which once again represses the trauma. Modernity was the setting for the Holocaust, rationalization did set out to order the world. But modernity also denies the role of affect, and thus affect informs the process of ordering the world by its fascination with transgression and apocalyptic desire. When the two combine, the technological madness that results is the result neither of technology nor of madness, but of their explosive mixture.

Notes

1. Georges Bataille, "The Sacred Conspiracy," in *Visions of Excess: Selected Writings, 1927–1939*, trans. Allen Stoekl, Carl R. Lovitt, and Donald M. Leslie Jr., ed. Allen Stoekl (Minneapolis: University of Minnesota Press, 1985), p. 179.

2. Saul Friedländer, "Martin Broszat und die Historisierung des Nationalsozialismus" in *Mit der Pathos der Nüchternheit: Martin Broszat, das Institut für Zeitgeschichte und die Erforschung des Nationalsozialismus*, eds. Klaus-Dietmar Henke and Claudio Natoli (Frankfurt am Main: Campus Verlag, 1991), p. 166.

3. The phrase comes form Luce Irigaray, "The Power of Discourse and the Subordination of the Feminine," in *The Irigaray Reader*, trans. various, ed. M. Whitford (Oxford, Basil Blackwell, 1991), p. 126.

4. Wulf Kansteiner, "From Exception to Exemplum: The New Approach to Nazism and the 'Final Solution,' " *History and Theory* 33, no. 2 (1994): 169.

5. Cf. William Gass's "The Origin of Extermination in the Imagination," *The Philosophical Forum* 16, nos. 1–2 (Fall–Winter 1984–85): 26.

6. Arno J. Mayer, "Memory and History: On the Poverty of Remembering and Forgetting the Judeocide," *Radical History Review* 56 (Spring 1993): 7.

7. Jacques Derrida, *Writing and Difference* (London: Routledge, 1978), p. 282.

8. See the discussions of Zitelmann in Karl Heinz Roth, "Revisionist Tendencies in Historical Research into German Fascism," *International Review of Social History* 39 (1994): 429–55, and Wulf Kansteiner, "Emplotment and Historicization: Some Recent German Histories about National Socialism and Modernity," *Storia della Storiografia* 25 (1994): 65–87.

9. Rainer Zitelmann, "Die totalitäre Seite der Moderne," in *Nationalsozialismus und Modernisierung*, eds. Michael Prinz and Rainer Zitelmann (Darmstadt: Wissenschaftliche Buchgesellschaft, 1991), p. 17; idem, *Hitler: Selbstverständnis eines Revolutionärs* (Hamburg: Berg, 1987), pp. 196 and 462.

10. Kansteiner, "Emplotment and Historicization," p. 79.

11. Götz Aly and Susanne Heim, "Sozialplanung und Völkermord: Thesen zur Herrschaftsrationalität der nationalsozialistischen Vernichtungspolitik," in *Vernichtungspolitik: Eine Debatte über den Zusammenhang von Sozialpolitik und Genozid im nationalsozialistischen Deutschland*, ed. Wolfgang Scheider (Hanburg: Junius, 1991), pp. 19–20; idem, "The Economics of the Final Solution: A Case Study from the General Government," *Simon Wiesenthal Center Annual* 5 (1988): 38–39.

12. Götz Aly and Susanne Heim, *Vordenker der Vernichtung: Auschwitz und die deutschen Pläne für eine neue europäische Ordnung* (Frankfurt am Main: Fischer Taschenbuch Verlag, 1993), p. 485.

13. Ibid., pp. 184–85. Aly and Heim's work has now been complemented and partially superseded by Debórah Dwork and Robert Jan Van Pelt, *Auschwitz 1270 to the Present* (New Haven: Yale University Press, 1996).

14. Götz Aly, *"Endlösung": Völkerverschiebung und der Mord an den europäischen Juden* (Frankfurt am Main: S. Fischer Verlag, 1995), p. 25.

15. Ibid., p. 381.

16. Aly and Heim, "Economics of the Final Solution," p. 4. See also their essay "The Holocaust and Population Policy: Remarks on the Decision on the 'Final Solution,' " *Yad Vashem Studies* 24 (1994): 45–70.

17. Again in Kansteiner's words, they "present a consistent one-dimensional tragic plot that insists—to speak with [Hayden] White—'on the gain in consciousness for the spectators' of the disaster of Nazism. . . . This argument falls within the category of mechanistic explanation among historians. Being most familiar and therefore more easily convinced by the formist and the contextualist type of argumentation we perceive the cognitive limits of Aly's/Heim's mechanistic explanation more clearly, for instance their failure of conceiving of any socially responsible effects of science in postwar Germany." "Emplotment and Historicization," p. 81.

18. See the critiques of Aly and Heim in *Yad Vashem Studies* 24 (1994): Dan Diner, "Rationalization and Method," pp. 71–108; David Bankier, "On Modernization and the Rationality of Extermination," pp. 109–29; Ulrich Herbert, "Racism and Rational Calculation," pp. 131–45. See also Michael Burleigh, "A Political Economy of the Final Solution? Reflections on Modernity, Historians and the Holocaust," *Patterns of Prejudice* 30 (1996): 29–41, for a critique of Aly and Heim as well as of the very concept of "modernity" as a heuristic tool. Other useful critiques include Hermann Graml, "Irregeleitet und in die Irre führend," *Jarhbuch für Anti-Semitismusforschung* 1 (1992): 286–95; Christopher Browning, "German Technocrats, Jewish Labor, and the Final Solution: A Reply to Götz Aly and Susanne Heim," in idem, *The Path to Genocide: Essays on Launching the Final Solution* (Cambridge: Cambridge University Press, 1992), pp. 59–76; Martyn Housden, "Population, Economics, and Genocide: Aly and Heim versus All-comers in the Interpretation of the Holocaust," *Historical Journal* 38, no. 2 (1995): 479–86.

19. Detlev J. K. Peukert, *Inside Nazi Germany: Conformity, Opposition and Racism in Everyday Life* (London: Penguin, 1989), henceforth ING; idem, *Max Webers Diagnose der Moderne* (Göttingen, Vandenhoeck und Ruprecht, 1989), henceforth MW; idem, "Alltag und Barbarei: Zur 'Normalität' des Dritten Reiches," in *Ist der Nationalsozialismus Geschichte: Zu Historisierung und Historikerstreit*, ed. Dan Diner (Frankfurt am Main: Fischer, 1987), pp. 51–61, henceforth AB; idem, "The Genesis of the 'Final Solution' from the Spirit of Science," in *Nazism and German Society, 1933–1945*, ed. David Crew (London, Routledge, 1994), pp. 274–99, henceforth GEN; idem, "Rassismus und 'Endlösungs'-Utopie. Thesen zur Entwicklung und Struktur der national-sozialistischen Vernichtungspolitik," in *Nicht nur Hitlers Krieg: Der Zweite Weltkrieg und die Deutschen*, ed. Christph Klessmann (Düsseldorf: Droste Verlag, 1989), pp. 71–82, henceforth RAS.

20. Cf. GEN, p. 278: "what was new about the 'Final Solution' in world-historical terms was the fact that it resulted from a fatal racist dynamic present within the human and social sciences . . . a scheme for a high-technology 'solution' based on cost-benefit analysis." And RAS, p. 76: "The decisive particularities of this policy to annihilate the Jews cannot be explained by traditional anti-Semitism alone, but through its radicalization through the biologism of the 'racial hygienists,' through the departmentalization [*Arbeitsteilung*] of the bureaucratic apparatus, and through the generalisation of a racist medical doctrine, at first called 'euthanasia,' which in the alleged interest of the entire Volk [*Volksganzen*] undertook the 'therapeutic' killing of individuals, who were stigmatised as 'inferior.' "

21. Cf. MW, p. 68, where Peukert writes of the speed with which belief in progress and cultural pessimism, utopian dreams and totalitarian "coordination" [*Gleichschaltung*] could merge into one another. And RAS, p. 80, where Peukert says that "under certain conditions of crisis, mass murder and modernity are elective affinities [*wahlverwandt sind*]."

22. See David Schoenbaum, *Hitler's Social Revolution: Class and Status in Nazi Germany, 1933–1939* (Garden City: Anchor Press/Doubleday, 1966), and Ralf Dahrendorf, *Society and Democracy in Germany* (London: Weidenfeld and Nicolson, 1968). See also Norbert Frei, "Wie modern war der Nationalsozial-

ismus?" *Geschichte und Gesellschaft* 19, no. 3 (1993): 367–87, and Axel Schildt, "NS-Regime, Modernisierung und Moderne," *Tel Aviver Jahrbuch für deutsche Geschichte* 23 (1994): 3–22.

23. Zygmunt Bauman, *Modernity and the Holocaust* (Cambridge: Polity Press, 1989), p. 13, henceforth MH. In RAS, p. 80. Peukert also writes that with "Final Solution" utopias we are "dealing not with a necessary, but with a possible development." Cf. Jürgen Habermas, "Modernity: An Incomplete Project," in *Modernism/Postmodernism*, ed. Peter Brooker (London: Longman, 1992), pp. 125–38.

24. Zygmunt Bauman, *Intimations of Postmodernity* (London: Routledge, 1992), p. 178.

25. Apart from *Intimations of Postmodernity*, see also *Postmodern Ethics* (Oxford: Blackwell, 1993), and *Life in Fragments* (Oxford: Blackwell, 1995), which are attempts to grapple with what Bauman believes to be the new realities of social life without resorting to hackneyed and out-of-date sociological concepts developed to explain the old, modern world.

26. Similarly, Peukert writes (RAS, pp. 77–78) that "It is certain that the key figures in the 'Final Solution' utopia were party ideologues of the highest decision-making levels like Hitler and Himmler. But left to those levels, without the dogged plan-hatching [*Projekteschmieden*] of scientific experts, the *Krankenmord* would have been neither thinkable nor realisable."

27. See RAS, pp. 75 and 77 where Peukert talks of "cumulative radicalization."

28. Bauman avoids these dimensions of the Holocaust by maintaining a distinction between ancient and modern forms of barbarism, the latter being characterized by the existence of barbarism within society, the former by barbarism being an external threat. See his essay "Gewalt—modern und postmodern," in *Modernität und Barbarei: Soziologische Zeitdiagnose am Ende des 20. Jahrhunderts*, eds. Max Miller and Hans-Georg Soeffner (Frankfurt am Main: Suhrkamp Verlag, 1996), pp. 42–43.

29. See Dan Diner, "Between Aporia and Apology: On the Limits of Historicizing National Socialism," in *Reworking the Past: Hitler, the Holocaust and the Historians' Debate*, ed. Peter Baldwin (Boston, Beacon Press, 1990), pp. 135–45; idem, "Historical Understanding and Counterrationality: The *Judenrat* as Epistemological Vantage," in *Probing the Limits of Representation: Nazism and the "Final Solution,"* ed. Saul Friedländer (Cambridge, Mass.: Harvard University Press, 1992), pp. 128–42; idem, "Rationalisierung und Methode: Zu einem neuen Erklärungsversuch der 'Endlösung,'" *Vierteljahrshefte für Zeitgeschichte* 40 (1990): 359–82; Dominick LaCapra, *Representing the Holocaust: History, Theory, Trauma* (Ithaca: Cornell University Press, 1994); Hayden White, "Historical Emplotment and the Problem of Truth," in Friedländer, *Probing the Limits of Representation*, pp. 37–53; Hans Kellner, *Language and Historical Representation: Getting the Story Crooked* (Madison: University of Wisconsin Press, 1989); idem, "'Never Again' is Now," *History and Theory* 33, no. 2 (1994): 127–44.

30. Walter Benjamin, "N [Theoretics of Knowledge; Theory of Progress]," *The Philosophical Forum* 15, nos. 1–2 (Fall–Winter 1983–84): 14.

31. Mark Levene, "Is the Holocaust Simply Another Example of Genocide?" *Patterns of Prejudice* 28, no. 2 (1994): 8 and 10.

32. See Benno Müller-Hill, *Murderous Science: Elimination by Scientific Selection of Jews, Gypsies, and Others, Germany 1933–1945* (Oxford: Oxford University Press, 1988), p. 89.

33. Andreas Huyssen, "Mapping the Postmodern," in *Feminism / Postmodernism*, ed. Linda J. Nicholson (London: Routledge, 1990), p. 255.

34. Bauman, *Intimations of Postmodernity*, p. xvii.

35. James R. Watson, "Auschwitz and the Limits of Transcendence," *Philosophy and Social Criticism* 18, no. 2 (1992): 176.

36. Daniel Pick, *War Machine: The Rationalization of Slaughter in the Modern Age* (New Haven: Yale University Press, 1993), p. 187.

37. Herbert Marcuse, *Negations: Essays in Critical Theory*, trans. Jeremy J. Shapiro (Harmondsworth: Penguin, 1972), p. 10 and passim.

38. LaCapra, *Representing the Holocaust*, p. 94.

39. Ibid., p. 93.

40. Although in a different way from LaCapra, who calls for a sensitive historicization of the Holocaust that respects its status as limit-case. This goal, he believes, will best be achieved through a process of mourning which would give the Holocaust a "'proper' burial" (p. 193), unlike those historical approaches which prefer to deal with it as if already "dead" and finished.

41. Georges Bataille, "The Psychological Structure of Fascism," in *Visions of Excess*, p. 143.

42. See Georges Bataille, *The Accursed Share: An Essay on General Economy, Volume I*, trans. Robert Hurley (New York: Zone Books, 1991), p. 21. Andrew Benjamin writes that "the crisis of modernism can be described as resulting from the impossibility of sustaining the homogeneous and therefore of excluding the heterogeneous." *Art, Mimesis and the Avant-Garde: Aspects of a Philosophy of Difference* (London: Routledge, 1991), p. 63.

Remembering and Forgetting
The Social Construction of a Community of Memory of the Holocaust

Alan Milchman and Alan Rosenberg

> Should the enemies of the dead be victorious,
> even the dead would not be safe from victors
> who do not cease to score victories.
>
> —Walter Benjamin

As a transformational event, that is, one which has altered the human landscape in a decisive way, the Holocaust constitutes an urgent summons to think about its meanings and implications. The Holocaust, of which Auschwitz is emblematic, has bequeathed to our modernity the death-world, ". . . a new and unique form of social existence in which vast populations are subjected to conditions of life simulating imagined conditions of death, conferring upon their inhabitants the status of the living dead."[1] Such death-worlds remain an "objectively-real possibility," to use a concept of Ernst Bloch's, on the "Front" of our technoscientific civilization.[2] The prospect of new death-worlds on the Front of history leads us to grapple with the Holocaust as an integral component of what the French thinker Michel Foucault designated a "history of the present." By virtue of its insistence on problematizing present historical configurations, its focus on the genealogy of contemporary social structurations or practices, and its rejection of a suprahistorical perspective which insists on the necessity of the present, such a history of the present immerses us in concerns which are distinctly political. In that sense, Arno J. Mayer's view on how to approach the Holocaust is both consonant with a Foucauldian conception of a history of the present, and can guide our own inquiry into the question of memory and the Holocaust: "In sum, it is not enough to emotionalize and 'dwell on [the] horrors' of Auschwitz. Instead of allowing these horrors to 'paralyze' our critical intelligence, they should be read with a view to discerning 'political contexts' and mobilizing 'political passions' relevant to present-day concerns."[3] Indeed, it is in this way that we understand what Holocaust survivors meant when they uttered the phrase "never again!" which resonates with the concerns not only of those who were the specific targets of the Nazi genocide, but of all potential victims of emerging death-worlds. The need for such a mobilization of political passions was poignantly evoked by Elie Wiesel, when—speaking for the community of survivors—he asserted that: "Nothing has been learned, Auschwitz has not served as a warning. For more detailed information, consult your daily newspapers."[4] The horrors inflicted on the Bosnian Muslims or the Rwandan Tutsis are a grim confirmation of both Wiesel's plaintive cry and of the present-day concerns which motivate our efforts.

What is entailed by the need to "speak Auschwitz," to remember the Holocaust? We are compelled to return to the horror of the Shoah in the service of life. As Terrance Des Pres recognized, what leads us back to the death-world is the same basic assumption that has motivated so many survivors to bear witness:

> The assumption is that good and evil are only clear in retrospect; that moral vision depends on assimilation of the past; that man as man cannot dispense with memory. Wisdom depends on knowledge and it comes at a terrible price. It comes from consciousness of, and then response to, the deeds and events through which men have already passed. Conscience, as Schopenhauer put it, is "man's knowledge concerning what he has done."[5]

The assimilation of the past is integral to the construction of a community of memory of the Holocaust. We owe the term "community of memory" to Edith Wyshogrod.[6] However we are refunctioning this term, and using it in a very different sense than does Wyshogrod. For Wyshogrod, a community of memory is based largely on nostalgia for the past, with very strong overtones that what is involved is "a self-deception that purports to dig up an original that never existed."[7] For us, by contrast, a community of memory is prospective, not memorializing; its memory is in the service of future transformations, not a mythicized past; its history is critical, not monumental. A community of memory, as we seek to discuss it here, problematizes the present rather than sacralizing the past. Moreover, its memories are pluralistic, not monolithic; it makes room for difference rather than insisting on identity. Such a community of memory, we believe, can incorporate beliefs that allow humankind to confront its past and thereby begin to reshape its life-conditions.

This essay is divided into three parts. In part one, our concern is twofold: to explore the ways in which a preoccupation with the past, in this case the Holocaust, is mediated by *present* concerns, and has a distinctly *political* dimension, and to examine the debate swirling around the question of the relationship between *remembering* and *forgetting*. This latter question revolves around the insistence of thinkers such as Primo Levi that the great danger is that we will forget the horrors of Auschwitz, that it will be expunged from our memory, even as thinkers such as Charles Maier have raised the prospect that we may already suffer from a surfeit of memory, that our very preoccupation with the Holocaust carries with it its own dangers. Here then, our concern will be on whether or not a focus on the past can be obsessive and disabling. In the course of our own examination of this issue, it became clear to us that many of the thinkers with whose ideas we were engaged used the terms "memory" and "history" without any concern to distinguish between them, as general markers or designations for the way in which we think about and recollect the past. Thus, Maiers's trope of a surfeit of memory could easily be replaced with a surfeit of history; and for Levi's concern about a danger of a falsification of memory, one could just as well substitute a falsification of history. The looseness or lack of precision in the terminology here is not a problem at this point, inasmuch as our concern at this stage of the argument is over the competing claims of the implications of remembering or forgetting the past, in this case the smokestacks of Auschwitz, and not the specific modalities or ways in which the past shows up, as memory or history. In part two, our focus is on the ways in which our recollection or memory of the past is culturally or socially *constructed*. We do not have unmediated access to the past; we do not "see it" as it "really was." Rather our own culture, and our own present, contingent concerns are elements in the mix out of which our image of the past is shaped. In part three, we will discuss the way in which the past "shows up" for us phenomenologically; and how its taken-for-granted form can become disrupted. Here, we will examine the ways in which the discipline of history has generated the very categories through which we "see" the past today, memory and history. In the course of exploring the ways in which certain historians and social scientists have sought to make precise distinctions between memory and history, we shall *problematize* these concepts and show how they relate to a community of memory of the Holocaust.

Part I

For Primo Levi, ". . . the entire history of the brief 'millennial Reich' can be read as a *war against memory*, an Orwellian falsification of memory. . . ."[8] Beyond their determination to exterminate Jews and other *Untermenschen*, the Nazis were no less concerned to eradicate the memory of those particular deeds. Alvin Rosenfeld has illuminated this dimension of the Shoah:

> Apart from its genocidal aims, what distinguished the Nazi crime against the Jews was the intent of the criminals to leave behind no witnesses and, hence, no record at all. The Holocaust was to be a total, silent deed—in the words of one of its key perpetrators, "an unwritten and never-to-be-written page of glory." The fact that Himmler's will in this regard has not prevailed is owing in the first place to the determination of his victims, who found the courage and the means to persist against him as recording witnesses.[9]

One such witness was Chaim Kaplan, the memoirist of the Warsaw ghetto, who said of his diary: "It is difficult to write, but I consider it an obligation and am determined to fulfill it with my last ounce of energy. I will write a scroll of agony in order to remember the past in the future."[10]

The shapes of memory which emerge on the basis of the efforts of memoirists such as Kaplan, Jean Améry, and Primo Levi can become elements of a politics of memory which can orient us in the face of the threat of new death-worlds which confronts our late modernity as an objectively-real possibility. Memories, particularly group memories, are politically charged. As Arno Mayer has pointed out:

> . . . both memory and history tend to be used and misused for political ends. Through the ages, historical narratives and interpretations have served numerous functions other than the advancement of scholarship. They have been—and continue to be—shaped and instrumentalized to exalt rulers, to generate founding legends, to promote national identities, to brace belief systems, and to rationalize abuses of power. . . . Indeed, the purpose of heralding a collective memory is less to preserve an immutable receding past than to readjust and enliven it for use in arguments over policies for today and tomorrow. . . .[11]

Whether used to bolster or to challenge prevailing ideologies and orthodoxies, memory cannot escape becoming the object of a political battle. The struggle in France over the memory of Vichy, renewed in the light of the revelations of François Mitterand's own youthful engagement on behalf of the "national revolution";[12] the ongoing debate in Germany over how to remember a past scarred by the enormity of the Extermination and the role of ordinary Germans in it;[13] and the way in which the memory of the Holocaust has shaped Israeli politics[14] and hangs over the peace process today, all serve to alert us to the fact that more than a half century after the death camps ceased producing corpses we are still engaged in what Tom Segev has aptly described as "the battle over the memory and meaning of the Holocaust."[15] Indeed, memory is a decisive element of most political struggles. As Michel Foucault pointed out: "Since memory is actually a very important factor in struggle (really, in fact, struggles develop in a kind of conscious moving forward of history), if one controls people's memory, one controls their dynamism. And one also controls their experience, their knowledge of previous struggles."[16]

The perpetrator's concern to keep his crimes secret, and the concomitant need of the victims to record their memories, and their conviction that remembering is in the service of the future, characterize not just the Holocaust and its survivors, but the whole experience of humankind with totalitarianism and state power in twentieth-century modernity. As Milan Kundera has persuasively argued, it is forgetting that every totalitarian state seeks to impose upon its subjects. Thus, Kundera in his novel *The Book of Laughter and Forgetting*, has Mirek say: "The struggle of man against power is the struggle of memory against forgetting."[17] Indeed, besides the physical liquidation of a people and the destruction of the very memory of the deed, which the Nazis attempted in the Final Solution, the totalitarian state can also liquidate a group without physically exterminating it. As Kundera points out, speaking through his character, Hübl:

> You begin to liquidate a people . . . by taking away its memory. You destroy its books, its culture, its history. And then others write other books for it, give another culture to it, invent another history for it. Then the people slowly begins to forget what it is and what it was.[18]

In both cases, the totalitarian state must eradicate memory, make people forget. Indeed, as Tzvetan Todorov has pointed out, one of the characteristics of the totalitarian regimes of the twentieth century, in contrast to premodern tyrannies, is the use of their unprecedented control of information and communication to attempt to systematically bring about the destruction of memory.[19] Moreover, it can be argued that the liberal democracies of the West are also contributing to the destruction of memory, albeit in a different manner than totalitarian regimes, by virtue of the veritable barrage of information and images unleashed by the mass media, with their unremitting focus on the present moment, to the exclusion of any historical context. As Todorov has provocatively put it: "Here, memory would be threatened not by the obliteration of information, but by its overabundance. Thus, in a less violent, but ultimately more effective manner, because not provoking our resistance, but, on the contrary, making us the consenting agents of this march towards forgetfulness, the democratic states lead their population to the same goal as the totalitarian regimes. . . ."[20] The point, of course, is not to put an equal sign between totalitarian and democratic regimes, but to acknowledge that beyond the significant distinctions between the several political forms which occur within it, the trajectory of modernity, with its fixation on the new, is to cut humanity adrift from its past. Indeed, Theodor W. Adorno opined that "the terrifying image of humankind without memory [einer Menschheit ohne Erinnerung] is the veritable hallmark of modernity; of an advancing bourgeois society which involves the "liquidation" of memory and recollection.[21]

If the heroic efforts of memoirists such as Chaim Kaplan summon us to remember the Holocaust in all its horrific detail, what are we to make of the question raised by the historian Charles S. Maier: "Can there be too much memory?"[22] How are we to react to Arno Mayer's concern that the Holocaust may have contributed to a "rage for memory," which can have retrogressive political consequences?[23] Are these simply calls for closure, an insistence that it is time to get past the Holocaust, to remove ourselves from its shadow? If that were the case, then our response might take the form of the following comment by Geoffrey Hartman: "The call for closure, though understandable as an expression of hope (that a deep wound is finally healing), remains premature. Wherever we look—at a potentially murderous racial politics, or at the work of mourning, or at public education (which now includes the media and multiplying networks of information)—wherever we look, the events of 1933–1945 cannot be relegated to the past. They are not over. . . ."[24] However, neither Maier's concern about a surfeit of memory nor Mayer's fears about a rage for memory can be summarily dismissed. Indeed, each of them ultimately compels us to reflect upon a dimension of forgetting far removed from Nazism's war against memory, or the way totalitarian regimes seek to liquidate a people evoked by Hübl in Kundera's The Book of Laughter and Forgetting, or even the concern about a premature closure evoked by Hartman; an aspect of forgetting first illuminated by Friedrich Nietzsche precisely in the service of humankind's historical present and future.

What has provoked such concerns about a negative role played by memory is the link perceived between a growing mythicization and sacralization of memory, and its mobilization in the service of an ideology of victimization, claims based on ethnicity and the recrudescence of xenophobia. Specifically in the case of the memory of the Shoah, Charles Maier has pointed to the danger that the lesson "taught" by Holocaust museums may be a demand for respect and recognition based on the victimhood of one's group rather than a concern for new outrages now being perpetrated on other groups.[25] For Maier, this is but one facet of a growing fixation on ethnicity which permeates late modernity, and which is accompanied by a preoccupation with memory.[26] As a result, Maier believes that what he terms a "canonization of memory," an "addiction to memory," which increasingly shapes our historical present, "can become neurasthenic and disabling."[27] For Arno Mayer, the memory of the Judeocide, enshrined in such sites of memory as Yad Vashem and its Wall of Remembrance, where memory is sacralized, may be a goad to the repression of the Palestinian Arabs and to Israeli expansionism.[28] Indeed, for Mayer, such a use of memory is by no means peculiar to the Holocaust and its Jewish victims:

> Today's innumerable national(ity), ethnic, and cultural conflicts, many of them intensified by religious fervor, are unthinkable without the driving engine of institutionalized social memory: in Israel and the Occupied Territories; in the lands of yesterday's Soviet Union and Yugoslavia; in Kashmir and Sri Lanka; in the Sudan and Somalia; and more. Many neighborhoods of our planet are threatened by volcanic eruptions of highly selective, sectarian, and sacralized social memories. Although in the recent past men and women died "for the fatherland" . . . in this fin de siècle they are dying, and killing, "for memory."[29]

While such an obsession with memory seems to clash with Levi's conception of Nazism's war against memory or the Adornian image of modernity characterized by a humanity without memory, the cultivation of sectarian memory, with its xenophobic thrust, to which Mayer is responding, in its manipulation of past victimization and focus on phantasies of revenge, is quite compatible with a civilizational complex in which recollection of the past is largely controlled and circumscribed by the state or mass media. Neither a regime of the Nazi or Stalinist type, nor a liberal democratic regime have sought to simply extinguish memory. Rather, they have been obsessed with controlling and shaping it, through an omnipotent censorship and state organs of propaganda, in the former cases, or through the mass media in the latter case. If this has entailed the extirpation of certain memories (Levi's trope of a war against memory, Adorno's image of humankind without memory), it has also involved the enhancement, cultivation, and mythification of other memories. What is at stake, then, is the content of the memories which are sanctioned, and the uses to which they are put.

The danger that memory may be mobilized in the service of genocide, or, at the least, distance us from the horrors perpetrated on others, while we define ourselves by our own past victimhood and the demand for recognition and respect based exclusively on it, has led Arno Mayer to assert that: "The world is haunted less by 'the specter of man without memory' than by the specter of man without forgetting."[30] As a result of this danger, both Charles Maier and Arno Mayer have had recourse to Nietzsche's insight into the need for humans, as historical beings, to forget. Maier, concerned about what he sees as an addiction to memory and a concomitant preoccupation with history, shares Nietzsche's concern that "history might become a cloying excuse not to act and not to accept the fullness of life in the present: a sort of post-Victorian neurasthenia."[31] For Mayer, "[i]n Nietzsche's view, life was 'absolutely impossible' without unremembering. Indeed, he held that memory unalleviated by wise forgetting was a 'festering sore.' "[32] What would such a "wise forgetting" entail? We are not speaking here so much of the content (what to forget), as the process (how individuals and, more particularly, a culture come to forget). One cannot eliminate a certain voluntarism and intentionality from certain processes of "forgetting," those that proceed from state censorship and official histories, or the recent expressions of Holocaust denial, for example. However, Nietzsche's wise forgetting does not seem to proceed from state fiat or even the volition of a subject, but rather through a more complex and manifold process by which a culture works through the social wounds of its past.[33]

Nietzsche's own thoughts on what it means to be historical and his reflections on remembrance and forgetting contained in the second of his *Untimely Meditations*, the finely crafted "On the uses and disadvantages of history for life," can perhaps help us to grasp why the capacity to forget may be a vital component of life in a world increasingly shaped by ethnic hatred and warfare. Nietzsche raises the question of what it means to be historical, and in what sense history is necessary for humans, insisting that we need history "for the sake of life and action."[34] To be historical means not to be bound to the past, but rather to play a role in shaping the future, to be futural. To that end, Nietzsche argues that a delicate balance between remembrance and forgetting is necessary.

To see forgetting as a vital component of history may seem paradoxical at first glance. However, it is precisely here that Nietzsche's insight into the problematic of the historical is most powerful. Nietzsche insists on the need to forget, lest we be so consumed by the past that action oriented to the future is precluded; a part of the past must be forgotten "if it is not to become the gravedigger of the present. . . ."[35] For Nietzsche, future possibilities will be shut off if we lack the capacity to heal old wounds, an essential element of which is the ability—judiciously used—to forget. If such an ability is not present, there is the very real risk that a culture will be obsessed with revenge, trapped by an impotent rage or tormented to death by a horror that it cannot surmount. A dose of forgetting is necessary for human beings, not to obliterate their past, but to prevent themselves from being trapped by it; to be able to overcome it. This is an integral part of what Nietzsche terms "the *plastic power* of man." For him, its lack is disastrous: "There are people who possess so little of this power that they can perish from a single experience, from a single painful event, often and especially from a single subtle piece of injustice, like a man bleeding to death from a scratch. . . ."[36] How much greater is the danger of sacrificing the future to the past in the case of an injustice as gigantic as that of the Holocaust? Nazism would indeed have achieved a belated victory if its victims—and their spiritual offspring—in their obsession with its horrors, and under the spell of what Tom Segev has termed "a bizarre cult of memory, death, and kitsch,"[37] were to recreate the death-world in a new historical space and time.

Shortly after the outbreak of the Intifada in the late 1980s, such a danger, directly linked to the inability to forget, was specifically raised by Yehuda Elkana, director of the Institute of Science and Ideas at Tel Aviv University and himself a survivor, as a child, of Auschwitz:

> An atmosphere in which an entire nation determines its relation to the present and shapes its future by concentrating on the lessons of the past is a danger to the future of any society that wishes to live in relative serenity and relative security. . . . I see no greater danger to the future of Israel than the fact that the Holocaust has been instilled methodically into the consciousness of the Israeli public, including that very large part that did not endure the Holocaust, as well as the generation of children that has been born and grown up here. . . . What is a child supposed to do with these memories? For a great many of them, the horror pictures were likely to be interpreted as a call for hatred. "Remember" could be interpreted as a call for long-standing, blind hatred. . . . We . . . must forget. . . . The rule of historical remembrance must be uprooted from our lives.[38]

While we share Elkana's fears—which echo Nietzsche's—that a sacralization of memory and a *ressentiment* over historical wrongs can lead a people to perpetrate the very horrors on Others which their obsession with past atrocities inflicted on themselves was intended to prevent, we do not accept his injunction that we must uproot historical remembrance from our lives. There is a kind of remembrance which is frankly *revanchist*, and which can lead to the creation of new death-worlds. However, one avoids such an outcome not through historical amnesia, but through a kind of remembrance that allows one to work through the horrors of past experience. That is the conclusion reached by Charles Maier:

> The answer to obsession is not forgetting, but overcoming; the basis for consensus is not obscuring but repairing so far as is possible, and avoiding the categorizing of species that lay at the origin of "life unworthy of life." Thereafter let the historian insist that Auschwitz was not the end of history; it was not the entelechy of the twentieth century. . . . It is possible to make a fetish of Auschwitz. Granted, the distinction between mourning, honoring, analyzing—all legitimate ends for the historian—and fetishizing is a hard one. . . . History should contribute to reconstructive effort, efforts by, as well as on behalf of, earlier victims.[39]

Similarly, Nietzsche's warnings about the need to forget should not be seen as a repudiation of the important role of memory in history. Remembrance is also a crucial element in what Nietzsche terms a "critical history":

> If he is to live, man must possess and from time to time employ the strength to break up and dissolve a part of the past: he does this by bringing it before the tribunal, scrupulously examining it and finally condemning it. . . .[40]

If forgetting is an aspect of such a critical history, memory is no less vital to it. Such a critical history, as Nietzsche proposes, involves a process of working through the horrors of the past as a precondition for dissolving elements of it. And such a process is impossible without memory.[41]

It is out of just such a dialectic of remembrance and forgetting that a community of memory of the Holocaust can be constituted. A community of memory focused on the working through of the experience of past injustice and crimes, by virtue of its futural orientation, gives rise to a politics of memory and a critical history. Before we discuss what such a community of memory of the Holocaust, its politics and critical history, might look like, we want to address two important issues, the elucidation of which are vital to our inquiry: the cultural or social character of memory; and the distinction between memory and history.

Part II

The sociological discussion of memory had its inception with the Durkheimian school, and in the period between the two World Wars was advanced through the pathbreaking work of Maurice Halbwachs. It was Halbwachs who insisted that all memory is ineluctably shaped by the group or collectivity to which the individual belongs, that it has an indubitably cultural or social dimension:

> To be sure, everyone has a capacity for memory [mémoire] that is unlike that of anyone else. . . . But individual memory is nevertheless a part or an aspect of group memory, since each impression and each fact, even if it apparently concerns a particular person exclusively, leaves a lasting memory only to the extent that one has thought it over—to the extent that it is connected with the thoughts that come to us from the social milieu. One cannot in fact think about the events of one's past without discoursing upon them. But to discourse upon something means to connect within a single system of ideas our opinions as well as those of our circle. It means to perceive in what happens to us a particular application of facts concerning which social thought

reminds us at every moment of the meaning and impact these facts have for it. In this way, the framework of collective memory confines and binds our most intimate remembrances to each other.[42]

Inasmuch as memory, even one's most personal memories, manifests itself through language, and through the tropes, signs, symbols, and meanings that are specific to a particular social group, it bears the imprint of a given collectivity or culture. Once memory is stored linguistically or in narrative form, it is already a cultural memory even when it is the personal memory of my own experience. Arno Mayer, too, argues that memory is inescapably social in character: "... since individuals are 'never really alone,' they construct their autobiographical recollections in reciprocal relation with the no-less constructed reminiscences of others. Ultimately, then, individual and collective or social memories are a seamless web, whose patterns are imprinted with later understandings and concerns, and whose articulations are ordered and symbolized in accordance with conventional yet changeable codes of narrative exposition."[43]

In pointing to the constructed character of memory, particularly social memory, Mayer—perhaps inadvertently—alerts us to the danger of attributing an intentionality to the construction of memory. Any conception of a social or cultural memory carries the risk of its hypostatization. As Amos Funkenstein has said, there is a "tendency to ascribe an independent existence to collective mentality, to the 'spirit of the nation,' or to language itself, which thinks, as it were, by means of the individual. . . ."[44] Such a conception easily slides into an attribution of intentionality to such a collective mentality, which purportedly deliberately and consciously contructs its own memory. While attempts to so construct or shape a social memory, by the action of either the state or the mass media, are one hallmark of our late modernity, the complex and multiple processes by which a cultural memory arises and is formed are not reducible to the intentionality of state, mass media, or a hypostatized collective mentality.

Halbwachs, like Mayer, generally referred to such memory as "collective memory." We prefer to speak, however, of a social or cultural memory, eschewing the term collective memory for two basic reasons. First, the term collective memory is today overdetermined by its association with images of Jungian archetypes of the collective unconscious, with their biological or racial transmission of memory. Second, even to the extent that collective memory can be extricated from that kind of biologism, it seems to be most consonant with archaic or traditional communities, and their patterns of memory, enshrined in rituals and symbols which are virtually unchanging over many generations. Such a collective memory of archaic communities is also constructed, though not with the intentionality which is a component of the cultural memory of modern societies. However, the collective memory of such traditional communities has been virtually destroyed, or largely eroded, by the advance of modernity, which is characterized by what Geoffrey Hartman designates as "public memory." In contrast to the seemingly static, organic, and monolithic character of the collective memory of traditional communities, public memory is unstable and based on a plethora of rapidly changing images and symbols generated by the state or the mass media. Indeed, for Hartman, "unlike the older type of communal or collective memory," public memory "has no stability or durée, only a jittery, mobile, perpetually changing yet permanently inscribed status."[45] For Hartman, collective memory is today in danger from two sources: It is weakened because public memory, with its frantic and uncertain agency, is taking its place; and because a politicized collective memory, claiming a biological or mystical permanence, tries to usurp the living tie between generations."[46] Hartman's "politicized collective memory," no less than his public memory, arises with the demise of collective memory and the traditional communities in which they were constructed. What links these different ways in which people(s) remember is that each one is a social or cultural memory. Moreover, if memory is socially or culturally constructed, culture is itself inextricably bound to memory. As John Dewey pointed out, it is remembering that marks "the difference between bestiality and humanity, between culture and merely physical nature. . . ."[47]

This social or cultural character of memory can also be articulated by tracing its genesis out of the concrete experiences of human being. Memory is a recollection of lived experience, and any phenomenological inquiry into the elements which constitute memory should begin with the injunction of the young Martin Heidegger: "Let us immerse ourselves in the lived *experience*" (Versenken wir uns . . . in das Erlebnis).[48] Lived experience is not solipsistic; it occurs in what Heidegger terms an "environing world" (*Umwelt*), one which is historically and culturally specific, so that the experience itself is already structured by meaning.[49] Far from being an incoherent blur of sensations, experience, for adults, is typically encoded through the modalities of language.

Moreover, the meaning of these memories is socially or culturally mediated, by virtue of their intralinguistic character and the signs and symbols that are integral to their very structure. Thus, as Amos Funkenstein has put it: "No memory, not even the most intimate and personal, can be isolated from the social context, from the language and symbolic system molded by the society over centuries."[50]

Specific social groups recollect and imaginatively construct their past each in its own way. Whatever the bases for the group's unique sense of its own identity, whether this comes from within or is imposed by others, a particular social or cultural memory will bind its members to one another.

Such a social memory, will be structured by a congeries of cultural objectivations, which constitute what Jan Assman terms its fixed points: "These fixed points are fateful events of the past, whose memory is maintained through cultural formation (texts, rites, monuments) and institutional communication (recitation, practice, observance). We call these 'figures of memory.' . . . In cultural formation, a collective experience crystallizes, whose meaning, when touched upon, may suddenly become accessible again across millennia."[51] The cultural objectivations which become the crystallizations of a social memory can include traditions, myths, artifacts, monuments, places, ceremonies, testimonies, or symbols. What they all have in common is being the repository of a cultural memory.

Beyond its crystallization in figures of memory, in cultural objectivations, social memories are transmitted through a complex process of socialization, to which members of the group are exposed, and from which they derive a sense of belonging, and an awareness of the group's specificity.[52] As Assman points out: "The objective manifestations of cultural memory are defined through a kind of identificatory determination in a positive ("We are this") or in a negative ("That's our opposite") sense.[53]

The social memory, successfully transmitted and crystallized in its cultural objectivations, activates the individuals who make up the determinate social group: race, nation, religion, ethnos, class. When the mnemonic process serves to mobilize the group, and its members, for social action, a politics of memory is generated. The figures of memory on the bases of which such a politics arises, however, are not static. Indeed, it is precisely here that we take issue with Assman, for whom figures of memory are "fixed points," whose cultural meaning seems to be unchanging. We believe that a culture has the capacity to shift the meaning, to refunction, its figures of memory. Indeed, figures of memory are typically contested; they are the objects of acrimonious political debate and even the occasion for violent struggles. We need only think, for example, of the *lieux de mémoire*, the realms of memory, analyzed by the French historians working under the direction of Pierre Nora. The memory of the French Revolution, or of the Vichy regime, to take but two such sites of memory, remain subject to pluralistic interpretations, the objects of bitterly contested and ever changing meanings.[54]

In his penetrating analysis of the way in which Nazism appropriated the image of the "Third Reich" for its own purposes, Ernst Bloch shows how a political movement can consciously refunction a figure of memory in the service of death. As Bloch indicates, in the sixteenth century the Third Reich had incarnated the projective memories and images of emancipation from oppression:

> in its original form the Third Reich had denoted the *social-revolutionary ideal dream of Christian heresy*: the dream of a Third Gospel and the

world corresponding to it. . . . . The more the situation of the peasants and
ordinary urban citizens worsened . . . the more powerfully the prophecy
of a new, an "evangelical" age necessarily struck home. . . .[55]

The Nazis orchestrated a politics of memory which, as Bloch makes
clear, refunctioned such cultural objectivations with lethal results: "The
Nazi was creative, so to speak, only in the embezzlement at all prices
with which he employed revolutionary slogans to the opposite effect.
With which . . . he used the dark lustre of old phrases and gave a patina
to the revolution which he claimed to be making."[56] While such a refunctioning of figures of memory can be deliberately undertaken by a political movement or a regime, utilizing the instruments of propaganda and
the mass media, it can also emanate from more spontaneous social
processes, from the convergence of the multiple strands of lived experience, and emerge from "below." Such a politics of memory can be xenophobic, as in the case of Nazism, and produce the death-world symbolized by Auschwitz and its smokestacks, or it can be animated by recon-
structive efforts on the part of, or for the sake of, the victims of historical
injustice. The structure of such a politics of memory will be linked to the
kind of historical narrative that shapes it, and here some comments on
the relationship of memory and history are in order.

Part III

In Martin Broszat's "plea" for an "historicization" of National Socialism,
and his subsequent discussions with Saul Friedländer about this issue,
the question of the relationship of memory and history occupied a central place.[57] In this discussion, it becomes clear that Broszat and
Friedländer are not using the terms "memory" and "history" as general
markers for the way in which we recollect the past, as did Levi, Mayer,
or Maier, for example, but in a very precise sense, in which the distinctions between the two terms become important. It is this issue, and its
wide-reaching implications, that will be our focus as we proceed with
this discussion. What concerns us here is not the possibility that historicization can lead to a relativization or normalization of Nazi crimes,
and even to apologetic tendencies, which is not the outcome toward
which Broszat's argument is directed. Rather, it is the contention, which
Broszat champions, that the time has come to treat the Nazi epoch of
German history in the manner in which historians treat other epochs
and regimes; that the study of the Hitler-state should be subject to the
same canons and protocols that shape any historiographical endeavor.
What underlies Broszat's plea is the belief that memory always carries
with it a moral-political stamp, and has a pronounced tendency to mon-

umentalization, while history as a reconstruction of the past, i.e., historiography, results in objectivity; in short, memory tends to be at odds
with "authentic historical reconstruction."[58] Whether he is speaking of
"official memory" incarnated in the state or the memory of those who
have had direct or indirect experience, victims of the Holocaust and
their children, for example, Broszat sees memory as "nonscientific" and
"mythical"; by contrast, historiography yields "rational understanding."[59] Broszat is certainly prepared to acknowledge a place for mythical
memory:

> in their nonscientific way, many such literary, mythical images of the
> Nazi experience furnish us with insights. Such insights are, in the best
> sense of the term, "intelligent," and are thus quite compatible with the
> growing need for a better scientific understanding of the past.[60]

Yet, while memory may be compatible with the work of the historian, for
Broszat it is not the same; indeed, it is difficult not to conclude that, for
Broszat, mythical remembrance can at best be ancillary and, in the final
analysis, subordinate, to the scientific comprehension produced by historiography; and this despite his statement about compatibility. There-
with lies the urgency of Broszat's plea, after forty years, to permit the
historicization of Nazism.

Friedländer rejects Broszat's claims for historicization, though he
fears that historians will one day, perhaps in another generation, cross
"the line between an existentially determined perspective and a
detached scientific point of view,"[61] that is, from memory to history.
While such an outcome seems normal to Friedländer in the case of other
historical events, the unique horror of the Shoah is such that it is difficult for him to accept the prospect of its becoming the object of a "purely
scientific distancing from that past."[62] Nonetheless, Friedländer does not
really challenge Broszat's distinction between a memory that is moral-
political and a historiography that is detached and scientific, only his
contention that even in the case of Nazism and the Holocaust, there is
now an urgent need for the latter. Moreover, such assumptions about history, its scientificity and objectivity, are widely accepted in the modern
historiographical community.

It is just that distinction between a memory that is moral-political
and a history that is scientific and objective which we want to problematize. Indeed, it seems to us that history is no less moral-political
than the way in which Broszat and Friedländer see memory. In short, we
are not prepared to accept a vision of history which sees the past "the
way it really was," which, because it is "objective," makes it possible for
the "facts" to speak for themselves. The conception of objectivity which
underlies such a vision would mean that history, in contrast to memory,

is not socially mediated and structured by its cultural determinants. We do not intend to eliminate the notion of objectivity altogether, but we do reject a conception of objectivity with a capital "O," a conception which is suprahistorical and transcendental. Our concern is that a vision of history which purportedly yields Broszat's "authentic historical reproduction" may be burdened by just such a conception. The historian's objectivity, the way in which she elicits the "facts," is bound by what Michel Foucault terms the "regime of truth," on the basis of which the facts are permitted to show up. According to Foucault:

> Truth is a thing of this world: it is produced only by virtue of multiple forms of constraint. And it induces regular effects of power. Each society has its régime of truth, its "general politics" of truth: that is, the types of discourse which it accepts and makes function as true; the mechanisms and instances which enable one to distinguish true and false statements, the means by which each is sanctioned; the techniques and procedures accorded value in the acquisition of truth; the status of those who are charged with saying what counts as true.[63]

What counts as truth, objectivity, and fact, the very protocols and canons to which the historian is normally subject seem inextricably yoked to the specific culture in which they are produced.

The question we must briefly address is whether history can free itself from the cultural mediations that shape our memories; whether, as Michel de Certeau puts it, on the bases of its analytic procedures, technical methods, and interpretative techniques, historiography can, indeed, credit itself with having "a special relationship to the 'real' because its contrary is posited as 'false.' "[64]

As Hayden White points out: "Prior to the French Revolution, historiography was conventionally regarded as a literary art. More specifically, it was regarded as a branch of rhetoric and its 'fictive' nature generally recognized."[65] However, the fictive character of history did not mean that it yielded error, rather than truth. Indeed, truth was not then equated with "fact," and the "imagination no less than the reason had to be engaged in any adequate representation of the truth. . . ."[66] In the nineteenth century, however, historiography as a discipline counterposed itself to fiction: "it became conventional . . . to identify truth with fact and to regard fiction as the opposite of truth, hence as a hindrance to the understanding of reality rather than as a way of apprehending it."[67] Historiography's scientific turn has transformed it into a modern version of dogmatism. As de Certeau argues:

> It has slowly been losing its foundation in social operativity and transforming its products into representations of a reality in which everyone must believe. I call this dogmatizing tendency "the institution of the

real." It consists of the construction of representations into laws imposed by the state of things.[68]

Modern historiography thus insists that there can be a direct, unmediated relation between the writing of the historian and the "facts," between words and the past events they depict. However, the relationship between history and fact may not be so direct. History may not function as a mirror in which the past is reflected so much as a construction, socially mediated, of the historian. What the historian with his pretensions to scientific objectivity overlooks, as White asserts, is "that the facts do not speak for themselves, but that the historian speaks for them, speaks on their behalf, and fashions the fragments of the past into a whole whose integrity is—in its representation—a purely discursive one."[69] Even the simplest description of a historical event, the mere register of the facts, is by its discursive character and narrative form, an interpretation on the part of the historian. Moreover, the narrative form itself, the mode in which history is emploted by the historian, is culturally mediated, and politically charged. As de Certeau persuasively argues, historiography, "[i]n pretending to recount the real, manufactures it. It is performative. It renders believable what it says. . . ."[70]

Perhaps the greatest danger of modern historiography is its inability to recognize its own dogmatizing tendencies. Convinced by their own hegemonic claims to scientificity, historians do not acknowledge the sociocultural, and institutional constraints and practices which shape their production. On this issue, de Certeau's comments are particularly acute:

> Expressed bluntly, the problem is as follows: a *mise en scène* of a (past) actuality, that is, the historiographical discourse itself, occults the social and technical apparatus of the professional institution that produces it. The operation in question is rather sly: the discourse gives itself credibility in the name of a reality which it is supposed to represent, but this authorized appearance of the "real" serves precisely to camouflage the practice which in fact determines it. Representation thus disguises the praxis that organizes it.[71]

The distinction between memory and history does not seem to correspond to a mythical-fictive character of the former and the objective-scientific character of the latter. The fictive, emplotment, is an integral part of history, however diverse its forms. And if histories as myth are no longer constructed today, that is because of cultural transformations attendant on the spread of modernity, and not because of anything inherent in the "nature" of the writing of history. Moreover, we are convinced that, despite its pretensions, history no less than memory, and the experiences of which it is a recollection, is shaped and mediated by the environing world, Heidegger's *Umwelt*, the ambient culture. Indeed, it seems to us that the very distinction between a mythical-fictive and an objective-scientific way of articulating the past is one way in which, in the course of history in the making, the historical discipline, historiography, has understood and constructed itself. We are making our own choice not to base ourselves on such a distinction, and are instead adverting to another way of articulating the past, one whose contours have been shaped by thinkers such as Foucault and Hayden White.

If history is to be distinguished from memory, the basis for such a distinction, as we have seen, would not be that memory is culturally mediated while history, being objective, is not. A distinction based on the time that has elapsed between what happened, what is conventionally designated as the historical event, and its representation may seem more promising. On this basis, memory would be direct and personal, the recollection of those who lived it, and those to whom they directly transmitted it; it is "hot," the events that are remembered are still "alive." Memory, in this sense, would be limited to perhaps no more than two or three generations, and, therefore, one could assert that the memory of the Holocaust is now passing into history. History would "take over" when memory had run its course, and the events that had been remembered could then become the objects of "cool," dispassionate, or objective representation. Such a vision would thereby limit memory to both a narrow temporal horizon, and to what can be directly communicated or received through everyday intercourse. It would leave no room for what we have termed a social memory, encapsulated in cultural objectivations and figures of memory whose durée is not limited to just a few generations.

Yet how can such a social or cultural memory be distinguished from history? After all, as Pierre Vidal-Naquet has asserted "memory is not history: not that the latter follows the former through some unidentifiable mechanism, but because history's mode of selection functions differently from that of memory and forgetting. Between memory and history, there can be tension and even opposition."[72] Doesn't the existence of such a tension or opposition presuppose our ability to arrive at a precise definition of the terms memory and history? Yet it is precisely such definitions that elude us, even as we find ourselves constantly utilizing terms such as memory and history. Rather than proposing new definitions for such terms, perhaps we should acknowledge, as does Barbara Herrnstein Smith for the term "meaning," that memory and history are "idiomatically indispensable" though "theoretically intractable"; that the use of such terms "dominates all informal talk of human action and experience and frustrates all effort at formal definition and determination."[73] We need to utilize these terms and concepts, even as we recognize that while we cannot do without them, neither can we proffer precise definitions for them. It is in such a fashion that we need to see "memory" and "history."

If precision and formal definition prove elusive, however, we can nonetheless point to the situation in the lived experience of human communities where the discipline of history has imposed such distinctions. We humans find ourselves within a "world." A world is the complex of practices, technologies, institutions, beliefs, and understandings shared by the members of a given group or community; in short, the "reality" in which a person "lives." But a world is not simply the totality of all that surrounds us; a world is not the social environment such as we conceptualize or thematize, it. Rather, in the words of the young Martin Heidegger: "The world comes not afterward but beforehand, in the strict sense of the word. . . . The world as already unveiled in advance is such that we do not in fact specifically occupy ourselves with it, or apprehend it, but instead it is so self-evident, so much a matter of course, that we are completely oblivious of it."[74] Indeed, we can subsequently thematize this world because we are already in it.

This world includes a past. To utilize and refunction, a Heideggerian trope, we are always already with a past. Whatever the contours or content of the world in which we find ourselves, the past shows up. One dimension of our world, therefore, is a past. This past which shows up can be designated the "heritage" of a given "we." And such a heritage is an amalgam which includes what Broszat separates into "memory" and "history," as well as myth and all the components of Assman's "figures of memory." Moreover, what shows up as our past, our heritage, like the rest of our world, has a taken-for-granted character; it is not something we ordinarily think about, let alone question. The past which shows up for some "we" remains unquestioned until it becomes problematized. This problematization of the past can be the result of a social or cultural shock to the community, which comes from without (a defeat in a war, for example), or is the result of the activity of its own members who challenge the taken-for-granted way in which the past shows up, religious prophets, revolutionary heroes, or—increasingly in modernity—intellectuals, those who constitute the members of a discipline, such as history, who "make" the very categories and narratives through which the past is articulated.

A recent example of such a problematization of the way in which the past shows up concerns the relationship of neutral Switzerland to Nazi Germany during World War II and its reaction to the Holocaust. For more than half a century that past showed up to most Swiss as that of a nation which had been prepared to defend its neutrality at all costs, despite being surrounded by the Axis powers, a beleaguered outpost of freedom. However, for the past ten years or so, a new generation of young Swiss historians has been at work challenging the heritage of Swiss resistance and redescribing the national past so that it includes cooperation with the Nazis, including a considerable role in facilitating the looting of financial assets from occupied Europe, and in particular those of Europe's Jews.

The distinction between memory and history, the former as subjective and the latter as objective, with which historians such as Broszat and Friedländer work, is an example of how the discipline of history, or historiography, thematizes and conceptualizes the taken-for-granted way in which the past shows up, thus making it, for example, into Broszat's mythical-fictive and objective-scientific articulation of the past. Other contemporary historians have chosen to categorize the way in which we see the past differently. Thus Pierre Nora, whose multi-volume *Realms of Memory* has done so much to illuminate the way in which the past shows up for the modern French, distinguishes between "environments of memory" [*milieux de mémoire*], and "realms of memory" [*lieux de mémoire*]. The former, which he insists is characteristic of archaic communities, consists of customs, rituals, and traditions, whereas the latter, which he argues typifies modernity, are forged and articulated by the historians, whose narratives breathe life into them. For Nora, the environments of memory are privileged by virtue of the immediacy and authenticity of the way the past shows up, in contrast to the realms of memory, which are mediated by the deliberate constructions of historians. The claim of authenticity attached to Nora's *milieux de mémoire*, seems to us to constitute a romanticization of archaic communities, ignoring the fact that their articulations of the past are no less constructed (albeit in different ways) than those characteristic of modernity. If Broszat privileges history over memory, finding the latter to be hopelessly subjective, a form of knowledge inferior to that produced by history, Nora's position is, in one sense at least, its symmetrical opposite: memory is authentic and living, while history is no more than a pallid reconstruction, "always problematic and incomplete."[75] Both Broszat and Nora work with a set of binary oppositions, and it is precisely such a binary opposition between memory and history (whichever one chooses to privilege) which we want to put in question, even as we acknowledge that we will use these terms without the formal precision which the scientist regards as essential.

History as a discipline, historiography, produces the categories through which we articulate the past, through which, under determinate conditions, we problematize what has previously been taken for granted, that part of our world in which the past just shows up. Moreover, once the past has been thematized, categorized into memory and history, once the problematizations through which this occurs are over, it will become what just shows up for a succeeding generation. That past, which phenomenologically just shows up, a heritage, will, therefore, be a complex mix of memory and history; the result of previous problematizations, though now taken for granted until new social occurrences again result in a problematization and new modes by which history as a discipline thematizes the past.

Such a dialectic can be seen in the way the past shows up for most Israelis, and how that past has recently become problematized. The German-Jewish historian Dan Diner has argued that the Holocaust is the founding myth of the state of Israel.[76] For most Israelis, the past, the birth of the state of Israel, has shown up in terms of "Holocaust and rebirth," the outcome of a mythical process of "destruction and redemption."[77] It is only in the past two decades that this way in which the past shows up has become problematized by the so-called New Historians. For these historians and social scientists, the way the past shows up for most Israelis is the product of a Zionist historiography in which both the richness of Jewish life in the diaspora and the violence inflicted on the Palestinian "other" have been systematically occluded. Whether or not this problematization will transform the way in which the past shows up for Israelis will itself depend in large part on the outcome of this challenge to official history.

Not only do the debates within a discipline such as history shape the way in which we articulate the past, so that the Swiss heritage will be articulated differently today than it was only a couple of decades ago, or the way in which the past shows up for Israelis may be transformed, but the very categories through which that articulation of the past proceeds will themselves be configured and reconfigured through an agonal process internal to the discipline. Here we can apply Steven Shapin's insights about scientific knowledge to the knowledge articulated by the historian and to the categories appropriate to it. Shapin sees "the structure of knowledge making and knowledge holding *as social processes*."[78] Hence the very distinction between memory and history, the way it is configured, is up for grabs. These categories are not fixed but always in a state of flux, the object of debate and dispute. Nonetheless, such categories are "more or less" useful; never final, but good enough for historians to get by with until the occasion for their problematization arises. The historian makes use of such categories in order to produce a narrative articulation of the past. And it is such historical narratives which can become a part of the way the (unthematized) past shows up for any given "we."

Such historical narratives, like other cultural memories, contain within themselves what we have termed a politics of memory. However, a politics of memory, as we have suggested, can be based on a sacralization and memorialization of the past or on an effort to work through it. Thus, in the case of the Nazi genocide, a certain way of remembering, a memorializing memory, and a certain kind of history—what Nietzsche terms "monumental history"—far from contributing to the elimination of the factical-historical conditions that produced the death-world, will only perpetuate them. David Carroll has made this point in a particularly forceful way:

> simply remembering the past—at least a certain form of memorializing memory—is not a guarantee that the worst forms of injustice and dev- astation of the past will not be repeated in some form or other. In the case of extreme injustice—of which there is certainly no shortage in recent history—it is difficult to avoid writing history (and evoking memory) in a spirit of revenge, even if the resentment of revenge will undoubtedly repeat and perpetuate in a different form the past events one is attempting to represent in order that they never happen again.[79]

Carroll has called our attention to the concrete danger of such a memorializing memory of the Holocaust and of the politics to which it gives rise; it is worthwhile to cite him at length:

> In fact, the memory of the Shoah has often been evoked for the purpose of promoting distrust and fear among people and states. The Shoah is for many the sign that no people can trust any other people . . . and that aggressive "self-defense" at all costs must be the principle of the post- Shoah era. A profound distrust of others is thus rooted in the knowledge that anything is possible because the unimaginable in fact did occur. Rather than an increased sensitivity to the demands made by minori- ties and a willingness to accept the ever-increasing heterogeneity of "the people" constituting the modern nation or state, a dogmatic nationalist politics rooted in a certain memory of the Shoah and that aims at all costs to preserve the "identity" of a people can just as easily justify almost any action against ethnic and religious minorities, no matter how repressive or unjust. . . . The lesson of the Shoah becomes: Let us ensure that what happened to the Jews and gypsies of Europe will never happen in the future, or in the case of Israel, that it will never again happen to Jews. In that light almost any action against any "enemy" can be justified.[80]

While Carroll rightfully fears the rise of xenophobic and militaristic ele- ments within Israel, for whom the memory of the Holocaust is sacral- izing and has become the occasion for an authoritarian and bellicose pol- itics of memory, it is no less important to recognize and condemn the same xenophobia and militarism, the same memorializing memory, which animates much of the Palestinian political milieu. Indeed, the tragedy is that in late modernity the politics of memory seems to revolve increasingly around a regressive memorialization and its concomitant dreams of vengeance among the political regimes and movements that claim to speak in the name of the victims of injustice. A politics of memory embedded in the process of working through the past, by contrast, rejects revenge, and bases itself on a concern for the Other, any Other, any group or "race" who may be scorned and oppressed. Such a politics of memory, instead of sacralizing past victimization, utilizes it to attempt to transform the conditions of factical-historical existence which produce victimization in any form. Such a politics of memory is not obsessed with the past, but is prospective and futural. Whereas a memorializing memory cannot dispense with an Other as an object of vengeful fantasies, even generating a new Other where ancient ones have been liquidated,[81] a memory that is prospective in its thrust seeks to extricate humanity from the historical conditions in which an Other becomes the focus of rage and hatred, the conditions in which a death-world can arise. As Nancy Wood insists in her commentary on Pierre Nora's analysis of realms of memory: "This politics would seek to counter the 'commemorative obsession' of our times by putting memory back 'in its place,' by seeking a new balance of forces between the obligation to remember and the 'capacity to forget,' a capacity that ensures a society's ability to extricate itself from memory's incapacitating grip."[82] However, what can be incapacitating here is not memory *tout court*, but rather a particular kind of memory and its politics; a memorializing and monumental memory, which blocks any possibility of working through the horrors of the past.

The kind of politics of memory which establishes itself, the kind of community of memory which is constructed, depends, then, on the uses to which memory is put. Tzvetan Todorov has distinguished between two ways in which a group can remember its past: a "literal" and an "exemplary" recovery of the past or memory. A literal memory means that to the extent possible, the past "remains an intransitive fact, not leading beyond itself . . . I also establish a continuity between the being that I was and the one I am now, or of the past and present of my people, and I feel the consequences of the initial traumatism at every moment of my existence."[83] Such a use of the past does not permit the person or group to work through the experience of the past, to surmount it and go forward; instead the person or group remains stuck in its past, the sacralized memory of which becomes a prison, within which the person or group is trapped. With an exemplary recovery of the past, "I decide to utilize it . . . as one instance among others of a more general category, and I use it as a model for understanding new situations. . . . I open this memory to analogy and to generalization . . . the past therefore becomes a principle of action for the present."[84] Such a use of memory, by virtue of its ability to generalize and to draw analogies with the experience of others and to grasp new situations, has a prospective character in contrast to a literal memory.

What if a culture lacks the plasticity to forget in the Nietzschean sense; what if its memory is literal, and its remembrance, instead of allowing it to surmount the past, leads it only to phantasies of vengeance? What if its historical narratives, and its memory, leads only to an endless reliving of the past? Under such conditions, remembrance of the Holocaust would lead only to rage and despair, resulting in a possible self-destruction of the culture. The alternative to such an outcome is to try to work through the memories of that dark time so that we don't become imprisoned by them. That means attempting to construct a community of memory of the Holocaust in which remembrance is exemplary and not literal, prospective and not regressive.

How can history contribute to such a community of memory? Michel Foucault has provided us with important guidelines for the historical articulation of the Holocaust. His concept of an "effective" history rejects the efforts of historians to incorporate events into a suprahistorical and totalizing vision; to make them elements of an overarching and teleological process. According to Foucault:

> History becomes "effective" to the degree that it introduces discontinuity into our very being . . . "Effective" history deprives the self of the reassuring stability of life and nature, and it will not permit itself to be transported by a voiceless obstinacy toward a millenial ending. It will uproot its traditional foundations and relentlessly disrupt its pretended continuity. This is because knowledge is not made for understanding; it is made for cutting.[85]

Foucault's insistence here on discontinuity as an element of effective history is aimed against the prevalence of metahistorical narratives as one hallmark of modernity. Indeed, the discontinuity to which he refers is an antidote to the tendency to see history as a progressive or linear process. However, Foucault is no philosopher of discontinuity; he is quite critical, particularly in his later work, of any tendency to see "the present as being precisely, in history, a present of rupture, or a high point, or a completion or a returning to dawn, etc."[86] Foucault's concern, which underlies the work of effective history, is to "ask ourselves, 'What is the nature of our present?' . . . to describe the nature of the present, and of 'ourselves in the present.'"[87]

Beyond his rejection of philosophies of history, Foucault's understanding of how to approach what historians have taken for granted, the historical event, can also serve us as we grapple with ways in which to approach the Holocaust. Foucault adumbrates a conception of what he terms "eventalization," by which he means in the first place "a breach of self-evidence. It means making visible a *singularity* at places where there is a temptation to evoke a historical constant, an immediate anthropological trait, or an obviousness which imposes itself uniformly on all."[88] In addition, for Foucault, "eventalization means rediscovering the connections, encounters, supports, blockages, plays of forces, strategies and so on which at a given moment establish what subsequently counts as being self-evident, universal and necessary. In this sense one is indeed effecting a sort of multiplication or pluralization of causes."[89] Foucault's insistence on the importance of sensitivity to the contingent in history, and his rejection of monocausal and deterministic understandings of historical events can alert us to the dangers of certain kinds of historical narratives of the Nazi genocide.

Whatever the modes of figuration consonant with the construction of a prospective community of memory, it is important to recognize that no historical narrative will provide us with the Truth of the Holocaust. In one sense, the need to assimilate new evidence, to be open to new research, is something which few historians would dispute. Thus, Gordon Craig, one of the most discerning historians of modern Germany, has insisted "that there is nothing absolute about historical truth. What we consider as such is only an estimation based upon what the best available evidence tells us. It must be constantly tested against new information and new interpretations that appear, however implausible they may be, or it will lose its vitality and degenerate into dogma and shibbolith."[90] Beyond this, however, Martin Heidegger's thinking on the question of truth is especially important for us. In his "On the Essence of Truth" (1930), Heidegger articulates an understanding of truth, not as correspondence between judgment and judged, cognition and reality, but as *aletheia*, unconcealment, revealment. Yet, as Heidegger shows, there is a concealing in every revealing, inasmuch as there is no single meta-historical truth, no historical essences. Any historical narrative, no matter how comprehensive it aims to be in revealing its "truths," will conceal others. In that sense, every interpretation or judgment should be tentative, open to new possibilities; every truth should be partial. Heidegger's thinking on the question of truth has its reverberations in Hayden White's reflections on historical narration. For White, the historian's choice of a linguistic protocol, her mode of emploting an historical event, eliminates other choices, other possibilities. The best historians will recognize "that any linguistic protocol will obscure as much as it reveals about the reality it seeks to capture in an order of words."[91] This will be the case whether the historical narrative aims to reveal facets of the Holocaust or factors in the emergence of natural science. To take a concrete instance, Steven Shapin, in his history of the seventeenth century "scientific revolution," has argued that: "Since . . . there is no essence of the Scientific Revolution, a multiplicity of stories can legitimately be told, each aiming to draw attention to some real feature of that past culture. This means that selection is a necessary feature of any historical story, and there can be no such thing as definitive or exhaustive history, however much space the historian takes to write about any passage of the past."[92] However much the historian's narrative can reveal, the process of selection will entail that something else is concealed. In working to construct a community of memory of the Holocaust, we need to rid ourselves of the presumption that our historical narrative will provide us with a final truth. We need to acknowledge that however much we reveal about the horror of the Shoah and its meaning for us, the narrative we construct will also conceal other facets of the death-world.

The project of a community of memory of the Holocaust, therefore, also confronts modern historiography's claim to scientific univocity. Michel de Certeau has pointed out that historiography's pretension to provide us with a single, global representation of reality can be seen as "a mythic structure whose opaque presence haunts our scientific, historical discipline."[93] By contrast, the prospective community of memory about which we have been speaking will be self-consciously *pluralistic*. It will acknowledge that memory has many voices and narratives which demand expression, that remembrance is plural, not univocal. However, this rejection of univocity does not mean that all historical narratives are equally valid; that we must, in the name of pluralism, lend credence to the claims of Holocaust deniers, for example. A community of memory of the Holocaust should make room for difference, eschewing the totalizing discourses that dominate the current scene, but it also should set limits. The criteria for such limits will not be found in the mere assertion of "objective validity," but, as Barbara Herrnstein Smith argues, "in relation to measures such as applicability, coherence, connectibility, and so forth," measures which "depend on matters of perspective, interpretation, and judgment, and which will vary under different conditions."[94] Such criteria, however, in contrast to an insistence on a single Truth, will be respectful of difference. In order to contribute to the construction of such a community of memory and its many voices, we must be prepared to embark on a series of experiments in thinking the Holocaust.

Notes

1. Edith Wyschogrod, *Spirit in Ashes: Hegel, Heidegger, and Man-Made Mass Death* (New Haven: Yale University Press, 1985), p. 15.

2. Bloch's ontology privileges the category of possibility over that of actuality, thereby emphasizing both the openness of the historical process and the significance of the futural. "Objectively-real possibility" is that which is still in the process of formation, whose conditions are still developing; that which presages a new actuality. "Front" is where the new actuality is arising on the horizon, where the future is emerging. Ernst Bloch elaborates on these categories

in chapters 17 and 18 of his magnum opus, *The Principle of Hope* (Cambridge, Mass.: MIT Press, 1986).

3. Arno J. Mayer, "Memory and History: On the Poverty of Remembering and Forgetting the Judeocide," *Radical History Review* 56 (Spring 1993): 8. In the phrases in quotes, Mayer is citing Hannah Arendt's *The Origins of Totalitarianism*.

4. Elie Wiesel, cited in Alan Rosenberg, "The Crisis in Knowing and Understanding the Holocaust," in *Echoes from the Holocaust: Philosophical Reflections on a Dark Time*, ed. Alan Rosenberg and Gerald E. Myers (Philadelphia: Temple University Press, 1988), p. 387.

5. Terrance Des Pres, *The Survivor: An Anatomy of Life in the Death Camps* (Oxford: Oxford University Press, 1976), p. 47.

6. See Edith Wyschogrod, "Man-Made Mass Death: Shifting Concepts of Community," *Journal of the American Academy of Religion* 58, no. 2.

7. Ibid., p. 171.

8. Primo Levi, *The Drowned and the Saved* (New York: Vintage International, 1989), p. 31; our emphasis.

9. Alvin Rosenfeld, "Jean Améry as Witness," in *Holocaust Remembrance: The Shapes of Memory*, ed. Geoffrey H. Hartman (Oxford, U.K., and Cambridge, Mass.: Blackwell, 1994), p. 60.

10. *The Diary of Chaim A. Kaplan*, cited by Rosenfeld, "Jean Améry as Witness," p. 58.

11. Mayer, "Memory and History," p. 13. While Mayer in this instance doesn't distinguish between memory and history, what is important here for our puposes is his insistence on the political character of memory.

12. For an account of the late French president's youthful right-wing ideology and support for the Vichy regime, see Pierre Péan, *Une jeunesse française: François Mitterand, 1934–1947* (Paris: Fayard, 1994).

13. After the *Historikerstreit* of the late 1980s, the politics of memory has once again become a German preoccupation as a result of the translation of Daniel Jonah Goldhagen's *Hitler's Willing Executioners: Ordinary Germans and the Holocaust*. For an account of this controversy, see Josef Joffe, "Goldhagen in Germany," *The New York Review of Books* 43, no. 19 (November 28, 1996).

14. Perhaps the best account of the ways in which the Israeli people, and its governments, have remembered the Holocaust, is Tom Segev, *The Seventh Million: The Israelis and the Holocaust* (New York: Hill and Wang, 1993).

15. Ibid., p. 252.

16. Michel Foucault, "Film and Popular Memory," in Michel Foucault, *Foucault Live: Collected Interviews, 1961–1984*, ed. Sylvère Lotringer (New York: Semiotext[e], 1996), p. 124.

17. Milan Kundera, *The Book of Laughter and Forgetting*, trans. Aaron Asher (New York: HarperPerennial, 1996), p. 4.

18. Ibid., p. 218.

19. Tzvetan Todorov, *Les abus de la mémoire* (Paris: Arléa, 1995), pp. 9–11.

20. Ibid., p. 13.

21. Theodor W. Adorno, "Was bedeutet: Aufarbeitung der Vergangenheit" in Theodor W. Adorno, *Erziehung zur Mündigkeit: Vorträge und Gespräche mit Hellmut Becker 1959–1969* (Frankfurt: Suhrkamp, 1979), p. 13.

22. Charles S. Maier, *The Unmasterable Past: History, Holocaust, and German National Identity* (Cambridge, Mass.: Harvard University Press, 1988), p. 161.

23. Mayer, "Memory and History," p. 7.

24. Geoffrey H. Hartman, *The Longest Shadow: In the Aftermath of the Holocaust* (Bloomington and Indianapolis: Indiana University Press, 1996), p. 2.

25. Charles S. Maier, "A Surfeit of Memory? Reflections on History, Melancholy and Denial," *History & Memory* 5, no. 2 (Fall/Winter 1993): 144–45. The Israeli philosopher Adi Ophir has pointed to the danger of a sacralization of the Holocaust and its memory, which can make one impervious to the sufferings of others: "Biafra was only hunger, Cambodia was only a civil war; the destruction of the Kurds was not systematic; death in the Gulag lacked national identification marks. . . ." (Adi Ophir, "On Sanctifying the Holocaust: An Anti-Theological Treatise," *Tikkun* 2 [1987]: 62.)

26. Maier, "A Surfeit of Memory?," pp. 147–49. Whereas Maier sees these tendencies as a rejection of the Enlightenment tradition and the nation-state, it seems to us that ethnicity as the basis of politics may be the outcome of tendencies inherent in the nation-state as the locus of the political and of crucial strands of the Enlightenment project itself.

27. Maier, "A Surfeit of Memory?," p. 141.

28. Mayer, "Memory and History," pp. 13–14.

29. Ibid., p. 14. Mayer has explicitly linked memory and vengeance as motivating factors in contemporary conflicts, pointing out that when people "kill for memory, they do so furiously, savagely, and indiscriminately." Ibid., p. 15.

30. Ibid., p. 7.

31. Maier, "A Surfeit of History?," p.140.

32. Mayer, "Memory and History," p. 15.

33. The complex processes by which a culture can actually engage in such a "wise forgetting" remain beyond the scope of the present essay.

34. Friedrich Nietzsche, *Untimely Meditations*, trans. R. J. Hollingdale (Cambridge: Cambridge University Press, 1983), p. 59.

35. Ibid., p. 62.

36. Ibid. Shelby Steele's concept of "enemy-memory," articulated in his *The Content of Our Character* with respect to the black experience in America, a memory so fixated on a group's own catastrophe that they are overwhelmed by it, is quite close to the experience that Nietzsche is evoking here.

37. Segev, *The Seventh Million*, p. 11. Given Saul Friedlander's explicit linkage of kitsch and death to Nazism in his *Reflections of Nazism: An Essay on Kitsch and Death*, Segev's warnings about a new cult of death and kitsch arising from the memory of the Holocust itself takes on a particularly ominous meaning.

38. Yehuda Elkana, "For Forgetting," *Haaretz* (March 16,1988), cited in Seger, *The Seventh Million*, pp. 503–504.

39. Maier, *The Unmasterable Past*, p. 168.

40. Ibid., pp. 75–76.

41. What it means to "work through" the past, and the actual processes by which this can be accomplished, cannot be dealt with at length within the confines of the present essay. For a more thorough discussion of this issue, though one perhaps too psychoanalytically oriented in our view, see Dominick La Capra,

Representing the Holocaust: History, Theory, Trauma (New York and London: Cornell University Press, 1994).

42. Maurice Halbwachs, *On Collective Memory* (Chicago and London: the University of Chicago Press, 1992), p. 53.

43. Mayer, "Memory and History," p. 9. In his *On the Genealogy of Morality*, Nietzsche includes a genealogical account of how human memory is shaped, of how humans acquire their "technique of mnemonics," which for him is also socially or culturally constructed. See Friedrich Nietzsche, *On the Genealogy of Morality*, ed. Keith Ansell-Pearson (Cambridge: Cambridge University Press, 1994), pp. 41–42. We want to thank Nikolas Rose, who in his *Inventing Ourselves: Psychology, Power, and Personhood* (Cambridge: Cambridge University Press, 1996), first alerted us to Nietzsche's discussion of the technique of mnemonics.

44. Amos Funkenstein, *Perceptions of Jewish History* (Berkeley: University of California Press, 1993), p. 8.

45. Hartman, *The Longest Shadow*, p. 107.

46. Ibid.

47. John Dewey, *Reconstruction in Philosophy* (Boston: Beacon Press, 1957), pp. 1–2.

48. Martin Heidegger, *Zur Bestimmung der Philosophie, Gesamtausgabe*, vol. 56/57 (Frankfurt: Vittorio Klostermann, 1987), p. 68. This was Heidegger's first lecture course at Freiburg University, in the war emergency semester of winter 1919. The approach embodied at the very outset of Heidegger's project for a hermeneutic phenomenology can guide our effort today.

49. Ibid., p.71. Heidegger here refers to the experience of walking into class and seeing your desk, an experience of the environing world already full of meaning. Even the most uncanny experience—that of the death-world, for example—would not be meaningless.

50. Funkenstein, *Perceptions of Jewish History*, p. 5.

51. Jan Assman, "Collective Memory and Cultural Identity," *New German Critique* 65 (Spring–Summer 1995): 129. Massada can serve as an example of such a figure of memory for Jews, the Hermannschlacht for Germans; each can be activated across millennia for members of its own group. Moreover, as these examples can show, the political uses to which such figures of memory are put in the present need not be salutary.

52. In asserting that a cultural memory is transmitted through a process of socialization, we want to distance ourselves from visions of collective memory transmitted biologically or racially, as Jung claimed for his archetypes.

53. Ibid., p. 130.

54. See *Realms of Memory: Rethinking the French Past, Volume I: Conflicts and Divisions*, under the direction of Pierre Nora (New York: Columbia University Press, 1996), passim.

55. Ernst Bloch, *Heritage of Our Times* (Berkeley and Los Angeles: University of California Press, 1991), p. 118.

56. Ibid., pp. 117–18 (translation modified).

57. See Martin Broszat, "A Plea for the Historicization of National Socialism," and Martin Boszat and Saul Friedländer, "A Controversy about the Historicization of National Socialism," both in *Reworking the Past: Hitler, the*

Holocaust, and the Historians' Debate, ed. Peter Baldwin (Boston: Beacon Press, 1990).

58. Broszat, "A Plea," p. 85.

59. Broszat and Friedländer, "A Controversy," pp. 106–107.

60. Ibid., p. 107. Later in his discussion with Friedländer, Broszat puts it this way: "alongside the scientific-academic reconstruction of the Nazi period . . . there was also a legitimate claim by the victims for other forms of historical memory (for example mythical), and there was 'no prerogative of one side or the other.'" Ibid., p. 124.

61. Ibid., p. 130.

62. Ibid., p. 129.

63. Michel Foucault, "Truth and Power," in Michel Foucault, *Power/Knowledge: Selected Interviews and Other Writings*, ed. Colin Gordon (New York: Pantheon Books, 1980), p. 131. For a more thorough analysis of the relation between truth and power in Foucault, which is beyond the scope of the present essay, see Alan Milchman and Alan Rosenberg, "Michel Foucault, Auschwitz, and the Destruction of the Body" in *Postmodernism and the Holocaust*, ed. Alan Milchman and Alan Rosenberg (Atlanta and Amsterdam: Rodopi, 1998).

64. Michel de Certeau, *Heterologies: Discourse on the Other* (Minneapolis: University of Minnesota Press, 1986), p. 201.

65. Hayden White, *Tropics of Discourse: Essays in Cultural Criticism* (Baltimore: The Johns Hopkins University Press, 1978), p. 123.

66. Ibid.

67. Ibid.

68. De Certeau, *Heterologies*, p. 200.

69. White, *Tropics of Discourse*, p. 125.

70. De Certeau, *Heterologies*, p. 207.

71. Ibid., p. 203.

72. Pierre Vidal-Naquet, *Assassins of Memory: Essays on the Denial of the Holocaust* (New York: Columbia University Press, 1992), p. xxiii.

73. Barbara Herrnstein Smith, *Belief and Resistance: Dynamics of Contemporary Intellectual Controversy* (Cambridge, Mass., and London: Harvard University Press, 1997), p. 52.

74. Martin Heidegger, *The Basic Problems of Phenomenology*, trans. Albert Hofstadter (Bloomington: Indiana University Press, 1982), p. 165.

75. Nora, *Realms of Memory*, p. 3.

76. Dan Diner, "The Yishuv Confronting the Destruction of European Jewry," *Ha-Tziyonut* 13 (March 1988): 301 (in Hebrew), cited in Anita Schapira, "Politics and Collective Memory: The Debate over the 'New Historians' in Israel," *History and Memory* 7, no. 1 (Spring/Summer 1995): 17.

77. Ibid., p. 17.

78. Steven Shapin, *The Scientific Revolution* (Chicago and London: The University of Chicago Press, 1996), p. 9. (Original italics.)

79. David Carroll, "Forward: The Memory of Devastation and the Responsibilities of Thought: 'And let's not talk about that,'" in Jean-François Lyotard, *Heidegger and the "jews"* (Minneapolis: University of Minnesota Press, 1990), p. ix.

80. Ibid.

81. Though the physical elimination of most Jews from Central and Eastern Europe as a result of the Holocaust has not eliminated the hatred of the Jew as Other in these countries, the increasing role of the growing Gypsy population as an object of hate shows the way a new Other can be created.

82. Nancy Wood, "Memory's Remains: Les lieux de mémoire," *History and Theory* 6, no. 1 (Spring/Summer 1994): 147.

83. Todorov, *Les abus de la mémoire*, p. 30.

84. Ibid., pp. 30–31.

85. Michel Foucault, "Nietzsche, Genealogy, History," in *Michel Foucault, Language, Counter-Memory, Practice: Selected Essays and Interviews*, ed. Donald F. Bouchard (Ithaca, N.Y.: Cornell University Press, 1977), p. 154.

86. Michel Foucault, "Critical Theory/Intellectual History," in Michel Foucault, *Politics, Philosophy, Culture: Interviews and Other Writings, 1977–1984*, ed. Lawrence D. Kritzman (New York and London: Routledge, 1988), p. 35.

87. Ibid., p. 36

88. Michel Foucault, "Questions of Method," in *The Foucault Effect: Studies in Governmentality*, edited by Graham Burchell, Colin Gordon, and Peter Miller (Chicago: University of Chicago Press, 1991), p. 76.

89. Ibid.

90. Gordon A. Craig, "The Devil in the Details," *The New York Review of Books* 43, no. 14 (September 1996): 8.

91. White, *Tropics of Discourse*, p. 130.

92. Shapin, *The Scientific Revolution*, p. 10.

93. De Certeau, *Heterologies*, p. 203.

94. Smith, *Belief and Resistance*, p. 78.

Time's Impossibility
The Holocaust and the Historicity of History

Raj Sampath

I n a collection of masterful essays titled, *The Infinite Conversation*, Maurice Blanchot treats an array of topics from madness to ethics to speech/writing in the literary and philosophical traditions of the West. Pursuing those themes, he raises questions on historical judgment concerning our recent past.[1] In chapter five, "The Indestructible," lies a peculiar section titled "Being Jewish."[2] From this tiny yet profound piece, we can uncover an enigmatic temporal relation: we discover a split relation whose poles are themselves doubled. The polar relation lies between (1) the *Holocaust* constituted as a particular historical *event* and (2) the *historicity* of an ontological becoming, which ensues from the event, beckoning the question of legacy and *after-effect*; the latter includes the temporal nature of judgment on the past that comes from the future. The second pole concerns the historicity of the conditions by which the Holocaust as a (past) occurrence and a *figure* of time come to be thought as an event in history; the temporal horizon of those conditions exceeds the linear concept of historical time conceived as continuous emerging and passing away. What is the relation between the historicity of the Holocaust and the historicity of history? How does this chiasmic interlocking bind the philosophy of history with the unique temporalization of a future-guided philosophical meditation?[3]

If an ontological disruption of history takes place in the event of the Holocaust, then the nature of this disruption offers itself to a radical form of questioning. How does this *ontological* disruption operate by a certain modality of temporality? The *time* of historical becoming dilates within the event; the dilation or stretching of the event opens up a horizon of chronoleptic possibilities, which then effects how we conceive of the 'legacy'. *We temporalize what remains for us.* We put ourselves *in* time in so far as we open a relation to *a* time and thus the dual possibility of its memory and passage. Inversely, how we conceive of history leading up to the event, the historiographical function of ascertaining the past in its distance, is transformed; the possibility of relating a determinate image of time to a historiographical representation mutates within an ambiguous horizon. How does history continue or fail to continue to happen *in and for* us in the wake of the Holocaust? The event continues to shock the past that came before it and the future that will come. The event, which withdraws itself in transforming past and future, liquidates its own historical presence in a spiral of temporal indiscernibility: an affliction of time itself, the *traumatic event of a historizing time* at work in the event. In Blanchot's text, we experience the vertigo contained in some of the basic aporias of historical time given the double question of the historicity of the Holocaust and the historicity of history.[4]

Blanchot begins his essay by taking up a specific question: he raises the issue of what it means to be Jewish in both its ontological and historical registers. He collates being with a type of movement. Indeed, the semantic ambivalence of this movement relates to the opaque question of historical being in general. On the nature of being-Jewish, Blanchot states:

> it exists so the idea of exodus and the idea of exile can exist as a legitimate movement; it exists through exile and through the initiative that is exodus, so that the experience of strangeness may affirm itself close at hand as an irreducible relation.[5]

The Jewish identity is the identity of movement and exodus, and the existence of the identity persists through the "initiative" of exodus. The historical origin or 'initiative' is not one of a mere ahistorical beginning; rather, the origination of existence is structured by the movement, which is exodus—not the origin of movement but movement *as* origin. Movement *takes the place* of the Origin, which in turn guarantees the ethical reappropriation of the question of origin in its fundamental historicity. The origin of the origin *becomes* the movement of the question of the origin. The retreat of a determinate origin is proportionate to the movement of an "irreducible relation." The "strangeness" of the origin presents itself when movement originates the concept of a *historical* origin while affirming the impossibility of arriving at a universal historical identity, i.e., a dogmatic empirical/or ecclesiastic sense of Creation. For the *relation* to the origin is what moves. As such the historicity of history is guaranteed in its very impossibility only because the alterity marked in its own origin nullifies the possibility of its end.[6] What is strange is not the withdrawal of a concept of Origin but the relation to an original question, which evokes its own most possibility of 'movement'. The eschaton is annihilated in the movement of the question of the origin.

Being-Jewish sanctifies a specific temporal collision between two events: the *impossibility* of locating the origin and the *confirmation* of continuous exile from the very passing of nonsacral history. Eternity hides in a certain historicity, and historicity evokes the eternal question of the origin. The *relation* between the two events invokes another form of temporalization: neither an ahistorical event of origination of Time from eternity nor a deliverance from time in the embrace of a post-historical transcendental synchrony. Instead the movement *happens*; but the occurrence subsumes our intuitive understanding of origin and end in a deeper temporalization *beyond* both. Exile maintains a relation of distance with our normal understanding of history as the passage and retention of events *in* Time. The drift of this motile being submerses history in its very historicity so that the ontological relation between movement and time complicates the question of the 'origin' of History itself. To exile the origin from any concept of the Origin is to revive a metaphysic of movement based on an ethics of the exodus. The incalculable 'movement' of this being is the other which makes possible the equation of history with determinate movement (cycle, teleology, progression, etc). Again, this does not constitute the exodus from history; rather, one can speak of an exile from the *concept* that relates movement with confirmed historical passage (linear becoming), thus enlivening the question of the 'movement' of the historicity of History in its original occurrence.[7]

Given the question of the Holocaust, a certain violence disperses our meditation on the relation between being and movement in the Judaic figure of exodus. But in recovering ourselves from the dispersal, we can analyze a peculiar aporia of historical time. A question is born out of the event. At stake is the relation between a *type* of movement and a *historizing* time.[8] This relation comes alive given the question of a dilapidated origin. The estranged origin *is* the exile in *relation* to the material regeneration of its degenerate future (Holocaust). But since the future of origin (as exile) is never present, the materialization of a future that could not be imagined (Holocaust) takes the form of another event: one that continually destroys the possibility of its own origin and thus affirms the impossibility of placing the figure of the Holocaust in the traditional image of Historical Time. The inexplicable is inextinguishable. Exiled from the possibility of an innocent future that could continue the original thought on Exile, we speak of an ethical warp of time: a warp that has no time for an origin and has too much time for passage, and thus for pure forgetfulness.

A massive temporal complication arises. A contortion of time itself occurs between two 'ends': (1) the movement of exile as the exterior possibility of equating a visible time with the movement of history and (2) the historical event (Holocaust), which attempted to destroy the exile, where the impossible movement of exile other than History is caught within an immobile event that refuses reconciliation. The irreducible relation between an original exile from History (as self-consummating) and the inscription of extermination as an empirical void within modernity remains in its own denial of time: the 'before' and 'after' of modernity itself withdraws. If exile escaped from the eschatological notion of history (and thus its secular correlate in progressive history), then how does the attempt at *immobilizing* the event of exile in its very negation (Holocaust) rupture the possibility of a future movement?

For if the exile never retained a *determinate* image of movement of history, if it never had a dominant concept of temporality (that is already fulfilled), then the attempt to eradicate—that which has never existed—as such raises a peculiar problem. How does *crossing the event* of negation itself evoke another relation between the non-origin of exodus and the question of movement? The negation of negation disinters itself in the event. How does the 'historical' event of the Holocaust bear on the question of movement *as* origin, which animates the complex question of the historicity of history? Conversely, what is the immeasurable relation between movement and historical time given the question of the Holocaust? The event (Holocaust) marked the 'final' attempt to destroy the movement known as exile. The event tried to freeze historical time analogous to the catatonic figure of death in the gas chambers: the very expulsion of the possibility of exile from history resembles the very extermination of time from history and thus the possibility of history conceived as a succession of remembered evacuations, i.e., the shift of epochs. If one does not speak of a continuous succession of epochal horizons (ancient, Christian, modern), then the *relation* between the *threshold* to something other than succession (and thus simultaneity or coexistence), something other than time and eternity, and the *question* of exodus comes into being. Something awakens in the heart of destruction.

With respect to the double link between *movement* as the historicity of history—where exile constitutes the phantom origin of Time—and the *Holocaust* as an event which absorbed movement and thus mistook extermination for the final proof of History's visceral finitude, we find another perplexing question. As Blanchot states, it has to do with

> a denial so absolute, it is true, that it does not cease to reaffirm the relation with the infinite that being-Jewish implies, and that no form of force can have done with because no force is able to meet up with it (just as one can kill a man who is present, and yet not strike down presence as an empty never-present presence but rather simply cause it to disappear). The anti-Semite, at grips with infinite, thus commits him-

self to a limitless movement of refusal. No, truly, excluding the Jews is
not enough, exterminating them is not enough; they must also be struck
from history. . . .[9]

From the 'initial' definition of exile as the *movement* of the question of
the historicity of history, we can turn to a pathological phenomenology
of the event (Holocaust): the event as an attempt at transcendence in
institutionalized death as the imaginary pathogenic solution to the question of time. One can ask what is the relation of arresting movement in
the space of history with the liquidation of time in nature: how is this
chiasmic event constitutive of the historical horizon of the Holocaust in
its very historicity or rather its capacity for being-historical, which
exceeds the question of its origin in History? The inverse of the problem
is that as the event, it overflows the meaning of genocide, enforcing a
type of movement which is subordinate to an unnamable time; as such
it reinforces an alterity of irreducible historical magnitude, whereby the
unthinkable (technologically administered genocide) becomes the
infernal logic of being-past. When exile, which is *already* the dissociation
of time and historical memory of the origin, is "struck from history
itself," the problem of how history remembers its own 'historical' origin
is doubled. If exile is the other movement *in* history, other than the
origin and end *of* History by way of an absolute eschaton, then the negation of exile itself evokes another sense of end (and thus origin). The
movement of/at the origin is the exile of any relation between being and
time from an origin (and the parousia of the concept). But the negation
of the movement, which is already the negation of time and being,
returns us paradoxically to the question of origin minus the metaphysical geometry of History, such as origin and end/or even originless and
endless. The antinomies reincarnate another structure while movement
returns from the site of extermination. For reckoning with the infinite,
which is reckoning with the very historicity of History itself, for attempting to divorce movement from history by crossing out the Other, leads
us paradoxically back to the *mysterium tremendum*, which is the self-
concealing Absolute. Erasing movement may be possible, but erasure
itself is no guarantee that time has been solved. The dissolution of being
into death by way of the event coincides with the historical dissipation
of History itself into a time other than the End.

Certain questions become relevant at this juncture. If the Holocaust
perturbs a specific temporal horizon, a standing horizon in which the
historicity of history is determined by a certain relation between movement and exile, a relation which delivered the sense of *historical* time
against the mythological concept of an eternal origin, then how do we
conceive of the relation between 'movement' and 'time' when considering the *historicity* of the Holocaust? What is the temporal horizon by

which we ascertain the historicity of the very event (Holocaust), the latter of which constituted the attempt of purging from history a type of movement (exile) of a *historical* time (Jews)? As an event which erased the very condition of its existence in history by negating the relation between movement and historical process, the event *comes to be* anti-event; it *remains* as a recyclable void of a finite time. If one can speak of movement as exile prior to the event of the Holocaust, then the ontology of a movement (National Socialism) that tried to fix the exodus in the instant of its destruction is plagued by several paradoxes. Moreover, these aporias effect our understanding of the temporal distortion we spoke of originally; the event of the Holocaust continues to effect its past (History as exile) and its future—or our present as a disruption of movement given the question of the historicity of History. The murder of time *in* history is haunted by this dead time's return to a deeper historicity.

This movement from the origin (as exile) to the event (Holocaust) is like the dilated approach of light to the limit of the event-horizon of a black hole: the mysterious dimension between dimensions, between inside and outside, between life and death, where light disappears. The movement into disappearance constitutes a polar event of which the accretion that flows back, the residuum that cannot be absorbed, forms the silhouette of presence, a symptom of absence: as the only sign that disappearance is visible, it constitutes the after-effect, the legacy, a call for historical judgment about that which resists being historical, namely, History itself. Invisibility becomes the alibi of the visible when invisibility itself becomes 'historical'. The future that falls out from the event is nothing but our present *remaining* as a painful historical judgment on what history resists most, namely, its own historicity. When time dies, history still remains in the death event. For when the present cannot live in the full measure of its own singular presence, its own time divorced from the time of the Other, when the present does not become the remains of a future (like previous presents) but simply *remains* with an unmasterable past, then something occurs. Life seeks to restore itself, but this time around another relation between the three dimensions (past, present, future) and movement is born. Given this question of the historicity of history, the distinction between before (past) and after (future) collapses, just as the distinction between event and anti-event dissolves when considering the question of movement and time in the image of the Holocaust. The effective link between historical reality and its other side, its void, the alterity of monstrous nonbeing which is the unreality known as *historicity* (of History) awakens the question of the border, the very boundary of Time itself. To have experienced the end of exile from history is to be exiled to the continuous question of an end to the metaphysical concept of time (circle, line, instant, etc). But the *end* of the metaphysics of time relates to the *birth* of another logic of time's ontology: *historical time*.

In the final instance, we experience the knot of a fourfold temporal horizon: a horizon which binds (1) the movement of historical time with (2) exile in the figure of the historicity of history (or the historical destruction of the metaphysics of History conceived as continuous origination and ending) with (3) the impossibility of movement captured in the catatonic event (Holocaust) which summons (4) its future (our present) to return *beyond* the event *back* to the original question of the *historicity* of the Holocaust. The fourth dimension is conceived in terms of the problem of historical death.[10] The legacy of the Holocaust is our event, so to speak, an event which repels its opposite in complicating the concept of historical time. The new concept forces us to reconsider the relations of the three dimensions of time in the fourth dimension which unites their *movement as an event*. For the time being, we wrestle with the question of what constitutes the before (how it happened) and the after (why has it happened) of a non-event—or rather, the condition for an event to be present or absent in historical time when the historicity of history has become palpable. A negative transcendence occurs when writing the history of the movement of time to the event crosses the time of the end of movement embodied in the event, which awaits to be read. Inversely, the occurrence of transcendence in its negativity *moves* the exile's end back to the origin of the question of the historicity of history.

The demonstration of paradoxical inversions, which in turn forms the conditions for producing philosophical concepts, does not diminish, dilute, or dissolve the 'historical magnitude' of the Holocaust; it is, after all, an event in history whose primary legacy will elicit questions of causality and accountability for the remaining time. But this eternity is original: it is the question of time concerning its eternal return back to the event of its origin. However, the deepening of philosophical problems, the discovery of ever new complex forms, and the expansion of the philosophical imagination reflect the *historicity* of the event; it reflects the event in time, in transition, in the flux of generational change whose witnesses—who are only *secondary* witnesses to the immediate generation which survived the victims—are called back to an impossible origin. These are witnesses of the witnesses and thus have not witnessed anything. These witnesses—not of the event itself, but the event in time and the time of the event—testify *through philosophical invention* to the horrific possibility that lies at/in the event of the Holocaust, namely, its passage from memory. Future generations are witnesses *of time in a time* in which the event appears to absorb the possibility of narrative, time, history, experience, and memory. However, time speaks about *its own past*, and thus another one—other than the time that experienced its own death—comes into being. And this twilight is what speaks; death comes into being out of the eclipse of being, which still radiates the event. As such the relation between the event and the future elicits a negative transcendental reflection. Or rather, we speak of a transcendence lost in the darkest immanence of an 'inhuman' past which comes in the form of a 'human' experience of reflection. Philosophical genesis is a type of testimony to this event that resists its own temporalization but then falls within the flow of history. Thus an ontological disruption ensnares the possibility of a *death-movement* within the chiasmic horizon of the historicity of the Holocaust and the historicity of History when history is conceived as *the visible movement of time*.

The question of the witness of the witness emerges. The secondary witness witnesses the *legacy* of testimony on the event and not the testamentary structure of death that is the event itself. As such the secondary witness is among the blind progeny of the legacy. Moreover, the structure of this witness's being is temporalized differently; it involves the fourfold *relation* of the historicity of history and the historicity of the Holocaust. And this fourfold relation appears as an event. The event takes the form of the singularity of a threshold. The threshold is pierced by a relation of two poles, which are absolutely incommensurable *in their relation*. Inversely, the strength of their relation guarantees the possibility of understanding. One pole concerns the problem of exile as the problem of the historicity of history: that is the 'historical' origin of a relation between visible time and the movement of history, an origin itself which is irreducible to any relation between time and movement. It is more of a countermovement that makes possible transcendence from being-in-history as such. The other pole is the problem of the attempted death of exile itself: the latter of which is already a spectral being torn between the futurity of transhistorical redemption and the invisibility of being-in-history. As such the 'death' of exile, the death of an invisible historicity itself, becomes the ontological problem of *historical* death, which is irreducible to the equivalence of death as past, which is History. These two poles endure a relation which calls for its own singular testimony: the philosophical genesis of an idea of historical being-in-historical death. But the genesis of such an Idea in fact summons the great problem of historical time for the historicity of History. The threshold is the call of this question.

Hiding within the singular nucleus of the chiasmus—of the historicity of the Holocaust and the historicity of History—is a certain universe of time. For the witness (survivor) of the event, this universe withdraws itself in proffering the ethical possibility of a post-metaphysical relation to time and being. No dogmatic metaphysics or theology can usurp one's ownmost singular relation to death or one's ownmost singular relation to the death of the other, or even dying for the other. Even the reciprocal sharing of death, the 'impossibility of simultaneity and the simultaneity of impossibility,' stands watch against the possible return of the absolute concept of metaphysics. But the witness of this witness, which springs from the head of the witness itself, is not exactly the *same* creature; then again, it does not relish in an irreducible *difference*, which covets the secret eternity of its own decision to be (or not to be). Surviving the survivor has no choice but to reckon with the dialectic face to face. To temporalize the encounter with the dialectic, to face it head on without fear, to meet it with another logic, to invent the Relation of this encounter suggests a singular occurrence. The occurrence is one of a split-negativity. It refuses two available terms, which seem to persist with the event: the possibility of a pretranscendental metaphysical decision on time and history (end, transition, culmination, repetition, endlessness) and the impossibility of a posttranscendental critique beyond metaphysics (closure, dispersal, dissemination, rupture, discontinuity). Simply put, the relation of the encounter refuses the absolute Concept beyond time and eternity and the incessant deferral, which does not decide on any concept. In some senses the encounter faces two eternities *at once*. But the encounter is not part of some reckless abandon; nor does it found itself in a nonfoundational suspension. It lives and dies in its own element: the relation of the encounter between the *threefold* dialectic (negation, negation of negation, reconciliation) and the *four-dimensional* chiasmic movement of the historicity of Holocaust and the historicity of History persists.

Three versus Four: neither of which reduces itself to an empty abstract predicate or form, which cannot account for the simple consciousness of the movement its shares with its other. Both consider the movement of a relation, the possibility of transcending the history of metaphysics (time vs. eternity) *and* the metaphysical forms of history (circles, lines, instants, etc.). Both proffer the possibility of ensnaring any transcendental beyond incapable of conception as a moment within a certain self-actualizing movement. Both imagine the possibility of temporalizing the relation of passage, that is, the passage beyond the cosmological antinomies (of origin/end and originless/endless), and the passage occurring in the self-derived conception of its own event. The dialectic imagines an absolute idea in a circular becoming, in which end is latent goal at the origin and the original actualization is the end occurring: the circle of circles. The fourfold imagines a movement in which the relation between origin and end are not given in the history of metaphysical geometric forms (circles, lines). Likewise, crossing the event of negation, in which exile as the nonoriginal movement of the historicity of History (as determinate movement) is *struck* from history itself, calls us back to another metaphysical possibility: the possibility of thinking the origin once again. But this time, we metaphysicalize about the *relation* between 'origin' and 'end,' a relation lodged in the heart of the singularity that beats within the chiasmus. Passage *becomes* another question. When metaphysics meets its other, or rather, when the event of crossing over from metaphysics to the other *happens*, then a question is born. But this 'birth' is just the self-activation of another question, and thus another exile, another commitment to the infinite, whose movement seeks itself in the element of another origin: the origin of the origin.

Notes

1. Maurice Blanchot, *The Infinite Conversation*, trans. Susan Hanson, (Minneapolis: University of Minnesota Press, 1993). Originally published in French as *L'Entretien infini* in 1969.

2. Ibid., p. 123.

3. Postwar French thought has produced a profound rethinking of philosophical problems concerning memory, time, history, testimony, and events. In addition to Blanchot, one can mention the influential work of Emmanuel Levinas, Jacques Derrida, Jean-François Lyotard, Phillipe Lacoue-Labarthe, Jean-Luc Nancy, and Pierre Vidal-Naquet. These thinkers represent a complex distillation of French Hegelianism with Husserlian phenomenology and Saussurean structural linguistics coupled with the 'trinity' of Marx, Nietzsche, and Freud, and determined to a large extent by the looming horizon of Martin Heidegger's thought. For a general survey of twentieth-century French philosophy, see Vincent Descombes, *Modern French Philosophy*, trans. L-Scott Fox and J. M. Harding (Cambridge: Cambridge University Press, 1980). At one level, my essay will treat the impulses of this tradition. However, we have a specific aim, which in some senses tries to supersede the 'critiques' of metaphysics, ontology, and phenomenology in twentieth-century French philosophy. Our goal is to examine the *phenomenological temporality* engendered in the question of the Holocaust as an event *in* history and an event *of* memory.

4. Blanchot for the most part is characterized first and foremost as a novelist and literary critic whose theoretical and philosophical roots extend back to phenomenology, to the thought of Martin Heidegger and Emmanuel Levinas; psychoanalysis; surrealism; the Collège de Sociologie (Bataille, Leiris, Klossowski, and Caillois); the lectures of the Hegelian-Marxist Alexandre Kojève; and finally a range of poets, writers, and thinkers, such as Nietzsche, Mallarmé, Baudelaire, Char, Kafka, and Proust. My essay in some senses moves in the rhetorical interstices of Blanchot's own artistic mode of meditation; consequently strict philosophical and historical issues particularly concerning temporality and events are oftentimes barely perceptible in the themes of his work but no less profoundly registered at certain critical thresholds of the movement of his thought. Blanchot's poetics are distant sources of light out of which philosophical and theoretical rays extend far beyond their origin. For an economic description of Blanchot's life within the context of twentieth-century French intellectual history, see Martin Jay, *Downcast Eyes: The Denigration of Vision in Twentieth-Century French Thought* (Berkeley: University of California Press, 1993), pp. 551–55. For more on World War II and its impact on French intellectual life, see Mark Poster, *Existential Marxism in Postwar France* (Princeton: Princeton University Press, 1975), p. 109.

5. Blanchot, *The Infinite Conversation*, 125.

6. Here one should not imagine a continuous process based on the law of the line; rather, we must consider a continuous revision of the concept of process as movement based on the creative incommensurability of the relation of its two poles: 'beginning' and 'end'.

7. This peculiar complication concerns the temporal horizon by which we commence the very *act of historicization* of History itself: this includes the latter's basic assumptions of origin, movement, being, time, and history in the finite set of their interminable relations. The literature on philosophical questions that the Holocaust poses to epistemological dimensions of historiography is vast. For a detailed account of problems in the philosophy of history with respect to historiography, see Pierre Vidal-Naquet, *The Jews: History, Memory, and the Present*, trans. David Emes Curtis (New York: Columbia University Press, 1996). For a more abstract, philosophical outlook on contemporary theoretical problems of events and memory within the context of French phenomenology, see Jean-François Lyotard, *Heidegger and 'the jews,'* trans. Andreas Michel and Mark Roberts (Minneapolis: University of Minnesota Press, 1990); Phillipe Lacoue-Labarthe, *Heidegger, Art, and Politics*, trans. Chris Turner (Oxford: Basel Blackwell, 1990); and Jean-Luc Nancy, *The Experience of Freedom*, trans. Bridget Mcdonald (Stanford: Stanford University Press, 1993).

8. Initially we can separate historizing time from historicity, the history of time and the temporalization of history (cycles, eschaton, irreversible duration, and even ecstatic time). Historizing time concerns how one temporalizes the *event* of thinking the being of the *historicity* of history itself.

9. Blanchot, *The Infinite Conversation*, p. 129.

10. The fourfold consists of the historicity of history as a bipolar relation: the historical destruction of the metaphysics of History (conceived as continuous origination) and the historicity of the Holocaust conceived as the history of metaphysical destruction, which usurps the possibility of a new metaphysical origination. The temporal contortion of this fourfold requires a *fundamental* reevaluation of the relations between time, movement, event, being, death, origin, end, historicity, and History.

Part 5

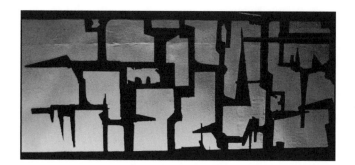

The Crisis of Representation

Introduction

F rans van Peperstratten's "Figure, Law, Silence: 'Auschwitz' and the crisis of representation" advances the hypothesis that "when a community or group shows an increased tendency toward representation of its identity in the form of figures, this goes hand in hand with a reinforcement of the mechanism by which others are excluded." The complex of figure/representation/identity leads to exclusion because it presupposes that "a rigorously delineated reality or identity exists and can be exposed by means of a clear figure or *Gestalt*." Such a figure need not be plastic. It can also be created by language, as in the case of Heidegger's figure/Gestalt—the struggle of world and earth in the work of art. In Kafka and Levinas, on the other hand, the law and the good remain transcendent, invisible, nonenclosing, nonexclusive, nonproprietary. We must remain in the desert, in perpetual exile, and always other than any and all fictioning of the people: "We hear *that* the law speaks to us, we know *that* we are obliged to do something, but we do not immediately know *what* it is we ought to do." We have to find out what we ought to do, we must speak, and yet we must do this without a figure or *Umriss* that represents the law and its anterior voice. Thus the crisis of representation and the silence surrounding Auschwitz.

In a careful review of Lyotard's "Auschwitz book," *Le différend*, Peperstratten refers to the five types of silence described in this text. With the fifth type of silence, which Peperstratten calls "ontological silence," we are placed on the verge of nothingness, yet within language: "We therefore have to conclude that there is no nothingness, there is no outside of the phrases. Decisive borders or incisive boundaries just do not exist." What is unphrasable in terms of existing idioms, the unrepresented, is still phrased as feeling. Stock phrases do not exhaust either language or politics. Politically we must represent the unrepresentable, but we must do so in the manner of Aaron (and Schönberg himself) in the opera *Moses und Aaron*—"never repeating anything unaltered." Only in this negative manner of representing the unrepresentable can there be a *mimesis* and politics not allowing of "grand-scale identification."

Auschwitz was the attempt to eradicate a "subjugated knowledge" (Jews) of the fundamental distinctions/boundaries between different kinds of sacrifice. It is not accidental, therefore, that the attempted murder of those transmitting these distinctions continues to be called "The Holocaust." Eve Tavor Bannet's "The Kampf for language: Holocaust, Shoah, and Sacrifice" attempts to differentiate the holy and unholy acts that are today muddled together in the word 'holocaust'. Bannet shows that Hitler's *Mein Kampf* demonstrates not only a good knowledge of the function of the scapegoat, but a step-by-step construction of the Jew as the German people's mimetic rival "for control of the language and for oratorical supremacy." The Jew is figured as both Hitler's monstrous double and the mimetic rival of the Aryan race. The Jew, then, can be sacrificed for the sake of Aryan redemption if, and this is implied by Bannet's analysis, if the German (and not just the German) Christian community is willing to depart from the (Jewish) Old Law which forbids human sacrifice. Unfortunately, we know that this was indeed the case. Do we today have ears to hear that "when we burn the Other, it is ultimately ourselves that we consign to the ashes"?

How do nations such as Germany, Austria, France, Italy, and the United States represent themselves after Auschwitz, during German "unification," during the formation of the European Community? Erik Vogt takes us to Austria's heading today and asks if the eagle has landed again. Austria is now remaking itself, reconstructing its past, resurrecting its hyper-German spirituality and culture—all in an amnesiac frenzy of a homogenizing and sanitizing self-understanding that would hope "to level out the rupture of Austro-German National Socialism." This politics of effacement and forgetting rests upon a simple revisionism: National Socialism in Austria was only the "errancy of the few." The *aigle*/eagle thus rises again nightly over the hidden graves and memorials of annihilated Jews and daily over the *Heldenplätze* of good Austrians killed in action against German barbarism. Austria remains decent precisely to the extent that its politics of forgetting successfully engenders a "forgetting the impossibility of forgetting." Does such a politics, advancing itself "as a heading for Central Europe which in turn advances itself as a heading for the universal essence of humanity," have any chances of success? The features of this new Austrian politics of representation resonate with specific writings of Hugo von Hofmannsthal, in which he attempted a restoration of the Catholic baroque and a narration of the Austrian people's history. Against this restoration and neo-baroque construction, Vogt, in the spirit of the Austrian resistance/underground, recommends an allegorical vision which fragments the attempted totality and closure, fissuring and splintering it with segments of barbed wire and filling its blanks with the absence of Auschwitz.

Karyn Ball situates George Tabori's play *Weisman und Rotesicht* amidst debates over the Holocaust's uniqueness and the specific figure this requires within competing modes of representation. The duel between Weisman and Copperface over whose victimization is more momentous is thus placed "in dialogue with theoretical treatments of the Holocaust" for the purpose of underscoring Tabori's paradoxical undermining and reconfirmation of "the exceptionality of Jewish victimization." This paradoxical interrogation of representations is also the crux of Lyotard's argument that the unrepresentability of Auschwitz underlies both the inadequacy of the traditional standards for testimonial evidence in the case of Holocaust survivors' testimonies and the fact that the survivors are often unable to speak "adequately" about their experiences. The singularity of suffering makes it unrepresentable. This presents an enormous problem illustrated by "Copperface," who simply has to declare that his victimization is exceptional (unrepresentable/unique) to make his case valid. If "Weisman," on the other hand, makes the same claim, we have an undecidable case (what Lyotard calls a *différend*). Copperface's case (his uncle was lynched in Disneyland) and Weisman's case (his aunt was burned to death in Treblinka) are both "exceptional" and in this regard comparable cases. Universal good intentions, which the Holocaust more than preceding horrors proved nothing more than illusionary, are the form which terrorism took yesterday and still takes today—both at Treblinka and Disneyland. Why then continue to defend the study of the Holocaust? Because we need to understand both how modernity betrayed its best intentions, and how these best intentions "themselves betrayed, and continue to betray, the worse illusions about the responsibilities attending modernity." Such is our postmodern condition.

A.R./J.R.W.

Figure, Law, Silence
"Auschwitz" and the Crisis of Representation

Frans van Peperstratten

Introduction

In May 1995, the fifty-year commemoration of the end of the horrors of World War II took place. It is a saddening thought that in the Netherlands, where I live, public attention during this commemoration again focused on the war as such rather than on the things that happened more or less behind the scenes of this war: the massive extermination by the Nazis of not only the Jews, but also gypsies, communists, homosexuals, and the handicapped. The battle of Arnhem was reenacted, there were veterans' parades and displays of old airplanes, there were resistance fighters being showered with honors—and only at an isolated, silent moment were those who never returned from the extermination camps remembered.

For obvious reasons, the "50th May" breathed new life into the debate about whether we should continue to commemorate, and if so, what and how. It would be a good thing if the focus could gradually shift from the war to the genocide. The fact is, for a long time now, the Netherlands and other European countries have agreed that henceforth there must be cooperation with a democratic Germany; therefore, it makes increasingly less sense to continue to dwell on the occupation of our country, long ago, by a totally different German regime. Moreover, the extremely painful historical event was not so much the war itself as "Auschwitz," the massive and efficiently organized extermination of specific population groups (although the speed of the Nazis' efficient extermination machine was surpassed by the even wilder carnage in Ruanda in April 1994).

Why should we continue to commemorate Auschwitz? Not because of Auschwitz's alleged uniqueness, but because Auschwitz—or genocide in general—is the extreme limit of what people can do to one another; because Auschwitz is a consequence of the combination of totalitarianism and racism; and because in present-day Europe, these phenomena, linked to xenophobia, nationalism, and idolization of the regional religion, language, and culture, are rearing their ugly heads again. The events in former Yugoslavia, but also the growth of the extreme right in, for example, France and Austria, are cases in point. Against this background it is clear that we must continue to commemorate Auschwitz because of the future. Especially now that the survivors are rapidly disappearing from the ranks of the living, the importance of remembering the past is shifting to our orientation toward the future. For the survivors themselves, the function of commemorating may be to reconcile themselves to the pain of the past, but for someone like myself, born in 1950, it should instead be to send the political message "Never again!" thus strengthening a common anti-totalitarian and anti-racist tradition.

Philosophers, too, have a task here. By the very nature of their discipline, it is not up to them to map the uniqueness of Auschwitz, but to elucidate the link between Auschwitz and the general characteristics of totalitarianism and racism, which is the aim of this paper. It will be necessary to delve into the field of culture, since I believe that tendencies toward totalitarianism and racism become all the more dangerous as they gain a firmer foothold in the culture of a people or group. My starting point is the relationship between the notions of *figure, representation*, and *identity*. This complex of notions is intricately interwoven with the above-mentioned tendencies of totalitarianism and racism. My hypothesis is that when a community or group shows an increased tendency toward the representation of its identity in the form of figures, this goes hand in hand with a reinforcement of the mechanism by which others are excluded.

It is no accident that in philosophy and the arts, there is currently a crisis of representation. A positive political aspect of this crisis is that it constitutes an obstacle to totalitarianism and racism, since these phenomena need representation. Representation usually presupposes that a rigorously delineated reality or identity exists and can be exposed by means of a clear figure or *Gestalt*. In the field of politics, the idea of representation implies that a specific identity is assigned to a group in such a way that there is a clear borderline between it and other groups. Thus, a certain constellation of the complex of "figure—representation—identity" implies exclusion. In that sense, the crisis of representation, or of figuration, can be welcomed as the crisis of the closed collective identity, which is at the root of totalitarianism and racism.

A notion opposed to the figure is the *law*, by which I do not mean the laws of the state, although these can exert a positive influence in this field, but ethical law, i.e., the highest ethical command. My point of departure here is the hypothesis that ethical law is that which, by its very nature, cannot be represented in a figure. The ethical obligation opens the identity, thereby undermining the breeding ground of totalitarianism and racism. At the same time, it is clear that in one way or another, the law either presents itself or is presented to us. Justice, after all, must be put into practice.

A link can also be established between the crisis of representation and the *silence* around Auschwitz. The silence that, even among some of the survivors, surrounds Auschwitz is caused by the feeling that Auschwitz cannot fully be represented. At this point, however, the crisis of representation cannot wholly be welcomed, since Auschwitz must be discussed—it must not be forgotten. We have often been reminded of the remarkable dialectic of remembering and forgetting with respect to Auschwitz. Here, I only wish to point to the analogy between this dialectic and the fact that ethical law can oblige us to commit acts that we may seem totally unable to commit. Hence, in analogy to this: even where we cannot remember, we must commemorate.

I shall now attempt to clarify the meanings of figure, law, and silence and their mutual relationships. My material is mainly taken from recent French philosophers, who have done a great deal of work on such matters as identity and representation. I shall, however, arrive at a fairly conventional conclusion, viz., that the tension between representation and the unrepresentable must be demonstrated—which requires representation. At the end of this article, I shall illustrate my argument with a reference to the opera *Moses and Aaron* by Arnold Schoenberg.

The Figure of Totalitarianism

In fact, because of its two different meanings, we can distinguish two ways in which identity is related to totalitarianism: identity in the sense of a plurality of things being identical and in the sense of the character of some entity, for instance, the identity of a person or of a people as a whole.

In the political philosophy of Claude Lefort, we find an elucidation of the connection between totalitarianism and the first meaning of identity.[1] In Lefort's view, totalitarianism is typified by the "logic of identification." This logic in the Stalinist version is the following: the people = the working class = the communist party = the leader = Stalin. Of course, this logic of identification is also applicable to Nazism. In this case, we get: the people = the Aryans = the National Socialist party = the leader = Hitler.

However, I do not think Lefort's "logic of identification" suffices to describe the Nazi type of totalitarianism. Nazism not only posits identity in the sense of an equation of different elements of society, it also postulates an identity in the second sense, a character. In Lefort's equation, this character appears if, instead of the Marxist concept of "the working class," we now read "the Aryans." However, Lefort's formulas do not show the enormous difference between the concepts of "working class" and "Aryans." The working class is a cosmopolitan concept without a very specific content. For Marx, the working class is almost a synonym for humanity. The term Aryans, however, stands for a local, limited identity, a specific character that is supposedly proper to a natural race.

The work of Philippe Lacoue-Labarthe and Jean-Luc Nancy is helpful in elucidating how the formation of such a limited identity comes about. Their starting point is the idea that the essential question of politics is identification, or better, self-identification, on a national scale. Furthermore, this self-identification proceeds by *mimesis*, imitation, and this imitation needs a model. Their text *The Nazi Myth* (1990) shows how, since the end of the eighteenth century, the problem of German identity had become acute, how the solution for this problem was sought mainly in aesthetics; and how, within this aesthetical politics, myth played an eminent role. As early as 1795, Hölderlin, Hegel, and Schelling asked for a "new mythology." In Nietzsche, we find this desire to "overturn Platonism," which means that in Plato's opposition between *logos* and *muthos*, the balance would have to be shifted in favor of *muthos*. Myth here is not to be seen as a story about the ancient world, but as a plastic art, as fiction in the literal sense of formation, a power that creates a model, an exemplary figure, to be imitated by the people in order to start a new world. Wagner, who proposed the idea of the *Gesamtkunstwerk*, the total work of art, is also important. This idea soon includes politics, with the result that the nation is seen as a work of art that has to be produced by some politician-artist.

Lacoue-Labarthe and Nancy quote such Nazi ideologists as Goebbels and Rosenberg to prove that Nazism was a response to this German predilection for myth as a means to identification. Alfred Rosenberg wrote a book entitled *The Myth of the Twentieth Century*. In his view, myth designates an identity taking shape with exclusive differences, and as dreamed. Germany, Rosenberg says, has never dreamed its dream, which is why there has never been a real German state. Rosenberg believes that the dream, that is, the freedom of the soul, always assumes shape in a figure, a *Gestalt*. He takes two more crucial steps: first, he explains that the figure assumes plastic boundaries, and second, he says that these boundaries are determined racially. "Race," Rosenberg states, "is the outward image of a resolute soul."[2]

We understand that the boundaries of this figure exclude something:

the Jew falls outside the figure that is going to be dreamed, or rather produced as a work of art. The Jew is the embodiment of ugliness. The Jews, for their part, reject myth, reject the creation of a world of their own modeled on a figure; they do not have their *Gestalt* of the soul, as Rosenberg says. They are formless, they are devoted to abstract and universal ideas instead of assuming a concrete and specific identity. As a matter of fact, for Rosenberg, this is also true of liberalism and Marxism. With their talk of either the individual or humanity, liberalism and Marxism also lose themselves in lifeless and abstract principles. In Rosenberg's opinion, it is nature that wants the exclusive differences; it is nature that dreams itself in figures. So, the formless Jew, or universalism in general, is not wanted by nature.

I would now like to turn to Heidegger's text "The Origin of the Work of Art."[3] In 1934, Heidegger stepped down from the rectorate and thus from an active role within the Nazi regime, although he never withdrew his sympathy for and membership in the party. This text on art, dating from 1936, should give us an indication whether any distance has arisen in those two important years between Nazi ideology and Heidegger's thinking.

Heidegger also brings art and politics very close to each other. He understands a work of art as something in which *truth* happens. The truth has set itself to work in the work of art. He then adds that the act of founding a state is another way in which truth presents itself. So, for Heidegger, the essence of the state is the same as that of a work of art. He also calls art the origin of the historical existence of a nation. Art is the foundation of history, but, to his mind, always in a specific way for each specific nation. Finally, he states that the question is whether the Germans are just now inaugurating their history through art.

In particular, truth establishes itself in a work of art as a struggle between light and dark, between revealing and concealing. Heidegger interprets this as a struggle between world and earth. World is the openness in which a nation fulfills its destiny; here the essential decisions are made about victory and defeat, mastery and slavery, what is sacred and what is not. Earth, then, is concealedness; it is the traditional ground on which a nation lives, the material on which the world is built. As we see, both world and earth are defined by Heidegger in a very conservative way. But what is even more important, from these notions of world and earth, Heidegger comes to the idea of a *Gestalt*, a plastic figure. The struggle between world and earth appears as a line (*Riss, Umriss*) producing a delineated figure, a *Gestalt*. For Heidegger, truth is fixed in the *Gestalt*.

In my opinion, the crucial point in this issue of figuration, as in many philosophical problems, is the question of the borders or boundaries. I am curious to know whether Heidegger, like Alfred Rosenberg, sees the *Gestalt* as enclosed, and thus as something that excludes; and whether Heidegger has race in mind as a natural ground for the figure. To begin with the latter question, Heidegger's figure does not seem to be incorporated by a race. He avoids the biologism and thus the racism of the Nazi ideology. He does not focus on nature, but on the way in which earth, or the Greek *phusis*, comes into the open, and for him, this is essentially done by language. He is therefore mainly interested in *Dichtung*. For Heidegger, in *Dichtung*, which means poetry as well as creation, we have the original naming of things, the saying what it is that beings come into the open as, the saying of the unconcealedness of beings. This saying (in German: *sagen*) Heidegger calls *Sage*, which is also myth.

However, the fact that Heidegger's figure is created by language, by myth, does not make it an open figure. Myth indeed excludes. In Heidegger's view, it is in myth that a historical nation gets the concepts of its essence preformed and determined, the concepts that express the specific way this nation belongs to world history. Myth is the way a nation opens *its* world, starting from *its* earth on which this nation is grown. Therefore, it is not *Blut und Boden*, blood and soil, that is crucial for Heidegger, but the German language defined as the exclusive property of the people (the *Volk*) as a specific and local entity. Perhaps the Jews, as they spoke German, were not immediately excluded from this entity, but I wonder if they really belonged to the historical nation Heidegger envisaged. It seems they could only belong to it if they completely assimilated themselves to the German world and the German earth.

In 1956, Heidegger wrote an epilogue to his text on art in which he, not coincidentally, felt the need to return to the question of the *Umriss*, the boundaries of the figure. He argues that the boundary in the Greek sense—he refers to the Greek word *peras*—does not enclose. This seems to be a mystification, produced by Heidegger twenty years later, in order to create a distance between his 1936 text and the Nazi ideology. I cannot understand how a figure could appear without the boundaries that draw a dividing line between what belongs and what does not belong to this figure.

The Law

There is a short story by Kafka entitled "Before the Law," which, for all its conciseness, addresses the relationship between man and ethical law in a brilliant manner.[4] I shall try to give the essence of the story, which begins as follows: "Before the law there is a guard. This guard is approached by a man from the country who requests access to the law." The guard, however, refuses the man admittance. He warns the man that, if he does try to enter nonetheless, he will be confronted by ever more powerful guards from hall to hall. The man decides to wait until he is given permission. At the end of his life, still waiting, the man asks the guard, "Surely everybody tries to gain access to the law? How can it be that, in all these years, no one else has requested permission to enter?" The guard answers the dying man, "It was impossible for anyone else to be admitted here, since this entrance was intended for you alone. I shall now leave and lock it."

The law, therefore, is *transcendent*, both spatially and temporally. The law is not to be found "outside." Whether anyone turns to the law at all, depends on that particular person. It begins with someone wanting to go from outside to inside. But wanting is not enough. It is impossible to coincide with the law (or the good, or justice). The law continues to elude us, but it is precisely for this reason that we go on trying to get closer to it. A problematic aspect to this story is, incidentally, that the man never does anything, he just waits on a stool. His relationship to the law remains pure only because he does not act.

This story by Kafka seems to be a literary rendition of Kant's philosophy. In the phenomenal world of space and time, ethical law is unreachable; unlike the natural laws, ethical law belongs to the noumenal world, the world that can only be reached by thought and then takes the shape of ideas. According to Kant, our knowledge of the phenomenal world, of nature, can at best indicate that nature, especially man's nature, is constituted in such a way as to make acting in accordance with the law possible. There is thus a bipolar structure: a transcendent ethical law, on the one hand, and nature, the phenomenal world in which we live and in which a positive attitude toward—but not a coinciding with—the law is possible, on the other. We find the same bipolar structure in Levinas' thinking. Levinas is the critic of the Western tendency to overrate the knowledge of being, to find the law or the good within a knowable reality, and thus to ignore the transcendency of the law, personified by Levinas in the Other. At the same time, Levinas' thinking is directed at elucidating how the phenomenal world, for example, the economy or language, is turned toward the reception of the Other.

This bipolarity is maintained by both Kant and Levinas. Thus, in reality there may be visible signs that refer to the law, but the law itself is not visible and cannot be made visible as such. Therefore, any figuration is limited in principle. The *figure*, as delineated, cuts itself off from transcendency. The figure belongs to the order of finite reality and therefore can never represent the law as such.

This is the thesis that is at the core of Jean-François Lyotard's critique of Heidegger, formulated in his book *Heidegger and 'the jews'*.[5] Scholarly opinion has it that in the mid-thirties, Heidegger's thinking underwent a so-called *Kehre*, i.e., a change of course. However, Lyotard denies that a fundamental change took place in Heidegger's thinking. According to Lyotard, Heidegger only repeats the Western exclusion of the law; this he does by allotting, in the human condition, the central place to truth conceived of as a relationship to Being; or more particularly, by sticking to the idea that knowledge forms the basis for political decisions. And, as we have seen, knowledge, for Heidegger, takes shape in a figure.

If the *Kehre* also stands for Heidegger's reflection on his politics, and if politics is indeed the molding or fictioning of the people as a mimetic work of art, then, Lyotard argues, Heidegger could have seen that all figures, all models for this fictioning are equally worthless. Heidegger should then have concluded that the people can also refrain from the fictioning, from the figuration, that they can remain in the desert or in the diaspora. Then Heidegger would have come close to Jewish thinking, in which there is not the primacy of Being, but the primacy of the law. In Jewish thinking, Lyotard writes, God does not express himself in nature, in some representation, in a figure, but in a book. The interest of the Jews is not knowledge with which to create the final figuration, but endless interpretation. However, Lyotard writes, this exodus toward the law did not take place in Heidegger. Heidegger kept looking for signs of Being, for instance, in the poetic figure, and forgot the law. That is why Heidegger never paid attention to the fact that the Nazis wanted to destroy the Jew as the witness of the law, of the difference between good and evil, of ethical obligation.

We have to remember that the law is not a figure. With Lacan, we could speak of the law of the father, but this is not the figure of the father. Lacan's work on the imaginary and the symbolic order seems to oppose image and word; only the imaginary order would bring us the illusory satisfactions of desire, whereas the symbolic order (the order of the words) would be the space of ethical law. I'm afraid I cannot believe in this opposition between image and word. Language is not essentially more open than images. As both the Nazi ideologists, in the strict sense, and Heidegger have shown, it is possible to create an enclosed figure, a *Gestalt*, with language, particularly in myth, and to use this figure to organize a national self-identification, on the one hand, and exclusion, on the other. We do not have a simple opposition between figure and law because of the supposed fact that the figure is a visible image and the law is articulated in words. In itself, the law is not a representation at all, not even in language, although, of course, the law has to be presented in some way.

Here I would like to refer to the conversation between Elisabeth Weber and Lyotard about the way the ten commandments were received.[6] Lyotard supports the story from the Jewish tradition which supposes that Moses heard all ten commandments, whereas the common Jewish people were only able to hear the *aleph*, the laryngal beginning of sound, the quasi-letter with which the first commandment starts in Hebrew. Lyotard comments that the proclamation of the law by this *aleph* does not clearly state what we should do; this is something which we have to discover time and again. We hear *that* the law speaks to us, we know *that* we are obliged to do something, but we do not immediately know *what* it is we ought to do.

Thus, I conclude that the law is almost unspoken. Ethics is on the edge of language. Again, we see an essential link between the ethical law and the crisis of representation. Why crisis? Why not simply say the law is unrepresentable? Because the law speaks, silently or not, we have to do something and we have to find out what; so we have to present at least something related to the law. To be sure, silence poses the same problem, especially the silence surrounding Auschwitz: this silence refers to unrepresentability.

Silence

Several French philosophers have already focussed on the question of silence. The reasons for this are related to a certain distrust of the logo-centric discourse of, for example, Hegel, but also that of Sartre and, to a degree, of structuralism—the discourse that pretends to be able to artic-ulate and represent everything. It is clear from this distrust that silence cannot simply be conceived of as the negation of speaking, a negation that must be canceled out again in speaking—or thinking. Two examples follow.

In his later work, *The Visible and the Invisible*,[7] Maurice Merleau-Ponty continues to hold on to the aim of phenomenology to give expres-sion to "the things themselves," from the depth of their silence, as Mer-leau-Ponty says (4). The language needed for this expression remains connected to the mute things it interpellates (125). What takes place is a transition from the mute world to the speaking world (154). Conse-quently, language is born from silence, but since language makes thought possible, it also leads to silence again. "Silence," Merleau-Ponty writes, "continues to envelop language, the silence . . . of the thinking language" (176). This is why Merleau-Ponty defines philosophy as "the reconver-sion of silence and speech into one another" (129).

Maurice Blanchot distinguishes between two different types of silence. The first type may be called trivial; this silence occurs when lan-guage is really superfluous, when communication can, for example, also be realized by silently slipping some money into the other person's hand. The second type of silence carries much more weight: this occurs when language is essential. In its essential quality, language causes the world of things to evaporate; and not only things, but also words can again and again be negated by language. The essential language, therefore, tends toward the nothing, to silence; but at the same time, Blanchot makes the emphatic point that silence can only be approached via the—audible or visible—words.[8] This is why Michael Holland speaks of "the dialogue between speech and silence which makes up Blanchot's writing."[9]

Now that we have grown familiar with some ways in which language and silence can be interwoven, I want to return to Lyotard, who in this respect was certainly influenced by both Merleau-Ponty and Blanchot. For Lyotard, the most important reason for mentioning "the end of the great narratives," or "postmodernism," a term he first used in 1979, is Auschwitz. When Lyotard presented his new postmodern philosophy to his French colleagues in 1980, he did not refer to postmodernism, but chose the title "Phrasing after Auschwitz." Lyotard's main work, *The Differend*, published in 1983, is the elaboration of this question. This work could therefore be called an "Auschwitz book."[10] The book opens with the observation that "the survivors rarely speak about it" (3). It is immediately clear that the theme of Lyotard's book is not only the speaking (the "phrasing") but also the silence after Auschwitz. In Lyotard's view, it is this silence which makes the continuation of the Hegelian dialectical discourse impossible.

"The silence that surrounds the phrase 'Auschwitz was the extermination camp,' " Lyotard writes, "is the sign that something remains to be phrased which is not" (57). Lyotard understands the silence imposed by the crime of Auschwitz as indicating "that something which should be able to be put into phrases cannot be phrased in the accepted idioms" (56). There is a slight difference between these two statements: something is not or cannot be said.

We learn more about this "is not said" in Lyotard's example of the journalist who interviews a survivor of Auschwitz (13–14). There is a chance that this survivor will remain silent. He may have different reasons for not speaking: (1) He thinks he is unworthy to speak. After all, he was lucky and escaped. Compared with the others, the survivor's situation was not that extreme. He is not allowed to speak on behalf of the deceased. (2) The survivor thinks the journalist unworthy: the journalist is too young, too well equipped, not serious enough, unable to understand, and likely to make a superficial article out of the survivor's story. (3) The survivor cannot remember the experience very well. The referent of his memory has grown too uncertain to speak about it. (4) The survivor may just think that Auschwitz was a complete absurdity about which no meaningful sentence can be produced. In fact, these silences say something, something negative, about the addresser, the addressee, the referent, and the sense. Lyotard calls these silences negative phrases. We could also call them meaningful or *speaking* silences. They make up the first type of silence I discern in *The Differend*.

The second type of silence occurs when people do not speak because *violence* or the threat of violence is committed against them (10–11). Thirdly, people may remain silent because what they want to say has to be said in a specific *genre* of discourse, but they already know that this genre is *not* socially *recognized*. Other genres dominate, so they may think it is useless to speak. Fourthly, we have to acknowledge that behind the "is not said" may lie a "cannot be said." Lyotard's notion of a "differend" includes the situation in which somebody has a point of view which cannot be articulated because the adequate idiom or genre does *not yet exist* (13). A person remains silent because there is no language with which to express his or her point of view. In Lyotard's view, one should try to find new idioms to remedy this problem. Thus, Lyotard praises Marx because he heard the silence of the workers and tried to develop a new idiom in which to phrase this silence (171–72). A pursuit like this corresponds to Kant's famous definition of Enlightenment, the emergence out of the inability to speak up publicly. Lyotard clearly supports this Kantian version of Enlightenment which is why it is rather short-sighted to create an opposition between Lyotard's postmodernism and Enlightenment. Lyotard's basic assumption seems to be that whoever is silent should be able to speak.

However, in *The Differend* we also find a fifth type of silence, which cannot be remedied by any actual or future ability to speak and express. I suggest calling this an *ontological* silence, for Lyotard writes that the occurrence of a phrase is a question of Being or Non-Being, that each new phrase arises out of nothingness, out of the abyss of Non-Being which is opened after each phrase (66). He adds that this silence between phrases does not belong to the negative phrases or speaking silences (75). It does not refer to the addresser, or the addressee, etc., but to the occurrence of a phrase. Will the next phrase ever come? This silence places us on the verge of nothingness, where, waiting for the arrival of the next phrase, we experience a feeling of suspense.

Strangely enough, even in this ontological context, Lyotard says that silence, and even nothingness itself, is a phrase. He states explicitly, "that the absence of a phrase (a silence, etc.) or the absence of a linkage (. . . nothingness, etc.) are also phrases. What distinguishes these particular phrases from others? Equivocality, feeling, . . . , etc." (68).

We therefore have to conclude that there is no nothingness, there is no outside of the phrases. Decisive borders or incisive boundaries just do not exist. Certainly, there is silence, there is no speech, but this no speech is *in* speech. Similarly, there is unrepresentability, but in discussing it, we present it in language, although very equivocally, without a clear content. With this reflection, Lyotard turns to the famous last words of Wittgenstein's *Tractatus*: "What we cannot speak about we must pass over in silence." Lyotard replies by saying: "It is already phrased, as unphrasable in the existing idioms, as feeling" (80). At least the ontological silence cannot be called a representation of anything, but it appears as a phrase anyway. To return to the problem of the figure in politics, this would mean we cannot have no figure at all; a nonfigurative politics cannot exist. The real problem is, which figures do we have? And in which settings?

Moses and Aaron

The opera *Moses and Aaron* was written and composed by Arnold Schoenberg between 1930 and 1932 and was intended as a protest against Nazism. Partly because the opera was never finished (only the first two acts were completed), performances of the piece were not given until after Schoenberg's death in 1951. A truly brilliant performance took place in Amsterdam in 1995 under the direction of Pierre Boulez, with stage management by Peter Stein.[11]

Quite rightly, George Steiner called *Moses and Aaron* "an opera about opera."[12] In my opinion, both the music and the text turn this work into a critique of the figure. One might say that in this opera, Schoenberg has already integrated the crisis of representation and put it to use against Nazism. The opera plays on the paradoxes of the representation of the unrepresentable in a very serious manner.

In a musical sense, Schoenberg underlines the well-known question originally raised in the biblical story by deciding not to use euphonious tonality. Nowhere better than in this opera does the method of "twelve-tone" or "serial" composition developed by Schoenberg fall into place. Since in this composition, Schoenberg adheres to the principle of never repeating anything unaltered (the principle of continuous variation or varied repetition), stock musical phrases do not get a chance. Also, with Aaron singing and Moses producing a kind of sung speech (*Sprech-stimme*), the division of roles between Moses and Aaron as described in the Bible is given a remarkable musical form.

Schoenberg himself wrote the libretto, rewriting the medieval German of the Lutheran Bible. Therefore, the words, too, with their tonality and rhythm, have, in a way, been composed, hand in hand with the music. In comparison with the Bible, the story has also been given a sharper edge by Schoenberg. Therefore, I shall discuss here not the Bible text, but Schoenberg's.[13] This text can be looked upon as an exercise in Kantian thinking. God is called omnipresent and omnipotent, and therefore beyond human representation, at any rate in the form of images. God only appears in Moses' *thinking*, but as the latter is not a talented speaker, his brother Aaron is assigned the task of being Moses' voice. God's unimaginability is held to be the specific difference between the "new" God of the Israelites and the "old" God of the other peoples. God is beyond both representation and the intellectual, human calculation of cause and effect, of crime and punishment, of sacrificing and thus acquiring God's mercy.

In every respect, Aaron is the intermediary between Moses and the people. "My Moses," Schoenberg wrote in a letter in 1933, "is not human at all."[14] Whereas Moses stands for the law ("the unrepresentable law of the unrepresentable God"), for inflexibility (the staff), and for thinking; whereas Moses simply declares that the people must serve God, Aaron opts for love, flexibility (the snake), and representation through word and image and deeds (miracles) and seems to care mainly for the people's salvation. The political aspect is clearly present: according to the text of Act III, Aaron defends himself before Moses with the argument that he acted for the freedom of the people, "so that they would become a nation." Moses' answer is as follows: "To serve, to serve the divine idea, is the purpose of the freedom to which this people has been chosen." The people themselves are unstable in their opinions, varying according to circumstances, but at the creation of the golden calf, they exult at gods that act as "masters of our senses," that are "earthly and visible," that have "borders" and are "measurable," and that "do not ask for that which is denied to our hearts."

As is generally known, the story reaches a climax when Moses comes down from Mount Sinai with the stone tablets on which God's finger is said to have written the ten commandments. Moses destroys the golden calf, saying, "Begone, you image of powerlessness to enclose the boundless in an image finite!" Aaron, however, states that the people cannot grasp more than an image; in his view, "the image expresses the perceivable part of the whole idea." And, Aaron continues, "These tablets, they are also images, just part of the idea." These words of Aaron seem to hit Moses hard—and to convince him. He smashes the Tablets of the Law to pieces and cries in despair: "Then I have fashioned an image too, false, as an image must be. Thus I am defeated! Thus, all was but madness that I believed before, and can and must not be given voice. O word, thou word that I lack!"

In my view, the first important feature of the opera is the fact that there is not one figure, one hero, but a plurality of very different figures. These figures are presented as possibilities, as open to choices by the people. We have the golden calf as an image of the divine. There is Aaron with his fluent speech, who seems to represent communicative language as the means to unite the people. And there is Moses who is hardly able to express his immediate experience of God in words and who needs Aaron to do this. Moses, and this is the second feature, represents unrepresentability. For a moment, Moses thought he had a representation of the law, but he soon admitted that this representation was also inadequate. The third important point is that the opera is itself a figuration. It goes too far to say, as Albright does, that "the opera itself is like the golden calf." But it is a figuration indeed, in which we are confronted with different figures, including a figure stating that the highest Being cannot be represented.

Steiner is completely wrong to say that the dramatic conflict is "one between a man who speaks and a man who sings."[15] The essential conflict, or better, the unresolvable problem, is between any kind of representation, on the one hand, and the unrepresentable, on the other, a problem that can only be shown by means of representation. As Albright rightly observes: "the commandment against graven images was itself a graven image and has annulled itself."[16] The final question Moses asks himself is the same question Schoenberg as a composer is asking himself: Isn't the opera wrong to try to express unrepresentability, to express transcendence? Thus, the opera is a representation of the problems of representation.

These problems can be clarified with the help of the aesthetics of the sublime. The sublime is opposed to Heidegger's conception of art, that is, to *Gestalt* and myth, in the service of a delineated identity of the People. The sublime comes about when human imagination, which is the faculty of representing, aims at representing infinite size or power—and necessarily fails. The sublime feeling arises when we encounter something that turns out to be boundless; in other words, when there is a formless representation, without a *Gestalt*. The representation refers to to the fact that something unrepresentable exists, which causes a strange combination of delight and unease in the human heart. As Kant saw, a link can be established between the aesthetics of the sublime and the ban on images known to Judaism, Islam, and Protestantism.[17] Kant adds in explanation that, in the case of the sublime, the *Darstellungsart*, the manner of representing, is wholly negative with respect to the senses. This does not detract from the fact that it remains a manner of representing. This representation, however, no longer meshes with the familiar idea of *mimesis*. If, in the sublime, *mimesis* can exist at all, it is a *mimesis* without model, a *mimesis* that does not allow grand-scale identification.

If these features of art, as revealed by Schoenberg's opera, could be transposed to politics, a link between art and politics would not be that bad at all. This manner of representing does not shut itself in; rather, it points beyond itself, to the unrepresentable, to that which is different. This manner of representing is not self-complacent, but also immediately shows its own restrictedness. However, we should also realize that the way in which we can commemorate Auschwitz will always be restricted. There is no perfect way to commemorate Auschwitz.

Notes

1. Claude Lefort, *L'invention démocratique. Les limites de la domination totalitaire* (Paris: Fayard, 1981), pp. 167 ff.
2. Cited in: Philippe Lacoue-Labarthe and J.-L. Nancy, "The Nazi Myth,"

Critical Inquiry 16 (Winter 1990): 306. Very instructive also is Philippe Lacoue-Labarthe, *Heidegger, Art and Politics. The Fiction of the Political* (Oxford and Cambridge: Basil Blackwell, 1990), and his "Transcendence Ends in Politics," in *Typography; Mimesis, Philosophy, Politics* (Cambridge and London: Harvard University Press, 1989), pp. 267–300.

3. Martin Heidegger, "Der Ursprung des Kunstwerkes," in *Holzwege* (Frankfurt a. M.: Klostermann, 1950), pp. 7–68. The English translation, "The Origin of the Work of Art," appears in *Poetry, Language, Thought* (New York: Harper and Row, 1971), pp. 17–87.

4. This story has been published separately, but is also completely cited in Kafka's novel *The Trial*.

5. Jean-François Lyotard, *Heidegger and 'the jews'* (Minneapolis: University of Minnesota Press, 1990). See mainly nos. 21–23.

6. *Jüdisches Denken in Frankreich*, ed. E. Weber (Frankfurt a. M.: Jüdischer Verlag, 1994), pp. 161–64.

7. Maurice Merleau-Ponty, *The Visible and the Invisible*, ed. C. Lefort (Evanston: Northwestern University Press, 1968).

8. A.-L. Schulte Nordholt, *Maurice Blanchot. L'écriture comme expérience du dehors* (Genève: Droz, 1995), pp. 69–70.

9. *The Blanchot Reader*, ed. M. Holland (Oxford and Cambridge: Basil Blackwell, 1995), p. 3; this volume includes two essays published in 1962, "Being Jewish" and "Humankind," in which Blanchot, a friend of Levinas, wrote about Judaism and the Nazi camps.

10. J.-F. Lyotard, *The Differend: Phrases in Dispute* (Manchester: Manchester University Press, 1988). Some additional reasons to call this an Auschwitz book: It starts with a discussion of the French "revisionist" historian Faurisson, who says he cannot find any proof that the gas chambers really existed (3), which, of course, is ridiculed by Lyotard. In every chapter of the book, Auschwitz is referred to as a crucial event. Lyotard calls Auschwitz the most real of all realities, insofar as reality always entails possible, yet unknown, senses (57–58); so, there is a lot to say about Auschwitz, without the certainty that it fits in Hegel's speculative rationality: "This crime at least, which is real . . . , is not rational" (179).

11. The recording (the second under the direction of Pierre Boulez) is released on CD by Deutsche Grammophon GmbH 1996, 449 174-2 GH2.

12. George Steiner, *Language and Silence: Essays on Language, Literature and the Inhuman* (New York: Atheneum, 1977), p. 132.

13. I used the English translation (with some adaptations) in the booklet that accompanies the 1996 CD's. This translation is based on A. Schoenberg, *Moses und Aron. Oper in drei Akten. Textbuch* (Mainz/London/New York/Tokio: Schott, 1957).

14. Cited in D. Albright, *Representation and the Imagination* (Chicago: The University of Chicago Press, 1981), p. 41.

15. Steiner, *Language and Silence*, p. 132.

16. Albright, *Representation and the imagination*, p. 44.

17. Immanuel Kant, *Kritik der Urteilskraft*, B 124.

The Kampf for Language
Holocaust, Shoah, and Sacrifice

Eve Tavor Bannet

I would like us to begin to alter what we remember when we hear the word "holocaust." Borrowed from the language of sacrifice, where it means an offering which is wholly burnt on an altar to God, this word "holocaust" now also recalls the crematoria in the camps, their black smoke rising to heaven as a society's victims dwindled to cinders and ash. Muddled together in this word "holocaust," then, are holy and unholy acts. We have conflated them, and dismiss them both as barbarities. But this is something we can no longer afford to do, if we want the barbarity to stop. For what I've described is not just the accident of a word. Conflation of sacrifice and sacrifice is engrained in Western culture, Western language, and Western thought—so deeply engrained, in fact, that it persists even after Nazism, which might be portrayed as one of its effects. This is not a minor matter if, as René Girard insists, all human societies are founded on sacrifice and held together by actual or symbolic repetitions of that originating act.

I will argue in this paper that when we blur the boundaries between different kinds of sacrifice—when sacrifice of the Other is fused with sacrifice of the Self and confused with the sacrifice of animals, as has been the case in the West almost from the first—societies are founded on a *pharmakon*, that unstable medium where medicine turns into poison and evil into good; and barbarity is never very far away. I'm going to argue that the Jews who burned through the centuries and the Jew who died on the Cross as "victims who founded societies" for others, also represented a "subjugated knowledge" which has always already insisted that elementary but fundamental distinctions between sacrifice and sacrifice be inscribed, defended, and preserved. My aim is to show that, from this point of view, Hitler was perfectly right in representing his *Kampf* as a *Kampf*, or struggle, for language and for the words we use.

Girard's theory of sacrifice has "successfully" been used to "explain" the Temple cult of the Israelites, as well as a variety of human and animal sacrificial cults among the Greeks, the Romans, the Canaanites, and others.[1] To foreground the ongoing confusion about sacrifice and to suggest the extent to which it is rooted in a certain tradition of Western language and Western thought, I will apply René Girard's theory of sacrifice where it has not been overtly applied before: to Hitler's *Mein Kampf* and to Christianity's doctrine of "vicarious sacrifice." Finally, I will try to indicate what the Jews (even those ancient Israelites) understood that they did not.

Girard's theory argues that social groups deflect the violence which threatens to tear them apart when conflicts and rivalries emerge, by turning that violence outward onto a surrogate victim.[2] All sacrifice is, therefore, a form of victimage or scapegoating. While releasing its own violence cathartically upon the body of the victim, the group bonds together against its victim so that unity and unanimity, peace and harmony, are restored. The *pharmakos*, or scapegoat, thus often comes to figure in history and myth as a *pharmakon*. First criminal, then saviour; first enemy, then redeemer, the scapegoat is both poison and cure, both the source of evil and the source of good.

For this redemptive scapegoating mechanism to work, Girard insists, it does not matter if the scapegoat is human or animal—the victim has only to be marginal, vulnerable, incapable of reprisal, and capable of being treated as a surrogate for the self or substitute for the group. There must, in other words, be sufficient resemblance between victim and sacrificers for the sacrificers to be able to construct their victims as their own "monstrous double." While representing the victim as an enemy who is bringing whatever evils plague the sacrificing individual or community into it from outside, the sacrificers project their own monstrous traits onto the victim, and expel, kill, and burn them by expelling, killing, and burning their surrogate.

Mein Kampf indicates how well Hitler understood the scapegoating mechanism that Girard describes; indeed, sacrifice is a word that recurs throughout his book. "To win the masses for a national resurrection," Hitler insists, "no social sacrifice is too great."[3] Germany's national resurrection must inspire "faith bordering more or less on religion, combined with a similar spirit of sacrifice" (102); for the resurrected "volkish state" was to be founded "not on material egoism, but on a spirit of sacrifice and joyful renunciation" (423).

The German word *Opfer* fuses victim, agent, and sacrificial act;[4] but the particular form that the German people's sacrifice and joyful renunciation were to take were made quite clear in the book. "Germanism" was being "exterminated" (141), Hitler says, by geographical divisions which exiled the Hitlers and 10 million other German-speakers outside the German Reich and subjected them to "foreign nations" who "gnaw at our nationality" and expected them to "bear inconceivable sacrifices in taxes and blood" (15). In the Reich itself, "national awareness" was precluded by social and political divisions, like the growing division between rich and poor, which were being exploited by the Communists, while the German people's commitment to democracy and universal suffrage was undermining its single-minded determination to fight for *Deutschland über alles*. The way to get the Germans to "unite and fight for the preservation of their species" once more, Hitler explains, is by means of violence and propaganda: violence because "like a woman," the masses always submit to force and brutality and willingly "sacrifice others" to preserve their own safety and peace (42-3); and propaganda to identify the enemy and unite the masses against a common foe:

> The art of all truly great national leaders at all times consists primarily in not dividing the attention of a people, but in concentrating it on a single foe. . . . It belongs to the genius of a great leader to make even adversaries far removed from one another seem to belong to a single category. (118)

In the course of his book, Hitler therefore shows his genius as a leader by making the Jews the foe responsible not only for the German people's lack of "Germanism," but also for "Western democracy" and "universal suffrage," for Communism and Social Democracy, for International Finance and the gap in Germany between rich and poor. National unity, unanimity, and awareness could then be achieved by sacrificing the Jews, so that all these German evils could be expelled, exterminated, and joyfully renounced in the surrogate person of the Jew.

But why the Jews? I trust that we are not assuming that it is just normal and natural that it would be the Jews. For even Hitler did not do that. Nazi propaganda for the masses later identified the Jews with rats and other vermin, thus with the lowest kind of animal; but Hitler took another route. *Mein Kampf*'s autobiographical narrative painstakingly describes the process by which young Adolf "discovered" that it is the Jew (not himself) who dominates language, and through it, the German people; the Jew (not himself) whose oratory carries everything and everyone before it.

Scene by autobiographical scene, *Mein Kampf* constructs the Jew as Hitler's "mimetic rival" for control of the language and for oratorical supremacy. Here is young Adolf in his native Braunau, a small, forgotten corner of the Austro-Hungarian Empire, priding himself on his "orator-

ical skills [as] a pugnacious boy" at school (6) and using them to surround himself with "husky" bullies. Here is young Adolf newly arrived in
Vienna: Mr. Noone from Nowhere, a penniless outsider whose small-town
brogue is all but incomprehensible even to the meanest inhabitants of
the big city. Here is young Adolf, working on construction sites, developing what he considers brilliant arguments about history and politics at
night, trying out his great oratorical talents during the Communist Agit-
prop at lunchtime—and for his pains, getting himself thrown off the construction site by "husky" construction workers,[5] not once, but time after
time, on job after job. Here is young Adolf noticing that Jews best him at
arguments:

> A Jew could never be parted from his opinions. . . . I talked my tongue
> sore and my throat hoarse, thinking I would inevitably succeed in con-
> vincing them . . . but what I accomplished was often the opposite. . . .
> Gradually I began to hate them. . . . How hard it was, even for me, to get
> the better of this race of dialectical liars! (62, 63)

And here is Adolf several years later in Germany—where he is delighted
to find they understand his accent better[6]—enjoying his first oratorical
victory. He is speaking *against the Jews*, and for the first time since his
pugnacious boyhood, he manages to carry most of his audience with him:

> and the thing that I had always presumed from pure feeling without
> knowing it, was now corroborated: I could "speak." (215–16)

"I could speak"—not a minor matter for a man who saw that:

> the power which has always started the great religious and political
> avalanches in history has from time immemorial been the magic power
> of the spoken word, and that alone. (106–107)

"I could speak"—not a minor matter, either, for a man who conceived of
"the language struggle" as "a struggle for the soul" of a people (12).
Hitler's *Kampf* for power in Germany is therefore represented as a
"*Kampf* for language"—a *Kampf* for the "holy right to [his] mother
tongue" (11). And one might therefore say of Hitler what he said of the
Jew: "His whole Germanism rests in language alone" (312).

Inscribing the identity of language, nation, and (political) culture in
the fabric of his text, Hitler goes on to project his own monstrous political program onto his perceived rival in the language struggle, the Jew. It
is of the Jew that Hitler writes:

> With every means he tries to destroy the racial foundations of the
> people he has set out to subjugate. (325)

The Mosaic religion is nothing other than a doctrine for the preservation of the race. It therefore embraces almost all sociological, political
and economic fields of knowledge which can have any bearing on this
function. (150–51)

The great master of lies understands as always how to make himself the
pure one, and to load the blame on others. Since he has the gall to lead
the masses, it never enters their heads that this is a betrayal also.
(318–19)

[He] is Lord of the Reich. (314)

[He] dreams of world domination. (313)

His spreading is a typical phenomenon of all parasites. Wherever he
appears, the host people die out after a shorter or longer period. (305)

Projecting onto the Jew his own goals and political ambitions, as well as
his own long-time identity as a member of a "foreign people" in the
Austro-Hungarian Empire and as an outsider in Germany, Hitler argues
that it is the Jew (not himself) who belongs to a "foreign people" (61) and
bears no physical resemblance to the Aryans among whom he now lives;
the Jew (not himself) who is "no German" (56); the Jew (not himself)
who has brought dreams of world domination and of racial purity into
Germany from the outside; the Jew (not himself) who is an "agitator misleading the nation" (169), the "villainous poisoner" (42) of the German
people, and a monstrously impure and unhealthy "parasite." In Girard's
terms, therefore, Hitler constructs the Jew as his own monstrous double.

And it is as Hitler's monstrous double and other I that in Hitler's text,
the Jew also becomes, by extension, the double and mimetic rival of the
Aryan race: "The mightiest counterpart of the Aryan is represented by
the Jew" (300). The fate of Aryan and Jew is therefore inextricably
linked: "His Star of David rose higher and higher in proportion as our
people's will for self-preservation vanished" (329). The swastika has to
triumph over the Star of David, and the Aryan over the Jew because the
Aryan can rise only by eliminating his rival and sacrificing his counterpart. Ironically, however, according to the complex logic of surrogation
and substitution at work in this text, this also meant that, having identified himself with Hitler's *Kampf* against Hitler's own surrogate, the Aryan
was "preserving" himself by turning his violence outward onto Hitler's
"monstrous double." The Aryan would thus restore "healthy social conditions" to Germany by exterminating Hitler's effigies, and "cleanse"
himself and the German nation by sacrificing Hitler's surrogates in the
person of the Jew.

We hardly need to be reminded that sacrifice is also central to Christianity's "struggle for the soul" of people. The problem here, as Girard
himself has come to realize, is that the Church's doctrine of "vicarious

sacrifice" could well be said to conform to Girardian theory in almost every respect. For the Church, Christ has always been a *pharmakos*, both human victim and sacrifical lamb, as well as the proverbial *pharmakon*, first criminal and then savior, first poison and then cure. Christianity's doctrine of salvation through Christ's "vicarious sacrifice" could be said to teach that sacrifice of an other, as a surrogate for oneself or one's group, is the only means of attaining salvation. As Horace Bushnell says, vicarious

> is a word that carries always a face of substitution, indicating that one person comes in place, somehow, of another. . . . The Christian salvation is a vicarious sacrifice. . . . Vicarious sacrifice belongs to the essential nature of all holy virtue.[7]

And, as E. O. James has pointed out:

> Christ as propitiary victim . . . has always been a cardinal doctrine of Christianity, finding expression in a sacrificial tradition and a sacramental system.[8]

This means that the Church can also figure as the very type of a society founded on the sacrifice of another human being and held together by symbolic repetitions, in the Mass and the Eucharist, of that originating act. Walter Burkert, an important German scholar of sacrifice, argues that the centrality of sacrifice in Christianity is grounded or accompanied by a certain fascination with violence:

> those who turn to [Christianity] for salvation from the so-called evil of aggression are confronted with murder at the very core of Christianity: the death of God's innocent son.
> Thus blood and violence lurk fascinatingly at the very heart of religion.[9]

And this "fascinatingly," in turn, suggests the ease with which those anodyne, ecclesiastical, symbolic reenactments of a vicarious sacrifice which was supposed to put an end to sacrifice for all time, could be translated into actual reenactments of the bloody deed on the tortured bodies of heretics and Jews. As Girard has observed, "Christianity took on a persecutory character as a result of the sacrificial reading of the Passion and the Redemption."[10]

Girard, himself a believing Christian, has been sufficiently disturbed by this possible reading of Christianity as a celebration of his theory's deadly trinity—violence, victimage, and surrogation—to write a book, *Things Hidden Since the Foundation of the World*, to say that his theory does not apply to Christ.

> The sacrificial interpretation of the Passion must be exposed as a most
> enormous and paradoxical misunderstanding. . . . Mankind relies on a
> misunderstanding of the text that explicitly reveals the founding mech-
> anism, to reestablish cultural forms which remain sacrificial and to
> engender a society that, by virtue of this misunderstanding, takes its
> place in the sequence of all other cultures, still clinging to the sacrificial
> vision that the Gospel rejects.[11]

Girard's argument in the book is that the "sacrificial reading of historical
Christianity" has been a misreading of Jesus, whose death *reveals* the sacrifical mechanism at the foundation of all cultures and religions in order to
render it inoperative; that Christ's act was not a sacrifice at all; or if it was,
it was a sacrifice designed, like the sacrifices in the Old Testament, to
unmask and critique the evils of sacrifice from the point of view of the
victim. Clearly, we're still in the *pharmakon*, with victimage being unmasked by an inversion of it, which mirrors it and can be mistaken for it.

Girard is not alone, among recent scholars, in going back to to the
Old Testament to read Jesus as a Jew and to recognize rejection of the
"sacrificial mechanism" in the Old Law "superseded" by the Church. But
to recover that subjugated knowledge which divided *pharmakon* from
pharmakon and poison from cure, we also need to allow the difference
of an other's tradition to intervene between the "Old Testament" and its
"completion" in the New, and to permit the *écart* of an other's history to
interrupt the repetition of the same.

For those who live under the strictures of the Old Law, there is no
proximity between between sacrificing another human being and sacrificing an animal. The first is absolutely forbidden.

> Blood pollutes the land and no expiation can be made for the land, for
> the blood that is shed in it, except by the blood of him who shed it.[12]

Maimonedes and Abrabanel say that animal sacrifice was introduced in
the Temple to wean the people from pagan cults requiring human sacrifice, like the sacrifice of children to Moloch. Here, there was clearly a
moment of substitution, as R. Banaiah illustrates in his commentary on
Abraham's sacrifice of the ram in place of his son Isaac:

> As Abraham burned the ram, he said: Do Thou regard this as though the
> ashes of my son Isaac were heaped up on top of the altar before Thee.
> So, during each and every step of the sacrificial service, as he did some-
> thing to the ram, he would say: Do thou regard this as though it were
> being done to my son Isaac.[13]

In the context we have been discussing, this should be read with the rab-
binical injunction in mind that if one is not strong enough to defeat the

evil impulse outright, one had best throw it a sop that will stop it from accomplishing its aims. In other words, if people need a scapegoat, if they cannot help but seek a victim, if they must sacrifice *something*, let it be a sheep, a cow, a goat, that it may not be a man or a child. If people need to project their own evil onto a sacrificial victim, let the sacrificer's sin be transmitted to the animal through the ritual laying on of hands, so that this problematical, and, according to Girard, unconscious moment of displacement and projection of one's own monstrous faults onto an innocent "other" can be made conscious, memorized, and marked. And let the victim be a "clean" animal, one that we would normally kill for food, so that people can share its meat, and live, and rejoice before their God.

For the analogy actually operative in the Temple was not between sacrificing an animal and sacrificing a human being; it was between offering up an edible domestic animal and offering up grain, wine, oil, salt, spices, the first fruits of one's harvest, and the first fruits of a tree. The semiology of sacrifice in the Temple was *alimentary*: sacrifice was to be a physical reminder that life and food, in all their forms, come from God, and are not ours to take as we will. In the semiology of the Temple, the binary opposition lay not between the Raw and the Cooked (almost everything was roasted!); it lay between fast and plenty, between the offering wholly burnt to ashes and the offering shared out as meat, between the complete surrender and the complete enjoyment of (physical and spiritual) food.

For those who still live under the strictures of the Old Law, offering up another human being is absolutely proscribed; but it is absolutely commanded that one be ready to offer *oneself* up rather than violate the covenant with God. That is why there is a long Jewish tradition of self-offering in response to religious persecution—a tradition of *Mesirut Nefesh* and *Kiddush Ha-Shem*, which involves surrendering the body to the rack and the pyre as if one were being sacrificed on the altar, while elevating the soul and dedicating it to bear witness, for the Consecration of the Name. Twentieth-century scholars who read Jesus as a Jew try to place him in this long line of suffering servants, which leads from the Book of the Maccabees and Rabbi Akiva through the persecutions of the Middle Ages, the rigors of the Inquisition, and beyond. They find historical links and similarities of sentiment, for instance, between this prayer of the dying Ezra in *The Book of the Maccabees* (IV) and readings of Jesus's sacrificial self-offering in the early Church:

> Be merciful to your people. . . . Let my blood serve as their purification and accept my life as a ransom for them.[14]

But then, each of us has prayed that he would be the last. Each has prayed that the spilling of *his* blood, the charring of *his* flesh, and the memory of his ashes upon whatever manmade altar, would be weighed against the sins of the generation, and that the merits of his act would be remembered when God came to judge us, so that God would be merciful to his people. Each has cried out to God in the midst of suffering, destruction, and death: why, God, have you abandoned us? And it is to *this* tradition of suffering servants that the word *Shoah* (which in Hebrew supplies the place of the word "holocaust") may be linked. *Shoah* means destruction, catastrophe, darkness, the abyss; and by the shift of a single silent letter, it becomes *shavah*, a cry, the victim's cry for help and immemorial outcry to God:

> The Israelites cried out [in Egypt] and their cry for help rose to God.[15]

Each, in this long line of suffering servants has received the yoke of Heaven from the example of those who came before—as we still do, every day in the morning liturgy, when we read the order of sacrifices in the Temple and the first lines of the *Shema*,* while trying to prepare ourselves, through our *kavanot*,† for such surrender of the self and dedication of the soul. For there is no other who can offer herself in my place. In the language of the Qumran texts, which iterates that of the Prophets:

> The offering [*olah*] of the lips in accordance with the law shall be as an agreeable odour of righteousness, and perfection of way shall be as a voluntary gift [*minchah*] of a delectable oblation [*korban*]. . . . Each man should make his own sacrifice to God: the offering of a life completely dedicated to a striving for perfection before Him.

There is no surrogate for this offering of my lips and of my life, no vicarious elevation and perfection of a person's own "way."

Two kinds of sacrifice—one of the Other, and one of my Self—with completely different outcomes, confused in the same words. Jesus did not end with his cinders, and neither did I, the Jew. Cinders—what falls to the earth, dissipates, and blows away—are the fate of empires like Rome or the Third Reich, which sacrifice the Other—to remind those who have ears to hear and eyes to see that when we burn the Other, it is ultimately ourselves that we consign to the ashes. The sentence we pass on others sooner or later rebounds on ourselves, for as Girard says, "the culture born of violence must return to violence."[16]

Jesus did not end with his cinders, and neither did I, the Jew. I have always already been sacrificed for the sins of the world—sacrificed by the sins of the world, and because of my own sins too—but I arise each

---

*"Hear oh Israel," said several times each day and the last thing a Jew says before she dies.

†Direction of attention, sacred intention, from the vocabulary of piety and mysticism.

time anew. I live again in every generation, with my strange folkways and stranger tongue, to mark the place where the *Kampf* of the soul of a people becomes a *Kampf* for language against the lips and the languages which conflate holy with unholy acts.

Notes

1. For examples of this confusion of different sacrificial objects and sacrificial cults, see for instance the essays in *Le sacrifice dans l'antiquité*, eds. Jean Rudhardt and Olivier Reverdin (Geneva: Hardt, 1980), or in *Sacrifice*, eds. M. F. C. Bourdillon and Myer Fortes (New York: Academic Press, 1980). See also Henri Hubert and Marcel Mauss's still classic *Sacrifice: Its Nature and Function*.

2. René Girard, *Violence and the Sacred* (Baltimore: Johns Hopkins Press, 1977/1972); see also the discussion in *Violent Origins*, ed. Robert G. Hamerton (California: Stanford University Press, 1987).

3. *Mein Kampf* (Boston: Houghton Mifflin, 1971), p. 337. Page numbers to this edition will be given in parentheses in the text.

4. I'm indebted to Helga Madland for this point.

5. "I argued back, from day to day better informed than my antagonists, until one day a few of the spokesmen on the opposing side forced me either to leave the building at once or to be thrown off the scaffolding. . . . Poverty meant I had to go back [to the construction work at another site] whether I wanted to or not. The same old story began anew and ended very much the same as the first time." (40, 41)

6. "The German of my youth was the dialect of Lower Bavaria; I could neither forget it nor learn the Viennese jargon. . . . A German city! . . . In addition, the dialect, much closer to me, which particularly in my contacts with Lower Bavarians, reminded me of my childhood" (123, 126).

7. Horace Bushnell, *The Vicarious Sacrifice Grounded in Principles of Universal Obligation* (1866), pp. 39, 40, and 53.

8. E. O. James, *Sacrifice and Sacrament* (New York: Barnes & Noble, 1962), p. 11.

9. Walter Burkert, *Homo Necans: The Anthropology of Ancient Greek Sacrificial Ritual and Myth* (Berkeley: University of California Press, 1983/1972), pp. 1–2.

10. René Girard, *Things Hidden Since the Foundation of the World* (Stanford: Stanford University Press, 1987), p. 225.

11. Ibid., pp. 180, 181.

12. Numbers 33:35.

13. Shalom Spiegel, *The Last Trial* (New York: Pantheon, 1967), pp. 61–62.

14. S. K. Williams, *Jesus's Death as Saving Event: the Background and Origin of a Concept* (Montana: Scholars Press, 1975), p. 176.

15. Exodus 2:23.

16. Girard, *Things Hidden*, p. 148.

Austria's Heading
Has the Eagle Landed Again?

Erik M. Vogt

Two eyes, then; two gazes, two visions . . .

A *pensée de survol*, winged, a bird's eye view, imperial and totalizing the trajectory of Austria's identity in the twentieth century by lifting up its different ends: the end of the Habsburg monarchy; the end of the First Republic; the end of the Corporate State; the end of the Ostmark; pronouncements here and there concerning the end of the Second Republic and the dawning of a Third Republic apropos the German "unification," the political transformations in Eastern Europe, the formation of the European Community (and Austria's newly acquired membership in it).

Noiseless flights and easy passages over, above all, its difference with itself,[1] its Austro-German self by turning this hyphenated self-identity/difference into simple oppositions and binarisms. Internal oppositions characterized both the Austrian empire (although people of German descent presented a minority, the Habsburg empire had a German common denominator, a German leadership whose identity had been derived from its German significance, that is, from national categories that had been foisted on this old empire—categories that ultimately became identical with those of Austro-German nationalism) and the First Republic (the idea of *Anschluss*) as well as the fascist Corporate State (Austria as the "better Germany") with its claims of being a more effective mediation of "German spirituality and culture." In all these nationalist narratives, Austria was conceived as difference not to Germany, but rather to a particular form of Germanness. In other words, Austria appeared as a reduit, as a reserve for true and authentic Germanness that, as Ostmark, was brought home into the Third Reich.

These internal oppositions were then externalized by means of the Second Republic's strategies of in-differentiation written by model pupils of a continuist hermeneutics who, in the raging grip of homogenizing self-understanding, have aimed at the ultimate height of the always already retroactively posited unity of the Austrian spirit (whose flag is the eagle-*aigle*), reinvoking *Ganzheitsdenken* (a notion of totality and wholeness) with its harmonious contemplation of reality in order to level out the rupture of Austro-German National Socialism, the turbulences of Austria's difference-with-itself, and to "transcend" them in form of a recursive loop of endless endings directed by the transcendental warrant of the Austrian nation-thing. On the basis of redressing the hyphen having marked the Austro-German past in terms of a simple and pacified national opposition, this hermeneutic furor of totality has then reaffirmed Austria's spiritual "inner truth and greatness" and exported the piles of past waste it, too, had produced, to Germany, thereby allowing the Austrian spirit to sublate-forget its other *Geister*, ghosts, ashes.

In other words, Austrian "post"-Auschwitz politics reveals itself as a politics of effacement and forgetting that, for the sake of the community and its legitimacy, has required the removal of all traces of extermination. Some reminders:[2]

—The disciplinary-educational dispositive dictating the legitimation discourse of the Second Republic was based on a dual sleight of hand— its discourse argued that Austrians were not members of a Greater German nation and that they had been a collective and resisting victim of National Socialism.[3] And whatever the reasons for the acceptance or support of the *Anschluss* by parts of the population in 1938, in the following years a collective educational process had taken place in the course of which this very population had become aware of their national identity as Austrians and had consequently rejected Nazi theory and practice. The difference between Austrians and Germans was therefore "national and ethical." And the education of the youth was to stress the Austrian national and state consciousness "against the pretentious invocation of an unproven status of the Germans as a chosen people," the positive and authentic Austrian values of "amiability, decency, politeness, conciliatoriness," as well as a self-critical awareness of the negative ones: "excessive malleability, sensibility, affectionateness."[4] The recultivation of the awareness of an Austrian *Heimat* and *Kultur* (home and culture), the removal of "war damage" and the importance of harmony and conciliation as central virtues of Austrian identity emphasized the necessity of linking the now having again become "authentic" Austria with other European "Kulturnationen."

—This very nationalizing discourse[5] fusing tradition(s) and horizon(s), was made possible and regulated by a proprietary texture woven by strategic in-differentiations. Die *Entlastungsgesetze* (compensatory

laws) revealed themselves as instantiations of the Lyotardian *tort* exon-
erating (*entlasten*) Austria—Jews were either nationalized or turned into
foreigners according to the indifferentiating principle of equal treatment;
victims of Nazi euthanasia, enforced sterilization as well as gays/lesbians
and gypsies were deprived even of the possibility to testify to the litiga-
tions, to articulate their validity claims: the Austrian version of *Schad-
ensabwicklung* (damage control).

On the other (same) hand, the generously granted claims of the
zealous ones having conscientiously followed the path of duty, thus were
entitled to *Kriegsopferfürsorge* (war victim assistance). And this became
operative as another *Wink* (sign and hint) for the revisionism inherent
in Austria's (semi-)official historiography with its historically structured
distinction between the war as *the* historical event and National
Socialism as "errancy of the few." Moreover, this revisionism allowed not
only for the creation of the effort necessary to cover the crime, but also
for the establishment of a continuity and for the performance of an easy
passage leading straight from the "resistance fighters" of the 1934–45
period to those who, in the *Geist der Lagerstrasse* (spirit of the camp),
founded later on the Second Austrian Republic. Thus, de-Nazification
and its lawful enforcement, perceived as *Alliierten-Zwangsgesetze* (the
laws forced by the Allies) and the *Rachejustiz* (vengeful justice) by the
majority of the Austrian population as well as many politicians, if effective at all, was turned into an instrument for the purification of the Austrian National Socialists from accusations.[6]

This perspective of continuity informing the political semantics of
the 2nd Republic—for instance, its designation of the war between 1939
and 1945 as "Second World War" suggesting a mere continuation of the
Great War in terms of a European battle for power and, therefore, meaningfulness by not attaching significance to the effects of National Socialism—is also operative in Austria's dealings with memorials.[7] A brief
glance reveals that Austria still wants to leave the commemoration of the
victims of National Socialism to private individuals—the official participation in the remembrance of NS-victims is usually still limited to ritual
exercises, to few memorials in the larger cities. Whenever diplomatic
and foreign-policy considerations play no role, the requests and demands of those formerly persecuted remain without echo. Not only is
there but limited interest in extending the material remainders of concentration camps to memorials, the respective relics are still rather
razed to the ground or converted to another use.

Less difficult than the remembrance of the NS-victims is that of
those fallen in action or those dead who were not annihilated for political or "racial" reasons. Thus, while war memorials remembering those
killed in action can be found in central places (both in cities and smaller
towns and villages), graves and memorials remembering the annihilated

Jews, prisoners of concentration camps, and deserters are hidden away or marginalized. And if memorials of the Nazi atrocities are inscribed onto Austria's *Heldenplätze* (places of the heroes) these sites commemorating both sites of memory and the "people of memory" are themselves destroyed.[8]

Accordingly, the discourses and imagery having constituted and made up the web of the 2nd Austrian Republic's politics of (self)representation have to be read in terms of the imaginary with its appearance of continuity and harmonious totality. A true *Verbändestaat* (state consisting of both associations and bandages), therefore, handing over all disruptive wounds to time, so that the rising eagle not be disturbed in its continuous flight.

This handing over has never been simply a matter of forgetting, but of forgetting the impossibility of forgetting. Disastrous continuities and compulsion to repeat—in Austria this reads: tradition.[9] Their popular variations displaying cynically, for instance, in newspapers that the Austrians have remained decent, that is, undamaged in their being throughout the process of annihiliation prove Wiesel's statement: "Nothing has been learned, Auschwitz has not served as a warning. For more detailed information, consult your daily newspaper."

However, this Austrian politics of forgetting by compulsively repeating a supposedly homogeneous tradition has to be varied constantly. One of its latest variations can be read as a heading back to the future—of *Mitteleuropa* (Central Europe).

When, in 1989 and 1990, the borders of Austria were opened toward Hungary and Czechoslovakia, certain perceptions of and projects for Central Europe, having started to appear from the mid-1980s,[10] seemed to have found their material basis: Central Europe.

Central Europe: somewhere and somehow between Germany and Russia, between Italy and the Baltic Sea. A geographically and politically not definable territory with shifting names: *Mitteleuropa, Zentraleuropa, Zwischeneuropa, Osteuropa, Südosteuropa, Donauraum, Europa dazwischen, Zentralmitteleuropa, Ostmitteleuropa, Mittelosteuropa*. And nonetheless, somewhere and somehow with Austria as its center—and if not with Austria, then at least with Vienna.

Manifold desires with changing undertones have capitalized on Central Europe: there is a Western desire with anti-Russian undertones in the Eastern countries; a neutralist and nationalist desire with anti-American undertones in German speaking countries; a regionalist desire for autonomous relations in Italy. And Austria's desire—once again informed by the matrix of Austro-German self-difference/identity: Central Europe as periphery of the German territory and as delimitation from the German center in form of a circumlocution for the old Austrian empire.[11] In other words—words evoked by the Austrian government, its state discourses: "In my opinion, we have today the role of the good neighbor and interpreter. We attempt to translate how the current state of thought is in those countries"[12]—Austria's desire for Central Europe appears to have taken on the shape of a re-embarking to a Europe of origins that, under the Austrian heading, needs to be restored, rediscovered, and reconstituted. The heading toward Central Europe with Austria as avant-garde describes a return to its history and its imaginary geography, an Odyssean homecoming somewhere and somehow between nostalgic retrospective and utopian anticipation.

This Central European heading, this Austrian heading over regions of enduring ethnic and religious intolerance, marked by bitter quarrels, murderous wars, and frequent slaughter on a scale ranging from pogrom to genocide, toward Central Europe, presented as the other heading (of Europe), as heading of the other (Europe),[13] is not defined by geography or empirical history. Referring essentially to the imaginary memory-space of the former Habsburg monarchy, it presents itself as a spiritual figure of Central Europe invoked against the crisis of Spirit, the crisis of Europe, of European identity, and more precisely of European culture marked by "Americanization, materialism, hedonist nihilism, de-Christianization."[14] The spirituality of a Central Europe without the assignment of a geographical or territorial outline, the new spiritual forces from this middle place, are mobilized as central-europo-centrist mission, as "metaphor of protest" against the heteronomy of Europe, against the East-West oppositions, against "the hard reality of power politics,"[15] as unity of spiritual life, action, and creation. Consider this statement by an Austrian historian:

> For all these reasons I am in favor of making a virtue of necessity. Since there is no definable Central Europe, one has the freedom to postulate a utopian one. One may call the incantation of such a vague unity like Central Europe which contradicts the historical circumstances a utopian projection because the search for Central Europe arises from the same suffering from the bad reality and, like each utopia, strives to save man from the inevitable power-political embrace through the leap into other dimensions negating experience. Let us thus admit that this Central Europe—weak in history, fugitive in the present, more than uncertain in the future—is a cipher for that which is not, but ought to be, a spiritual attitude, an ethos.[16]

And this spirit is inflamed, it already burns again in the "living consciousness of the Austrian people": "I believe that in the Austrian underground, which has been rarely illuminated, processes of a new manner of living have been forming and also restless motions in what was called the soul. But even if there is no soul, it exists at least as a psychical process, . . . , as a center of unrest, as volcano, as fire in man. Even if one suppresses this fire, it nonetheless is alive and it is remarkable how many fires are still burning and burning again under the ashes in Austria."[17] The spirit gathers itself in conflagration, it burns as the fire of Central Europe, and the Austrian eagle rises up again above the stench of burning flesh, the decomposing dead, and interiorizes itself toward authentic homecoming.

This appropriative Austrian project of Central Europe instrumentalizes a rhetoric of plurality, multinationalism, transregionalism, and openness[18] (a rhetoric that, however, apropos the migration effects in the wake of the opening of the borders in 1989 and 1990, was immediately renounced and replaced with the image of Austria as the "fortress of Europe"), which advertises itself as a farewell to modernity, as an affirmation of postmodernism. However, a closer examination brings to the fore rather a modern antimodernism—the Austrian coinage being a "postmodernism with a view"[19]—with an *identitas in diversitate* that stages the relationship between nationalism and philosophical nationality, between national or supranational identity and the logic of identity itself, according to the logic of exemplarity. For the diversity of Central Europe receives as its heading the example or exemplar of Austrian diversity, thereby inscribing a particular place and discourse in the name of the universal:

> Austrians are especially used to living completely different perspectives, hopes, anxieties, worries, even unified in one human being. As we have realized: completely different political perspectives can coexist. Why should man, and in particular the Austrian, be a hot-pot, when he never was one even during his greatest times—the Austrian was never a hot-pot, even when he was obsessed and stricken by *morbus austriacus*, even when he lived as a confused and difficult one. He never was a hot-pot and in his best contributions to world culture he did not offer hot-pots but diverse menus from Mozart to Freud. For this very reason, one has to take into consideration that many Austrians today and also tomorrow live in deep inner uncertainty.[20]

The Central European Spirit thus figures as an exemplary value for humankind and the Austrian as an exemplary value for Central Europe.

And what is more, the *eidos* of Central Europe is inscribed into the unexamined axiomatics of a simplified—and highly Catholicized—idea of philosophy that, at a certain moment, has come to converge with the destiny and existence of the Austrian people. Let us re-mark the moment of convergence, for example, in the sophisticated naïveté or the crude sophism of a philosophical discourse on Austrian philosophy entering the stage of geopolitics in terms of "an expression of Austrian identity"[21] by limiting ourselves to what concerns the general structure of its indispensable idiom of historical conflation:

- Austrian philosophy differs from German or Western European philosophy in its taste for the complex, the manifold, the plural, and thus is constitutive of a tradition ending in postmodernism.
- This tradition has its origin in the Catholic baroque with its harmony of oppositions, its attempt to level out and overcome oppositions and contradictions, its universalism.
- The specific form of "humanitas austriaca" has to be considered as the cultural medium of a Central European, multinational and trans-regional spirituality.
- The autonomous Austrian tradition of philosophy is identical with that of Central Europe.[22]

The property of the Austrian idiom, oscillating continually between these two irreconcilable discourses, advances itself as a heading for Central Europe which in turn advances itself as a heading for the universal essence of humanity. Austrian cultural identity would thus be responsible for the Central European today and, thus, as always, for the trans-Central European. It would be responsible, in particular in its Catholic dimension, for the universe, for "the restoration of the dignity of humankind . . . against the Western idols of consumerism and the Eastern idols of power."[23]

And recent politico-institutional strategies of Austria's foreign cultural policy, often obscene in their euphoria, have strived to implement this metaphysical projection of a symbolic center—Vienna[24]—at the heart of this Central Europe. This struggle for hegemonic centrality, for Vienna as metropolis, as point in which Central Europe gathers and converges, has taken place on the stage of geopolitics not only in form of the organization of various symposia and conferences on Central Europe, the establishment of a new university space (the establishment of Donau-Universitäten and Academies for Central Europe in Austria),[25] the rapid dissemination of Austrian Cultural Institutes in the former Eastern European countries, but also in form of a consensus of the media fueled by the internationalization of Austrian Broadcasting (Radio Danubia, Radio Adria) and new newspaper or magazine consortiums. Moreover, this stage is animated by an aesthetico-political discourse reinvoking theater and theatricality (in particular, the tradition of opera and operetta) and a certain Austrian (cultural) landscape (in terms of the *Naturschönes*) as the representational means for asserting this Austrian cosmology as formal, cohesive, and absolute totality.

If nature can no longer be captured immediately, all images of nature are marked by history. In the last instance, nature itself is a product of historical processes. Cultural landscapes are, in other words, exemplifications of natural history. They generate an aesthetic experience of natural beauty because they stimulate images that are to reconcile natural conditions and cultural activities. What is esteemed in cultural landscapes is the utopian figuration of a reconciliation of nature and culture, a utopian semblance.

The canon of images used by the central-europo-centrist missionaries to represent the cultural landscape as symbol of the Second Republic betrays an uncanny identity with several books of illustrations of the Austrian landscape edited around 1938 with the intention to emphasize the beauty that the Ostmark had brought into the German Reich.[26] For those images present it as beautiful *physis*, as organic totality, as harmonious consonance of landscape, historical architecture and culture, with a particular dominance of baroque tradition and custom.

Rural subjects dominate, while the contemporary urban realm remains excluded; cities are almost exclusively represented by historical, that is, baroque buildings. And the (not so) different images of cultural landscape evoke the sphere of unalterable values, unity, and simplicity by following the logic of growth cycles and the ecclesiastical year. Thus, a stage with a cultural fluid is established, marked by traditional aesthetic concepts such as *Schein*, beauty, aura conjuring up images of natural immediacy and completeness, of a divinely ordered and meaningful cosmos.

It is on this very representational stage that this particular reservoir of ideal, perfect images, timeless and undamaged, forge a connection between landscape, geopolitical position, national character and a certain idea of the state. And this in the spirit of a certain Austrian metaphysics embodied in the program of various festivals embedded in the summer landscape.

Catholicism, baroque totality, cosmology, organicity—Austria as miniature of the Creation—auratic images signed by the Austrian discourse on Central Europe returning to the "common focus towards which, between 1919 and 1939, the discourses of worry gather or rush headlong: around the same words (Europe, Spirit), if not in the same language."[27]

A theatrical speech is therefore called upon, a speech before the theater of the world, of history, and of politics, that rehinges the age and brings everything back in order, readjusts it. And although the theatrical and representational (aesthetico-political) means characterizing the recent Austrian evocations of Central Europe as latest national(ist) cosmology present themselves again, anew, as the new, they rather exhibit the features of repetitive memory of and anamnetic capitalization on an apotheosis of Austria put forth by Hugo von Hofmannsthal in various writings from 1906 to 1929. In order to show that it is in this particular discourse of worry that the Austrian present resonates, let me thus redraw the schematic contours of the mythical narrative that I supposed to provide Hofmannsthal's (neo)baroque invention of the Austrian idea with a certain organicity.

Hofmannsthal's attempted restoration of the Catholic baroque, in particular in the context of the Salzburg Festival[28] as "visible symbol" of the Austrian "summoning of spiritual strength,"[29] stipulates the sensuous unity of spirit and nature, that is, the possibility of symbolically[30] transcending polar opposites. Brought, moreover, onto the theatrical stage, this aestheticization of the theological transfers the metaphysics of the disclosure of Spirit into the language of beautiful appearance. The result is then a 'transposition of the inherently mythic character of symbolic expression"[31] from a religious-mythic discourse to an aesthetico-political discourse: "We are not concerned with the foundation of a theater, with the project of dreamlike fantasies or the local affairs of a provincial town. We are concerned with European culture, and one of eminently political, economic, and social significance."[32]

Therefore, the term "baroque" emerges in this metaphysical mimetology not simply as a periodizing label or as an artistic style, but rather as a cosmology representing theological, aesthetic, and political principles of the Counterreformation. And Hofmannsthal institutes himself as its storyteller recounting to the Austrian people their history, that is, the story of their origin—the story founding the intimate being of the Austrian community on the theatrical stage. Salzburg as spiritual space of the nation which is simultaneously "possessed of a true spirit of cosmopolitanism"[33] is the scenography of this indefinite, regular repetition through which a truly mything Austrian people with its cosmopolitan-nationalist mission of a convergence of "the idea of Europe"—which needs "an Austria: a structure of unartificial elasticity, yet a structure nonetheless, a true organism, suffused with an inner religion of its own"[34]—and the "Austrian idea" become truly Austrian in this mythation: a true cultural organism opposed to and transcending the crisis of material civilization: "Even this material civilization will no doubt continue to develop, but—we can at least hope—under another star, with the possibility of self-transcendence. . . . The talk must now be of the appearance of a new authority, not the authority that lies in official capacities, but rather one that will be embodied in purely psychic and spiritual forms, unanimous with the reawakening of religious meaning, so that the concept of the mass, this frightful and dangerous concept . . . might be transcended and definitively replaced with the higher concept of the Volk."[35]

As such, the very program of the Salzburg Festival is characterized by embracing "both the poetico-ethnological nostalgia for an initial *mything* humanity and the wish to regenerate the old European humanity by resurrecting its most ancient myths."[36]

The baroque is resurrected in both Hofmannsthal's mimetological discourse and its recent recirculation in the form of a discourse on Central Europe in terms of a complicity between the example and the universal, between cosmopolitanism and nationalism, representing the entire cosmos from the vantage point of a Catholic center that controls the principles and the process of representation. In both instances, neobaroque theatricality, functioning as the representational aesthetic means toward a national cosmology, is thus constitutive rather than reflective of cultural and political (Austrian) identity. Both operate then closed economies of mimesis that, with their appeal to an aesthetico-symbolic totality as the site of dwelling for a spiritual community, engender a certain aestheticist politics.

What, however, happened to a look at the underside of this attempted mythical restoration of the Catholic baroque world with its theatrical insistence on symbol, coherence, totality, closure? What, in other words, happened to an eye's glance that, scanning the apparently smooth, seamless, and beautiful surface of this cosmology's narratives and images, suddenly got cut up by them, thus revealing the latter to be products of fissures and violent sutures, abrupt descents and broken contours? How could it ever gather itself again, splintered by the barbed wires forcing image and narrative into line? Would it not rather be fragmented, carried away by its own sight, perhaps hurled outside of itself—an uprooted eye pouring into and losing itself no longer in the *schöne Land* (beautiful land), but, filled with the blank, the absence of Auschwitz, rather in the deathzone of the Austrian landscape, until it finally turns—in an inversion—from a glance at the dead into a dead glance?

An allegorical vison,[37] then, that freezes the Austrian landscape, mortifies the aesthetic spirit, thereby disrupting the easy passage from "nature to stone to spirit."[38] Images of (natural) beauty, tinged by "past real suffering,"[39] become images of a "memento"[40] in the face of the historical catastrophe, the unparalleled physical violence and destruction, and exhibit fragments and ruins that "extinguish the *eidos*,"[41] that is, the false semblance of totality.

Anti-Heimat, anti-nature, anti-art.[42]

Historical constellations of nature are mobilized against the naturalized image of nature (as reservoir of civilization's garbage and sanctuary of "recreational activities") that decipher nature as commodity, in its artificiality produced by disciplinary technologies of cleansing, hygiene, and health.[43] "Naturalness" and artificiality merge, they reverse roles. The origin imitates its reproduction, its medial representation.

The replacement of the emphatic concept of natural beauty with that of natural ugliness—excrement, illness, hideously deformed bodies—empties out all mimetological variants of mimesis (of an allegedly originary nature) by producing grotesque-allegorical modes of writing and imaging that draw ever new connecting lines between corporeality, nature, violent phantasms, and media images. These drawings translate into fragmentary scenarios that could best be described as the imagery of the imagery of a slaughterhouse. Bodies decline into ruins; they dissolve through (not so) natural processes into split open wounds that do not find their *telos* in some authentic death veristically captured and glorified, for example, as eternal face. If, "after" Auschwitz, each claim of positivity for death is but an injustice to its victims—and death is no longer what is most horrible[44]—then literary depictions of individuality, death masks—taken before the stiffness and the beginning decomposition—and their easy photographic reproductions have to be read as suppression of the forces of destruction: for as harmonious appearance they still suggest that the voice of life could speak unmistakably in them, claiming the aura of inviolability. An aesthetically performed horror, working in the ever-widening abyss between figure and flesh, body and person, physical appearance and selfhood, destroys the reified and commodified expressivity of death by writing, painting, scrawling all over it.[45] Non-mimetological mimesis of the dead, protesting against the aestheticized horror, those modes of writing/imaging become the "sites of an *endless mimesis*, which is both interminable and inorganic, producing no art and achieving no appropriation."[46]

Notes

1. Jacques Derrida, *The Other Heading: Reflections on Today's Europe*, trans. P. A. Brault and M. B. Naas. (Bloomington: Indiana University Press, 1992), p. 9.

2. The following texts have been the hosts of my parasitic meandering through the Second Republic: Josef Haslinger, *Politik der Gefühle: Ein Essay über Österreich* (Darmstadt: Luchterhand, 1987); Robert Menasse, *Das Land ohne Eigenschaften: Ein Essay zur österreichischen Identität* (Vienna: Sonderzahl, 1993); *Kontroversen und Österreichs Zeitgeschichte: Verdrängte Vergangenheit: Österreich-Identität, Waldheim und die Historiker*, eds. Gerhard Botz and Gerald Sprengnagel (Frankfurt/New York: Campus, 1994); *Österreich 1945–1995*, eds. R. Sieder, H. Steinert, E. Talos (Vienna: Verlag für Gesellschaftskritik, 1995); *Schwieriges Erbe*, eds. W. Bergram, R. Erb, A. Lichtbleu (Frankfurt/New York: Campus Verlag, 1995).

3. This according to the selective (mis)reading of the Allies' Third Moscow Declaration from 1943, which had declared Austria as the first free country to have fallen victim to Hitler's politics of aggression.

4. Robert Knight, "Education and National Identity in Austria after the Second World War," in *Austrians and Jews in the Twentieth Century*, ed. R. S. Wistrich (New York: St. Martin's Press, 1992), pp. 178–95.

5. For this logic of "nationalizing," see *Nationalism and Nationalities in the New Europe*, ed. Ch. Kupchar (Ithaca: Cornell University Press, 1995).

6. See in particular the articles by Gerhard Botz and Hans Safrian in *Kontroversen um österreichische Zeitgeschichte*.

7. I follow here Josef Seiter, "Vergessen—und trotz alledem—erinnern:

Vom Umgang mit Monumenten und Denkmälern in der Zweiten Republik," in *Österreich 1945–1995*, pp. 684–705.

8. See also James Young, *The Texture of Memory: Holocaust, Memorials and Memory* (New Haven: Yale University Press, 1993), and Anton Pelinka, "Vom Umgang mit der Geschichte: Denkmäler und historische Erinnerung in der Zweiten Republik," in *BMUK, Denkmal und Erinnerung* (Vienna, 1993).

9. Menasse, *Das Land ohne Eigenschaften*, p. 63.

10. See Milan Kundera, "The Tragedy of Central Europe," *New York Review of Books*, 26 April 1984; Edgar Morin, *Penser l'Europe* (Paris: Gallimard, 1987); H. M. Enzensberger, *Ach Europa* (Frankfurt: Suhrkamp Verlag, 1987); for the Austrian version of this discourse see, in particular, *Aufbruch nach Mitteleuropa*, eds. E. Busek and G. Wilfinger (Vienna, 1986) as well as *Projekt Mitteleuropa*, eds. E. Busek and E. Brix (Vienna: Ueberreuter, 1986). A common theme to emerge from these "new" self-reflections in Europe on Europe is the emphasis on Europe's *essence* being in its diversity, its complexity, its lack of a single center and absence of uniformity. However, as will be demonstrated, what is problematic with regard to the Austrian intervention in this debate is to distil from these (supposedly Austrian national) characteristics a European essence which is then presented as the ordinary and genuine meaning of Europe.

11. See *The History of the Idea of Europe*, eds. K. Wilson and J. van der Dussen (London and New York: Routledge, 1993).

12. Quoted in Daniéle Renon, *Les représentations géopolitiques de Mitteleuropa chez Erhard Busek* (Paris: Gallimard, 1994), p. 91.

13. See Jacques Derrida, *The Other Heading*, p. 15.

14. *Projekt Mitteleuropa*, p. 15.

15. Ibid., p. 17.

16. Ibid., pp. 125–26.

17. Ibid., p. 138.

18. Ibid., pp. 67–69.

19. Ibid., p. 165.

20. Ibid., p. 138.

21. Peter Kampits, "Österreichs Philosophie als Ausdruck österreichischer Identität," *Revue d'Allemagne et des pays de langue allemande*, 1992/4: 477–85.

22. Kampits, "Österreichs Philosophie als Ausdruck österreichischer Identität," p. 477.

23. *Projekt Mitteleuropa*, p. 131.

24. Ibid., pp. 145–47

25. Ibid., pp. 157–59

26. See the excellent article by Wolfgang Kos, "Imagereservoir Landschaft: Landschaftsmoden und ideologische Gemütslagen seit 1945," in *Österreich 1945–1995*, pp. 581–98. See also Lucca Chmel, *Bilderbuch Österreich* (Vienna: Globus, 1947), for a particularly impressive case of how Austrian cultural politics began to rewrite history immediately after the Second World War by portraying landscapes, monuments, relics, and people in terms of a "beauty" not carrying any traces of destructive history. Here are only two examples from the preface asserting continuity for Austria: "The history of our people is the history of struggle for its freedom." "Austria lived, it lives, and it will live." It is also important to observe that the notes to this volume of images were written in four

languages, thus already preparing for the selling out of Austria as the country of tourism *par excellence*.

27. Jacques Derrida, *Of Spirit: Heidegger and the Question*, trans. G. Bennington and R. Bowlby (Chicago and London: University of Chicago Press, 1987), p. 61.

28. The relevant writings by Hofmannsthal attempting to (re)establish (German) Austria as the "spiritual bridge" between West and East, North and South, can be found in Hugo von Hofmannsthal, *Gesammelte* Werke, 15 vols., ed. H. Steiner (Frankfurt, 1945–55), *Prosa III* and *Prosa IV*. Their intertextuality is quite complex—references can be found not only to Nietzsche's *Birth of Tragedy* and Thomas Mann's *Reflections of a Nonpolitical Man*, but even more important, to the respective programs of Bayreuth and Oberammergau. The following pages are deeply indebted to the excellent study by Michael P. Steinberg, *The Meaning of the Salzburg Festival: Austria as Theater and Ideology, 1890–1938* (Ithaca: Cornell University Press, 1990). Steinberg's reading of the "ideology" of the Salzburg Festival is succinctly captured in the following passage: "As an exercise in cultural planning, Salzburg is a romantic redefinition of society as a community, an aesthetic totality. It stands between, on the one side, the rationalistic planning of Mannheim, and, on the other, the deromanticized, de-aestheticized politics of totality of Carl Schmitt. . . . There is . . . an intellectual continuity between the aestheticizing totality of the Salzburg ideology and the de-aestheticized totality of Schmitt and Nazism in general. Hence the intellectual—and in many cases political—continuity between Salzburg ideology and Austrian Nazism," p. 78. Other texts dealing with Hofmannsthal's conception of the "Austrian idea" are Wolgang Mauser's article "Die geistige Grundfarbe des Planeten, Hugo von Hofmannsthals 'Idee Europa,'" in *Hofmannsthal Jahrbuch: Zur europäischen Moderne* 2/1994 (Freiburg: Rombach Verlag, 1994), pp. 201–24; Jacques Le Rider's "Hugo von Hofmannsthal and the Austrian idea of Central Europe," in *The Habsburg Legacy: National identity in Historical Perspective*, eds. R. Robertsen and E. Timms (Edinburgh: Edinburgh University Press, 1994), pp. 121–35; Frederick Ritter, *Hugo von Hofmannsthal und Österreich* (Heidelberg: Lothar Stiehm Verlag, 1967).

29. Quoted in Steinberg, *The Meaning of the Salzburg Festival*, p. 57.

30. Max Pensky, *Melancholy Dialectics: Walter Benjamin and the Play of Mourning* (Amherst; University of Mass. Press, 1993), p. 112.

31. On the abundant secondary literature on Hofmannsthal and symbol(ism) see Matthias Mayer, *Hugo von Hofmannsthal* (Stuttgart: Verlag Metzler, 1993), pp. 184–98.

32. Quoted in Steinberg, *The Meaning of the Salzburg Festival*, p. 57.

33. Hofmannsthal, *Prosa III*, p. 185.

34. Ibid., p. 406.

35. Ibid., p. 505.

36. Jean-Luc Nancy, *The Inoperative Community*, ed. P. Connor, foreword by Ch. Fynsk (Minneapolis: University of Minnesota Press, 1991), p. 46.

37. Walter Benjamin, *The Origin of the German Tragic Drama*, trans. John Osborne (London: NLB, 1977).

38. This phrase was coined by Hermann Bahr.

39. Theodor Adorno, *Aesthetic Theory*, trans. and ed., R. Hullot-Kentor (Minneapolis: University of Minnesota Press, 1997), p. 64.

40. Ibid.

41. Benjamin, *The Origin of the German Tragic Drama*, p. 175.

42. The reference is to the "genre" of *Anti-Idylle or Anti-Heimatroman* that has dominated Austrian literature for almost forty years. The number of the authors writing in this very "genre" would be too vast to list them here. That this literary discourse is, actually, a *mésalliance* blurring the traditional laws of genre is demonstrated in my "What Are Poets For—in Austria—'After' Auschwitz," *History and Memory: Suffering and Art* ed. H. Schweitzer, special issue of *Bucknell Review* 42, no. 2 (Fall 1998). In this very context, those *mésalliances* are read as allegorical unwritings of a certain "aesthetic ideology" (Paul de Man, *The Resistance to Theory* [Minneapolis: University of Minnesota Press, 1986], p. 78) ranging from the early Nietzsche to the restorative spirit of the catholic baroque in the contemporary (Austrian) discourse.

43. It is, above all, Elfriede Jelinek who has repeatedly exhibited these links in her texts. See, for example, *Oh Wildnis, oh Schutz vor ihr* (Reinbeck bei Hamburg: Rowohlt, 1994); *Totenauberg* (New York: Continuum, 1997).

44. This in the shadow of Adorno's "Meditations on Metaphysics" in his *Negative Dialectics* (New York: Continuum, 1997).

45. I am thinking of Arnulf Rainer whose painting-overs could be read as allegorical exercises of mortification (*Abtötungsübungen*).

46. Philippe Lacoue-Labarthe, *Heidegger, Art, Politics* (Oxford: Basil Blackwell, 1990), p. 38.

"You can't make
a full evening out of
being a Yid anymore"
George Tabori and the Limits
of the Holocaust's Uniqueness

Karyn Ball

When Holocaust scholars insist on the Holocaust's historical singularity, they are asserting that its status as a moral trauma
transcends other traumatic events in Western history. This argument is
charged with the horror that surrounds the Jewish genocide as a specifically modern, technologically and bureaucratically produced mass
murder. The "Final Solution" unleashed unimaginable statistics on an
enlightened Europe, statistics that called into question the moral
assumptions underlying the Rights of Man and their attendant
humanism. The singularity argument also serves to remind the Western
world of the debt of respect and mourning owed to survivors and the
bereaved while underscoring the exceptionality of survivors' experiences
in the death camps. These experiences are presumed to transcend the
intersubjective structures of normal civilized life, and thus attest to the
unbearable solitude of surviving. In short, the uniqueness argument figures for scholars' desire to protect its meaning as a moral injunction to
respect the dead, the survivors, and their families; and to refuse complicity with future terror.

Given the traumatic character of Holocaust memory, it is not surprising that the singularity claim has produced considerable dispute
among scholars in recent years. This dispute culminated in the 1986
West German Historians' Debate (*Der Historikerstreit*) in West Germany
when the conservative historians Ernst Nolte and Michael Stürmer
argued for a revision of German history that would decentralize the
Jewish genocide and thereby provide the historical conditions for Germans to rebuild a positive national image.[1] For Charles Maier, Saul
Friedländer, and Hayden White, the West German Historians' Debate

raised the problem of where to set the limits of representation in keeping with the desire to protect the moral meaning of the Holocaust from the vicissitudes of ideology and forgetting.[2] For White, in particular, this question is affected by the "inexpungeable relativity of every historical phenomenon," a relativity that would seem to belie the recourse to the figure of uniqueness. This is the case insofar as the existence of competing modes of representation is a function of the polysemic character of discourse which undermines the effort to set standards intended to protect one perception of the Holocaust from sentimental appropriations or revisionist trivializations. Moreover, as his discussion of Art Spiegelman's testimonial graphic novel *Maus: A Survivor's Tale* suggests, the responsible *emplotment* of the Holocaust (i.e., its poetic configuration in narrative) can occur in a number of surprising venues that push the limits of absurdity in their mixture of "'low' genre with events of the most momentous significance."[3]

Against the backdrop of these debates, I would like to situate George Tabori's *Weisman and Copperface* (1990) as a play that dramatizes the provocative mixture of the absurd and the momentous that White describes.[4] Through a series of ironic linkages couched in laconic language, the climactic verbal duel between the male protagonists under the title "High Noon" presents the respective efforts of Weisman and "Copperface" to prove that the magnitude and quality of his victimization exceeds the other's. In this manner, the duel pressures the uniqueness claim as one that could responsibly reflect and respect the specificities of Jewish suffering under the Nazis and in general. By placing this duel in dialogue with theoretical treatments of the Holocaust, the subsequent analysis focuses on the ways in which Tabori paradoxically undermines and reconfirms the exceptionality of Jewish victimization. My aim is to illuminate how the improprieties of Tabori's "Jewish Western" deepen the aporias that surround the representation of traumatic history.

In framing and interrogating the exceptionality of Jewish victimization and the Holocaust, *Weisman and Copperface* is typical of Tabori's recent work which often focuses on the Nazi past. The play depicts the black-comic trials of the Jewish Arnold Weisman and his "mongoloid" daughter, Ruth, as they drive from California to New York, where Weisman intends to spread the ashes of his wife on Riverside Drive in accordance with her last wish. Unfortunately, Weisman loses his way and stops in New Mexico, where a hunter steals the car at gunpoint and leaves them stranded in the desert with nothing but the urn containing Mrs. Weisman's ashes. Their only hope for salvation arrives in the person of Joe Nakedass, or "Copperface" as he is identified in the dialogue. Copperface is a long-suffering Native American who has traveled to this spot to commit suicide. After hearing his life history, a sometimes delirious rant punctuated with anti-Semitic insults and insinuations, Weisman challenges Copperface to a verbal duel to determine who has suffered more. Weisman's daughter Ruth is at once referee, scorekeeper, and implicit prize since whoever wins will take her with him. In the end, "Copperface" appears to be winning, but concedes after Weisman confesses his attempt to drown Ruth when she was a small child. His victory is futile, however, since Ruth insists on eloping with the Native American, despite her father's qualms about her handicapped condition, her ability as a "mongoloid" to be a "proper" wife, and Joe's competence as caretaker. Ultimately, Weisman accepts his fate; but after saying goodbye and bestowing an ambivalent blessing on his daughter, he dies of a heart attack, at which point Ruth spreads her mother's ashes over her father and covers him with rocks. On their way toward Santa Fe, Joe Nakedass reintroduces himself as Geegee Goldberg while Ruth adopts his nickname for her, Turtledove, with the sun rising on their departure.

Toward the beginning of the duel, Weisman declares that he has not only been beaten by his family, by rabbis, and by "3000 young blacks with bicycle chains." He also submits that he is a widower, a batterer, and the nephew of a Treblinka victim. Copperface, on the other hand, has been "Electro-shocked in the Ku Klux Klan clinic," a testimony that provokes Weisman's denial. When Copperface counters this denial with "Exceptional case," Ruth grants him two points.

Weisman's denial and Copperface's defense in this instance of the duel highlight the problem of representing an atrocity when the witnesses themselves as well as the evidence of their death have been annihilated. This is a problem that leads Shoshana Felman and Dori Laub to identify a "crisis of witnessing" to describe the paralysis of the bystanders as well as the subsequent silence of survivors in the Holocaust's aftermath.[5] Their analysis of this crisis draws on Jean-François Lyotard's argument in *The Differend* where he suggests that the "unrepresentability" of Auschwitz is, in part, a measure of the fragility of testimonial evidence in a context wherein the competence and sympathy of the listeners is in question and the survivors feel prevented, unable, or inadequate to speak.[6] Accordingly, if for Felman, Laub, and Lyotard, the Holocaust is exceptional, this is because the victimization and isolation of the survivors is reproduced, not only by the Nazis' elimination of evidence, but also through the disbelief and denial that the survivors face when they attempt to narrate their experiences.

Ultimately, then, different standards of receiving and judging survivors' testimonies are in order if their suffering is not to be intensified. Here is where the hermeneutical distinction between meaning and facticity becomes relevant.[7] For if testimony respecting the Final Solution is to be validated irrespective of its facticity or of its capacity to point to concrete evidence (which the destruction of the crematoria and the burning of the dead to some extent preclude), then this is a product of the desire to safeguard appropriate respect for the memory of those who were murdered as well as for those family members and others who survived them.

This desire has sometimes driven Holocaust writers to affirm the unspeakability of the death camps as a means of recognizing the incommensurability between the horrors of surviving and the intersubjective structures that organize everyday life. In this view, the death camps belong to an order of experience wherein the ubiquity and imminence of death are impossible to disavow. In contrast, the world outside functions on the basis of such a disavowal. Citing this opposition, scholars who argue for the Holocaust's singularity claim that the universality of death and suffering in the camps precludes the translation of survivor experiences into the language of civilized existence. Their insistence on the Holocaust's "unrepresentability" produces a circular figure: the Jewish genocide is presumed to be unique because the barbarism it names exceeds imagination and consequently meets with disbelief; at the same time, the genocide is unrepresentable by virtue of its singularity.

The opening exchange between Weisman and Copperface ironically emphasizes this circularity. Copperface need only declare that his case is exceptional to win two points from Ruth. Insofar as Ruth's validation of his testimony transpires despite his statement's apparent absurdity, the exchange exposes the weakness of the arguments for the Holocaust's singularity on the basis of the denial it produces. Copperface is not, at this moment in the play, identifiable as a Jew; nonetheless, he can successfully deploy the "exceptional case" argument. His success undermines the uniqueness claim respecting the Jewish genocide, for if everyone who cannot produce evidence of her/his victimization assumes the status of an exceptional case, then the Holocaust's exceptionality loses its meaning.

This unraveling of the uniqueness argument contributes to the irony of Weisman's declaration that his aunt was burned to death in Treblinka following Copperface's statement that his uncle was lynched in Disneyland. The symmetry of their respective losses (for Copperface, an uncle, and for Weisman, an aunt) is seemingly undercut by the asymmetry between the reality of crematoria in Treblinka and the relative implausibility of a lynching in Disneyland. Yet there is another more complicated level of symmetry between them which Disneyland's improbability as a site of execution suggests. In our minds, both Treblinka and Disneyland are places set apart from everyday life: Treblinka by virtue of the thousands who were murdered there and Disneyland by virtue of the escapist interludes its pristine fantasy worlds permit. Through this comparison, then, the profound reality of Treblinka is made manifest through a laconic evocation of the sense of *unreality* that surrounds it. Crucial here is how this sense of unreality is produced: not because Treblinka embodied a departure from "normal" life, but because the capacity to orchestrate barbarism in the midst of populated areas is itself an operative feature of modern existence as such. Indeed, if Disneyland and Treblinka become at some level comparable here, it is because both are undeniable products of a specifically modern aesthetic: the will to engineer a utopic order and to apply all technological means available in the service of this will.

Interestingly, the implications of this improper linkage do not come to bear on the connection between Jewish and Native American victimization, which is never openly articulated. The obliqueness of this connection consequently functions to enunciate the literal silence surrounding the painful histories of other marginalized groups, including those belonging to Native Americans. In recent years this asymmetry in the play reflects a problematic reality: in American classrooms as well as in the popular media, the universally accepted and ubiquitously cited model of historical evil is Hitler's Germany. The consequence of this mode of arguing is that the history that produced the Holocaust overshadows the genocide, expropriation, and ghettoization of the various Native American tribes. This overshadowing is, perhaps, understandable given the Jewish genocide's relative recentness in Western history. Nevertheless, it should also be admitted that the effect of this tendency is to limit moral considerations of historical responsibility for oppression to comparisons with the Nazi regime's exemplary evil, thus deflecting such considerations from the United States' ongoing responsibility for the historical and political oppression of Native Americans, to name just one example.

Equally significant in this respect is the function of Weisman's daughter who acts as referee. Ruth's social marginality as a "mongoloid" woman is belied by her symptomatic exclusion from the "privilege" of debating the status of her suffering with her father and Joe Nakedass. Outside of the structural necessity of a third party playing judge and the narrative logic pitting her father's "snow-white piety" against his interlocutor's "copper humor," it is unclear why she does not participate more centrally in the duel. Moreover, while her mongoloid condition would seem to aggravate the aporia surrounding the question of who is the appropriate judge of historical oppression, in Ruth's case this competence never comes into question. Her marginality nevertheless becomes a crucial factor in her father's victory. If he wins in the end it is because he confesses to an attempt to murder his daughter precisely because of her handicaps.

Ultimately, then, both duelists define their victimization through confessions of their personal and sometimes self-inflicted miseries (Weisman is a batterer and Copperface is a divorced drug addict). The disclosure that pronounces Weisman a victor is thus the finale in a series

of seemingly gratuitous linkages between personal inequities and historical atrocities that indicate the potential banality of self-proclaimed victimization. For if oppressing others can be identified as an oppressive
burden in its turn, if not the supreme burden as Weisman's winning confession suggests, then perpetrators also retain the power to enjoin our
sympathy as victims of their own criminal acts. The category of traumatic victimization is, in this case, too easily conflated with that of personal suffering and both lose their efficacy as moral grounds for com-
manding sympathetic response.

The play on names reinforces this confusion. On the one hand, the
abstract figuration of Arnold Weisman and Joe Nakedass as the "white
man" and the "redface," ironically emphasizes the overdetermined
meaning of their skin color as a basis for eternal enmity, despite the historical, social, and personal circumstances that might otherwise connect
them. Ruth, on the other hand, is the name of a non-Jewish woman in
the Book of Ruth who converts to Judaism upon her marriage. After her
husband dies, her loyalty to her mother-in-law and her resolute efforts to
adhere to Jewish laws, earns her a heroic stature as a "good Jewish
daughter" whose honorary position in the biblical literature is reconfirmed by her identification as an ancestor of David. Yet while the biblical Ruth joins the Jewish community through marriage and obedience
to its traditions, Weisman's daughter renounces her name at will, and, by
implication, her Jewish ancestry in adopting her future mate's term of
endearment, *Turtledove*. The effect of this conjunction is to stress the
voluntary aspects of familial and community membership; Jewish identity and victimization consequently lose any essential and transhistorical value.

In contrast, Copperface's admission that he is actually "Geegee
Goldberg" at once subverts and reinforces the exceptional "essence" of
Jewish victimization. For while Copperface can alternately affiliate
and/or disaffiliate with Jewish history through a change of name, his final
act of self-identification compels the audience to read his personal history in light of his presumed Jewish ancestry (i.e., in light of his "Jewish-
sounding" name). Accordingly, the prejudice he faces by virtue of his
"copper" skin takes on the specificity of anti-Semitism. The implication
is that he must apparently bear the effects of this prejudice despite his
expropriation of Jewish identity and despite his own Jewish self-hatred.
By extension, Jewish victimization is, after all, "essential" insofar as
"Jews" must endure it even when their identity is veiled and/or dis-
avowed.

Finally, for Tabori, a Hungarian Jew who fled Europe during the Nazi
period, it would seem that the privileging of the Jewish genocide as a
transcendent trauma has reached its moral and logical limits. *Weisman
and Copperface* illuminates these limits through the character of the

ash-bearing Jewish wanderer, Arnold Weisman, who has assumed its meaning as an extension and reconsolidation of his victim status. These limits are also stipulated by the reality of other traumatic histories such as the expropriation of Native Americans that have been similarly marked by genocide and seclusion. Despite the power of the arguments favoring the Jewish genocide's exceptionality, it is still important to concede that the effort to reinforce the Holocaust's moral efficacy through recourse to an affirmation of its uniqueness may, in the long run, constitute a vain attempt to save memory from history, which is to say, to protect the possibility of memory's redemptive meaning from the banalities and short-circuitings of ideology. Admittedly, however, there is a certain level at which this position attests to a bad conscience or, at the very least, a loss of faith in the pedagogical and moral efficacy of treating the Holocaust as an event whose horror transcends all others. This skepticism, which could be said to haunt Tabori's play, also multiplies the contradictions involved in writing about the Holocaust, especially now, following the fifty-year anniversary of the liberation of Auschwitz. But not simply for reasons which are already obvious: that other "equally" traumatic events have since taken place and that a somewhat dismissive climate prevails in which many thinkers contest the Jewish genocide's continuing privilege in the Western cultural imagination. Such a climate makes this writing seem at best self-indulgent and at worst irresponsible. A less obvious difficulty stems from the sense that the very act of writing about such events cannot seem to avoid borrowing, if not exploiting, their pathos and profundity. This writing is often precious, overburdened with a conviction of its own urgency and relevance.

Ultimately, then, I must acknowledge that despite my feeling that the language of Tabori's play offers a literary alternative to this preciousness, the contradictions involved in continuing to write about the Holocaust, more than half a century after, will not, obviously, be reconciled by recourse to irony. But neither will they be "solved" by contesting the Holocaust's uniqueness, by claiming that all events are unique and that the Jewish genocide is simply one of many, deserving no special consideration in our reflections on the conditions for ethical behavior in the current era.

Granted, many of those who criticize the uniqueness claim do so with legitimate grounds. They worry that focusing on the Holocaust's exceptionality allows us to escape thinking about other genocides that should demand our attention.[8] But this position effectively misses the point. The uniqueness argument is a rhetorical figure for the crisis in values to which the Holocaust contributed. This is the case insofar as the Holocaust is an event that brought home, more so than the preceding barbarities accompanying the slave trade, imperialism or colonialism, the illusions grounding Western claims to universal good intentions. It would therefore seem that renouncing this specificity feeds both historical irresponsibility and history as automatism.[9] In contrast, to argue that the Holocaust is unique is to see it as a reminder of the denial that permitted the Final Solution as well as a demand for the humility that citizens of Western nations should subsequently evince in future perceptions of our own agency in recognizing and hopefully fighting oppression. How the implications of this denial and the injunction of this humility are to shape future conceptions of responsibility in current affairs, is a problem that the position challenging the Holocaust's uniqueness fails to address. For to accept the Holocaust's singularity in this sense is, paradoxically, to avow the likelihood of continuing complicity in contemporary humanitarian crises.

This undesirable complicity might be understood as a postmodern plight insofar as it is aggravated by the proliferation of mass communications that force us to bear constant witness to the multiple terrors of the times. Needless to say, while the Holocaust's singularity cannot be blamed for our implicatedness in these events, neither is writing about the Holocaust likely to prevent future atrocities. Indeed, as Zygmunt Bauman acknowledges, the Holocaust "has changed little, if anything, in the course of the subsequent history of our collective consciousness and self-understanding. It made little visible impact on our image of the meaning and historical tendency of modern civilization."[10] Why then, must Bauman, like myself, feel compelled to defend the study of the Holocaust? Ultimately, it is because writing about the Holocaust has a moral impetus: it assumes that citizens of Western nations should attempt to understand both how the genocide derails the best intentions of an Enlightened society and how these very intentions themselves betrayed, and continue to betray, the worst illusions about the responsibilities attending modernity.

Notes

1. The *Historikerstreit* began with the June 6, 1986, publication of Ernst Nolte's "The Past That Will Not Pass" in the *Frankfurter Allgemeine Zeitung*. Here, the former student of Heidegger argued against the monolithic "demonization" of the Nazi genocide of the Jews and for a more "normal" (meaning less "obsessive") view of the Holocaust, for a revision, in other words, which "properly" locates the Holocaust within the broader context of genocide as a whole. Within this framework, he also contends that the Gulags in the USSR were more "original" than the Nazi crimes and that, in fact, Hitler's decision to eliminate the Jews can be linked to his fear that the "Jew-infested" communist regime would commit the same offense against Germany if Hitler did not act first.

Jürgen Habermas responded with "A Kind of Settlement of Damages: The Apologetic Tendencies in German History Writing" (*Die Zeit*, July 11, 1986), in which he reprimands Nolte and other conservative historians for seeking to revise history with the intent to normalize and thereby rationalize the Holocaust through comparisons with other genocides. For Habermas, the question of whether German responsibility for the Holocaust should be kept alive in memory is a question of how one is to deal in the present with "ambivalent inheritances." Along these lines, the critical appropriation of historical traditions is possible only on the basis of *post-conventional identity*, an ideal of cosmopolitan respect for reciprocity and justice for individuals. In John Torpey's words, this identity ideal is aimed at producing "a critical perspective toward the life context in which one is raised and toward the barbarism out of which it may have been created" ("Introduction: Habermas and the Historians," *New German Critique* 44 [1988]: 5–24). In sum, the ideal of post-conventional identity promotes universalism at the expense of nationalism while affirming the necessity to remember and to reflect on the German past.

2. See Charles S. Maier, *The Unmasterable Past: History, Holocaust, and German National Identity* (Cambridge, Mass.: Harvard University Press, 1988), and the collection of essays introduced and edited by Saul Friedländer entitled *Probing the Limits of Representation: Nazism and the 'Final Solution'* (Cambridge, Mass.: Harvard University Press, 1992). Hayden White's essay, "Historical Emplotment and the Problem of Truth," which I discuss above, is included in this collection, pp. 37–53.

3. Hayden White, *Probing the Limits*, p. 42.

4. George *Tabori, Weisman und Rotgesicht, Theaterstücke II* (Frankfurt am Main: Fischer Taschenbuch Verlag, 1994), pp. 205–39.

5. Shoshana Felman and Dori Laub, M.D., *Testimony: Crises in Witnessing in Literature, Psychoanalysis and History* (New York: Routledge, 1992).

6. Jean-François Lyotard, *The Differend: Phrases in Dispute*, trans. Georges Van Den Abbeele (Minneapolis: University of Minnesota Press, 1988). In this situation, silence is rhetorical, an index that one or more of the addresser, addressee, signification and referent instances of a phrase have been neutralized or denied. Lyotard enumerates these four possibilities as follows:

> Silence does not indicate which instance is denied, it signals the denial of one or more of the instances. The survivors remain silent, and it can be understood 1) that the situation in question (the case) is not the addressee's business (he or she lacks the competence, or he or she is not worthy of being spoken to about it, etc.); or 2) that it never took place (this is what Faurisson understands); or 3) that there is nothing to say about it (the situation is senseless, inexpressible); or 4) that it is not the survivors' business to be talking about it (they are not worthy, etc.). Or, several of these negations together. (*The Differend* 14, section 26)

7. In his chapter entitled "Testimony and Historical Truth," in *Testimony: Crises in Witnessing in Literature, Psychoanalysis and History* cited above, the psychoanalyst Dori Laub observes how, among a group of historians, psychoanalysts, and artists attending a conference on education and the Holocaust, "a lively debate ensued" after a videotape of a woman giving testimony was played. The historians argued that the "inaccuracy" of the testimony was very troubling

given the importance of such accuracy in combatting historical revisionists who might "discredit everything." The psychoanalysts, on the other hand, argued for an alternative understanding of historical truth which assumed that the meaning and function of the woman's testimony were more important than its facticity. See Felman and Laub, *Testimony*, pp. 59–63.

8. This is a position eloquently articulated by Peter Haidu in "The Dialectics of Unspeakability: Language, Silence, and the Narratives of Desubjectification." He writes:

> Exclusive stress on the uniqueness of the Event, combined with its sacralization, results in its disconnectedness from history. The evolution of a cult of remembrance into a sectarian exclusionary ritual "[separates] the Jewish catastrophe from its secular historical setting." The Event's uniqueness is reified; it is conceived as entirely *sui generis* and unprecedented: decontextualized, it therefore must escape historical comprehension. . . . Worse, such a historical *hapax* also leads to dismissal of the event as irrelevant: if the Holocaust is entirely unique and disconnected from human historicity, what can be its relevance for the perplexed, engaged in making historical and moral choices?

Friedländer, ed. *Probing the Limits of Representation*, p. 291, with citations from Arno Mayer's *Why Did the Heavens Not Darken? The "Final Solution" in History* (New York: Pantheon, 1988) pp. 16–19 and Saul Friedländer's "The 'Final Solution': Unease in Interpretation," *History and Memory* 1 (1989): 71–73.

9. As Geoffrey Hartman writes:

> Even if "nothing human is alien to us," the burden of the *Shoah* . . . cannot be overcome because it cannot be reduced to familiarity. The Holocaust remains human and alien at the same time. The worst attitude we could take is to persuade ourselves that it might not happen again or that it is something that happened before—that the Holocaust was one catastrophe among others.

See Geoffrey Hartman's Introduction to *Bitburg in Moral and Political Perspective*, ed. Geoffrey Hartman (Bloomington: Indiana University Press, 1986) p. 7.

10. Zygmunt Bauman, *Modernity and the Holocaust* (Ithaca: Cornell University Press, 1991) p. 85.

Notes on the Contributors

KARYN BALL received a master's degree in creative writing from Syracuse University in 1990 and the Academy of American Poets Award for a short selection of poems that same year. In 1993, she completed a second Masters in Comparative Studies in Discourse & Society at the University of Minnesota in Minneapolis. A 1995–1996 stipend from the German Academic Exchange Service (DAAD) enabled her to conduct research on the German reception of Spielberg's *Schindler's List*. A Wallace Fellowship from the University of Minnesota has allowed her to continue research in Germany, as well as begin work on her dissertation, entitled "The Vicissitudes of Memory: The Traumatic as a Genre of Discourse." She was awarded a 1997–1998 Charlotte W. Newcombe Doctoral Dissertation Fellowship by the Woodrow Wilson National Fellowship Foundation.

EVE TAVOR BANNET is professor of English and women's studies and chair of English at the University of Oklahoma. Her books include *Scepticism, Society and the Eighteenth-Century Novel; Structuralism and the Logic of Dissent*; and *Postcultural Theory*.

DEBRA B. BERGOFFEN is professor of philosophy and women's studies at George Mason University. Her writings draw on the work of Nietzsche, Freud, Beauvoir, Sartre, Irigaray, and Lacan to address questions of truth, subjectivity, and justice. She is the author of *The Philosophy of Simone de Beauvoir: Gendered Phenomenologies, Erotic Generosities*, and co-editor of *Prospects for Continental and Postmodern Philosophy of Science* and *Other Openings*.

JAMES BERNAUER is professor of philosophy at Boston College. He received his Ph.D. from the State University of Stony Brook and other degrees in philosophy and theology from Fordham University, St. Louis University, Woodstock College, and Union Theological Seminary. He studied with Michel Foucault in Paris for two years. Dr. Bernauer is the author of *Michel Foucault's Force of Flight: Toward an Ethics for Thought* (Humanities Press, 1990) and is editor of *Amor Mundi: Explorations in the Faith and Thought of Hannah Arendt* (Martinus Nijhoff, 1987) and co-editor, with David Rasmussen, of *The Final Foucault*. His current research project is an analysis of German Christian moral formation in the period before the Holocaust.

KLAUS DÖRNER holds both a doctorate in philosophy and a degree in medicine. He was the leading physician at the Psychiatric Hospital in Gütersloh and held the chair of psychiatry at the University of Witten-Herecke until 1996. Among his numerous publications are *Irren ist menschlich: Lehrbuch der Psychiatrie* (Bonn: Psychiatrie-Verlag) and *Tödliches Mitleid* (Gütersloh: Verlag Jakob van Hoddis).

JENNIFER N. FINK is a visiting assistant professor at the Pratt Institute, and is an adjunct professor at New York University. She is co-editor of the collection *Performing Hybridity* (Minnesota, 1998). She is also the author of the novel *The Mikveh Queen*, the short story collection *Thirteen Fugues*, and a forthcoming academic study of the performance work of Anne Sexton. She received the *Georgetown Review*'s 1996 Fiction Award.

ROGER FJELLSTROM is associate professor of moral philosophy in the Department of Philosophy and Philosophy of Science at Umeå University, Sweden. Beside philosophy, he has published several collections of poetry, and has had exhibitions of his paintings.

RUTH LIBERMAN is an artist who has exhibited in the United States, Canada, England, and Venezuela. She is a Ph.D. candidate at New York University, currently working on her dissertation on humor in artistic representations of the Holocaust.

DR. BURKHARD LIEBSCH has since 1997 been a fellow at the Cultural Sciences Institute in Essen and at the Center for Sciences in Nordrhein-Westfalen. His publications include *Zu denken gebe: Identität und Geschichte* (1997) and *Geschichte als Antwort und Versprechen* (1998).

DETLEF LINKE is professor of neurophysicology and neurosurgical rehabilitation at the University of Bonn.

ALAN MILCHMAN teaches in the department of political science at Queens College, CUNY. He is currently writing a book (with Alan Rosenberg) on Michel Foucault, psychoanalysis, and the disciplinary society. Among his recent publications are *Postmodernism and the Holocaust*, co-edited with Alan Rosenberg (Atlanta: Rodopi, 1998); "Martin Heidegger und die deutsche Universität: Radikalismus und Konformidät," in Wolfgang Bialas and Georg G. Iggers, eds., *Intellektuelle in der Weimarer Republik* (Frankfurt: Peter Lang, 1996), "Michel Foucault, Auschwitz and Modernity," in *Philosophy and Social Criticism* 22, no. 1 (1996); and "The Philosophical Stakes of the Heidegger Wars," *The Journal of Value Inquiry* 27 (1993) and 28 (1994), all with Alan Rosenberg.

FRANS VAN PEPERSTRATEN is an associate professor in the philosophy of culture and society at Tilburg University, the Netherlands. He has published several books in Dutch on social philosophy, the history of philosophy, and Lyotard's postmodernism. He has written several articles and reviews on the representation of "Auschwitz."

ALAN ROSENBERG is associate professor of philosophy at Queens College, CUNY. He is writing a book (with Alan Milchman), *Experiments in Thinking the Holocaust*. He is the co-editor (with Alan Milchman) of *Martin Heidegger and the Holocaust* (New Jersey: Humanities Press, 1996). He has also co-edited *Echoes from the Holocaust: Philosophical Reflections on a Dark Time* (Philadelphia: Temple University Press, 1988), and *Healing Their Wounds: Psychotherapy and Holocaust Survivors* (New York: Praeger, 1989). Among his recent publications are "Martin Heidegger and the University as a Site for the Transformation of Human Existence," *The Review of Politics* 59, no. 1 (1997), "Resoluteness and Ambiguity: Martin Heidegger's Ontological Politics, 1933–35, *The Philosophical Forum* 25, no. 1 (1993), and "The Unlearned Lessons of the Holocaust," *Modern Judaism* 13 (1993), all with Alan Milchman.

RAJ SAMPATH was born in Madras, India and immigrated to the United States as an infant. Holding a B.A. in history from the University of California, Berkeley, and a Ph.D. in European intellectual history from the University of California, Irvine, he is currently researcher and lecturer at the University of California, Berkeley. Professor Sampath's current work is an attempt at a synthesis of twentieth-century continental philosophies of history and historical time with developments in theoretical physics, particularly Einstein's General Theory of Relativity. His major publication is the "The Historicity of Archaeology: Historical Time in Foucault's *The Order of Things*," in *The Histories of Michel Foucault*, ed. Jeffrey Di Leo (Bloomington: Indiana University Press, 1995).

PAUL SARS has studied philosophy and German language and literature in Nijmegen (the Netherlands) and Munich (Germany). His Ph.D. dissertation concerned the Rumanian poet Paul Celan. He is chairman of the Dutch Paul Celan Society and editor of *Meridianen*, the Dutch Celan yearbook. Paul Sars is assistant professor in the department of philosophy of the University of Nijmegen in the Netherlands and president of Studium Generale, a series of lectures on topics of general interest. His publications include *Paul Celan: Gedichten* (Dutch translation of twenty-five Celan poems by Frans Roumen and an extensive commentary by Paul Sars) (Baarn, 1988), and *Ich bin es noch immer: Zur Konstistenz in der Lyrik Paul Celans*—Diss. 3 volumes, in German (Nijmegen, 1993).

HANS SEIGFRIED is a professor of philosophy at Loyola University of Chicago. Among his recent publications are "Autonomy and Quantum Physics: Nietzsche, Heidegger, and Heisenberg," *Philosophy of Science* 57 (1990); "Zur Ambivalenz des Fortschritts bei Nietzsche und Heidegger: Wissenschaft und Technik als Vermittler," *Allgemeine Zeitschrift für Philosophie* 16 (1991); "Dewey's Critique of Kant's Copernican Revolution Revisited," *Kant-Studien* 83 (1993); and "Heidegger at the Nuremberg Trials: The 'Letter on Humanism' Revisited," in A. Milchman and A. Rosenberg, eds., *Martin Heidegger and the Holocaust* (Atlantic Highlands, N.J.: Humanities Press, 1996).

THOMAS W. SIMON received his Ph.D. from Washington University (1973) and his J.D. from the University of Illinois College of Law (1991). He was a liberal arts fellow in philosophy at Harvard Law School (1987–1988) and received a certificate of study from Hague Academy of International Law (1995). His publications include *Democracy and Social Injustice* (Rowman & Littlefield, 1995) and a forthcoming anthology, *Law's Philosophy* (McGraw Hill). His articles include "Defining Genocide," *Wisconsin Journal of International Law* (1996), and "Group Harm," *Journal of Social Philosophy* (1995). He edits an interdisciplinary electronic journal, *Injustice Studies*. Currently, Dr. Simon teaches philosophy at Illinois State University and practices law, including consulting for Rwandan refugees on genocide cases.

DAN STONE is Junior Research Fellow in modern history at New College, Oxford. He is the author of several articles on Holocaust historiography, and recently completed his doctoral thesis entitled "The Construction of the Holocaust: Genocide and the Philosophy of History." He also worked on the exhibition "Representations of Auschwitz" which was shown in Cracow, Oldenburg, and Weimar in the summer of 1995. Dr. Stone is the editor of a forthcoming book from Rodopi on theoretical interpretations of the Holocaust.

PETER STRASSER, born in 1950, is professor of philosophy in the department of philosophy, sociology and informatics of law [Institut für Rechtsphilosophie, Rechtssoziologie und Rechtsinformatik] at the Karl-Franzens-University, Graz (Austria). Among his publications are: *Verbrechermenschen: Zur kriminalwissenschaftlichen Erzeugung des Bösen* (Frankfurt am Main/ New York: Campus 1984); *Die verspielte Aufklärung* (Frankfurt am Main: Suhrkamp 1986); *Philosophie der Wirklichkeitssuche* (Frankfurt am Main: Suhrkamp 1989); *Geborgenheit im Schlechten: Über die Spannung zwischen Kunst und Religion* (Vienna: Deuticke 1993); *Das Menschenmögliche: Späte Gedanken über den Humanismus* (Vienna: Deuticke 1996).

ERIK M. VOGT, who received his Ph.D. at the University of Vienna, is assistant professor of philosophy at Loyola University in New Orleans. He has published *Sartre's Wieder-Holung* (Vienna: Passagen Verlag), numerous translations from and into German and English, as well as articles on modernism/post-modernism, political philosophy, and aesthetics. He is general editor of the series "Neue Amerikanische Philosophie" (Vienna: Turia+Kant).

JAMES R. WATSON is a professor of philosophy at Loyola University in New Orleans, Louisiana. He is the author of *Thinking with Pictures* (1990), *Between Auschwitz and Tradition* (1994) (German translation, *Die Auschwitz Galaxy* [1997]), *Kontinentalphilosophie aus Amerika: 22 Photogrammische Porträte* (1998); *Portraits of American Continental Philosophers* (1999); and is the co-author of *Louisiana Labor: From Slavery to "Right-To-Work"* (1985). He is president of the Society for the Philosophical Study of Genocide and the Holocaust.

ANDREW WEINSTEIN is writing his Ph.D. dissertation on representation of the Holocaust in contemporary American art at the Institute of Fine Arts, New York University. He teaches art history at the Cooper Union and at the Fashion Institute of Technology, State University of New York. An essay of his appears in *Jewish Experiences in Modern Art* (Rutgers University Press, forthcoming in 2000).